1985

History of Central Africa

Volume one

History of Central Africa

VOLUME ONE

edited by
David Birmingham and Phyllis M. Martin

Longman
London and New York

Longman Group Limited
Longman House
Burnt Mill, Harlow, Essex, UK

Published in the United States of America
by Longman Inc., New York

First published 1983

British Library Cataloguing in Publication Data

History of Central Africa
Vol. 1
1. Africa, Central—History
I. Birmingham, David II. Martin, Phyllis M.
967 DT352.5

ISBN 0-582-64673-1
ISBN 0-582-64674-x Pbk

Library of Congress Cataloging in Publication Data
Main entry under title:

History of Central Africa.

Bibliography: v. 1, p.
Includes index.
1. Africa, Central—History. I. Birmingham David.
II. Martin, Phyllis.
DT352.5.H58 1983 967 83-745
ISBN 0-582-64673-1 (v. 1)
ISBN 0-582-64674-X (pbk. : v. 1)

Printed in Singapore by
Kyodo Shing Loong Printing Industries Pte Ltd.

Cover photograph of fishing village of M'Pila, Brazzaville, Zaire, supplied by J. Allan Cash.

Contents

		Page
	List of maps	vi
	Preface	viii
1	Society and economy before A.D. 1400 *David Birmingham*	1
2	The savanna belt of North-Central Africa *Dennis D. Cordell*	30
3	The peoples of the forest *Jan Vansina*	75
4	The paradoxes of impoverishment in the Atlantic zone *Joseph C. Miller*	118
5	The societies of the eastern savanna *Thomas Q. Reefe*	160
6	The Indian Ocean zone *Alan K. Smith*	205
7	The Zimbabwe plateau and its peoples *D. N. Beach*	245
	Sources and further reading	278
	Acknowledgements	297
	Index	298

List of maps

	Page
Central Africa in the twentieth century	xii
1:1 The regions of Central Africa	2
1:2 The languages of Central Africa c. 1400	7
1:3 Crop domestication in North-Central Africa	10
1:4 Iron Age industry in South-Central Africa	18
1:5 Cattle-keeping in Zimbabwe	23
1:6 The kingdom of Kongo	28
2:1 North-Central Africa	31
2:2 Language groups and principal languages, North-Central Africa	33
2:3 Northern Muslim states and their slave-raiding zones	46
2:4 Bandia and Avongara states, late nineteenth century	53
2:5 Muslim slave-raiding and conquest, late nineteenth century	62
2:6 European exploration and conquest, North-Central Africa	71
3:1 The forest zone of Central Africa	76
3:2 The rain-forest	78
3:3 Political organisation in the forest zone, late nineteenth century	90
3:4 The Atlantic trade, c. 1875	101
3:5 War and population movements, c. 1800–1880	104
3:6 Estimated rural population in the forest zone, c. 1880	110
4:1 West-Central Africa	120
4:2 The Gulf of Guinea in the sixteenth century	130
4:3 Kongo and adjoining regions	136
4:4 The Mbundu region	138
4:5 Central and southern Angola	142
4:6 East of the Kwango and the Kwanza rivers, nineteenth century	154
5:1 The eastern savanna: flood plains and natural resources	162
5:2 Kingdoms of the savanna, 1700–1850	176
5:3 Traders and raiders of the eastern savanna, 1830s to 1890s	195

6:1 The Indian Ocean zone 206
6:2 Ethnographic distribution within the Indian Ocean zone 207
6:3 Eighteenth-century trade routes, Indian Ocean zone 226
6:4 The Indian Ocean zone during the nineteenth century 235
7:1 The Zimbabwe plateau before c. 1800 249
7:2 The Zimbabwe plateau in the nineteenth century 250

Preface

Central Africa is one of the largest regions of the tropical world, larger than India, larger than the Amazon, larger than South-East Asia. It includes the great 'Congo basin' of the Zaire river, the coastlands of the South Atlantic, the northern savannas of Cameroun and the Central African Republic, the southern plateaux of Angola and Zimbabwe and the Zambezi lowlands of the Indian Ocean. It is twice as large as West Africa on one flank, or East Africa and the Horn on the other, though population is more thinly scattered. The northern boundary touches the Muslim world of the Sahara about ten degrees above the Equator. The southern boundary runs into the desert fringes of the Kalahari from the Atlantic to the Limpopo. Modern Central Africa encompasses a dozen countries, from Malawi and Mozambique in the east to the tiny island republics of São Tomé and Equatorial Guinea in the west.

The geographical unity of Central Africa is both physical and human. Two great river systems, Zaire and Zambezi, tap the northern and southern halves of the region. The watershed runs along an old and rich belt of copper mines at the heart of the continent. All of Central Africa's three million square miles lie within the tropics, but the five-thousand-foot highlands of the south moderate the heat and reduce rainfall to thirty inches and below. The two great savanna belts of north and south sandwich a dwindling rain-forest, the last refuge of hunters and river-dwelling fishermen.

The three ecological layers of Central Africa are inhabited by modern peoples who are historically related to their neighbours, both west and east. The northern belt is peopled by Sudanic farmers who are among the world's oldest tropical cereal cultivators; many of them are linked to the lowland and plateau peoples of West Africa. The southern savanna, and much of the forest, is occupied by Bantu-speakers who are related by language and culture to the lakeland and highland peoples of East Africa. Throughout their history Central Africans have demonstrated their vitality and adaptability. The first volume of this work explores how they have experimented with new technology in pottery, in metal-working, in wood-carving; with new economies in fishing and in farming and in commerce; with new social organisation in families and in lineages and in states; with new religious worship, through ancestors and shrines and sacred kings. It is a history both rich and varied which provides illuminating contrasts and parallels with the histories of both West Africa and East Africa.

The last thousand years have seen the opening of Central Africa's three main frontiers to international influence. The eastern front, on the shores of the Indian Ocean, was the first to attract long-range maritime traders. From the tenth century A.D. Swahili, Indian and Arab merchants came with increasing regularity to seek iron and copper, ivory and gold, from South-Central Africa. A few centuries later Islamic domination of this trade was challenged by the rising Christian power of Europe. The friar João dos Santos became one of the early chroniclers of South-Central African history.

The second, northern, frontier of Central Africa was more slowly penetrated by new influences and ideologies. By the fifteenth century, however, the Muslim scholar Leo Africanus was able to describe North-Central Africa to geographers at the papal court in Rome. Close contact with the Muslim world came later, with the new military and commercial dynamism of the nineteenth century. It was then also that European travellers such as Barth, in the north-west, and Schweinfurth, in the north-east, studied North-Central African society.

The third and last frontier of Central Africa, on the western ocean, remained closed until the fifteenth century. It was first opened not by Muslims but by Christians who came to the South Atlantic in Portuguese caravels. In 1483 the kingdom of Kongo became the first Central African nation to open maritime communication with Europe. This transport revolution later resulted in the forced emigration of several million Central Africans. Most of them went to Brazil and the Caribbean. The traffic in slaves bit deeply into the continent and disrupted society on a wide front. This dark episode in the Atlantic zone's history continued until about 1860.

The nineteenth century was a peculiarly traumatic one in Central Africa. From mid-century a series of predatory commercial forces began to close in on all sides. Armed Khartoum traders came from the Nile in search of ivory. Nyamwezi caravans crossed the eastern frontier in search of copper mines and plantation workers for Zanzibar Island. Ovimbundu expeditions pressed inland from Angola seeking beeswax and red rubber. On each frontier African entrepreneurs responded aggressively to a rising demand for tropical commodities in a world-wide trading system. Their search left trails of destruction as they advanced the frontiers of exploitation towards the inner core of the continent.

By the end of the nineteenth century the painful, but indirect, penetration of international capitalism had been replaced by direct colonial conquest. Central Africa was partitioned four ways by its colonial powers, with Belgium and France taking the large northern spheres while Britain and Portugal gained the smaller southern ones. Only on the Bight of Biafra was the simple four-power quartering of the region interrupted by a tiny Spanish enclave and by Germany's initial thirty-year hold on Cameroun. The Belgians took over the great ivory and rubber fiefs of the forest. The French turned the old Atlantic ports into colonial markets for the extraction of cotton and timber. In the south-east, Britain extended the South African mining industry to the gold and copper reefs of Zimbabwe and Zambia. In Angola and Mozambique, Portugal's network of white shop-keepers became a plantation system where black conscripts grew coffee and sugar. Everywhere Central Africans lost their economic freedom of choice, saw their dignity eroded by racist ideology, and were forcibly moved from home and family to work for imperial masters.

The unity of historical experience in Central Africa was in some ways broken by partition. In other ways, however, the policies adopted by the main powers bear striking similarities, as volume two of this work demonstrates. The conquerors were too weak, or too reluctant, to impose expensive and uniform patterns of direct European government. Administrative and economic concessions were therefore awarded to companies who developed 'private' colonies within the national spheres of influence. Each of these territories had a different charter, but all tended to coerce their labour force a little more harshly than in formal colonies under metropolitan governments. The abuses of the Portuguese 'Niassa' company and of the Belgian 'India-Rubber' company became especially notorious, but British and French colonial practice in Central Africa was also harsh. The mining zones imposed particular burdens and dangers on surrounding populations. The advent of empire was an altogether more violent and disruptive affair in Central Africa than in West or East Africa.

During the high colonial period which followed the era of the concessions, a surprising degree of uniformity and comparability can be found in the Central African experience. The coercion of reluctant labour, the building of trans-colonial railways, the minimisation of mining costs, the imposition of compulsory crop-planting, the low investment of risk capital, all are common themes. The colonial powers not only adopted similar policies, but occasionally also collaborated across their own artificial lines of partition. Fruitful comparisons can be drawn regarding the use of female road gangs, the skilled training of miners, health measures against sleeping sickness and other epidemics, and plantation versus peasant production policies; each aspect enables Central Africa's twentieth-century history to be seen as an integrated whole rather than as a cluster of local experiences.

The colonial episode in Central Africa, although short, left indelible changes. Christianity had been introduced almost everywhere, and in several countries religious leaders came to play important national roles. The followers of Simon Kimbangu of Zaire set up their own well-organised church with several million members. Education in Catholic,

Methodist and Presbyterian schools gave new élites access to administrative power. The twelve colonial states were strengthened by the rise of nationalism, and even severe challenges to their territorial integrity and to their social structure did not cause them to wither away with independence. International economic relations often evolved in neo-colonial partnerships rather than seeking radical new directions. Even the large, post-colonial American involvement in Zaire had roots in the mining history of the early Belgian Congo. Portuguese decolonisation was a more drawn-out and disruptive affair than French decolonisation. It left young republics vulnerable to intervention by South Africa and anxious to seek new world allies. In Zimbabwe the rebellious truculence of quarter of a million white settlers postponed the ebb of the imperial tide. By 1980, however, all of Central Africa had achieved independence.

One long-term legacy of the four-way partition of Central Africa was intellectual and cultural fragmentation. Education and research became so linked to metropolitan nations in Europe that no broad view of the region's historical development emerged. Scholarship, like administration, was circumscribed by language boundaries of French, Portuguese and English. Whereas works of comparative historical synthesis were produced in West and East Africa, Central Africa remained divided. Two pioneering books of the mid-1960s, Vansina's *Kingdoms of the Savanna* and Ranger's *Aspects of Central African History*, dramatically improved the historical focus in the southern half of the region. Since then historical research has taken such forward strides that it has become possible to explore the common ground more fully. Courses in Central African history, comparable to those taught in West African history or East African history, can now be offered. In the present volumes, which constitute the first over-all survey to be published, efforts have been made to emphasise the wealth and range of available information. The footnotes and bibliographical essays are designed both to underpin the argument and to guide students, teachers and scholars towards further reading and new research.

The seventeen authors who did the actual writing of this history of Central Africa owe a boundless debt to their fellow historians. It is to these colleagues that this work is gratefully dedicated, to the committed Central African academics teaching in their own national universities, to the village sages with unrivalled knowledge of oral tradition, to the foreign research students seeing Africa with enquiring eyes, to the archivists who preserve five hundred years of documentation, and to the seventy-five million people of Central Africa. It is their story.

David Birmingham
University of Kent
Canterbury
July 1982

Phyllis M. Martin
Indiana University
Bloomington

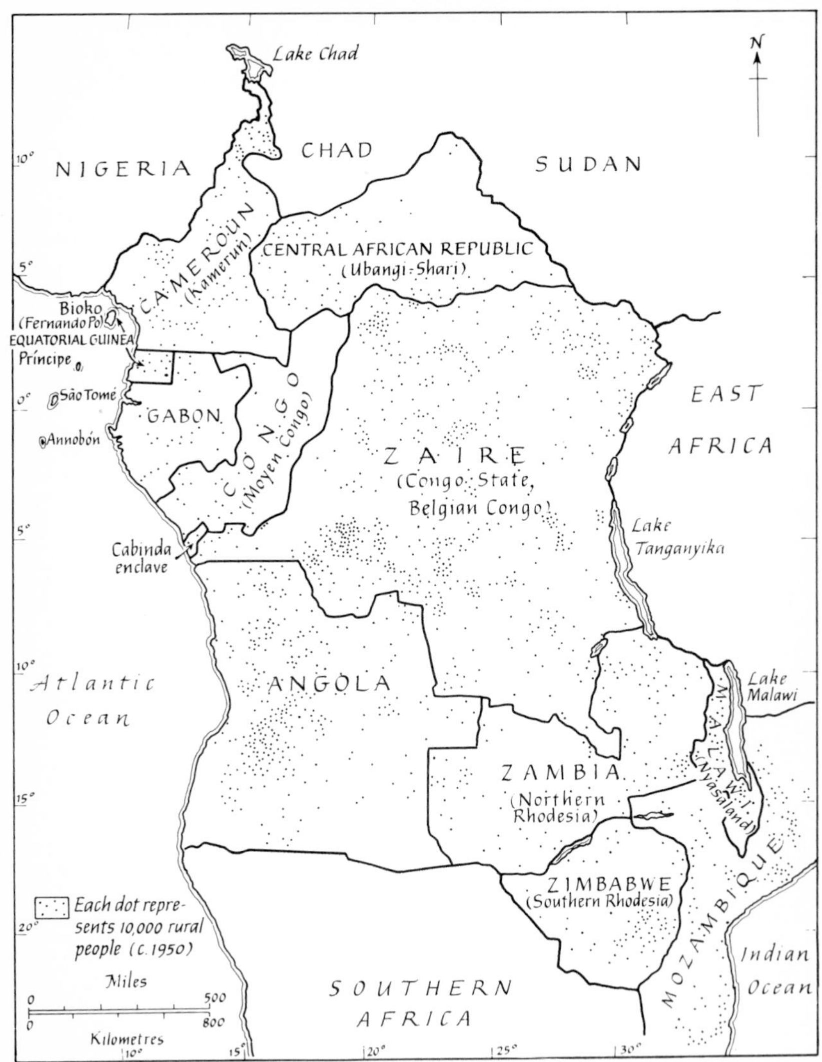

Central Africa in the twentieth century

CHAPTER 1

Society and economy before A.D. *1400*

DAVID BIRMINGHAM

Central Africa has a remarkable unity within the history of Africa. It is a world strongly unified by speech, and ninety per cent of its people use Bantu languages. It is a world equally unified by its economy. In the ten or fifteen centuries before the recent urban revolution ninety per cent of its people were farmers. Pre-colonial Central Africa was also a world curiously united by political experience. Most societies were managed on a small scale, and only rarely did the strands of power, religion and wealth intertwine to create centralised states. The exceptional states which did emerge, such as Kongo, Lunda and Zimbabwe, were fascinating examples of social ingenuity. In each case Central Africans demonstrated their ability to grasp new political ideas and economic opportunities. Adaptability and innovation are the hallmarks of Central African history.

By about the year 1400 the societies of Central Africa had acquired many aspects of their present-day culture. The Iron Age had reached a new maturity after a thousand years of development. Iron was regularly used for axes, hoes, blades, knives and needles. Copper and gold were in demand for jewellery and ornaments. Most people had become involved in the agrarian economy, yet hunting remained a significant skill. Important languages from Duala to Shona had almost acquired their modern form. Scattered homesteads were still the common pattern of settlement, though some larger villages had developed in the most fertile savannas. Exchange was still predominantly a household business, but markets flourished at economic meeting points. Trade had gained in importance as artisans became more specialised in fish-drying, in copper-mining, in salt-boiling, in palm-crushing and in sea-shell dredging. In some districts cattle herders had come to control the main source of wealth. Hunters, in their turn, had sometimes found new wealth by tracking elephants whose tusks sold well in the overseas markets of Asia.

The fifteenth century represents more than a point of economic achievement in Central African history. It was also a political threshold.

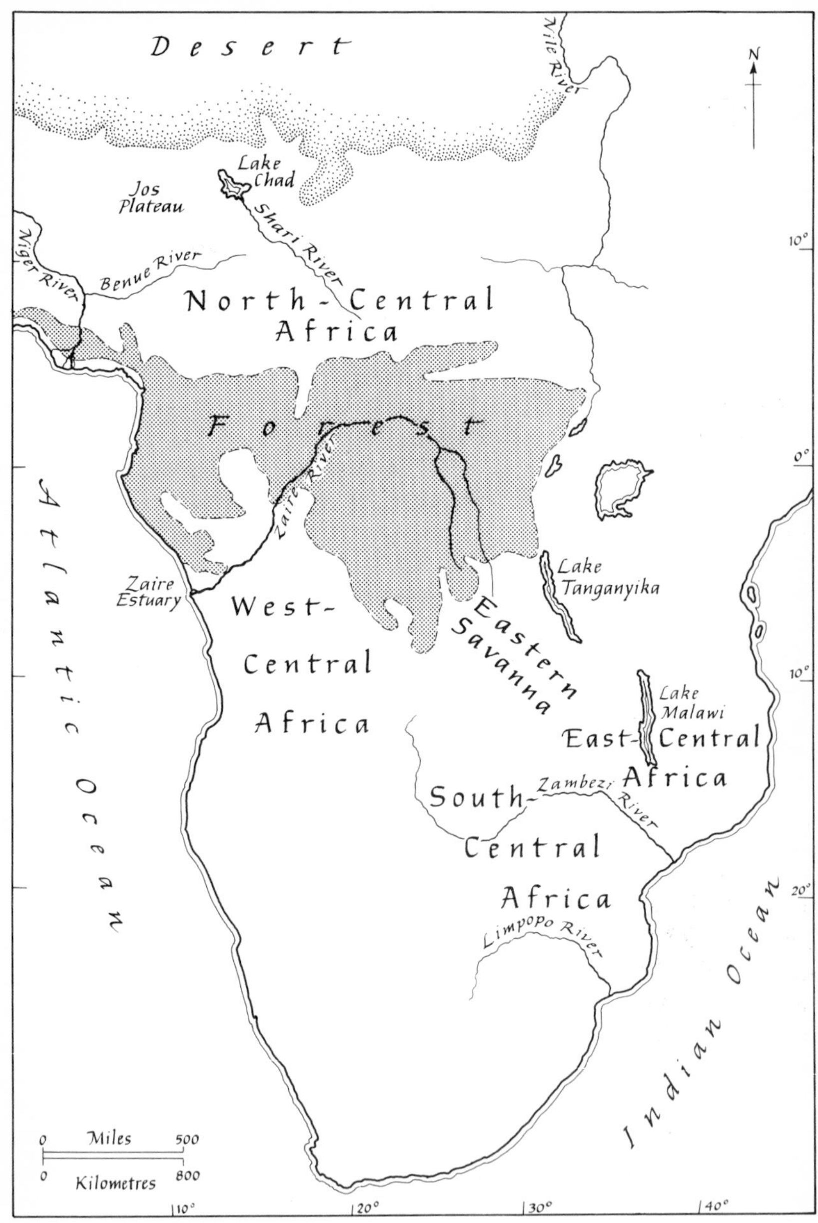

1:1 The regions of Central Africa

Some societies had the stability, the order and the continuity to reach down through five centuries to the present day. The earliest traditions contained in oral charters, camp-fire genealogies and heroic epics relate to the political experiments of five hundred years ago. The guardians of rain-shrines became village strong men; the priestesses of sky gods governed their followers from mountain-tops; the managers of caravan posts organised security for traders. Throughout Central Africa societies created new patterns of leadership as priests and elders and chiefs took charge of the affairs of man. The scale of social management began to grow, and power was added to economic privilege for the few. These economic and political changes were partly the result of new demographic trends. The most striking feature of Central Africa has always been the sparseness of its scattered population. Yet a demographic increase did occur before the fifteenth century, brought about by technological innovation, by economic skill, by centralised political leadership and by the diversification of mixed farming.

The rising and gently prospering population of Central Africa had adapted itself to four very different sets of climate and vegetation. In the hot, low woodland of North-Central Africa, the land dips gently towards the desert. Some of the rivers flow into the last of the great Saharan lakes, Lake Chad. In this open savanna country, stretching away to the Nile watershed, the time scale of human adaptation to changing methods of land use was long and slow. Population remained slight, and only on the western fringes of Cameroun did high densities compare with those of Nigeria.

The forest zone of Central Africa has always been even more thinly peopled than the neighbouring woodland. Although heavy rainfall made agriculture possible, soils were often poor or waterlogged. Dense vegetation and high tree cover made farming difficult. Yet the ecology provided an environment which favoured some specialised pursuits. Hunting bands maintained their distinctive life style, culture and economy. The rivers provided excellent opportunities for the spread of fishing communities, especially when the rivers of the southern Sahara dried up. By 1400, however, farming had become important in clearings, along river banks and in the attractive pockets of savanna which interspersed the denser galleries of high forest.

South of the forest lay another belt of savanna woodlands. In West-Central Africa there was a zone of real rural prosperity. In the central highland of Angola cattle-raising and crop-planting blended well in a region of reasonably reliable rainfall. An even more important area of demographic growth was the well-watered margin of the forest stretching through the southern Zaire basin and across the eastern savanna to lakes Tanganyika and Malawi. Although farmers prospered in the fertile valleys, their population never grew to the enormous densities reached in the higher, healthier and more fertile regions of East Africa.

In South-Central Africa the history of the Zambezi basin has been influenced by both climatic and mineral factors which distinguish it from the north and the west. Climatically South-Central Africa was the zone in which cattle could best flourish on a large scale. The absence of the tsetse fly enabled cattle barons to acquire a wealth not available in regions affected by cattle diseases. In Zambia the population was more thinly scattered, so that cattle-keepers and cattle-raiders were more mobile. The Zambian Copperbelt, on the other hand, became a major source of Central Africa's mineral wealth over the thousand years of its exploitation. The only other large mining industry to develop was on the Zimbabwean gold reefs. It was the gold-mining industry which from A.D. 1000 opened South-Central Africa to a steadily growing influence from the commercial world of the Indian Ocean zone. Metals, however, were not the most important geological feature of South-Central Africa. Fertility of the soil was always the primary concern of farmers. In the lowlands of Mozambique, and more especially in the southern highlands of Malawi, Central African farmers found conditions which were almost as good as those of East Africa. As a result, this region saw significant concentrations of Iron Age population by A.D. 1400.

The history of Central Africa is very much the history of a farming people. Farming, however, has not always been the prime activity of Central Africans. As an economic way of life it grew slowly by evolutionary stages. In order to understand fully the history of the centuries between 1400 and 1870 with which this volume is primarily concerned it is necessary to explore a remoter past, when the ancestors of those farming people won their living by gathering wild forest foods, by hunting savanna game and by netting fish. In studying the historical evolution of the remote past, it is also necessary to understand the two great innovations of Central Africa's prehistory. One was the managed production of domesticated food crops and animals. The other was the technological development made possible by metal-working skill. Each of these historic stages of growth contributed to the emergence of the rich and varied cultures of Central Africa in 1400.

TOOL-MAKERS, HUNTERS AND FOOD-GATHERERS

The earliest man in Central Africa was, of course, a tool-user, an unspecialised hunter, who probably preferred savanna country and the lighter woodlands of north and south to the dense forest of the Equator. For a million and a half years Central African hunters, like hunters throughout the western part of the Old World, used as their main tool the Acheulian 'hand axe'. They camped along streams and rivers, around lakes and on the sea-shore. Their preferred terrain would give good grazing for herbivorous game and a reliable water-course for the ambushing of animals while they drank.[1] Their camps consisted of two to five dozen people. At Kalambo Falls, near the south end of Lake Tanganyika, they built themselves wind-breaks for shelter. Home bases suitable for the butchering of meat were occupied continuously or seasonally over thousands of years. Food-gatherers ranged for miles around the camp collecting fruits, nuts, snails and good stone for tools. Cutting and scraping tools were made of stone, but many other implements were made of wood and have long since decayed. Gradually the hunters of Central Africa learned to use fire for warmth, for cooking and for driving game through the long dry grass.[2]

One interesting question of early prehistory concerns the first use of language. The good organisation of societies requires a precise form of communication. It is likely that the beginnings of language were associated with the old hunters during their tenuous occupation in Central Africa. Their skills in speech may, however, have been rudimentary.[3] That could be one reason why they underwent a major transformation, perhaps a complete replacement, about 100 000 years ago. Soon after that time the technology of Kalambo Falls, and of most other inhabited parts of Central Africa, underwent radical change. The new technology belonged to a more advanced man, *Homo sapiens sapiens*, who has survived until the present.

Homo sapiens, unlike the old hunters, was able to live in some parts of the tropical forest which periodically covered the equatorial zone according to the shifting phases of tropical climate. He was a much quicker learner than his predecessor. Intellectual and technological change accelerated as he matched his wit to the challenge of living in the African tropics. The first of his new stone tools in the Zaire and Zambezi basins were heavy Sangoan ones. Later, more specialised Lupemban adzes and gouges were developed in the forest.[4]

Man continued to camp out in the open, but where possible he sought refuge in rock shelters. At the Twin Rivers shelter in Zambia he soon became partial to eating cooked wart-hog and zebra. He developed the manufacture of precise, composite 'microlithic' tools. Stone cannot be beaten into a desired shape, like hot iron, but a good craftsman can chip it to serve hundreds of different purposes. In Angola this skill has survived until recent years, and modern gunsmiths make gun flints in what seems to be a traditional way. The flint is held between the heels and flaked with a horn punch and a wooden hammer. Tshitolian stone-knappers probably

1 J. Desmond Clark, *The Prehistory of Africa*, London, 1970, pp. 93–4.
2 The full archaeological record is in J. D. Clark, *Kalambo Falls Prehistoric Site*, Cambridge, 1974.
3 J. D. Clark, *The Prehistory of Africa*, pp. 102–3.
4 *Ibid.*, pp. 107, 114, 117.

practised this skill in Angola 20 000 years ago.[5] In Zambia it was an increase in rainfall that was responsible for a change in tool technology. At Kalemba, on the Mozambique border, the climate got warmer and wetter, and the vegetation grew thicker, around 15 000 years ago. The large grazing animals moved away to the drier regions of the Angola grassland. The local Nachikufan hunters had to learn to track down smaller prey. They ceased to throw heavy projectiles and adopted bows and arrows with sharp stone tips. They also learned to glue small stone chips on to wooden handles to make a wide range of special-purpose cutting tools.[6]

The specialist hunters of Central Africa were not, however, solely concerned with the economics of survival. They probably had rather more leisure time than the farmers of a later period. Although their songs, folk tales and dances are lost in the past, their rock art, their ornaments and their ochre cosmetics are known. On ceremonial occasions a hunter was a fine figure of a man, his chest neatly painted, bead charms around his neck, shells woven into his hair and decorations sewn to his cloak of skins. On the walls of his shelter he drew pictures of himself, proud and male, bow in hand, eyeing a herd of antelope. This tradition of rock art was so deeply rooted in the culture of Zimbabwe that it survived. It was Iron Age Zimbabweans, and not Stone Age hunters, who actually drew the elaborate rock paintings nicknamed 'Diana's Vow'. They had inherited a very long tradition.[7]

THE FISHERMEN OF NORTH-CENTRAL AFRICA

Hunting has remained important in Central Africa, but it has gradually ceased to be the central economic occupation. Slowly, over ten thousand years or so new ways of producing food have been learnt, shared and spread among neighbouring societies. The first important change to affect the production of food was not concerned with tools and technology but with cooking. It has been called, half-humorously, the 'fish-stew revolution'. With engaging exaggeration the culture of the fish-stew cooks was nicknamed the 'aquatic civilization of Middle Africa'.[8]

The great advantage that fishermen have over land hunters is that they need to roam less widely to catch their prey. They find it less difficult to settle down for longer periods of time. They can own more heavy objects, utensils, bowls, fishing baskets, net weights and traps because they do not have to carry them from camp to camp. The northern rivers, ponds and

5 *Ibid.*, pp. 138, 154–64.
6 D. W. Phillipson, *The Later Prehistory of Eastern and Southern Africa*, London, 1977, p. 31.
7 *Ibid.*, ch. xi; coloured illustrations may be found in Roger Summers *et al.* (eds), *Prehistoric Rock Art of the Federation of Rhodesia and Nyasaland*, Salisbury and London, 1959.
8 J. E. G. Sutton, 'The aquatic civilization of Middle Africa', *Journal of African History (JAH)*, xv, 1974, 527–46.

streams of Central Africa, now mostly dried up, were an excellent place for fishermen to prosper. Their bone harpoons and line-sinkers are to be found far into what is now complete desert. Between 10 000 and 5 000 years ago the peoples of Chad and the Central African Republic probably built reed rafts and dug-out canoes to carry home to the village their Nile perch, cat-

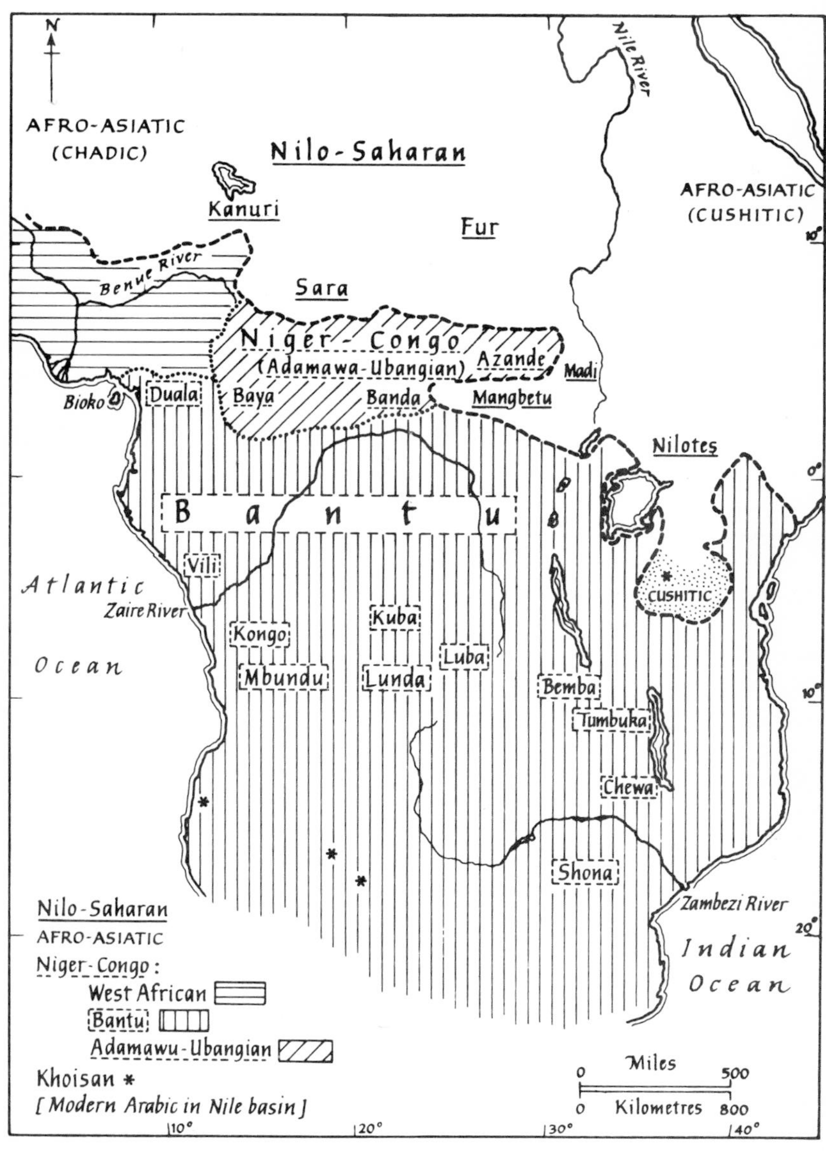

1:2 The languages of Central Africa c. 1400

fish, turtles and baskets of wild seed and water-lily root.[9] Zimbabweans of the same period either had to carry meat home on their heads, or to roast it where it fell after the chase.

The big technical discovery of the waterside peoples was the use of clay for making pottery. All previous Central African cookery involved roasting as there were no heat-resistant vessels. The invention of the clay pot made possible the stewing of fish and a whole 'revolutionary' development of stews and soups and porridges. Some of the first south Saharan pots were decorated with distinctive wavy-line designs. The lines were drawn with combs made of fish spines, animal bones and wood. The idea of pottery in general, and of wavy-line decoration in particular, might have been an independent local invention which spread beyond the boundaries of North-Central Africa into West Africa and down to the lakes of East Africa. It may also have spread toward the forest through the Shari and Ubangi basins, though traces of it have not yet been found.

Fish was certainly one of the foods cooked in the new-style pots. One important artefact which survives in the abandoned waterside 'villages' is the harpoon. Harpoon heads were carved from bone, given a serrated edge and fixed on to a shaft. They were probably used to spear fish and waterfowl and even crocodiles. Stone tools were less common in a marsh environment, where stone could be scarce. None of the ways in which reeds, nets and wood were used in the economic exploitation of the waterside environments can be rediscovered because the material decays beyond recognition. Only the harpoons remain.[10]

The fishermen of the northern rim of Central Africa probably spoke Nilo-Saharan languages.[11] This great family of languages is still spoken by the Songhai boatmen of the Niger in West Africa, by the Kanuri of Lake Chad and by the Nilotic peoples of the East African lakes. In North-Central Africa their old habitat dried up, and the Nilo-Saharans had to take to the green hills of Wadai and Dar Fur. Many more moved south to become the modern Central Sudanic peoples – the Sara, the Madi, the Mangbetu. As they did so they were under great pressure to perfect their food-gathering techniques.

THE BEGINNING OF TROPICAL FARMING

The pressure of climate which forced the people of North-Central Africa to modify their food-gathering practices slowly led to the development of agriculture. This development was a fundamental contribution to the

9 *Ibid.*, 535.
10 *Ibid.*, 529–30, 533.
11 Joseph H. Greenberg, *Languages of Africa*, The Hague, 1963, presents the revised Greenberg language classification which underpins this discussion.

economic history of Africa. In North-Central Africa farming was not introduced by the diffusion of foreign ideas and skills but by local ingenuity and innovation. The region became the cradle of a major tropical crop.

The origin of cereal farming is a complex historical event. Many peoples of the world learned about agriculture, along with the necessary seeds and tools, from their neighbours. In Central Africa the diffusion of such learning was difficult. Barley and wheat, which grew well in North Africa, were not suited to the climate of Central Africa. The peoples of North-Central Africa therefore had to domesticate their own tropical grasses. They had long gathered wild seed on sweeping plains bordering the Sahara. When desiccation of the land began 8 000 years ago, they actively sought ways in which to encourage tropical seeds on the most favourable surviving locations, and began regularly to harvest them when ripe. The almost accidental domestication of cereals can no longer be interpreted as a skill learnt once and for all, but as part of an evolutionary process which progressed in fits and starts. North-Central Africa was an ideal place for such an evolution to occur since it had plentiful wild sorghum. The gatherers naturally collected the largest seeds, the ones least likely to shatter over the ground, the ones with the fastest germination and the greatest resistance to drought. They unconsciously gave preference in their collecting to varieties whose heads all ripened at once rather than slowly over the season. Each of these selective processes took the gatherer one step nearer to evolving a domestic species with large, non-shattering seeds which could be planted and harvested.[12] The kind of sorghum first domesticated is called *bicolor*. It is the one closest to wild sorghum. Although it was first grown in the belt between Lake Chad and the Nile, it spread outward to West Africa and to India. In each area domestication continued to evolve, and new 'races' of sorghum became the local speciality. In North-Central Africa continuing sorghum evolution led to a local 'race' called *caudatum*. It became the crop of the old Nilo-Saharan fishermen and food-gatherers.[13]

The human manipulation of plant genes in order to obtain desirable varieties of crops is matched by changing human attitudes to plant care. At first plants were merely protected while growing spontaneously, but later active encouragement resulted in deliberate planting. Over most of Africa between the Sahara and the Equator, people experimented in plant protection and plant selection, thus ennobling African rice, finger millet and candle millet, in the same way in which peoples of North-Central

12 Jack R. Harlan, Jan M. J. de Wet and Ann B. L. Stemler (eds), *Origins of African Plant Domestication*, The Hague, 1976; editors' introduction on 'Plant domestication and indigenous African agriculture', pp. 3–4.

13 J. R. Harlan and Ann B. L. Stemler, 'The races of sorghum in Africa', in Harlan *et al.* (eds), *Origins*, pp. 465–77.

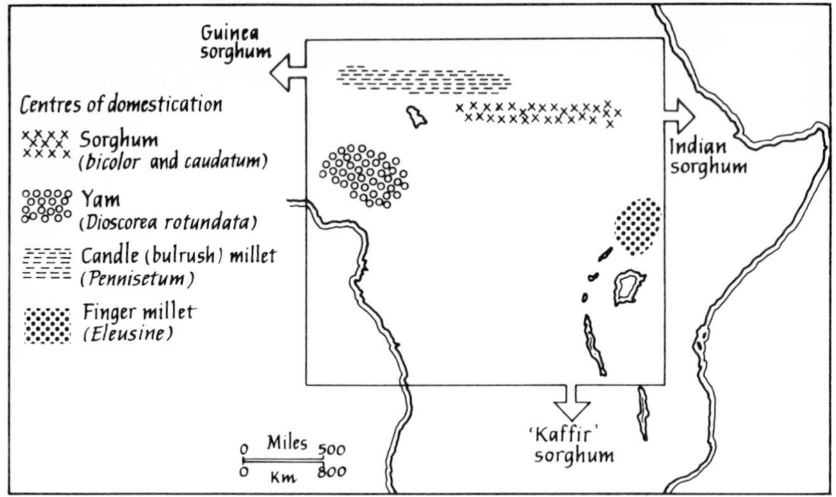

1:3 Crop domestication in North-Central Africa
Source: Adapted from J. R. Harlan, J. M. de Wet and A. B. L. Stemler (eds), *Origins of African Plant Domestication*, The Hague, 1976, pp. 336, 473, 477.

Africa ennobled sorghum.[14] Although the earliest agriculture developed naturally, and slowly, the intensification of agriculture was another matter and belongs to a more recent period, 4 000 years ago. It was then that the northern waterways rapidly dried up. Farmer-gatherers, who had been quite extravagant in their carefree use of extensive land, now had to concentrate intensively on the limited shores of shrinking lakes as each season's floodwater receded. Well-chosen seed could germinate before the soil dried out and ripen with very little moisture in years of drought. It was the pressure of climate which caused agriculture to replace foraging as North-Central Africa's source of plant food.[15] Foraging nevertheless remained an important economic activity everywhere, and twentieth-century farmers collected seeds of sixty different wild grasses to supplement their agriculture.[16]

14 See also Thurstan Shaw, 'Early crops in Africa: a review of the evidence', in Harlan *et al.* (eds), *Origins*, pp. 107–53; Lech Krzyzaniak, 'New light on early food production in the Central Sudan', *JAH*, xix, 1978, 159–72, gives the evidence for sorghum cultivation at Kadero, outside Khartoum, before 3000 B.C.
15 Harlan and Stemler, 'Plant domestication', in Harlan *et al.* (eds), *Origins*, pp. 15–16; see also Patrick J. Munson, 'Archaeological data on the origins of cultivation in the south-western Sahara and their implications for West Africa', in Harlan *et al.* (eds), *Origins*, pp. 187–209, which is illuminating for Central African parallels although actually about the northern ancestors of ancient Ghana.
16 Harlan and Stemler, 'Plant domestication', in *Origins*, p. 9.

Agriculture changed life styles and social organisation. Crops had to be protected from baboons and thieving neighbours. A settled way of life was necessary to tend and harvest plants and to defend the village granaries. Village chores had to be allocated among men, women and children. As agriculture spread from the easy alluvial lake soils to the rougher ground beyond, community efforts were needed to clear land with fire and stone axes, and till it with weighted wooden digging sticks or stone hoes. The broken plot was used for several years while its fertility lasted, thus encouraging stability and the building of more permanent houses. A fixed abode did enable families to accumulate more material possessions such as beer pots, sleeping mats, grindstones. When land was exhausted, or population increased, or drought and locusts destroyed the farms, villages split apart or moved communally to the nearest available land. Although the spread of farming communities was rather slower than the spread of hunting or fishing communities, they did spread a few miles at a time, a few tens of miles in a generation; and although they were frequently in conflict with hunters needing open tracts, they nevertheless colonised very large areas of the huntsman's under-populated northern savanna.

While cereal agriculture was evolving on the southern borders of the Sahara, a similar, equally revolutionary, process was taking place with regard to animal food supplies. Although hunting remained an important source of meat, the peoples of North-Central Africa acquired domesticated chickens, goats, sheep and cattle. Tame dogs helped with hunting, and northern groups later kept horses for riding.[17] Milking and butter-making became known, though meat-rearing was certainly an older skill. The domestication of these animals, and the origins of pastoral skills, did not develop within Central Africa, but further north. Eight thousand years ago, while fishing was proving so fruitful in the south Sahara, the peoples of the central Sahara were experimenting with cattle-keeping on the then green hills, and Sahara rock-artists drew pictures of long-horned cows in their shelters.[18] These cattle could have been domestic descendants of the wild cattle of North Africa, or they could have infiltrated the Saharan pastures from Asia. Their economic success was considerable, and a careful husbandman could increase his herd each year. In times of drought cattle could be moved to alternative pasture provided they were kept away from areas of trypanosomiasis or other disease. Cattle cushioned the short-term successes and disasters of a purely agrarian economy, as insurance, as wealth, as a source of prestige and influence. In very dry areas cattle specialists could live from their herds plus a little trade in grain. In most of

17 G. P. Murdock, *Africa: Its Peoples and Their Culture History*, New York, 1959, p. 228.
18 Angela E. Close, 'Current research and recent radiocarbon dates from northern Africa', *JAH*, xxi, 1980, 149–50, publishes the latest evidence for cattle and other domestic animals in Libya and neighbouring countries about 6000 B.C.; Henri Lhote, *The Search for the Tassili Frescoes*, London, 1959, provides illustrations, pp. 80–1.

North-Central Africa a mixed farming economy, with both crops and livestock, became the preferred pattern.

Historians spend much time exploring the history of food crops. They devote rather less time to the history of cooking. Yet cooking food probably required almost as much labour as growing it. The domestic tasks involved in food preparation were legion. Shelling, flailing, winnowing, peeling, gutting, and especially pounding all required hours of effort. The fetching of firewood was a particularly heavy chore often left to women. So too was the collecting, drying and cutting of dung fuel in areas where wood fuel was scarce. Cooking also involved the carrying of water which could require miles of trekking to perennial streams in the dry north. Water vessels had to be made and maintained for carrying, storing and cooking. One important if specialised form of food processing came to be beer-brewing, which used several fruits and grains but especially millet.

While the cereal revolution was getting under way in the northern savanna of Central Africa, a quite different food-producing revolution was beginning among the forest peoples of West Africa, where grain crops were difficult to ripen. One of the oldest food plants to be harvested in Africa was the yam. A whole variety of wild yams grew in the forest and northern woodland of both Central and West Africa. By gradually increasing the care and attention that was given to the collecting of wild yams, a natural process of tending them evolved. This vegecultural form of farming enabled gathering peoples to live more settled lives, to draw greater crops from the land, and to increase the forest population. This near-cultivation became especially important in Nigeria, where tubers up to two feet in length became a major source of food. The change from encouraging and harvesting spontaneous yams to the deliberate planting of the African *Dioscorea rotundata* created a truly domesticated plant evolved by human selection. One powerful incentive to specialising in *rotundata* yams was that they, unlike many other types, contained no poison which had to be extracted before cooking. Yam-gatherers and -planters perfected appropriate stone hoes for digging up their crop. Ritual, as well as technology, played a part in training societies to grow yams effectively. Once seasonal work patterns had been perfected, however, forest peoples could live well on yam agriculture.[19]

A second important crop of the forest was from the palm tree, *Elæis guineensis*. Oil palms have a fruit which is particularly rich in food value. A process of gathering wild palm nuts, and of protecting local palm trees, preceded the systematic harvesting of palm crops.[20] Palm-oil became

19 D. G. Coursey, 'The origins and domestication of yams in Africa' in Harlan *et al.* (eds), *Origins*, pp. 383–408, especially pp. 398–9 on ritual; Oliver Davies, *West Africa Before the Europeans*, London, 1967, pp. 118, 149, 206.

20 David R. Harris, 'Traditional systems of plant food production and the origins of agriculture in West Africa', Harlan *et al.* (eds), *Origins*, pp. 325–6.

particularly important in association with yam cooking. Although the evidence for early yam and palm cultivation is still quite slight, it would not be at all surprising if both tree cropping and tuber vegeculture were well advanced in Cameroun 4 000 years ago. It was in Cameroun that the two agricultural traditions of forest and savanna met.

The meeting of forest vegeculture and savanna cereal farming in the fertile uplands of the Cameroun–Nigeria border was associated with an important new stage in man's industrial development. This was the 'neolithic' polishing of heavy stone tools. The hunters continued to use stone-chipping techniques to make small sharp tools, but the farmers began to hone the working edges of their axes and hoes by grinding them. As they were driven by drought and rivalry to colonise the ever more heavily wooded and forested areas towards the Ubangi and Zaire basins, they required large numbers of ground axes which they manufactured from haematite rock and fitted with wooden handles.[21] These successful neolithic farmers of Cameroun did not speak the Nilo-Saharan languages of Central Africa but the Niger-Congo languages of West Africa. When they began to explore farming opportunities in Central Africa they carried their languages with them.

About 4 000 years ago, give or take a dozen centuries, the farmers of Cameroun began to feel short of land for their highly extensive forms of scattered farming. In their search for new territory they spread out on two very distinct fronts. One was the northern woodland front, into the Ubangi basin; the other was the western forest front, into the Zaire basin. The woodland front, which eventually 'colonised' a broad belt of North-Central Africa, originated in and around the plateau of Adamawa. Its people spoke the Adamawa-Ubangian branch of West Africa's Niger-Congo languages. In addition to the local sorghum, their crops probably included Guinea sorghum and finger millet. Their insurance against drought was probably bulrush millet.[22] Gradually the Ubangian peoples, ancestors of the Baya and the Banda and the Azande, spread east to the Nile watershed absorbing most of the woodland population whom they met. Even the most successful survivors from the hunting way of life, the northern pygmies, adopted the Ubangian languages to conduct trade, peace negotiations and marriage deals with their new neolithic neighbours.

The second front on which Cameroun farmers advanced into almost virgin territory was the forest front. There, western pioneers, from the southern part of the Benue basin, were more concerned with root and tree

21 H. van Moorsel, when showing visitors polished hoe heads in the Kinshasa museum, used to demonstrate their probable use with a similar, recent, hafted hoe from New Guinea; see also P. de Maret, F. van Noten and D. Cahen, 'Radio-carbon dates from West-Central Africa: a synthesis', *JAH*, xviii, 1977, 492–5.

22 Nicholas David, 'History of crops and peoples in Northern Cameroon to A.D. 1900' in Harlan *et al.* (eds), *Origins*, p. 245.

crops than with cereals, but were sufficiently versatile to adapt themselves to every economic challenge and opportunity which they met. Their success in practising the twin skills of vegeculture and agriculture was remarkable, and population grew. The language of the western farmers did not belong to the same branch of the Niger-Congo languages as did that of their northern neolithic contemporaries. In the west the new forest farmers spoke Bantu languages. Two thousand years later their descendants were to carry these languages right across Africa and down into South Africa.

The western neolithic culture adopted polished axe heads with an unusual neck feature. In the forest they had also used pottery of a distinctive style. The agricultural industry, and its associated early Bantu language, also spread from the Cameroun mainland to the large off-shore island of Bioko (Fernando Po). There Stone Age agriculture throve on the hillsides until recent centuries, unchallenged by the Iron Age which swept the rest of Central Africa fifteen hundred years ago. On the mainland the neolithic economy spread along the Gabon coast and into lower Zaire. A Kinshasa neolithic culture began to flourish in the southern savanna of West-Central Africa in the last centuries before Christ. The evidence of pottery and polished stone is not enough to guarantee that food producing, rather than advanced food gathering, had spread right through the western forest before the Christian era, but it seems likely.[23] It is also likely, but not yet proven, that the neolithic Bantu spread similarly through the eastern forest, or perhaps through its open northern margins, to reach the highlands on the borders of East Africa. Once out of the restricting forest environment the Bantu were free to use their agricultural flexibility to dramatic effect. Before they did so, however, new technological changes began to reach Central Africa. The Iron Age was at hand.

BLACKSMITHS, FARMERS AND THE FURTHER SPREAD OF BANTU LANGUAGES

The discovery, use and spread of iron marked an important stage in the history of nearly all the world's peoples, not least those of Central Africa. Metals are a versatile and efficient, if rather expensive, substitute for wood, bone and stone in the making of tools. The smelting of soft metals was first achieved on the northern side of the Mediterranean and rapidly spread to pharaonic Egypt, where copper and gold were used. The use of these soft metals did not initially spread to the rest of Africa. When, rather less than 3 000 years ago, the more difficult technical skill of smelting hard iron was perfected, the knowledge spread rapidly across Africa. Early tropical iron working was practised in two areas on the fringe of Central Africa. One

23 P. de Maret, 'The "Neolithic" problem in the West and South', in F. van Noten (ed.), *The Archaeology of West Central Africa*, Graz, Akademische Druk und Velagsanstalt, forthcoming, cited with kind permission of the author.

was on the Jos plateau in Nigeria. The other was in the kingdom of Meroe, on the middle Nile. Both places practised iron smelting about 2 500 years ago, just as it was spreading into Western Europe.

The skills required to make iron were complex and labour-intensive. Iron ore had to be gathered or mined, sorted and mixed with hardwood charcoal. It was then placed in either a pit or, better still, a furnace with a chimney. To increase the natural draught, bellows made of pottery and leather were set up around the pit or furnace and fixed to clay pipes which channelled air into the fire. A team of strong young men strenuously pumped the bellows for hours to the strains of work songs. In some places the furnace was in the middle of the village. In others the whole process had a flavour of ritual and was conducted in a remote place. Women were then not allowed near. In some societies, including many Bantu ones, iron-masters became persons of status and prestige in the community, rivalling the old hunt-masters for power and influence. When the iron-stone had 'cooked', and the waste slag had melted away, the craft-master took the spongy lump of 'bloom' from the furnace and carried it to the village forge. There it was reheated and hammered into usable wrought iron. The blacksmith became the great village artisan. He designed, manufactured, decorated and sold iron objects. Razors, jewellery, small blades and arrowheads were among the light objects made at an early date. Later knives, cutlasses and matchets replaced less wieldy stone cutting-tools. Later still, in some places only much later, the heavy tools, axes, mattocks and hoes, came to be made of iron. These new tools had the added advantage that they could be resharpened, and when the hoes were worn down the metal could be reforged.

The Iron Age probably reached the neolithic Bantu of Central Africa's forest from West Africa and from the Nile. The tradition could have spread from Nigeria to the neolithic communities of the western forest and hence out into the southern savanna. In West-Central Africa it is likely that iron smelting was based on pit furnaces. The archaeological evidence for the use of iron in the west dates from about the fourth century A.D. in western Zaire. The migrant Vili iron-masters from northern Kongo used pits to smelt iron in nineteenth-century northern Angola. Such pits remained in use in southern Angola as late as the 1930s.[24]

The iron industries of the eastern half of Central Africa are likely to have adopted their smelting furnaces from Meroe.[25] Already in the last centuries before Christ some iron working may have been practised on the farthest eastern side of Zaire close to the East African border. The effect of introducing iron to farmers in a fertile open area seems to have been almost explosive. Population grew rapidly, and Iron Age communities spread out

24 Ethnographic film at the Powell-Cotton Museum, Birchington, England, demonstrates the process.

25 See *Annual report of the British Institute in Eastern Africa*, 1977–8, 3.

to settle and farm the lake and hill regions in the corner of East Africa adjacent to the great equatorial forest. As they did so they acquired a new, third, agricultural tradition to add to their knowledge of cereal and root farming. This was the cultivation of the vegetable-banana. This crop had been domesticated in South-East Asia and probably reached the east coast with Indonesian seafarers at about the beginning of the Iron Age. Bananas became a staple food and a source of beer for the Bantu, and undoubtedly helped them spread their influence with amazing rapidity to the whole southern and south-eastern part of Central Africa.

The southern half of Central Africa had an early history which was very different from that of the northern half of the region. It was part of the great cul-de-sac of southern Africa into which the food-producing revolution spread, although very slowly. Until about two thousand years ago pottery was seldom if at all known in the Zambezi basin or in West-Central Africa. Neither cereal farming nor the tending of root and tree crops was widely practised among the dominant hunting population, though some polished stone axes had come into recent use in Katanga. It is possible that some sheep-rearing[26] may have filtered south in the very last centuries of the Stone Age, but domestic stock-keeping was certainly not widespread. All the great economic changes which had built up cumulatively in the last ten thousand years of the Stone Age reached the south suddenly. They did so more or less simultaneously with the arrival of iron-working skills. The change was so dramatic that it was associated with a wholesale cultural transformation. In the thousand years from about A.D. 400 to about 1400 the population of West-Central, East-Central and South-Central Africa not only increased dramatically but also changed; at the beginning of the period it was composed of Khoisan-speaking hunters and gatherers, who subsequently became Bantu-speaking farmers and herders. By 1400 the last Late Stone Age hunters had been outnumbered and absorbed in all but a few pockets of the southern savanna.

The eastern Bantu seem to have spread their ideas southward from the lakes region on two distinct fronts. One was the woodland front which brought the Iron Age to Zambia. The other was the coastland front which reached Mozambique by way of the coastal hills of Tanzania and then spread inland to Zimbabwe. The woodland Bantu may have been a little slower to respond to the draw of the south than the coastland Bantu. When they did begin to move into the southern savanna, however, they spread fast. Their languages did not have time to evolve all the distinctive characteristics of vocabulary and pronunciation which separated the older

26 Sheep and other pre-Iron Age animals in Central Africa require careful research, though it seems possible that sheep and pottery spread from West-Central Africa to the Cape area of western South Africa independently of the contemporaneous spread of iron and cattle from East-Central Africa to the Natal area of eastern South Africa; see T. C. Maggs, 'Some recent radiocarbon dates from eastern and southern Africa', *JAH*, xviii, 2, 1977, 171–2.

forest Bantu languages. Although the wide similarity of the woodland Bantu languages of Bemba and Luba and Kongo was once thought to be a sign of great antiquity,[27] the contrary is probably the case. The woodland languages are similar because they spread rapidly and above all recently. The dating of the spread of the woodland Bantu is a comparatively easy matter. Most archaeological sites with Early Iron Age pottery can be presumed to be associated with Bantu-speakers. The dates so far available from radiocarbon measurements cluster around the fifth century A.D.[28] Although the woodland was not an environment of first preference for early Bantu farmers, it was nevertheless one in which they could survive. The speed of their colonisation may reflect a constant search for better resources. One region, however, did prove especially attractive. This was the small lakes region of the Upemba basin through which the upper Zaire flows two hundred miles before entering the forest.[29]

The Upemba population of the fifth century grew rapidly around the lakes and absorbed the Late Stone Age peoples. Shelters gave way to solid houses, grindstones were placed in graves to provide flour in the after-life, iron hoes represented the practice of agriculture, and palm nuts were proof of tree-tending. Bones did not survive in the earliest village middens to indicate the relative importance of fish, game, goats and cattle. The early woodland farmers of south Zaire concentrated on survival and self-reliance, but some cross-fertilisation of ideas nevertheless took place. Artisans, for instance, were often travelling people who carried ideas. The salt-trade provided an example. Salt was an important necessity to an agrarian folk adapting itself to a diet of grain, but good salt was scarce. In the dry season expeditions were therefore organised to visit brine springs or salt lakes. The salt-panners gathered large quantities of wood for the purpose of boiling pots of salt water until they had dry cakes of salt to carry home. At the salt mines people met each other and exchanged ideas, crafts and decorated art forms. One such salt-manufacturing site was located at Kapwirimbwe, near to the modern capital of Zambia.[30]

The expansion of the lacustrine Bantu towards the hills and coastlands of the Indian Ocean began two thousand years ago. The great culture complex of new technology, new languages, new agrarian economies and new stock-rearing skills spread from one mountain 'island' to another

27 Roland Oliver, 'The problem of the Bantu expansion', *JAH*, vii, 1966, 361–76 is the key document which stimulated the collaboration of linguists, archaeologists and historians in search of an explanation for the expansion of the Bantu languages; the latest synthesis is Roland Oliver and Brian M. Fagan, 'The emergence of Bantu Africa' in J. D. Fage (ed.), *The Cambridge History of Africa*, II, Cambridge, 1978, ch. 6.

28 Phillipson, *Later Prehistory*, pp. 140–1.

29 Pierre de Maret, 'Chronologie de l'Age du Fer dans la Dépression de l'Upemba en République du Zaïre', Ph.D. thesis, Université Libre de Bruxelles, 1978, II, pp. 145 ff.; P. de Maret, F. van Noten and D. Cahen, 'Radio-carbon dates from West-Central Africa', 481–505.

30 Phillipson, *Later Prehistory*, p. 150.

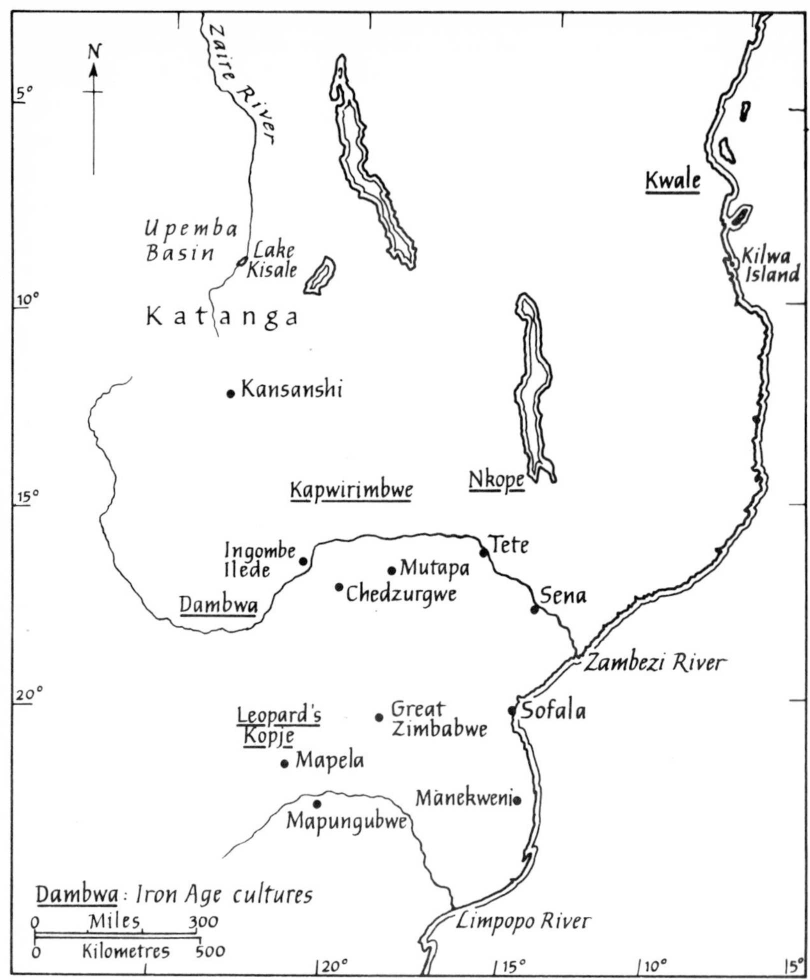

1:4 Iron Age industry in South-Central Africa
Source: Drawn from D. W. Phillipson, *The Later Prehistory of Eastern and Southern Africa*, London, 1977, especially figs. 59 and 64.

across the dry plains. By the second century A.D. the coast had been reached, and 'Kwale' pottery was being manufactured in villages all over the coastal hills of Kenya and Tanzania. By the fourth century a similar 'Nkope' style of pottery was in common usage in Malawi. The most ambitious and dynamic of the pioneers followed the coastland all the way to Natal in South Africa. Their success was partly due to the mobility provided by cattle ownership.[31]

31 Martin Hall and J. C. Vogel, 'Some recent radiocarbon dates from Southern Africa', *JAH*, xxi, 4, 1980, 431–55.

Between the Zambezi and the Limpopo the coastland Bantu spread inland on to the 5 000-foot African plateau. The highlands were free of malaria and tsetse flies, so that both people and cattle were healthier. The Zimbabwean Iron Age economy slowly began to flourish as agricultural settlements proliferated. One of these settlements briefly occupied the hill at Great Zimbabwe several hundred years before it became the centre of a kingdom.[32] In the sixth century the westward drift of Zimbabwean farmers reached the middle Zambezi and crossed into Zambia. At Dambwa they built larger and more permanent villages than before. Their houses, although small, were rectangular and solidly built of pole and *daga*. Their crops included beans and squashes. Cattle were certainly herded in the valley by the seventh century. By the eighth century, village elders had a range of material wealth and their funerary offerings included iron bracelets, copper bangles and even cowrie shells.[33]

CRAFTSMEN AND ELDERS IN THE EASTERN SAVANNA

About A.D. 1000 the age of exploration, settlement and conversion, as the Iron Age economy took hold, gave way to a later Iron Age with a growing level of material prosperity. The two themes which dominated the later prehistory of Central Africa were the development of new skills in mining, in craftsmanship, in farming and in cattle-range management and the perfection of social institutions to manage communities which were growing in scale and complexity. For the first time Central Africans saw real social distinctions develop between leaders and subjects. Priests, rain-makers, hunting-charm manufacturers, copper-mine owners, cattle barons, ferry-keepers, salt-pan guardians, blacksmiths, gold-carriers and commercial interpreters vied with one another for political influence.

One of the most interesting areas of prosperity was the Upemba basin of the upper Zaire which had so appealed to the early woodland Bantu. The inhabitants of Lake Kisale made pottery of a distinctive style from the eighth century, and within a couple of hundred years a fully-fledged 'Kisale civilisation' had emerged. Agriculture, chicken-raising and hippopotamus-hunting carried on as before, but a more specialised source of prosperity arose from the fishing industry. Cooperative groups of fishermen exploited the lakes systematically, cleaned old channels, dug new ones, and drained lakes from one to another to improve production. Canoes were developed to catch and carry fish, and special braziers were invented to cook fish on canoes. Fish-drying allowed the preservation, head-loading and long-

32 Peter Garlake, *Great Zimbabwe*, London, 1973, p. 182; for a short account of Zimbabwe in the Iron Age, see David Birmingham and Shula Marks, 'Southern Africa' in Roland Oliver (ed.), *The Cambridge History of Africa*, III, 1977, pp. 567–97.
33 Phillipson, *Later Prehistory*, pp. 124–5.

distance marketing of fish, a trade which became prosperous and drew Kisale people into contact with neighbours.

The external contacts of Kisale brought iron and salt from the north and copper from the south. They led to a regional exchange economy in agricultural and pastoral produce between lake-dwellers and farmers. Trade was profitable for the rich, and Kisale fish merchants became very rich by Central African standards. Their craftsmen made needles, fish-hooks and copper nails; their jewellers made personal ornaments for wives and children, and solid anklets of heavy copper; ivory and bone carvers decorated pendants to hang on copper chains. The rich grave-goods of some children suggested that they had been born to privilege and that wealth was inherited in families rather than won through individual enterprise. Important men were given sacrificial wives to accompany them in death. Metal specialists were buried with their anvils. As prosperity grew, the lake-side population expanded, the market for luxuries grew and trade goods from the Indian Ocean began to reach Lake Kisale.

One consequence of the growth of Kisale civilisation was the need for better political organisation to manage an increasingly stratified society of rich and poor. The evidence for political organisation is mainly conjectural. Elaborately decorated war axes were probably symbolic weapons associated with great chiefs. Small bells were probably items of political regalia, though none of the great double bells so widely used by Iron Age kings has been found. Public works probably involved the management of the river–lake system by a central administration. Although trade can grow without political initiative, political protection of both routes and markets is an advantage, and political families become important customers for luxury items. Above all, the density of population leads one to suppose that the Kisale societies needed political government on a scale hitherto unknown in Central Africa. Most woodland Bantu still lived thinly dispersed across the savanna. They were not usually tied to any particular territory, and when disputes split a community each party could go its own way in search of new land. The Kisale fishing nation could survive and prosper only in its very specific lake-side environment. When population pressure led to conflict, it was necessary to restore peace and order quickly. Thus did judges and kings evolve in a society which no longer had the age-old option of moving when social stress became intolerable.[34]

Where specific land and water areas were important, politics were about the control of territory. Elsewhere politics were more concerned with people and families, with lineages and religious affairs. The well-being of the ancestors was a constant preoccupation, and the gods intervened minutely in daily life. In central Malawi the high god of the Tumbuka was represented on earth by a great snake, Chikangombe. He travelled on the wind and was cared for by hill-top priestesses. An influential hierarchy of

34 de Maret, 'Chronologie de l'Age du Fer', pp. 347–54.

shrines developed, and shrine guardians became landowners. Gradually, however, a transition took place, and power shifted from the symbolic wives of a snake-god to male territorial chiefs.[35]

In southern Malawi people went to early Chewa shrines to pray and give offerings. They asked for rain, they asked for fertility, they feared flood and thunder, they sought success in the hunt and health for their children. People from different villages came to the great shrines whose influence cut across social and territorial boundaries. The guardians of the shrines became powerful priests. Shrine officials began to act as administrators and judicial arbitrators. A rudimentary political system had thus evolved in southern Malawi before kingship and its attendant fire rituals was developed by the Phiri clan after 1400.[36]

If fishing was a hallmark of development in southern Zaire, copper-mining became the distinctive feature of the later Iron Age in parts of Zambia. Small-scale mining and trading began early. At Kansanshi, on the western rim of the Zambian Copperbelt, seasonal immigrants carved green malachite from narrow seams by the fifth century. With simple hand tools they squeezed their way dangerously down the mines. Their small-scale, dry-season enterprise supplied many villages with copper jewellery before the industry became more standardised.[37]

By the fourteenth and fifteenth centuries the great copper mines of Zambia were in full production. No longer did output concentrate only on small items of luxury ornamentation. Copper was now cast into ingots. The Portuguese mariners who encountered these ingots on the Mozambique shore after 1500 described them as shaped like windmills. The bars were standardised into cross shapes of familiar sizes. They almost certainly came to be used as a form of money. Their worth was constant, their weight known, they felt good to handle, they did not wear away, and were easy to tie in bundles; in fact they had all the features of a good currency.[38] Currency, however, was used for social payments, for dowries, for tributes, rather than for daily purchases. A particularly fruitful market for the new copper ingots was among the Luba of southern Zaire. The thirteenth-century copper ingots were large and rather rare. A more plentiful, standardised supply of smaller ingots came into use a century later, to be followed by an abundant currency of small crosses. By the sixteenth century cowries had become sufficiently plentiful to serve as an alternative money, while in their purely decorative role cowries were partly replaced by foreign glass beads much prized by wealthy Luba.[39]

35 David Birmingham, 'Central Africa from Cameroun to the Zambezi' in Oliver (ed.), *The Cambridge History of Africa*, III, p. 532, drawing especially on J. M. Schoffeleers in B. Pachai (ed.), *The Early History of Malawi*, London, 1972.

36 T. O. Ranger, 'Territorial cults in the history of Central Africa', *JAH*, xiv, 1973, 581–97.

37 See Michael S. Bisson, 'The prehistoric coppermines of Zambia', Ph.D. thesis, University of California at Santa Barbara, 1976.

38 Phillipson, *Later Prehistory*, pp. 173–5.

39 de Maret, 'Chronologie de l'Age du Fer', pp. 254–7.

The Copperbelt was one of two areas in Zambia where a metal industry became important. The other was Ingombe Ilede, at the head of the lower Zambezi valley. In about 1400 a hill-top settlement became a trading emporium. Merchants and craftsmen visited it over several decades. The craftsmen received their copper in large, 7-pound ingots from northern Zimbabwe. The local workshops melted it down and drew it into wire. Some wire was sold in reels; some was finely coiled round fibre cores to make bracelets. The industry attracted other branches of trade as well. Ivory hunters brought their tusks to Ingombe Ilede to be carved for the luxury market or to be sold down-river to the Sofala coast. Ingombe Ilede became for a short time a gateway for imports of foreign cotton cloth and glass beads. The copper magnates probably gained political influence over both the valley trade and the village trade to north and south. But for some reason the site was less than wholly satisfactory, and before the fifteenth century was out it had been abandoned. The Chedzurgwe copper mines were conquered by the rising Zimbabwe kingdom of Mutapa.[40]

CATTLE AND GOLD IN SOUTH-CENTRAL AFRICA

The kingdom of Mutapa, which governed much of the northern Zimbabwe plateau from the fifteenth century, represents the political peak of the Iron Age in Central Africa. Its rulers succeeded earlier, and commanded more political and economic resources, than did their contemporaries in the Luba and Kongo kingdoms. The Mutapa empire of the northern Shona was built on two centuries of political expertise gained in the south, at Great Zimbabwe. It was also built on a growing overseas gold trade. But above all it was based on the solid domestic achievements of the South-Central African economy. The theme of this achievement was neither fish, as in Zaire, nor copper, as in Zambia, but cattle.[41]

The story of Zimbabwe's cattle economy, which was managed with such skill by the Shona ancestors, began on Leopard's Kopje sites, near Bulawayo, in the tenth century. Although cattle-keeping had been practised earlier, the role of cattle became more pervasive and more specialised. Ritual cattle figurines were baked of clay to symbolise wealth. Cattle-owners became more influential than other farmers, and chiefs emerged with large herds which their subjects tended for them. The Leopard's Kopje culture spread southward to the Limpopo and eastward almost to the hills of Manyika. Early cattle-keeping as a specialised way of life was also practised in the dry regions of neighbouring Botswana and south Angola, where agriculture was difficult. In the Zimbabwe highlands, however, cattle-keeping could be integrated successfully with the farming

40 See Oliver (ed.), *The Cambridge History of Africa*, III, chs 7 and 8.
41 P. S. Garlake, 'Pastoralism and *zimbabwe*', *JAH*, xix, 4, 1978, 479–93.

of sorghum, millet, peas and beans. The mixed economy of Leopard's Kopje therefore succeeded well, and in the twelfth century extensive new land was brought under cultivation. Villages became more permanent and drew in more of the scattered Early Iron Age farmers on the fringe. The most important agricultural development was the invention of terracing.[42]

Farmers in Zimbabwe soon found that fertility was often best at the bottom of slopes where top-soil had been washed down. The Leopard's Kopje farmers discovered that by building stone walls along hillsides they could increase the available area of steep, fertile agricultural land. Rainfall and damp hill mists were captured, and excessive erosion was avoided. At Mapela, near the Limpopo valley, a whole hill was entirely terraced for gardens, for houses, and for defence against jealous neighbours in the

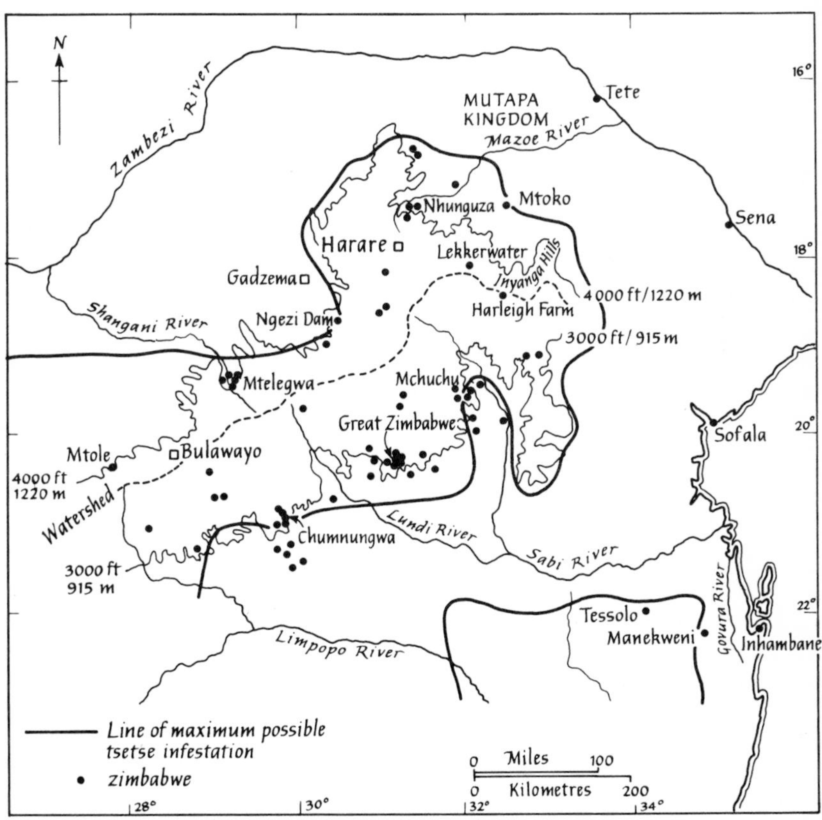

1:5 Cattle-keeping in Zimbabwe

Source: P. S. Garlake, 'Pastoralism and *zimbabwe*', *Journal of African History*, xix, 4, 1978, 484–5.

42 Garlake, *Great Zimbabwe*, pp. 155–6; T. N. Huffman, *The Leopard's Kopje Tradition*, Salisbury, 1974.

dryland. The building of terraces on the hills of Zimbabwe, like the digging of channels in the lakeland of south Zaire, required organisation and coordination. Hillside communities of terrace farmers evolved a hierarchical division of society. At Mapela the chiefs lived at the top of the hill. They ordered their houses to be built of solid *daga* laterite, with thick, decorated walls and floors. Their subjects lived in flimsy daub and wattle huts. The rulers of Mapela soon became linked to the trade networks, bought glass beads and became wealthy.[43]

The chiefs of Mapela, although prosperous, were not as prosperous as those of Mapungubwe. Mapungubwe is, along with Great Zimbabwe, one of the focal centres of the culture which grew out of the Leopard's Kopje communities. Around the foot of its hill, in the Limpopo valley, eleventh-century pastoralists cared for their cattle, built enclosures for them, made figurines of them, conducted burials with them. On the hill itself, possibly at a somewhat later date, the wealthier people ate beef in preference to game meat and grew terraced crops. Above all they were great traders. They dealt in locally mined copper, and in ivory; they bought gold beads for their chiefs, and Chinese celadon for their shrines. Their prosperity almost matched that of Great Zimbabwe.[44]

Great Zimbabwe lay on the eastern edge of the Leopard's Kopje culture zone. The surrounding country was dry, but the hill and its adjacent valley attracted adequate moisture. The site was continuously farmed from about A.D. 1200 to about 1450. The continuity is demonstrated by the uninterrupted evolution of the local pottery style, and the date is established from both foreign ceramics and radiocarbon measurements. The people of Great Zimbabwe, like those of Mapungubwe, became socially stratified as the more enterprising inhabitants dominated the terrace farms, built fine solid-walled houses, and monopolised the luxury trade in gold, porcelain, beads and cloth. The peoples of Great Zimbabwe discovered that stone walls were useful not only for terrace banks but also as free-standing boundaries and enclosures. Once stone masons had discovered this skill they rapidly improved the quality of the walls they made. Blocks of granite were broken, selected and trimmed. Decoration was included in wall design with chevron patterns or dark stones. The last great enclosure to be built at Great Zimbabwe rose 30 feet high, encircled the old complex of smaller stone compounds and dominated the walled households of the valley.

Great Zimbabwe was the capital of a kingdom, or the paramount chiefdom in a cluster of royal polities. Only a powerful ruler could have directed so much labour to stone-breaking, could have commissioned the services of so many skilled masons and could have surrounded the royal

43 Garlake, *Great Zimbabwe*, pp. 156–8.

44 Martin Hall and J. C. Vogel, 'Some recent radiocarbon dates from Southern Africa', 431–55.

dwellings with such monumental architecture. Great Zimbabwe was also involved in the gold trade, and mining became a large-scale industry across the granite hinterland. The few small workings of the Early Iron Age multiplied into thousands of mines. Some shafts were sunk a hundred feet before flooding and lack of air stopped the miner from digging his or her way even deeper into the earth. Rock was probably broken with fire and cold water. When hauled to the surface, the ore was crushed in mortars and washed to pan out the pure gold dust. Much of the gold was then traded to the east coast through Great Zimbabwe or the colonial outposts of its empire.[45]

Gold was the spectacular source of Shona wealth at Great Zimbabwe, but cattle continued to be the backbone of the daily economy. The royal herds were tended by clients who depended on the court for their status. Each ruler of a cattle district was permitted to build a small provincial court in imitation of the royal court, and royal masons were probably sent to design chiefly capitals.[46] The distribution of stone structures across the granite country was not random, but each local *zimbabwe* (or enclosure) was carefully sited near the edge of the plateau within cattle-walking distance of both summer and winter grazing. The enclosures were located away from tsetse infestation so that cattle could be drawn back from lowland foraging during the disease season. The management of the transhumant cattle economy, even more than gold-mining or terrace-building, led to differentials of wealth and to the emergence of kings.[47]

In about the eleventh century South-Central Africa began to experience a change of lasting economic and political significance. Its contacts with the world of the Indian Ocean grew in scale, regularity and importance. The east coast of Africa had supplied tortoiseshell, spices and perfumes to the later Roman Empire,[48] and rhinoceros horn and elephant tusks were regularly traded to India. Indirectly this trade percolated south to the coast of Mozambique, and Indian Ocean cowrie shells began to be imported. By the time Great Zimbabwe was built the trade had become organised, and affected the working lives of many people in South-Central Africa.

The traffic of the Mozambique coast grew steadily until A.D. 1500. Merchants could not sail from India or Arabia in a single monsoon season, and therefore established a half-way house on Kilwa island, north of the Mozambique border.[49] Swahili boatmen, who had learnt their navigational skills from the old Indonesian masters of the ocean, managed the cabotage trade. Swahili communities settled on the islands and bays of the

45 Garlake, *Great Zimbabwe*, pp. 183 ff.
46 P. S. Garlake, 'Rhodesian ruins – a preliminary assessment of their styles and chronology', *JAH*, xi, 1970, 506.
47 Garlake, 'Pastoralism and *zimbabwe*', 490–1.
48 *The Periplus of the Erythraean Sea*, which contains a description of trade in Roman times, is cited in G. S. P. Freeman-Grenville, *The East African Coast*, Oxford, 1962, pp. 1–2.
49 J. E. G. Sutton, *Early Trade in Eastern Africa*, Nairobi, 1973, pamphlet.

southern shore. Seasonal trading beaches and regular colonies grew up. The port of Sofala carried much of the traffic, and stone houses were built for the merchants. Market gardens were established to feed the ships' crews. Muslim dhows, down from Kilwa on the monsoon, had to be victualled before returning north with their cargoes of iron, copper and ivory and their coffers of Zimbabwe gold. The groves around Sofala were also planted with tree crops, and Swahili merchants enjoyed fresh citrus fruit and cooked their rice with locally-processed coconut oil.[50]

Far and away the most important import commodities in Central Africa's world trade were textiles. Cloth of many varieties, qualities and origins dominated the early trade of South-Central Africa; later, cotton materials became key features of Atlantic trade as well as of trans-Saharan trade to North-Central Africa. However much local textile industries expanded to meet the clothing needs of Central African societies, the market for foreign cloth continued to grow. On the Zambezi a local cloth industry developed from domestic cotton-growing. Cotton was spun by twisting it with clay weights and woven into *machira* squares which became the common currency of the valley. Control of this textile industry gave emerging chiefs in the lowlands new wealth and new power.[51]

The people of Zimbabwe used gold to pay for their imported cloth and for the occasional celadon dishes from China which were used by the kings who controlled the trade and by the priests who watched over the interests of the ancestors. The gold was carried over the mountains and down to the lowlands of southern Mozambique. There the traders built *zimbabwe* enclosures of rather inferior local stone but of typical highland design. At the enclosure of Manekweni the chief factor of the Shona trade used pottery decorated in the style of Great Zimbabwe. He probably also wore a leopard cloak, and many leopard claws were found on the great middens where they had been thrown out by the tanners. The élite at Manekweni ate well. The local countryside was tsetse-infested, but herds of cattle were pastured 70 miles away and young beef animals were brought in for the wealthy and privileged inhabitants of the enclosure. The lower classes at the trading station lived on the periphery of the settlement and relied on goats and small game for their more slender meat supply.[52] Manekweni was only 30 miles from the coast, but was well protected from sea-raiders by thick

50 João dos Santos, 'Ethiopia Oriental', in G. M. Theal (ed.), *Records of South-Eastern Africa*, Cape Town, reprint, 1964; see Birmingham and Marks, 'Southern Africa'.

51 For later Zambezi trade, see Nicola Sutherland-Harris, 'Trade and the Rozwi Mambo' in Richard Gray and David Birmingham (eds), *Pre-colonial African Trade*, London, 1970; Allen F. Isaacman, *Mozambique: the Africanization of a European Institution: the Zambezi Prazos 1750–1902*, Madison, Wisconsin, 1972; and especially M. D. D. Newitt, *Portuguese Settlement on the Zambesi*, London, 1973, ch. 10.

52 Graeme Barker, 'Economic models for the Manekweni *zimbabwe*, Mozambique', *Azania*, xiii, 1978, 71–100.

woodland and tall grass. In the sixteenth century two Portuguese travellers visited it, or a place very like it, from the port of Inhambane. The chief still ruled his domain, but his links with the highland had long since withered away.[53] An entirely new trade pattern had developed in South-Central Africa when the Zambezi was opened to Muslim and Christian traders after 1400 and new trading entrepôts were built at Sena and Tete. The gateway to the gold-bearing region moved from the southern end of the plateau to its northern rim; political power was transferred from Great Zimbabwe to the new northern kingdom of Mutapa.[54]

RAIN-PRIESTS AND RAFFIA-WEAVERS IN WEST-CENTRAL AFRICA

The Iron Age economy of West-Central Africa was similar to that of the east and the south, though the scale was often smaller. The farming population was mostly rather sparse. The copper mines in southern Congo and northern Angola were relatively small enterprises. The flood plains were small and scattered with no extensive lake systems. Cattle-keeping thrived at its best only in the highlands of southern Angola and along the plains of the Namibian border. Potters and blacksmiths confined their trade to the home community. Everyone, however, was concerned with the weather, and agriculturalists paid great attention to their rain-shrines.

The earliest known rain-shrines in Angola focused on carved wooden figurines called *malunga*. The custodians of these figurines, like shrine guardians in Malawi, could use their spiritual authority to exact tribute and loyalty from local farmers. Each deity dominated the people of a particular valley and lived in the stream which ran through it. The guardians became little chiefs, and their titles were incorporated into wider kingdoms. In the later kingdoms ancestors played a more important role than stream gods, and iron became the symbol of wealth and power. The Angolan kingdom of Kongo was just such a kingdom.[55]

The kingdom of Kongo was still in its first infancy in 1400. Political power was closely controlled by fertility priests and by custodians of the ancestral spirits. The material base for expansion was already present in the iron industry, but the major wealth of Kongo derived from its varied ecological surroundings. In the west the Kongo people had access to coastal salt lagoons and to shell fisheries where *nzimbu* currency shells could be dredged in the sand. In the east the Nkisi river resembled a tropical garden and was much favoured by millet farmers. In the forest raffia palms grew abundantly and provided the raw material for the Kongo textile industry. Squares of woven raffia became the major commodity of regional trade

53 Theal, *Records of South-Eastern Africa*.
54 See chapters by Smith and Beach below.
55 Joseph C. Miller, *Kings and Kinsmen: Early Mbundu States in Angola*, Oxford, 1976.

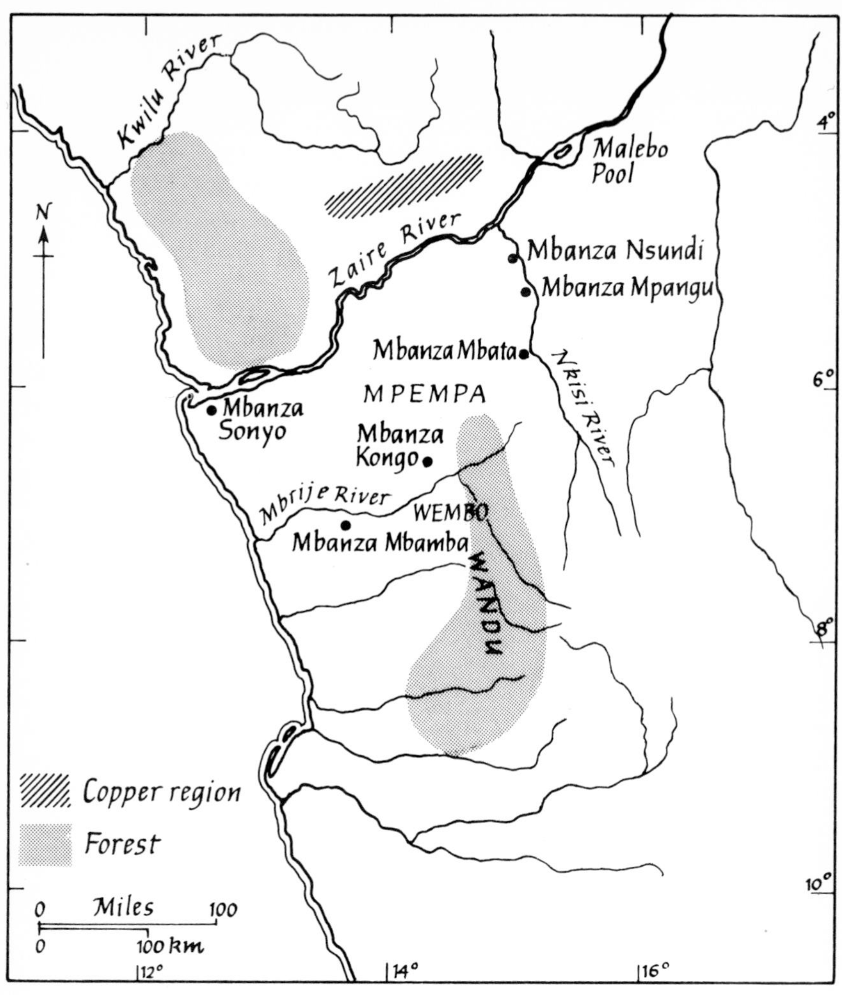

1:6 The kingdom of Kongo
Source: Anne Wilson [Hilton], 'The Kongo Kingdom to the mid-seventeenth Century', Ph.D. thesis, London University, 1977.

and a regular measure of market prices. Control of the raffia markets was a source of Kongo's political and economic influence.[56]

By 1400 all but one of the major historical factors which influenced the history of Central Africa had been set. The three main types of agriculture, based on cereals, roots and bananas, had spread to their zones of greatest effectiveness. The mining and manufacturing of iron, copper and gold had

56 Anne Hilton, *The Kingdom of Kongo to the Seventeenth Century*, Oxford, forthcoming.

spread to the major mineral zones and created networks of long-distance trade and communities of market-oriented craft-producers. The growth of the Muslim world economy had brought occasional foreign contacts to North-Central Africa and regular sea-faring commerce to the Indian Ocean zone of South-Central Africa. The only major transformation which had not yet occurred was in the west. In 1400 the Atlantic was still a closed sea, and West-Central Africa had its back to the ocean. After 1400 this situation changed dramatically. The maritime nations of Europe explosively expanded into the outer world at the end of their Dark Age. Overnight the Atlantic became a zone of opportunity for Central Africans. New crops were added to their agricultural repertoire, new religious and political ideas became available to their leaders, and new luxury goods were offered to their merchants. The price, however, was high; the opening of the south Atlantic brought new diseases, new weapons, new enemies and four hundred years of European slavery.

CHAPTER 2

The savanna belt of North-Central Africa

DENNIS D. CORDELL

North-Central Africa is an enormous area, stretching from the Adamawa plateau of central Cameroun to the Upper Nile, and from the Sahel to the fringes of the Zaire forest. The diversity of the region is also impressive. Its peoples speak a great variety of languages, they have many forms of social and political organisation, and they belong to different and shifting cultural and economic zones. A lack of research in the face of this heterogeneity creates problems for the historian. Sparse sources and the scattered distribution of extant studies have made it difficult to compose a unified perspective. In addition, North-Central Africa has often been a victim of balkanisation, its regions suffering superficial treatment as the little-regarded fringes of West Africa, the Muslim Sahel, the Nile valley and the Zaire basin. The societies of North-Central Africa did have links with these disparate areas, but their history is also one of increasing contact among themselves and with the larger world.

Changing patterns of ethnicity illustrate this theme. Ethnic groups are not discrete entities, but open groups whose membership and identity shift constantly. Not only do groups expand and contract, but also their characteristics alter through time. As in other parts of the continent, ethnic groups in North-Central Africa formed and disappeared; most are amalgams. The history of the Azande, initially a mixture of various peoples living south of the Mbomu river, is the history of an ethnic group in formation. Other groups have all but disappeared. The Sabanga of the Central African Republic (CAR), took the language and characteristics of the Banda in the early nineteenth century. Today they are largely 'Banda-ised', and their earlier identity is but a vague memory in the minds of old informants.[1]

1 Gillier, 'Les Bandas: notes ethnographiques', *L'Afrique française: renseignements coloniaux*, xxiii, 10, 1913, 392, n.1; Félix Eboué, 'Les peuples de l'Oubangui-Chari: essai d'ethnographie, de linguistique, et d'économie sociale', *L'Afrique française: renseignements coloniaux*, xlii, 11, 1932, 405; Eric de Dampierre, *Un Ancien Royaume bandia du Haut-Oubangui*, Paris, 1967, p. 173.

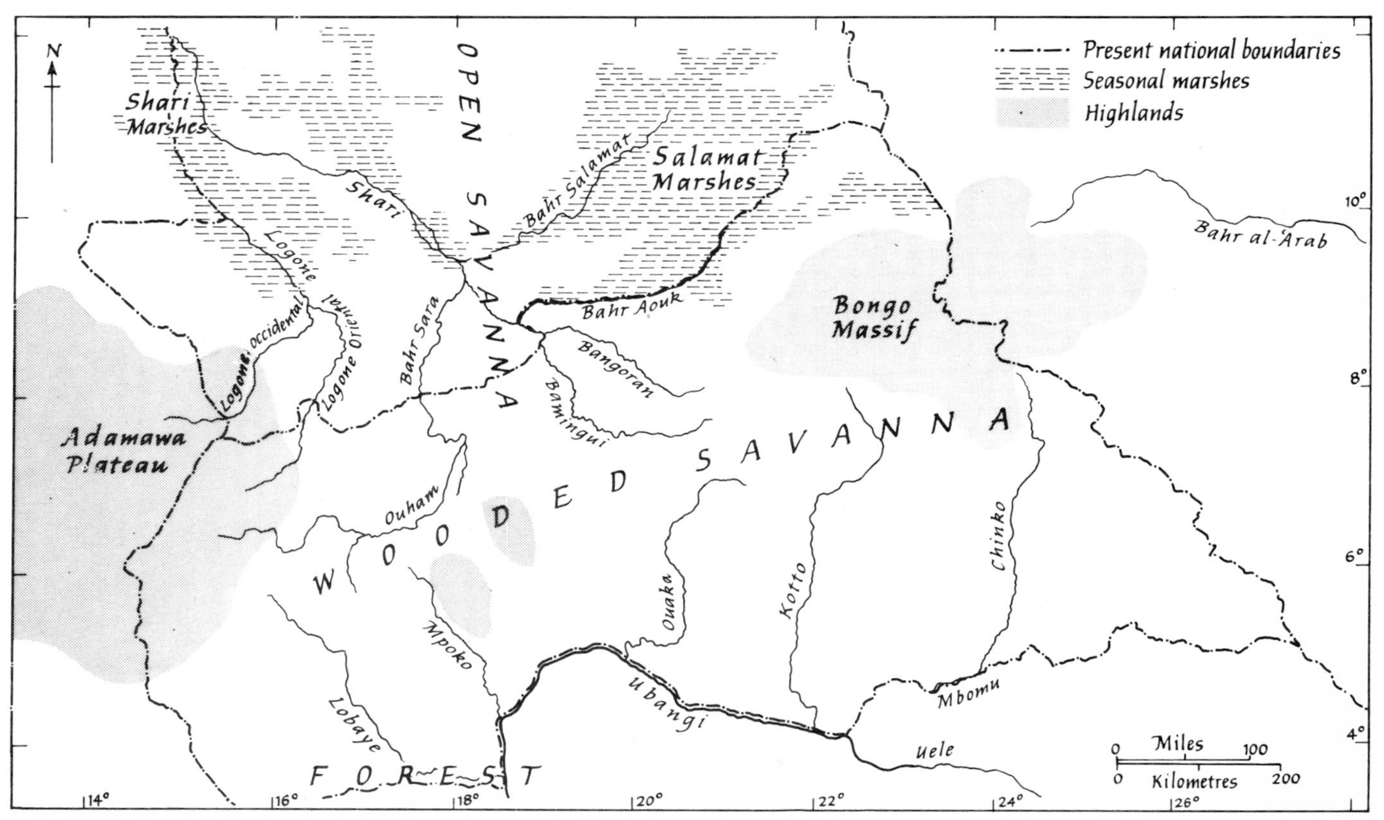

2:1 North-Central Africa

The economic and political fortunes of a group also affected its longevity. An ethnic group, like a state, a lineage, or a labour force, had to reproduce itself socially and biologically. The Bobangi traders on the Ubangi, for example, maintained their identity and their population by the absorption of outsiders.[2] Many of these people came into the society as slaves, taken in the interior and traded to the Bobangi for possible export to African and European traders on the Atlantic coast. By emphasising such ties across time and between societies, it is hoped to illustrate here that the basis exists for a unified view of North-Central African history over the last several hundred years.

THE LONG TERM : THE SAVANNA AND THE PHYSICAL ENVIRONMENT, 1400–1700[3]

Although the savanna seems open or limitless, North-Central Africa constitutes a discrete geographical unit. Most of the region falls into the Lake Chad and Zaire river basins, bordered by the Adamawa massif and Mandara mountains in the west and the highlands separating present-day Chad and CAR from the Sudan in the east. In the north, the swampy lowlands of the Salamat and the Shari separate the savannas from the Sahel and Sahara; in the south the tropical forest divides the region from the remainder of the Zaire basin.

Yet the region's geographical borders were not impermeable. The Adamawa massif, although more a part of the Benue–Atlantic zone, has had a prolonged and profound influence on the region. The peoples of North-Central Africa also interacted with others across the spine of hills separating the Zaire and Nile basins. Muslim societies in the Sahel became increasingly effective at extending their hegemony across the Shari and Salamat flood plains during the dry season. And in the far south, diverse influences bridged the border between savanna and forest.

Topographical variations within the region may also have affected the evolution of indigenous societies. The Lake Chad and Zaire basins are

2 Robert Harms, 'Oral tradition and ethnicity', *Journal of Interdisciplinary History*, x, 1, Summer 1979, 61–85.

3 Braudel suggests that history is the cumulative result of three kinds of influences, categorised by duration: the first, '*la longue durée*', or the long term, consists of those factors which alter at an almost imperceptible rate, but which affect human society most profoundly, mainly the physical environment and social structure. A second category encompasses developments of shorter duration, '*conjonctures*', which range in length from decades to centuries. Into this time-frame fit the phenomena of 'social history' described in this chapter. The third category is not made up of trends at all, but of individual events. This is '*l'histoire événementielle*', or conventional history, usually written at the level of individuals and events. Braudel argues that a true understanding of human history requires interlocking analysis of all three categories. See Fernand Braudel, *The Mediterranean and the Mediterranean World in the Age of Philip II*, trans. Sian Reynolds, New York, 1972, I, pp. 20–1, 23.

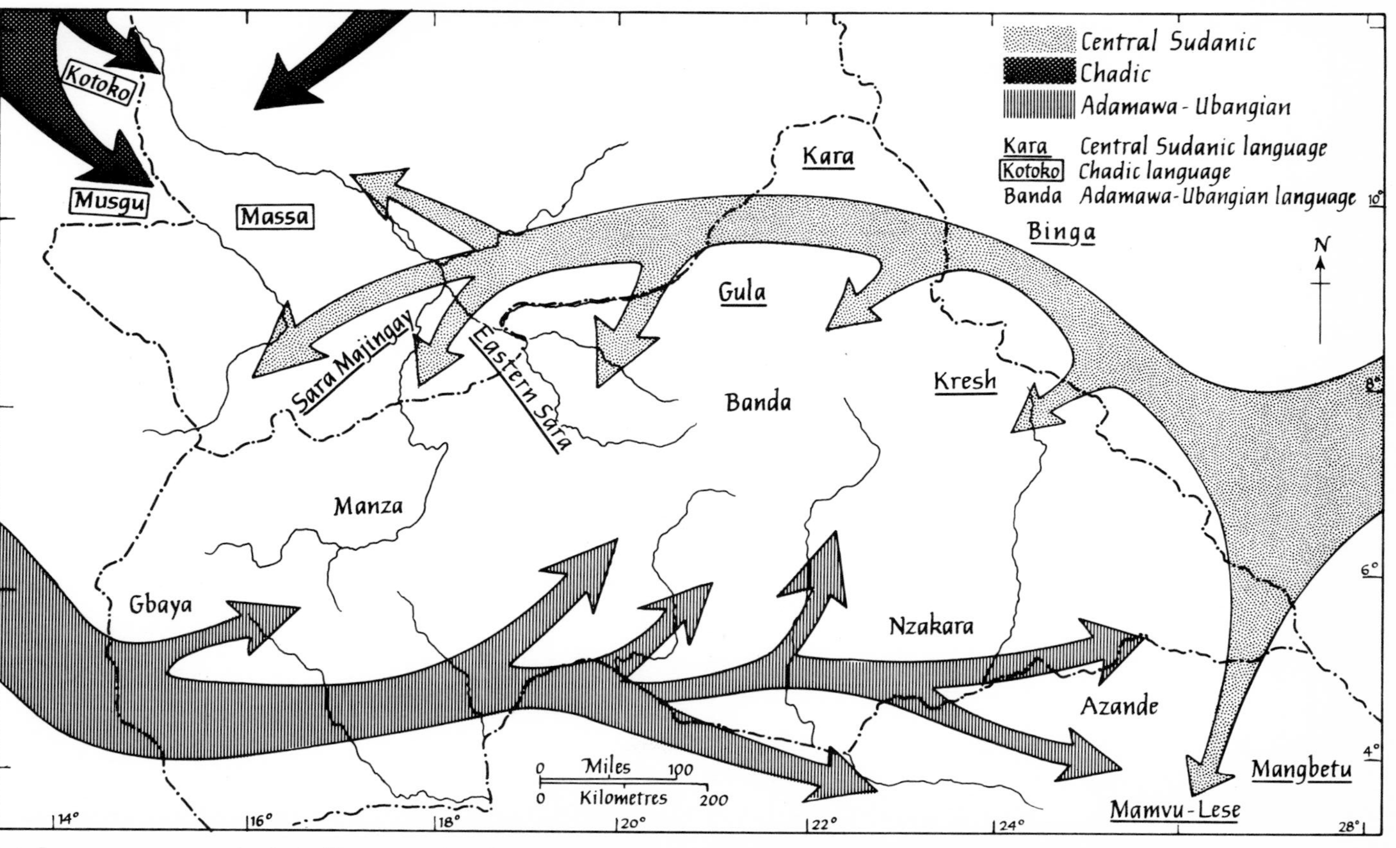

2:2 Language groups and principal languages, North-Central Africa

divided by highlands running from the Bongo massif along the Sudan border to the Adamawa plateau. In the east, most Banda peoples live to the south, between the highlands and the Ubangi and Mbomu rivers. Tributaries of these streams run almost directly north–south, serving as highways for local migration, and hence contributing to the emergence of a common culture. In present-day western and south-western CAR, the Gbaya peoples predominate south of the divide, although their settlements have also spread north-west on to the Adamawa plateau, and north into the Chad basin.

North of the Lake Chad–Zaire divide the ethnic map is not as easily summarised, but some over-all patterns are visible. The peoples living around the Shari headwaters speak closely related Central Sudanic languages. Further west, peoples along the middle Shari and upper Logone rivers speak similar languages, although groups from the Adamawa highlands may be found there as well. Although it is unlikely that these configurations reflect exactly the ethnic landscape of several centuries ago, their distribution nonetheless suggests that the Lake Chad–Zaire divide is a significant geographical feature. This may have been so long before 1400: several hundred megaliths were built perhaps two thousand years ago in the area between Bouar and Bozoum by an as-yet-unidentified civilisation. Many of them mark water sources along the crest separating the Lake Chad and Zaire basins.[4]

Other geographical features helped to shape the history of North-Central Africa. Enormous, abrupt, rock outcroppings are scattered from the southern edges of Lake Chad east to Wadai, and south to the CAR savanna. Significant enough to be clearly identified in the languages of all the peoples in the region today, these high, outwardly barren formations often contained inner recesses and hollows with enough water and soil to offer protection in time of conflict and to support permanent refugee populations.[5] The peoples and the archaeology of the outcroppings have not yet been studied in a systematic way, but both may provide important clues about the earlier history of North-Central Africa.[6] It is known, for example, that the non-Muslim Kenga who inhabit mountains near Mongo

4 Pierre Vidal, *La Civilisation mégalithique de Bouar: prospections et fouilles, 1962–1966*, Paris, 1969, pp. 22, 68; Vidal, *Garçons et filles: le passage à l'âge d'homme chez les Gbaya Kara*, Paris, 1976, pp. 42–3.

5 Pierre Prins, 'Les troglodytes du Dar Banda et du Djebel Mela', *Bulletin de géographie historique et déscriptive*, 1901, 12, 17–18, 26; P. H. Stanislas d'Escayrac de Lauture, 'Notice sur le Kordofan (Nubie supérieure)', *Bulletin de la société de géographie de Paris*, 4e série, i, 1851, 370–1; Georges Bruel, *La France équatoriale africaine: le pays, les habitants, la colonisation, les pouvoirs publics*, Paris, 1935, pp. 38, 54–55, 202; Pierre de Schlippe, *Shifting Cultivation in Africa: the Zande System of Agriculture*, London, 1956, p. 45.

6 Braudel, *The Mediterranean*, I, pp. 25–53; Vidal, *L'Archéologie et la vie: témoignage sur les sources de l'histoire en R.C.A.*, Bangui, 1974.

in the Sahel are a remnant group whose forebears migrated south to found the Muslim state of Bagirmi on the Shari.[7]

Resource endowment also influenced historical development. The irregular distribution of mineral deposits undoubtedly contributed to the rise of regional trade. Banda traditions suggest that a long time ago bridewealth was paid with large copper anklets from the east, and that people travelled far to acquire them. They probably went to Hufrat al-Nuhas in the Sudan, the only place where copper was mined in the pre-colonial era.[8]

The desire for rock salt also stimulated regional and long-distance exchange. Although small deposits exist in the CAR–Sudan–Zaire border area, most societies obtained this necessity by burning the leaves of certain kinds of plants and washing the ashes. But this process was time-consuming and produced a bitter mixture of sodium chloride and potassium sulphate. Thus purer mineral salt from the Sahel and Sahara found a ready market, first in the adjacent savanna and then further south. In the late eighteenth century, salt from deposits in Dar Fur, a state in the Sahel, made its way to non-Muslim lands in the south where a small quantity could be exchanged for a slave. Although the date when this trade began is unknown, a similar commerce further west in Kanem-Borno probably linked the desert with the savanna as early as the fifteenth century.[9]

Finally, there is the savanna itself, an open zone of high grasses and scattered trees. Not only did it have a great impact on societies within its confines, but it was itself the product of human interaction with the physical environment. In the CAR the land was originally covered by a thick, dry forest whose tall trees formed a closed canopy and prevented the growth of grass cover; similar conditions prevailed still further north. Such

7 Devallée, 'Le Baghirmi', *Bulletin de la société des recherches congolaises*, vii, 2, 3, 4, 1925, 15–16; Gustav Nachtigal, *Sahara und Sudan: Ergebnisse Sechsjähriger Reisen in Afrika*, Graz, 1967, II, pp. 679, 694–5.

8 In various places in this chapter, interpretations are partially based on oral testimonies collected in Ndele, the former capital of the Muslim slave-raiding state of Dar al-Kuti, now part of the CAR. These sources will be identified by number only; for a complete listing, see Dennis D. Cordell, 'Dar al-Kuti: A History of the Slave Trade and State Formation on the Islamic Frontier in Northern Equatorial Africa (Central African Republic and Chad)', Ph.D. thesis, University of Wisconsin, Madison, 1977. OA11.1; OA15.2/16.1; OA19.1/20.1; Georges Toque, *Essai sur le peuple et la langue Banda*, Paris, 1904; Ignatius Pallme, *Travels in Kordofan*, London, 1844, p. 351; Heinrich Barth, *Travels and Discoveries in North and Central Africa*, London, 1969, I, p. 521, II, pp. 141 and note, 488; R. Ciocardel, Birlea and Gbakpoma, *Eléments pour la géologie de l'Afrique*, Bangui, 1974, III, pp. 345–7.

9 Auguste Chevalier, *Mission Chari–Lac Tchad, 1902–1904: l'Afrique centrale française*, Paris, 1907, pp. 221–2; Charles Tisserant, 'L'Agriculture dans les savanes de l'Oubangui', *Bulletin de l'institut d'études centrafricaines (Brazzaville)*, nouvelle série, vi, 1953, 245; Muhammad ibn 'Umar al-Tunisi (Mohammed Ibn-Omar el-Tounsy), *Voyage au Darfour*, trans. S. Perron, Paris, 1845, pp. 317–18; al-Tunisi, *Voyage au Ouaday*, trans. S. Perron, Paris, 1851, p. 492; Paul E. Lovejoy, 'The Borno salt industry', *International Journal of African Historical Studies*, xi, 4, 1978, 629–32.

forests are generally resistant to fire, suggesting that agriculturalists produced the savannas as they slowly cleared the land to plant their crops.[10]

THE PEOPLING OF NORTH-CENTRAL AFRICA

Because the savannas are human-made and because their population was low and technology limited, their great area indicates a long history of human habitation. Indeed, excavations on the lower Logone and Shari rivers uncovered an important riverain civilisation, termed the Sao, dating from the end of the first millennium A.D.[11] Further south, the megaliths around Bouar probably date from between 500 B.C. and the beginning of the first millennium.[12] The enormous amounts of labour necessary to quarry, transport and erect these huge stone monuments suggest the existence of a settled agricultural society at an early date. Much further east, in river valleys north of the Mbomu, investigations have also unearthed stone implements confirming early settlement.[13]

Agricultural history generally supports this conclusion. Millets and sorghums were probably first domesticated on the northern fringes of North-Central Africa, whence they spread to the south-west and south-east.[14] Because these grains are among the oldest cultivated crops in Africa, it is possible that the people who grew them also cleared the savanna itself.

It is still not known if the present-day populations of the region are descended from these early societies. Historical studies of contemporary languages, however, suggest over-all stability.[15] Most major languages or language groups present today were probably found there in 1400. This does not, however, imply that North-Central African societies were moribund, awaiting external stimulation. The over-all configuration of language groups in Western Europe, for example, has remained relatively constant for several centuries past; yet empires have come and gone, the industrial revolution has occurred, and numerous wars have altered European societies.

10 R. Sillans, *Les Savanes de l'Afrique centrale: essai sur la physionomie, la structure et le dynamisme des formations ligneuses des régions sèches de la République centrafricaine*, Paris, 1958, pp. 258–9; Nicholas David, 'History of crops and peoples in North Cameroon to A.D. 1900', in *Origins of African Plant Domestication*, Jack R. Harlan, Jan M. J. De Wet, and Ann B. L. Stemler (eds), Paris and The Hague, 1976, pp. 230–2.

11 Annie M. D. Lebeuf, *Les Principautés kotoko: essai sur le caractère sacré de l'autorité*, Paris, 1969, pp. 37, 39, 42–44; Jean-Paul Lebeuf and Annie Masson-Detourbet, *La Civilisation du Tchad*, Paris, 1950, pp. 7–37.

12 Vidal, *Garçons et filles*, pp. 42–3.

13 Roger de Bayle des Hermens, *Recherches préhistoriques en République centrafricaine*, Paris, 1975, *passim*.

14 Stemler, Harlan and De Wet, 'Caudatum sorghums and speakers of Chari-Nile languages in Africa', *Journal of African History (JAH)*, xvi, 2, 1975, 166, 175–82.

15 Pierre Alexandre, 'Afrique centre-équatoriale et centre-occidentale', in *Histoire générale de l'Afrique noire*, Hubert Deschamps (ed.), Paris, 1970, I, p. 365; Christopher Ehret *et al.*, 'Some thoughts on the early history of the Nile-Congo watershed', *Ufahamu*, v, 2, 1974, 85–90, 96–97, 101–2.

In North-Central Africa, changes of similar magnitude undoubtedly took place within a context of relative linguistic stability. The movement, expansion and contraction of linguistic communities signalled shifts in earlier patterns of political, economic and cultural influence. Some languages disappeared altogether. In other cases, political change and economic activity brought peoples of differing linguistic backgrounds together. The association sometimes produced new languages – such as Kanuri, whose emergence paralleled the relocation of the Kanem state from the northern to the south-western side of Lake Chad in the late fourteenth century. The spread of Azande likewise heralded new political power.[16]

Longevity of a language does not necessarily imply a high degree of biological continuity among its speakers, although some continuity is likely since the transmission of an unwritten language demands that speakers pass it on and interpret it. Assuming that linguistic continuity implies a high degree of cultural continuity, a survey of the major language groups of North-Central Africa identifies the major nodes of culture that have shaped savanna history since 1400.

The Central Sudanic languages, found in the north and east, are the first group. The western subdivision of this group includes the major languages of today's southern Chad and northern and eastern CAR. The subdivision also extends south into the south-western Sudan and north-eastern Zaire.[17] These languages probably spread from south-western Sudan well before 1400. Sara Majingay and Bagirmi (Barma), for example, seem to have emerged as separate languages by A.D. 1000.[18]

Despite frequent local migration, the populations speaking these languages were apparently quite stable by 1400. They cultivated millet and sorghum, crops well-suited for the hot, dry climate. In fact, their initial expansion may be associated with the development of strains of millet and sorghums that could be grown in varied climatic zones. They also herded cattle and goats, and may have kept sheep. Their political institutions lacked positions of hereditary leadership. Nor did they practise

16 E. E. Evans-Pritchard, *The Azande: History and Political Institutions*, London, 1971, pp. 116–19; Douglas E. Saxon, 'Linguistic evidence for early contact between Saharan and Chadic speakers', paper presented at the annual meeting of the African Studies Association of the U.S.A., 1979, 20-24; Dierk Lange, 'Royaumes et peuples du Tchad', manuscript chapter presented to the Comité scientifique international pour la rédaction d'une histoire générale de l'Afrique, vol. 4, ch. 10, p. 14; H. J. Fisher, 'The eastern Maghrib and the central Sudan', in *The Cambridge History of Africa*, III, *c. 1050–c. 1600*, Roland Oliver (ed.), Cambridge, 1977, p. 291.

17 J. P. Caprile and J. Fedry, *Le Groupe des langues 'sara' (Republique du Tchad)*, Lyon, 1969; Stefano Santandrea, *A Tribal History of the Western Bahr al-Ghazal*, Bologna, 1964, p. 243; Santandrea, *Languages of the Banda and Zande Groups: a Contribution to a Comparative Study*, Naples, 1965, pp. 7–8.

18 Ehret *et al.* 'Some thoughts', 87–9.

circumcision, although body markings and the removal of lower incisors suggest passage rites.[19]

The second language group is Adamawa-Ubangian, subdivided into two branches, one centred on the Adamawa massif and the other extending eastward through the savannas along the rivers in the far south. This second branch is called Ubangian. These languages spread east into Central Sudanic territories, as well as south into the tropical forest. Other Ubangian languages such as Banda and Gbaya predominated in the savannas at the northern edge of the Zaire basin. As with the Central Sudanic group, the broad patterns of Ubangian language distribution were probably established by the end of the first millennium A.D.[20]

Contact and conflict between the cultural traditions represented by the Ubangian- and Central Sudanic-speakers is one of the long-term themes of North-Central African history. The linguistic map suggests patterns of interaction: Central Sudanic languages are found north, east and south-east of the Ubangian cluster. Until recently, this distribution has been widely accepted as proof of an Ubangian thrust from the west into a solid Central Sudanic zone. Although it is true that along the linguistic frontier in the north-east Ubangian groups such as the Ndogo and Banda have absorbed Central Sudanic-speakers, the Ubangian groups were already in the area when the Central Sudanic-speakers spread south. Their agricultural techniques, mainly of West African origin, had allowed them to exploit the wetter savannas of the Ubangi, Mbomu and Uele rivers along the fringes of the tropical forest in the south. They thus occupied a niche between the dry Chad basin in the north and the deep forest.

The peculiar distribution of the Central Sudanic societies may be partially explained by their dependence on cattle, millets and sorghums – all tolerating a relatively dry climate. These constraints led Central Sudanic-speakers to move around the wetter savannas bordering the southern river valleys. Resistance on the part of the Ubangian-speakers already present in the area may also have contributed to this pattern of expansion.[21]

The third major linguistic grouping in North-Central Africa is the Chadic language cluster found in the mountains of northern Cameroun, the plains bordering Lake Chad, and the lower Logone and Shari rivers. In this area, too, the evidence points to over-all stability. Although traditions of the Chadic peoples record much movement, most migration occurred within a relatively restricted area. In the plains, peoples such as the Kotoko, Musgu and Massa shifted residence repeatedly, mainly in search of shelter

19 Alexandre, 'Afrique centre-équatoriale', p. 365; Stemler, Harlan and De Wet, 'Caudatum sorghums', 175–82; Saxon, 'Linguistic Evidence', 14–15; Ehret *et al.* 'Some thoughts', 89, 101–2.

20 Ehret *et al.*, 'Some thoughts', 96. Also see William J. Samarin, 'Adamawa-Eastern languages', in *Linguistics in Sub-Saharan Africa: Current Trends in Linguistics*, vol. 7, Thomas A. Sebeok (ed.), Paris and The Hague, 1971, pp. 213–44.

21 Ehret *et al.*, 'Some thoughts', 99–100.

from slave raids launched by nearby Muslim states. Yet they never abandoned the region in large numbers. Written evidence from Borno in the sixteenth century suggests that the non-Muslims living along the rivers were the ancestors of present-day populations.[22]

These three major language groups have been the dominant features of the cultural landscape of North-Central Africa since at least 1400. This conclusion rejects much of the scattered narrative history which often posits large-scale migrations carrying whole peoples across the entire region or even beyond. It may appear to contradict oral traditions of many small-scale societies which refer to frequent migrations over what appear to be long distances. This contradiction is more apparent than real. North-Central Africa is, for the most part, a region of low population density. Arable land is extensive and of relatively uniform quality. Small groups have often split from larger ones to clear land and found settlements. Many of these groups also shifted settlement frequently to avoid attacks from more powerful centralised states on the northern and eastern fringes of the region. These states, such as Kanem-Borno or the problematic kingdom of Gaoga, increased from one or two in 1400 to more than double that number three centuries later with the rise of Dar Fur, Wadai and Bagirmi.

In this context of mobility, migration traditions often served as charters for new communities. Memories of even short moves were sometimes elevated to the status of foundation myths. These myths have often been interpreted as long-distance odysseys; most such traditions, however, probably record only local shifts of population.[23] Among the savanna peoples, fluid patterns of social structure combined with an hospitable environment to produce a similar pattern of short-range migration. Thus it was possible to have population mobility and long-term linguistic stability at the same time.

PHYSICAL ENVIRONMENT AND SOCIAL ORGANISATION IN THE SAVANNA

The prevalence of migration traditions in North-Central Africa and the important role they played as social charters implies substantial fluidity in social and political relationships. The Gbaya, Manza, Banda and some Sara lived in dispersed settlements; centralised authority was limited, and short-range migration common. In the case of the Gbaya at least, extreme exogamy reinforced these fissiparous tendencies. Most societies with these characteristics lived in the open savannas that cover the heart of North-

22 Bertrand Lembezat, *Les Populations païennes du Nord-Cameroun et de l'Adamaoua*, Paris, 1961, pp. 10–11; David, 'History of crops and peoples', pp. 239–41, 243. For the Kotoko, at least, A.M.D. Lebeuf would agree: see *Les Principautés kotoko*, pp. 53–80.

23 Harms, 'Oral tradition and ethnicity', 72–85; P. Van Leynseele, 'Les Transformations des systèmes de production et d'échanges de populations ripuaires du Haut-Zaire', *African Economic History*, vii, Spring 1979, 123, 126, 128.

Central Africa; different patterns of authority and settlement evolved among peoples living in the flood plains and mountains of the north-west and the forest fringes in the south. The varied forms of human society are too complex to be explained solely by geography; nonetheless, patterns of life in the savanna do suggest some tentative inferences about the relationship between human groups and their physical setting. A study of the Gbaya perhaps best illustrates the important role played by the environment.[24]

The Gbaya enjoyed a 'permissive social ecology', in which environmental constraints placed few restrictions on individual action.[25] The physical setting did not completely shape Gbaya society, but it certainly helped channel its development. The dynamics of social organisation, for example, were related to low population density and abundant land of acceptable quality. These combined to produce uncommonly high rates of mobility for an agricultural society. Social cohesion was correspondingly limited; people belonged to clans and sometimes defended clan territories, but at the same time they lived in dispersed hamlets. Fathers and sons and full brothers normally resided together throughout their lives in what might best be called extended family groupings. Beyond this level of genealogical grouping, however, residential composition and shifts were unpredictable.[26]

Gbaya economic organisation fostered similar independence. Each man controlled the labour of his household. Nuclear families usually worked alone, although in small hamlets men occasionally came together to help cultivate fields belonging to the hamlet leader. Because collective labour for the benefit of a single individual was infrequent, its product did not contribute to great economic inequality within the settlement. Private ownership of property such as huts, tools, domesticated animals and even some fields allowed most groups to be self-sufficient. Separate spheres of exchange, demanding special currencies available only to certain classes, were not a feature of the pre-colonial economy. Hence members of the

24 Ellen notes that the internal dynamics of social organisation sometimes cause societies to evolve in ways that are not necessarily in harmony with their environment. See Roy F. Ellen, 'Introduction: anthropology, the environment and ecological systems', in *Social and Ecological Systems*, Philip Burnham and Roy F. Ellen (eds), New York, 1979, pp. 8, 14. Burnham has studied the Gbaya most extensively. See *Opportunity and Constraint in a Savanna Society: the Gbaya of Meiganga, Cameroon*, New York, 1980; 'Notes on Gbaya history', in *Contribution de la recherche ethnologique à l'histoire des civilisations du Cameroun*, C. Tardits (ed.), Paris, in press; 'Permissive ecology and structural conservatism in Gbaya society', in Burnham and Ellen, *Social and Ecological Systems*, pp. 185–202; 'Raiders and traders in Adamawa', in *Asian and African Systems of Slavery*, J. Watson (ed.), Berkeley and Los Angeles, 1980, pp. 43–72; '*Regroupement* and mobile societies: two Cameroon cases', *JAH*, xvi, 4, 1975, 577–94.

25 Burnham, *Opportunity*, p. 68.

26 *Ibid.*, pp. 19–24; Burnham, 'Permissive ecology', pp. 187, 200, n.3; Burnham, personal communication, 6 Nov. 1980.

society enjoyed more or less equal access to the few prestige goods available. Nor were craft occupations like smithing the special province of particular groups, although clans possessing iron deposits did try to limit their neighbours' access to them.[27]

Extreme exogamy also contributed to the dispersed nature of Gbaya society. The marriage of a man of one clan to a woman of another precluded other marriage ties between these groups in succeeding generations, or as long as the tie was remembered. As in other parts of the continent, clans sometimes joined together or shared territories as an expression of political solidarity, and marriage alliances often reinforced these associations. But among the Gbaya the growth of institutionalised links between clans was undermined by marital prohibitions which forced the allies to forge new external links.[28] Consolidation and continuation of clan alliances over several generations were unlikely.

Political leadership was not well institutionalised. Each clan had an earth priest who represented the 'owners' of the land, but his duties were limited to ritual. He presided over ceremonies to ensure the fertility of the soil and the protection of its inhabitants. The position offered a possible avenue to centralised power, provided a priest could enlarge his sphere of authority, though this rarely happened.[29] Furthermore, succession was open, and the death of such a leader often provoked changes in alliances within clans:

> ... we are not dealing with a formal, enduring office of chiefship at the head of a stable territorial and administrative structure. Instead, the Gbaya political system consisted of a shifting pattern of alliance between small clan segments, leaders rising and falling in relation to their longevity, their personal qualities, their warfare successes, and their manipulation of exchange relations, marriage and descent ties, and other interpersonal links. In these conditions, successful men did not 'fill' pre-existent offices so much as 'create' leadership roles.[30]

The role of war leader among the Gbaya was thus an alternative avenue to power. Although individuals sometimes used the position to expand their influence, their powers were also limited. Mechanisms of dispute settlement were weak, and in the face of serious disagreements small groups left their leaders and settled in new territories.[31]

Characteristics of Gbaya society are found elsewhere in North-Central

27 Burnham, *Opportunity*, pp. 38–9.

28 *Ibid.*, pp. 26–8.

29 *Ibid.*, pp. 22, 25–6. For a somewhat different description of this aspect of Gbaya society, see John Hilberth, *Les Gbaya*, Uppsala, 1962, pp. 29–31.

30 Burnham, *Opportunity*, p. 36.

31 *Ibid.*, pp. 23–6; Burnham, 'Permissive ecology', p. 87. Studies of leadership roles in highland New Guinea are instructive here. See J. A. Barnes, 'African models in the New Guinea Highlands', *Man*, Nos. 1, 2, Jan. 1962, 5–9.

Africa. The concept of a 'permissive social ecology' is applicable to other Adamawa-Ubangian groups as well as to Central Sudanic-speakers in the CAR. Shifting to the east, for example, the Banda, like the Gbaya, were extremely decentralised, living in small groups of related males and their dependants. The clan was the only institution of broader scale. It provided an occasional mechanism for bringing groups together. A European who travelled among the Banda in the late nineteenth century reported that when hamlet leaders felt threatened, they called for assistance with piercing whistles; within minutes, as many as a hundred men would appear, while women and children disappeared into the bush. Hamlets followed similar procedures when they took the offensive; the ringing of bells called the men together to plan the attack. Nevertheless, despite the impression these combined actions sometimes made on Europeans, they were not institutionalised and probably occurred only intermittently. During the intense Muslim slave-raiding of the second half of the nineteenth century, visitors reported that people of one settlement would often stand by and allow the inhabitants of a neighbouring village to be carried off. The preservation of one's own hamlet superseded wider responsibilities. Nor were hamlets themselves very cohesive: dissatisfied Banda households often moved off to establish new homesteads.[32]

Leadership roles were similarly limited. Elected war leaders exercised considerable authority during campaigns. Afterwards their authority usually lapsed, although the personal qualities of a few men allowed them to become informal leaders, arbitrating disputes and offering advice. Other potential leaders included the earth priest and the chief initiator, along with sorcerers and blacksmiths, but, again, their activities were limited to particular realms. Some expanded their sphere of influence, but such successes stemmed from personal prowess and not institutional support.[33] Those who did become important rarely succeeded in transmitting their authority to chosen successors.

A cursory look at the Sara, a Central Sudanic people, and the Manza, another Adamawa-Ubangian society, further emphasises the decentralised character of social organisation in the savanna. The Sara peoples are spread from the Logone river valley in today's south-western Chad to the upper

32 Emile Leynaud, 'Parenté et alliance chez les Banda du district de Bria, région de la Kotto, Dar-el-Kouti', *Bulletin de l'institut d'études centrafricaines (Brazzaville)*, nouvelle série, vii–viii, 1954, 111–12, 115–16, 125–6, 156–7; Tisserant, 'Le Mariage dans l'Oubangui-Chari', *Bulletin de l'institut d'études centrafricaines (Brazzaville)*, nouvelle série, ii, 1951, 75–9, 81; Gillier, 'Les Bandas', 348; Albert Nebout, 'La Mission Crampel', *Bulletin de la société normande de géographie*, xiv, 1892, 236; Tisserant, *Dictionnaire Banda–Français*, Paris, 1931, p. 149; Tisserant, *Essai sur la grammaire Banda*, Paris, 1930, p. 8; al-Tunisi, *Voyage au Ouaday*, p. 274.

33 Tisserant, *Essai*, p. 3; Toque, *Essai*, 2; Tisserant, *Ce que j'ai connu de l'esclavage en Oubangui-Chari*, Paris, 1955, pp. 41–3; P. Daigre, 'Les Bandas de l'Oubangui-Chari', *Anthropos*, xxvi, 1931, 658.

Shari and its tributaries in the northern CAR. Like the Banda, they are divided into numerous smaller groups, and they, too, speak closely related languages but have never been united. Moreover, they had no sense of common identity. Most people lived in small, isolated settlements, and all made war among themselves.[34] Positions of leadership were restricted in the familiar ways. More centralised authority existed only among the Majingay in the northern Sara lands, where more than a dozen chiefs combined the roles of initiation leader and agricultural priest. However, such centralisation was probably a response to outside stimuli.[35]

The Manza, whose homelands lay between the Banda and the Gbaya, displayed similar characteristics. They describe their past as the repeated movement of small groups over short distances to escape famine or attacks by their neighbours and outsiders. Linguistic evidence suggests sustained contact with the forest peoples beyond the Ubangi in the south, but in the last several centuries they have lived in the central CAR. Organised into loosely united patrilineal clans, the Manza, too, lived in dispersed settlements. They were divided into chiefdoms, but each territory was small, and its leader's authority limited. The chief's position was not hereditary; when one died, a new leader was chosen on the basis of his exploits in war and knowledge of religious ritual. Groups sometimes combined under able war chiefs to hold off enemies, but such united efforts rarely outlived the 'big men' who initiated them.[36]

Although the social organisation of savanna societies inhibited the growth of centralised authority, several mechanisms did promote short-term collective action. Most, however, joined individuals rather than groups. They enabled 'big men' to extend their influence, but did not foster enduring institutions. Blood partnership and marriage alliance were two such mechanisms. Initiated by the exchange of blood or other bodily substances according to established rituals, blood partnership enabled individuals of different kinship or ethnic groups to pool their energies in work, war or commerce. Powerful individuals also employed these rituals to forge patron–client relationships with weaker rivals or conquered groups. Such accords theoretically bound the participants and their kinsmen for ever; in fact, most lapsed with the deaths of those who

34 Paul Brunache, *Le Centre de l'Afrique–autour du Tchad*, Paris, 1894, p. 218; Joseph Fortier (ed.), *Le Mythe et les contes du Sou en pays Mbai-Moïssala*, Paris, 1967, pp. 11–16; Modat, 'Une Tournée en pays Fertyt', *L'Afrique française: renseignements coloniaux*, xxii, 7, 1912, 275.

35 OA7.2/8.1; OA12.2; OA20.2; OA20.3; Fortier, *Le Mythe*, pp. 21–2; Brunache, *Le Centre de l'Afrique*, p. 218; Mario J. Azevedo, 'Sara Demographic Instability as a Consequence of French Colonial Policy in Chad (1890–1940)', Ph.D. dissertation, Duke University, Durham, N.C., 1976, pp. 32–45.

36 F. Gaud, *Les Mandja (Congo-Français)*, Brussels, 1911, pp. 92–5; A. M. Vergiat, *Moeurs et coutumes des Manjas*, Paris, 1937, p. 23; Suzanne Renouf-Stefanik, *Animisme et Islam chez les Manza (Centrafrique): influence de la religion musulmane sur les coutumes traditionnelles manza*, Paris, 1978, p. 22; Chevalier, *Mission Chari–Lac Tchad*, p. 115; Chevalier, 'De l'Oubangui au lac Tchad à travers le bassin du Chari', *La Géographie*, ix, 1904, 349.

concluded them.[37] Marriage alliances also enabled enterprising individuals to enlarge their followings. But once again, these links only lasted the lifetimes of the marriage partners; dispersed settlement, frequent movement and rules of exogamy undermined their potential to produce centralised institutions.

Secret societies also linked scattered settlements. By participating in secret rituals, individuals of different hamlets joined together, usually for specific ends. Initiation societies assembled boys from neighbouring villages for religious instruction and ceremonies marking the transition to manhood. Among the Banda and Kresh of the Sudan border region, women from different settlements joined societies whose aims were to improve the status of women in a male-dominated virilocal environment.[38]

The impact of the physical milieu on the organisation of savanna societies is further highlighted by a brief survey of societies found in more restricted environments. Settlement was often more compact, and authority more centralised. This is particularly true of the Kotoko, who lived in the plains adjacent to the Logone and Shari rivers in the north-west. Rainy-season floodwaters limited the land available for settlement, and the Kotoko tended to live in compact city-states built on occasional ridges and hills. In the more important settlements, government was in the hands of individuals of a royal lineage combining political and ritual duties. The basic elements of Kotoko culture derive from the ancient Sao who lived in the same region, and the Kanuri who lived south and south-west of Lake Chad. The Sao, too, lived in compact settlements on higher land.[39]

The physical environment did not shape everything: defence needs also influenced settlement patterns. The earliest Sao cities were compact but not walled, whereas substantial earthen walls encircled the later sites.[40] More recently, the Kotoko also lived in fortified settlements, probably to protect

37 On blood partnership and its uses among the peoples of North-Central Africa, see Evans-Pritchard, 'Zande blood-brotherhood', *Africa*, vi, 1933, 369–401; Cordell, 'Blood partnership in theory and practice: the expansion of Muslim power in Dar al-Kuti', *JAH*, xx, 3, 1979, 379–94; Riverain peoples also forged alliances through blood partnership. See Jacqueline Thomas, *Les Ngbaka de la Lobaye*, Paris and The Hague, 1963, pp. 113–14; Harms, 'Competition and capitalism: the Bobangi Role in Equatorial Africa's Trade Revolution, ca. 1750–1900', Ph.D. thesis, University of Wisconsin, Madison, 1978, pp. 161–6.

38 Robert Jaulin, *La Mort Sara*, Paris, 1967; Vidal, *Garçons et filles*, pp. 93–265; Eboué, 'Les Sociétés d'initiés en pays Banda', *Bulletin de la société des recherches congolaises*, xiii, 1931, 3–15; Daigre, 'Les Bandas', 689; Vergiat, *Les Rites secrets des primitifs de l'Oubangui*, Paris, 1951; J. Zugnoni, 'Yilede, a secret society among the G'Baya (Kreish), Aja, Banda tribes in the Western District of Equatoria', *Sudan Notes and Records*, xxvi, 1, 1945, 105–11.

39 A. M. D. Lebeuf, *Les Principautés kotoko*, pp. 14, 53–4, 232–51. Kanuri culture is itself a hybrid, a result of the interaction between indigenous peoples and the Kanembu, many of whom migrated into the area from north of Lake Chad following the decline of Kanem in the fourteenth century. See Fisher, 'The eastern Maghrib and the central Sudan', p. 291.

40 A. M. D. Lebeuf, *Les Principautés kotoko*, pp. 53–4.

themselves against the Muslims of Borno who began raiding for slaves in the area after 1200.

The Massa peoples along the Logone and Lake Toupouri were similar. Their lands, too, are essentially flood plains, leading them to settle on the rare stretches of higher ground. The environment made dispersed settlement impossible, but centralised leadership does not appear to have been a feature of early society. The major figure of authority was an earth chief with important ritual duties. Later, however, as conflict with Muslim states and their clients to the north increased, some Massa united under stronger leaders.[41]

Centralised leadership did emerge just beyond the western limits of North-Central Africa, among the peoples of the Bamenda hills and the highlands of eastern Cameroun. The land was more open than among the Kotoko or Massa, although more restricted than in the savanna further east. States developed such as the Tikar kingdoms, and those of Kom, Bum, Bafut, Bali and Bamum. All had influential men's associations, and a sacred ruler presided over their officers and numerous state officials.[42] Population was undoubtedly one factor in the evolution of these patterns of authority; these areas have long been densely populated, much more so than the savanna to the east.

The environment, population and external stimuli all encouraged more tightly organised societies. Among the most important of the outside influences between 1400 and 1700 was the expansion of Islam and the trans-Saharan commercial network. Somewhat later, the growth of the Atlantic slave-trade had similar effects on societies in the south-west. These two economic systems affected only the fringe areas of North-Central Africa before 1700; eventually, however, they had a dramatic impact throughout the region.

THE TRANS-SAHARAN NETWORK

The trans-Saharan network began to influence societies on the northern fringes of the savanna well before 1400. Initial stimuli came from Kanem, a large state north of Lake Chad, on the southern reaches of a major Saharan route linking the Chad basin with the oases of Fezzan and the Mediterranean coast. Along this and parallel routes in West Africa and the Nile valley, Muslims from North Africa and the Sahara made their way to black Africa. Muslim Berbers probably traded with Kanem as early as the ninth century. The rulers of Kanem adopted the faith two centuries later, and by the mid-thirteenth century the pre-Islamic royal cult and the élites

41 Igor de Garine, *Les Massa du Cameroun : vie économique et sociale*, Paris, 1964, pp. 23, 26–8, 224.

42 T. Eyongetah and R. Brain, *A History of the Cameroon*, London, 1974, pp. 36–42; Alexandre, 'Afrique centre-équatoriale', pp. 361–3.

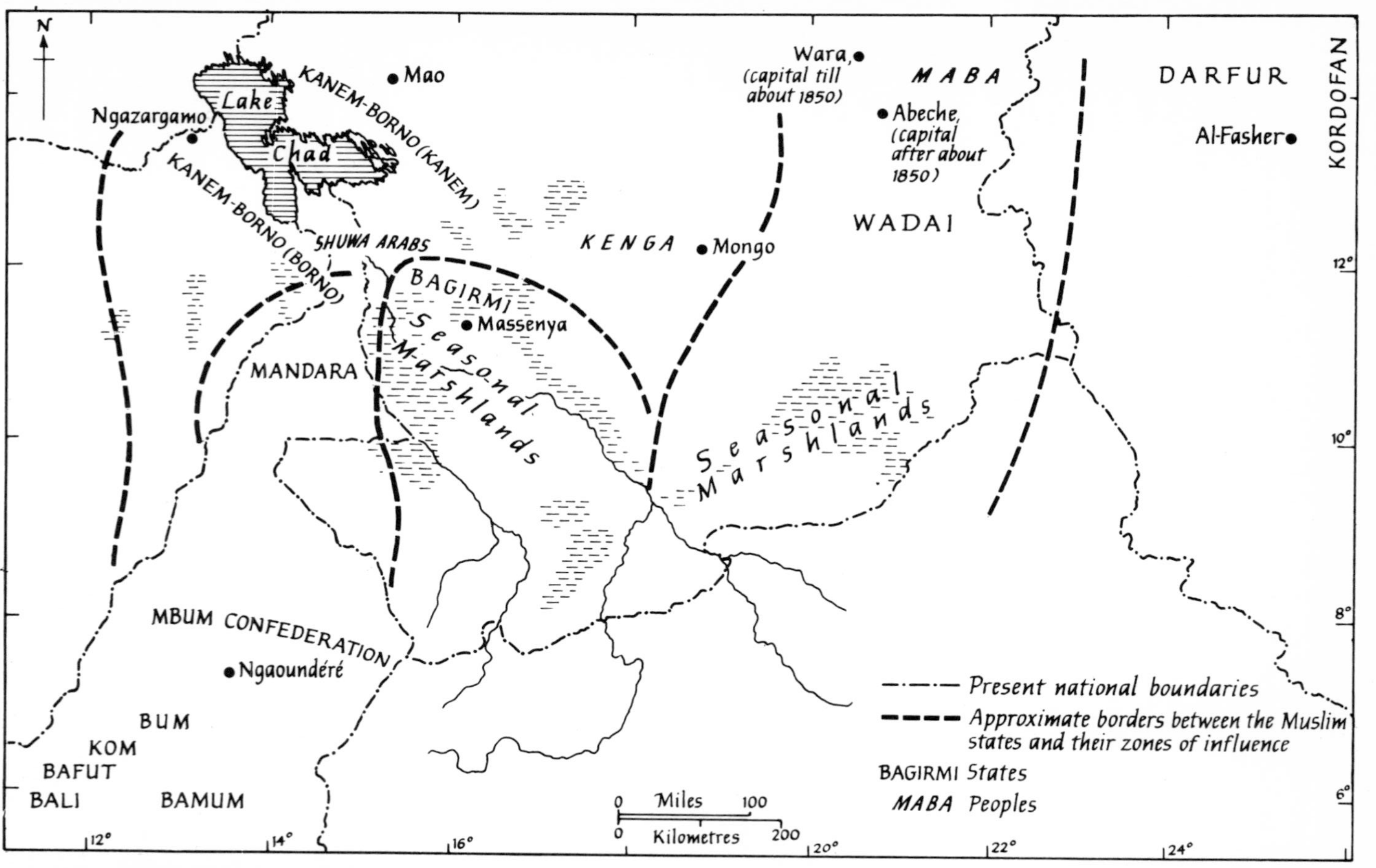

2:3 Northern Muslim states and their slave-raiding zones

associated with it had lost influence. The faith spread to the population at large.[43]

Although Kanem directed primary attention northward, going so far as to conquer and rule the Fezzan in the thirteenth century, the economy became increasingly tied to the non-Muslim lands south of Lake Chad along the lower Shari and Logone. Because the kingdom's primary export to North Africa was slaves, and because Muslims could not legally enslave one another, raiders were forced southward beyond the Islamic frontier. As early as the ninth century, commerce in black captives flourished in the Fezzan. Later Muslim visitors to Kanem noted that many of these slaves came from the Lake Chad region.[44] Kanem also raided directly to the south in Bagirmi, and the zone of raiding expanded to keep pace with a rising North African demand. Continued and growing imports may have been linked to high infant mortality in the Sahara and North Africa; slaves were thus necessary to replenish the population.[45]

Just before 1400, a major change in political orientation implicated Kanem even more directly in non-Muslim lands. Its rulers abandoned the area north of the lake for Borno to the south-west. Over the previous centuries, groups from Kanem had drifted in this direction, seeking more fertile land and greater security from drought and attacks by desert nomads. The new focus of political power, essentially a recognition of long-term demographic change, brought the state into closer contact with North-Central Africa. It also initiated a long-term process: Borno, later called Kanem-Borno as the new state reasserted control over its old homeland, first expanded its frontiers to embrace the Sao and Kotoko, and then began to play king-maker in areas still further south. In some cases, the rulers of Borno placed clients on the thrones of indigenous states. In other situations, the threat of slave-raiding stimulated the centralisation of power.[46]

While the trans-Saharan system initially affected only the north-west part of North-Central Africa, it later impinged on other regions. Bagirmi, for example, fell prey to slave-raiding in the early fourteenth century. By the sixteenth century, however, the Bagirmi élite had become Muslim,

43 Lange, 'Progrès de l'islam et changement politique au Kanem du XIe au XIIIe siècle: un essai d'interprétation', *JAH*, xix, 4, 1978, 498, 503–6, 513, 517.

44 John E. Lavers, 'Trans-Saharan trade before 1800: towards quantification', paper presented at the Second International Symposium of the Libyan Studies Centre: Trans-Saharan Trade-Routes, Tripoli, in press. See also Lange, 'Royaumes et peuples du Tchad', pp. 10, 12.

45 Lange, 'Royaumes et peuples du Tchad', pp. 9, 12; Fisher, 'The eastern Maghrib and the central Sudan', pp. 273, 275–6.

46 Fisher, 'The eastern Maghrib and the central Sudan', pp. 290–1, 313; Fisher, 'The central Sahara and Sudan', in *The Cambridge History of Africa,* IV, *c. 1600–1790*, Richard Gray (ed.), Cambridge, 1975, pp. 63, 129–31; Henri Moniot, 'Le Soudan central', in *Histoire générale de l'Afrique noire*, I, p. 341.

and, in turn, sponsored raids among the non-Muslim Sara of the middle and upper Shari.[47]

In Dar Fur, beyond the north-east borders of North-Central Africa, long-term developments paralleled those in Kanem-Borno and Bagirmi. A centralised Fur state appeared probably between 1100 and 1200. Islam played no apparent role in the kingdom during the reigns of its first two dynasties, but by the late sixteenth century a familiar process began to unfold: leaders consolidated power by installing a bureaucracy and codifying laws and customs. By the late seventeenth century, the state found itself at the southern terminus of the 'Forty-Day Road', a long-distance trade route that ran north-east to the Nile. Islam followed, becoming the state religion in the seventeenth century. But the new faith spread only gradually; the population tenaciously held to pre-Islamic rituals, and relapses were common. Yet Dar Fur, like Kanem-Borno, slowly became part of the Saharan economy and the Islamic world. Also like its illustrious western neighbour, Dar Fur supplied the trans-Saharan network with slaves from non-Muslim populations, taken first within its own borders and then in lands to the south. The first extensive campaigns beyond the Islamic frontier came in the late seventeenth century. Such operations remained a royal prerogative for the next two hundred years.[48]

Between Dar Fur in the north-east and Kanem-Borno in the north-west, Wadai developed similarly. Born of a revolt against Dar Fur, it emerged as an ethnically homogeneous state in the early seventeenth century. Over the next two centuries, the state expanded in all directions, becoming a multi-ethnic empire similar to so many others along the sub-Saharan Islamic frontier. It did not lie at the end of a desert trade route until the nineteenth century, when an enterprising sultan inaugurated a direct itinerary to Benghazi on the North African coast. But even before this, Wadai's ties to the Kanem–Tripoli and Nile routes integrated it into the trans-Saharan network.[49] Wadai, too, provided areas north of the Islamic frontier with slaves taken from the non-Muslim societies of North-Central Africa. As time passed, growing external demands for captives, and the need for prestige items for domestic redistribution, stimulated Wadai's expansion into the southern savannas. At the same time, competition with Kanem-

47 Lange, 'Royaumes et peuples du Tchad', pp. 9, 12; Fisher, 'The central Sahara and Sudan', pp. 132–4.

48 Rex S. O'Fahey and J. S. Spaulding, *Kingdoms of the Sudan*, London, 1974, pp. 108–24; Fisher, 'The eastern Maghrib and the central Sudan', pp. 303–5; al-Tunisi, *Voyage au Ouaday*, pp. 467, 487–8.

49 For a history of this route, see Cordell 'Libya, Wadai, and the Sanūsīya: A Ṭarīqa and a trade route', *JAH*, xviii, 1, 1977, 21–36.

Borno, Bagirmi and Dar Fur for territory and control over desert trade routes brought east–west expansion.[50]

The trans-Saharan network eventually affected most of North-Central Africa. Before 1700 its impact on the societies of the region remains unknown, although the effects were probably similar to those in later, better-documented eras. Intrusion undoubtedly promoted violence and flight in many regions. It also probably encouraged the growth of centralised authority as savanna societies such as the Sara sought to protect themselves.[51]

The expansion of the trans-Saharan system into North-Central Africa had yet another major effect. Unlike the Atlantic system it brought no major new food crops with it; but increased contact brought new diseases. The population movements, and denser settlement associated with slave-raiding, stimulated disease transmission and epidemics. Smallpox, syphilis and measles reached sub-Saharan Africa probably by 1600 as a result of contact with Muslims, Asians and Europeans. Judging from the better-recorded effects of these diseases on non-immune populations elsewhere, Africa must have experienced significant depopulation.[52] Even after the new diseases became endemic in black Africa, epidemics provoked by shifts in settlement further ravaged local populations.

It is not known just when and how such cosmopolitan diseases first afflicted North-Central Africa. Smallpox may have arrived with trans-Saharan trade.[53] Other diseases probably spread similarly. Slaves arriving in Dar Fur from further south often died of smallpox and other maladies uncommon in their homelands, leading traders to hold their captives for six weeks in the Fur capital to acclimatise them to the new disease environment. Those who survived were worth more. In Borno in the mid-nineteenth century slaves from Bagirmi were less expensive than those from further north because they were more susceptible to disease. And in Wadai, captives from southern regions such as the Banda and Kresh were

50 See Nachtigal, *Sahara and Sudan IV: Wadai and Darfur*, trans. Allan B. G. and Humphrey J. Fisher, London, 1971, pp. 205–29; Jeffrey E. Hayer, 'A Political History of the Maba Sultanate of Wadai, 1635–1912', M.A. thesis, University of Wisconsin, Madison, 1975; Anders J. Bjørkelo, 'State and Society in Three Central Sudanic Kingdoms: Kanem-Bornu, Bagirmi, and Wadai', Ph.D. thesis, Universitet i Bergen, 1976; al-Tunisi, *Voyage au Ouaday*, pp. 276–7, 280–1.

51 Maurice Delafosse, *Essai sur le peuple et la langue Sara*, Paris, 1897, pp. 9–10.

52 K. David Patterson and Gerald W. Hartwig, 'The disease factor: an introductory overview', in *Disease in African History: an Introductory Survey and Case Studies*, Hartwig and Patterson (eds), Durham, N.C., 1978, pp. 8–9, 15.

53 Azevedo, 'Sara demographic instability', 117; Azevedo, 'Epidemic disease among the Sara of southern Chad, 1890–1940', in Hartwig and Patterson (eds), *Disease in African History*, pp. 120–1, 134.

more vulnerable than those from further east, suggesting that their homelands were more recently exposed to slave-raiding.[54]

New diseases, flight, centralisation and new commercial opportunities were merely the more dramatic effects of the incorporation of North-Central Africa into the trans-Saharan network. Slower processes were also at work. All along the Islamic frontier, aspects of Islamic culture began to influence non-Muslim societies. The earliest contacts between the Muslim world of the Sahara and Sahel, and lands further south may have been the work of Muslim clerics who settled beyond the Islamic frontier. And even in the Sahel, common adherence to the faith fostered cohesion in multi-ethnic states such as Kanem.[55]

Muslim divination methods and medicine were often incorporated into well-developed non-Muslim traditions. Literacy in Arabic also had an important impact. In many regions it came to be associated with powers of divination and healing; thus Arabic charms, written on scraps of leather or paper and worn on the body, became common.[56] Literacy also provided a means of keeping records and communication. Much of what is known about the internal history of Kanem-Borno between the eleventh and early nineteenth centuries, for example, comes from the *Diwan*, a short chronology written in Arabic.[57]

It should not, however, be concluded that the cultural influences along the Islamic frontier flowed only one way. Unfortunately, an unbalanced view emerges from much of the literature, given that more is known about the Islamic world on the fringes of North-Central Africa than about non-Muslim societies further south. A few studies include examples of the impact of non-Muslim cultures on Muslim societies in the Sahel and North Africa. Such influences undoubtedly affected the Muslim areas adjacent to North-Central Africa as well.[58]

THE ATLANTIC SYSTEM

The Atlantic, or European, economy first impinged on the coastal forest

54 P. E. Lovejoy, 'The Long-Distance Trade of Wadai and Darfur, 1790–1870', seminar paper, University of Wisconsin, Madison, 1968, pp. 36–7, n.12; William George B. Browne, *Travels in Africa, Egypt and Syria from the Year 1792 to 1796*, London, 1806, p. 299; al-Tunisi, *Voyage au Ouaday*, p. 483; al-Tunisi, *Voyage au Darfour*, pp. 467–8; Barth, *Travels*, II, p. 514.

55 Fisher, 'The eastern Maghrib and the central Sudan', pp. 285–7, 327; Fisher, 'The central Sahara and Sudan', pp. 62–3, 93–7.

56 Fisher, 'The eastern Maghrib and the central Sudan', pp. 313–20; Alfred Adler and Andras Zempléni, *Le Bâton de l'aveugle: divination, maladie et pouvoir chez les Moundang du Tchad*, Paris, 1972, pp. 19–20, 63–4, 215; Fisher, 'Hassebu: Islamic healing in Black Africa', in *Northern Africa: Islam and Modernization*, Michael Brett (ed.), London, 1973, pp. 23–41.

57 For the most recent study of the *Diwan*, see Lange, *Chronologie et histoire d'un royaume africain*, Wiesbaden, 1977.

58 Fisher, 'Hassebu', pp. 27–8.

regions south-west of the savanna in the early sixteenth century. The fringes of North-Central Africa probably felt its impact in the following century. As with the trans-Saharan network, a major impetus for expansion was a search for labour, in this instance slaves to supply the American plantations. This demand was felt directly and indirectly. Direct contact quickly transformed coastal societies into intermediaries, providing captives from the immediate hinterlands to Europeans, Afro-Europeans and Africans on the coast. Such commerce became important in the Bight of Biafra by the sixteenth century and continued, with occasional interruptions, until abolition in the nineteenth century.[59] As time passed, the trade drew in societies further away from the coast, first stimulating regional commercial networks to provide captives, and then encouraging their extension deeper into the interior.

In the eighteenth century the Zaire river and its tributaries became integrated into this commercial system. The northern arm of the trade followed the Ubangi to the rapids at present-day Bangui, and then spread eastward to reach the open savanna.[60] In the late nineteenth century, when the first Europeans visited the area, the upper Ubangi and its eastern sources were divided into zones controlled by different river-trading groups. From the rapids at Bangui eastward to the Ouaka, the Banziri controlled commerce. Further east the Yakoma were the major traders as far as the Kotto river, where the Sango replaced them. The Sango link reached as far east as the Mbomu–Uele confluence.[61]

The Atlantic system also brought other changes. The Portuguese and other Europeans brought New World food crops with them which had a major demographic impact on African societies. Maize and cassava, in particular, spread to the North-Central African savanna, where they replaced or complemented indigenous crops such as millets and sorghums. Other influences from the Atlantic economy undoubtedly affected North-Central Africa before 1700. Although the desert system seems to have exerted greater influence over most of the region, further research in the riverain zones of the south may alter this impression. It is clear that both systems altered the shape of African society.

59 Philip D. Curtin, *The Atlantic Slave Trade: a Census*, Madison, Wisconsin, 1969, pp. 100, 128–30, 150, 157, 160, 170, 200, 221, 225, 247, 258; Eyongetah and Brain, *A History of the Cameroon*, pp. 51, 54–5; Engelbert Mveng, *Histoire du Cameroun*, Paris, 1963, pp. 138–40.

60 Dampierre, *Un Ancien Royaume bandia*, p. 59.

61 Archives du Musée Boganda (Bangui), No. 42 (Bangassou), L'adjoint-commandant du district de Ouango, 'Tableau de peuplades', 10 février 1910, 2–3; Archives Nationales Françaises, Section d'Outre-mer (Aix-en-Provence), 4(3)Dl, Gaillard, 'Rapport général sur le Haut-Oubangui (région au-dessus des rapides)', 31 octobre 1891; Jacques Marie de Crussol, duc d'Uzes, *Le Voyage de mon fils au Congo*, Paris, 1894; Pierre Kalck, *Histoire de la République centrafricaine des origines préhistoriques à nos jours*, Paris, 1974, pp. 61–2.

RECENT CENTURIES: SAVANNA HISTORY, 1700–1910

During the two centuries after 1700, although the long-term influences discussed in the preceding pages continued to channel historical development, it also becomes possible to distinguish more specific patterns of change, at least for some regions and for some periods.

First, political organisation and leadership became more centralised everywhere except in the central savannas and in the south-west. Second, the volume and importance of long-distance trade grew, particularly around the perimeter of the region. Links between these two sets of changes are obvious in some places; in others, they are less so. Further, in most instances they are related to a third theme: the growth of inequalities in wealth, rank and power within societies as well as between them. During these two centuries, many societies began or expanded the use of slave labour, significantly altering the distribution of wealth and influence. Important demographic changes also occurred after 1700. Many of these shifts were associated with the violence of Muslim slave-raiding and European conquest. Individuals and groups moved frequently, and people died in large numbers.

In this period, too, it is possible to trace the emergence of broad areas of common culture. In the west, north and east, Islam moulded small groups into larger ones, although in each area, Muslim world culture arrived in the garb of a different local tradition. In the west it came with the Shuwa Arabs, with the Fulani and with Hausa and Borno traders; in the north it was purveyed by transhumant Arab groups along with local agriculturalists such as the Bagirmi, Maba and Fur. In the east Islam came with petty traders from the Nile valley who drifted south in the eighteenth century. But such integration was not only the result of external influences. Along the Ubangi, Mbomu and Uele rivers in the south, the Azande and the Bandia emerged, bringing greater cultural unity and broader-scale political action to the forest-fringe societies.

THE WESTERN PLATEAUX AND SOUTHERN RIVERS

In the west the most notable development by 1700 was the rise of the Mbum. Organised into either several large chiefdoms or a loose confederation, the Mbum brought together most of the Adamawa plateau between the seventeenth and nineteenth centuries. Authority was vested in one or more theocratic figures called *belaka*. Their power was greatest in the Ngaoundéré region, but peoples beyond this zone also looked to them as major religious leaders. In the south-west, their sphere of influence extended to the Tikar states and the Bamileke chiefdoms of the Bamenda grasslands; in the east, it reached to the Mbere on the edge of the forest.

The Mbum states were perhaps part of a larger Korarafa empire which also included the Kona and Jukun confederations. These three clusters of peoples shared common religious traditions: the Kona confederation also drew smaller groups together under the aegis of religious leaders who resembled the *belakas* of Mbum. Indeed, the office of *belaka* may have been founded by a branch of the Jukun royal lineage.[62]

Little is known about how or why these confederations and the Korarafa empire came into being, although their location near the Benue suggests that they were commercial links between the desert-edge states and the Nupe and Yoruba kingdoms to the south-west. In any case, pressures of drought, famine and epidemics, as well as internal rivalries, combined to undermine the partial unity of the region in the mid-eighteenth century. The decline of the Korarafa empire soon followed.

No similar large-scale societies are known to have developed in the south-western forest margins of North-Central Africa. The influence of the Atlantic economy did, however, increasingly affect this region by stimulating trade along major rivers such as the Sangha and Ubangi.[63] Fed by tributaries from the savanna and the forest, rivers such as these became vital links between North-Central Africa and regions further south. As the many small-scale fishing societies of the area engaged increasingly in commerce, local and regional trading networks joined together to form ever-larger long-distance systems. Trade languages such as Lingala and Sango took shape on the middle Zaire and Ubangi rivers in the nineteenth century.[64] These languages and the regular exchange that produced them promoted a common culture.

Further east, beyond direct contact with the Atlantic system, but still in the river region, the rise of the Azande also brought greater cultural unity. The spread of the Azande is associated with the Avongara, a clan that came to dominate the peoples of the Mbomu and Chinko river valleys. Although oral traditions identify them as a foreign conquering group, the Avongara were probably an indigenous clan that subdued its neighbours. Ngura, the first identifiable historical leader, ruled an Azande group in 1750, and later rulers reckoned their descent from him. Led by the Avongara, the Azande subsequently spread to the east, south and west, conquering and absorbing

62 Eldridge Mohammadou, 'L'Empire de Korarafa, la Haute-Benue, et le plateau de l'Adamawa (XVIIe–XIXe siècles), unpublished manuscript, pp. 1–13. See also Mohammadou, *Fulbe Hooseere: les royaumes Foulbe de plateau de l'Adamaoua au XIXe siècle*, Tokyo, 1978; Burnham, review of *Fulbe Hooseere*, *JAH*, xxi, 4, 1980, 571; Burnham, personal communication, 8 May 1981.

63 Kalck, *Central African Republic: a Failure in de-Colonisation*, London, 1971, p. 5; Harms, 'Oral tradition and ethnicity', 71; Jan Vansina, *Introduction à l'ethnographie du Congo*, Kinshasa, 1966, pp. 10–11.

64 William J. Samarin, '*Lingua francas*, with special reference to Africa', in *Study of the Role of Second Languages in Asia, Africa, and Latin America*, Frank A. Rice (ed.), Washington, D.C., 1962, pp. 54–64; Samarin, 'Colonization and Central African *Linguae Francae*: a research report', Toronto, 1980, mimeographed.

other societies.[65] Expansion continued until the final decades of the nineteenth century when they came into conflict with Sudanese raiders, Egyptian colonial officials and Zanzibari slave-traders. Some Azande rulers preserved and even extended their authority through alliances with these outsiders, but expansion stopped. The halt became definitive at the end of the century when the Azande found themselves facing the Europeans. In the south and west they confronted the agents of the Congo State and the French, while in the north the British blocked their spread.

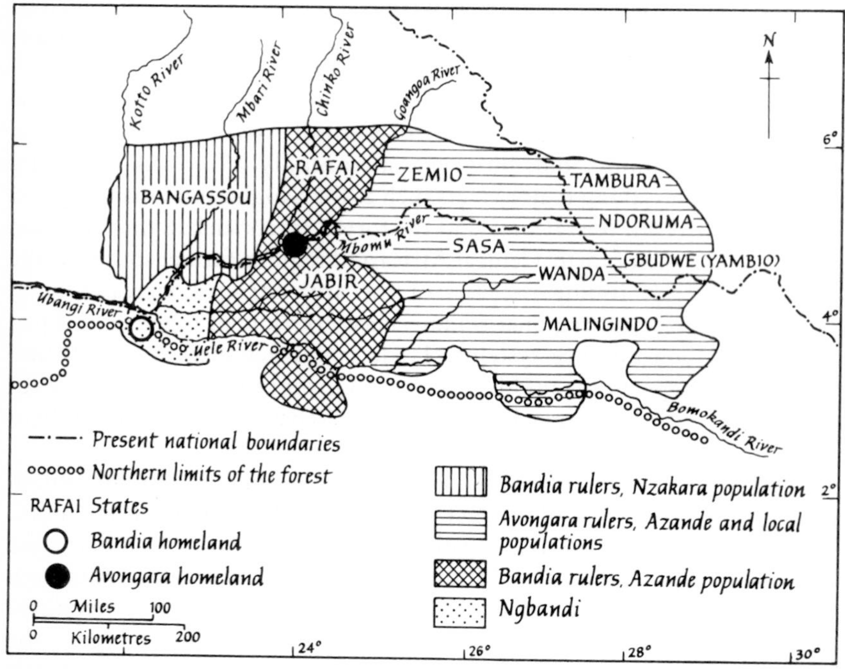

2:4 Bandia and Avongara states, late nineteenth century
Source: Partially based on Eric de Dampierre, *Un Ancien royaume bandia*, Paris, 1967, pp. 92–3.

How and why the Azande expanded is not known, although it is possible that their growth was linked to the arrival of American food crops, and was thus indirectly connected with the Atlantic system. Before the expansion the peoples of the region were partly hunters and gatherers, although fishing was probably also an important activity. The new crops may have contributed to population growth and to the consolidation of small-scale societies into larger chiefdoms. Increased agricultural productivity would

65 Evans-Pritchard, *The Azande*, pp. xi, 21–7, 37–8, 268, 271–2, 276, 296, 315–16, 421, 433; de Schlippe, *Shifting Cultivation*, pp. 6, 9–10.

also have made it possible to support an élite such as the Avongara.[66]

No distinct Azande 'nation' developed. Instead they founded a series of large chiefdoms spread through space and time. Ties with the Avongara clan legitimised each chiefdom, but expansion occurred through division and migration rather than through the growth of a unitary state. Azande rulers established their sons and allies as regional officials over conquered populations; each region also had its own local administrators. This pyramid organisation, unique in the area, was a source of Azande strength. It was also a source of weakness. Upon the death of a chief, subordinates often became independent, and competed with one another for jurisdiction over the often well-populated core district formerly governed directly by the chief. Each subdivision of the chiefdom was functionally autonomous because sons had their own followers and bases of economic and military support; hence recourse to warfare was frequent. Conflict brought migration, new conquest and a repetition of the process in new localities a generation later.[67]

Abundant land and growing population fuelled this cycle. Migratory expansion required sparsely populated territories. It also required followers to support claims, carry out conquests and pay tribute. Ample land was apparently available in the eighteenth and nineteenth centuries. As for people, they were available at a price. The hold of Azande chiefs over their followers was tenuous. Because population density was low and settlements scattered, rule by force was not possible. Leaders who were too demanding in their requests for labour, or too parsimonious in redistributing their wealth, lost their following. The balance was delicate. Only a few of the potential Avongara chiefs established states.[68]

The Azande expansion had two major effects: first, it encouraged broader unity. As the Azande conquered, they incorporated new peoples into their following through marriage, military service and blood partnership. Young men from many North-Central African societies became part of the Azande forces. Local allies became local administrators loyal to the Avongara. They prepared the population for direct Avongara rule, which usually began when the sons of conquerors attained adulthood and became administrators themselves. This long period of acculturation stimulated the adoption of the Azande language and elements of Azande culture.[69]

Nevertheless, assimilation was not total, and despite the emphasis placed

66 David Tyrell Lloyd, 'Changing Factors and Relations of Production among the Azande of Northeastern Zaire, c. 1800–Present', paper presented at the University of California at Los Angeles, 1974, pp. 14–15, 19–20; Evans-Pritchard, *The Azande*, pp. 72, 87–8; de Schlippe, *Shifting Cultivation*, p. 223.

67 Evans-Pritchard, *The Azande*, pp. 139–40, 157, 306.

68 *Ibid.*, pp. 215–16, 233–4; Lloyd, 'Changing Factors', pp. 12–13.

69 Evans-Pritchard, *The Azande*, pp. 21, 33; Dampierre, *Un Ancien Royaume bandia*, p. 13.

on 'Azande-isation' substantial variation existed within the Azande zone. Some differences grew out of the natural environment, which varied markedly from one region to another. Some Azande lived on the edge of the forest, whereas others had their homelands in the wooded savanna. Such different environments demanded different means of exploitation. Thus even though the expansion brought new food crops to most regions, many local agricultural practices persisted, and the newcomers adopted them.[70]

Local peoples influenced the emergence of 'Azande' culture in other ways. The Avongara and peoples from the heartland comprised a diminishing percentage of the population as conquest spread. Moving along the margin between savanna and forest, the Azande received and transmitted influences from both zones. From the forest, for example, they acquired the Mangbetu poison oracle. It became a central feature of Azande religion even though the vine that produced the poison did not grow in Azande territory. They obtained it through trade with the forest peoples. Eventually the oracle spread north beyond the Azande to the Banda, who associate witchcraft with *ondro*, nocturnal evil spirits which settle in the stomachs of their victims. The latter then become carriers of forces of ill-will that attack others in the community. Sorcerers identify *ondro* carriers by use of a poison ordeal. Similar associations of witchcraft and poison ordeals are found among forest peoples south of the Ubangi, suggesting contact across this ecological frontier. While the forest peoples identify the evil spirits with a different term, *likundu*, the characteristics are the same. The link between forest and savanna is provided by the river peoples. The same conception exists in the language of the Sango along the Ubangi river; it is also identified with the word *likundu*. Finally, from the north the Azande borrowed a wood shrine from the Madi. Circumcision came from the same direction. Divination is much more widespread in north-eastern Zaire than in the forest, and that, too, probably came from the savannas.[71]

A second major effect of the expansion was increased social stratification and inequality. The conquests, promoted by the larger scale of organisation and greater cohesion of the Azande rather than by technological superiority, created an élite. In addition to surpluses produced by higher-yielding crops, new patterns of labour mobilisation helped maintain the Avongara ruling group. The military units of conquest were often transformed into units of agricultural production. Warriors owed chiefs a complex mix of labour and tribute. For example, Gbudwe, a powerful

70 De Schlippe, *Shifting Cultivation*, pp. 184–90; Evans-Pritchard, *The Azande*, pp. 73–80, 119.

71 Evans-Pritchard, *The Azande*, pp. 97, 99, 105–10, 113, 119; Daigre, *Oubangui-Chari: souvenirs et témoignages, 1890–1940*, Paris, 1950, pp. 113–15; Gillier, 'Les Bandas', 392; Tisserant, *Dictionnaire*, pp. 354, 576; Vansina, *Introduction à l'ethnographie du Congo*, pp. 44, 50, 74.

ruler in the late nineteenth century, could call on seven hundred young men to work in the fields; other subjects also owed him labour. Communal labour in the Avongara fields, as well as agricultural tribute, brought greater concentration of wealth. Even though much of it was redistributed, the process reinforced the political and economic power of the Avongara since goods were channelled through them.[72]

Although Azande expansion was the most notable historical development on the south-eastern fringes of North-Central Africa after 1700, another related set of migrations and conquests suggests that the Azande phenomenon was part of a more extensive set of changes along the rivers separating savanna and forest. The Bandia, an Ngbandi clan from the river region west of the Azande, led another series of conquests.[73] In the seventeenth century, the Bandia had probably lived on the southern bank of the Ubangi, downstream from the Mbomu confluence. From there they spread north-east across Azande territory. Meeting remarkably little resistance, the Bandia by 1800 ruled a series of states on the forest margins north of the Mbomu river. In this area, the Bandia ruled Azande and a mixed collection of other peoples. Over time their culture changed accordingly.

This expansion, like that of the Azande, was characterised by conflict and competition. In the nineteenth century, these divisions allowed Muslim slave-raiders and slave-traders, as well as European intruders, to manipulate internal politics. In the eighteenth century, however, external forces posed no threat; dissatisfied subordinates and heirs of Bandia rulers simply moved on to new territories.[74]

The parallels between Bandia and Azande expansion are obvious. What is perhaps more instructive is how two similar groups from similar environments produced quite different types of states. The conquest of the Nzakara illustrates these differences. The Bandia crossed the Mbomu into Nzakara territory because they were attracted by the more open, richer and better cultivated lands of the savanna.[75] Once there, the Bandia, unlike the Azande, assimilated much of the culture of their subjects. They adopted the Nzakara language, and intermarried with a wide variety of subject clans. They also absorbed and redistributed women on a broader scale. These differences may be related to the smaller size of the Bandia migrations. The new arrivals were greatly outnumbered. In addition, the Bandia adopted major institutions, such as the ancestor cult, which integrated them into

72 Evans-Pritchard, *The Azande*, pp. 202, 215–16; Lloyd, 'Changing Factors', pp. 10–11, 32. On Gbudwe (Tambio) and the Azande in general, see Robert O. Collins, 'Yambio: independent Zande', *Tarikh*, ii, 2, 1968, 39–52.

73 Not to be confused with the Banda discussed earlier.

74 Dampierre, *Un Ancien Royaume bandia*, pp. 161–2, 179–81, 391–2.

75 *Ibid.*, pp. 156–8, 169, 172. See also Calonne-Beaufaict, *Azande: Introduction à une ethnographie générale des bassins de l'Ubangi–Uele et de l'Aruwimi*, Brussels, 1921; Armand Hutereau, *Histoire des peuplades de l'Uele et de l'Ubangi*, Brussels, 1922.

indigenous lineage organisation.[76] Finally, the Bandia state north of the Mbomu was far larger than any single Azande unit. Under Mbali and then Bangassou in the late nineteenth century, it extended northward into the savanna for 200 kilometres; its east–west axis was about the same.[77]

The more effective integration of the ruling élite, the greater similarity among groups within the state, and the greater ease of communication may have fostered growth of a larger state. However, despite these important distinctions, the Azande and Bandia-Nzakara shared many traits with the riverain cultures of the Ubangi-Mbomu-Uele region. The expansion of both groups further extended the zone of common culture, which, by the early nineteenth century, stretched from the forest margin to the Azande lands astride the Nile–Zaire watershed.

THE NILE–ZAIRE WATERSHED AND THE CHAD BASIN

The central geographical feature of the eastern part of North-Central Africa is the Nile–Zaire divide, which stretches nearly a thousand kilometres from the Chad region to the Mbomu headwaters. It separates the Nile and Zaire basins. Within this zone, the environment ranges from dry steppe across the divide in the Nile basin to tropical forest along the southern rivers. Savanna predominates in between. Linguistic evidence indicates that the present-day language groups have been there for a long time. The interplay among these diverse languages and environments over the centuries has created an ideal situation for studying cultural and economic change through language shifts and borrowings.[78]

The Central Sudanic peoples who lived north of the divide grew grain crops characteristic of the savanna. In most areas, animal husbandry was also an important activity. South of the divide, the Zaire basin more closely resembled the Azande and Bandia-Nzakara areas further south. Root crops were of prime importance, and riverain concepts of religion and other aspects of riverain culture prevailed.[79] Adjacent to the divide itself, people lived in dispersed homesteads, like the Banda and Gbaya to the west. For the most part, these societies did not develop large-scale political units. Some of these societies, such as the Binga, Kara, Gula, Kresh, Banda and eastern Sara, were known to the Muslim states of the desert edge by 1800.[80]

Along the divide in the south, near the Azande, lived the Ubangian peoples.[81] For many centuries, they had drifted northward along the

76 Dampierre, *Un Ancien Royaume bandia*, pp. 161–2, 285, 293–4, 417–20.
77 *Ibid.*, pp. 92–3.
78 See Ehret *et al.*, 'Some thoughts'.
79 D. E. Saxon, 'The History of the Shari river basin, ca. 500 B.C.–1000 A.D.', Ph.D. dissertation, University of California at Los Angeles, 1980, p. 32.
80 Browne, *Travels*, p. 356; John Lewis Burckhardt, *Travels in Nubia*, London, 1822, pp. 441–2; Pallme, *Travels*, p. 351, note; al-Tunisi, *Voyage au Ouaday*, pp. 280–1.
81 Ehret *et al.*, 'Some thoughts', 96–7.

Mbomu tributaries to settle in the savanna. Only marginally affected by slave-raiding, this movement continued through the eighteenth and early nineteenth centuries. Like the Azande and Bandia, who undoubtedly influenced them, the Ubangian peoples were poised between savanna and forest, and their culture reflected this intermediate position. They, too, became conduits of acculturation, passing aspects of southern religion and politics to the savanna societies, as well as adopting northern institutions and passing them southward. Leadership was more centralised than among their Central Sudanic neighbours, and yet more diffuse than among linguistically related groups further south. The Ubangians brought root crops with them, but also adopted grain cultivation common in the north. Yet differences remained. Whereas the Nile grain cultivators raised cattle, the presence of the tsetse fly in Ubangian areas made herding impossible.[82]

Whereas some Ubangian peoples moved north, Central Sudanic groups also drifted south. The Mangbetu and Mamvu-Lese made their way to the forest. There they adopted root crops, along with agricultural techniques necessary for a wetter environment. They also borrowed the rectangular house and village plan of their Ubangian and Bantu neighbours. Shortly after 1800, the only state founded by Central Sudanic-speakers developed among the Mangbetu.[83]

The history of the far northern savanna fringe after 1700 heralded events that would eventually disrupt all of North-Central Africa. Geographically, this zone is distinct, lying almost entirely within the Chad basin. The Central Sudanic languages found there are closely related to those along the Nile–Zaire divide. Fishing peoples from the east, attracted by the rich Shari waters, made their way into the basin as early as the first millennium. As in the riverain zone in the south, exchange promoted cultural homogeneity. Linguistic analysis shows that the migrants adopted many features of culture from peoples already living in the Shari valley.[84] With the exception of Bagirmi, the internal history of this area is very little known. Better understood, however, are its links with the Muslim zone immediately to the north.

THE MUSLIM ECONOMY AND MUSLIM POWER FROM THE EIGHTEENTH CENTURY

By the late eighteenth century, the major Muslim empires of the desert edge and Sahel had carved out raiding zones in the south. Their slaving activities had not only caused havoc in the Shari valley but had also

82 *Ibid.*, 90–6, 99 and note, 104 and n.26; Saxon, 'The history of the Shari basin', pp. 38–9; Santandrea, *A Tribal History*, pp. 71, 85–7, 95–6, 105, 107–17.
83 Ehret *et al.*, 'Some thoughts', 100. Also see Curtis Arthur Keim, 'Precolonial Mangbetu Rule: Political and Economic Factors in Nineteenth-Century Mangbetu History (Northeastern Zaire)', Ph.D. dissertation, Indiana University, 1979.
84 Saxon, 'The History of the Shari Basin', pp. 32–48.

stimulated the growth of centralised power. In the northern part of the valley, the Bagirmi, themselves early victims of raiding from Kanem-Borno, extended their influence. From Kanem-Borno they borrowed titles and offices, as well as patterns of military and family organisation. At the same time, they maintained older ritual ties with the non-Muslim Kenga.[85]

In the early decades of the nineteenth century, Bagirmi raiding and trading in the middle Shari valley had an important impact on non-Muslim populations. Items of Muslim culture such as dress, divining ceremonies and enclosed compounds spread among the Sara. Intrusion brought increased violence, which encouraged dispersed groups to come together under centralised leadership. From the Bagirmi, the Sara Majingay borrowed the office of *mbang*, a political and religious leader associated with manhood initiation. In the 1850s, several of these leaders governed large towns. By the end of the century, three large Sara confederations had appeared.[86] Traders and craftsmen from Bagirmi and other northern regions also made their way further south. Cloth became an important trade good; cloth garments became indicators of status.[87]

At the same time, new groups of Muslims associated with new centres of centralised power on the Islamic frontier infiltrated North-Central Africa. First came the *jallaba*, itinerant peddlers of diverse ethnic background from the Nile region north of Khartoum. In the mid-eighteenth century, they had spread west in commercial networks that linked Muslim lands such as Kordofan, Dar Fur and Wadai to the Nile. Perhaps attracted by the copper of Hufrat al-Nuhas, later diasporas carried them beyond the Islamic frontier among non-Muslim peoples such as the Kresh, Banda and, eventually, the Azande. Their numbers grew during the nineteenth century following Egyptian conquest of their homeland and the imposition of higher taxes. At first, relations between the *jallaba* and non-Muslims were pacific. These Muslims were not raiders. Lightly armed, they travelled in small groups with a few donkeys loaded with merchandise, depending on the willingness of their hosts to supply them with ivory and small numbers of slaves. Over time, their presence contributed to the spread of Arabic as a trade language, and the diffusion of Muslim culture.[88]

85 *Ibid.*, pp. 84–91, 104–9; Viviana Paques, *Le Roi pêcheur et le roi chasseur*, Strasbourg, 1977, pp. 1–5; M. Jomard, 'Préface', *Voyage au Ouaday*, p. xxxvi; Patterson, 'Bagirmi to the Nineteenth Century', seminar paper, Stanford University, 1968, p. 13.

86 Jaulin, *La Mort Sara*; Saxon, 'The History of the Shari Basin', pp. 94–5; Barth, *Travels*, II, pp. 678–9, 686, 689–92, map facing p. 347; Escayrac de Lauture, *Mémoire sur le Soudan*, Paris, 1855–6, pp. 98–9.

87 Barth, *Travels*, II, p. 686. This was also true in the late nineteenth century. See Brunache, *Le Centre de l'Afrique*, pp. 216 ff.

88 R. O. Collins, 'Sudanese factors in the history of the Congo and Central West Africa in the nineteenth century', in *Sudan in Africa*, Yusuf Fadl Hasan (ed.), Khartoum, p. 160; J. R. Gray, *History of the Southern Sudan, 1839–1889*, London, 1961, pp. 65–66; Browne, *Travels*, II, p. 488; Nachtigal, *Sahara and Sudan*, IV, pp. 353–4; Georg Schweinfurth, *The Heart of Africa*, trans. Ellen Frewer, New York, 1874, II, pp. 409, 415.

The second group of newcomers to North-Central Africa were Hausa and Borno traders, arrivals from the north-west who began trading in Adamawa early in the nineteenth century. Like the *jallaba*, the Hausa and Borno were peaceful peddlers in search of ivory. Arriving in small caravans, their success also depended on the hospitality of their non-Muslim trading partners.[89] These early Muslim traders, like the *jallaba* in the east, were not disruptive since slave-raiding and slave-trading were confined to the northern fringes of Central Africa at this time. Within the region, Muslims and non-Muslims coexisted. After the mid-nineteenth century, violence engendered by larger-scale slaving was to change all of this.

The second half of the nineteenth century was a time of great upheaval. Violence, conquest and migration altered many customary patterns of social organisation, political action and economic exchange. Although each region and society responded to these changes according to its own internal dynamic, external factors were the prime movers in North-Central African history after 1850. The upheavals had their origin in the north, in the expanding Muslim economy of the desert and the Nile. This expansion was not new, but the intensity of its impact after 1850 was unprecedented. As before, Muslims continued to move southward, but the nature of their dealings with non-Muslims changed. First, the numbers of Muslim traders, raiders and teachers who ventured beyond the Islamic frontier increased markedly. Second, more than ever before, Muslim economic and political institutions followed them. These factors brought the Muslims greater independence. The pattern before mid-century had been the assimilation of small groups of traders into non-Muslim societies; after 1850, ever-increasing numbers of non-Muslim chiefs, warriors and even ritual specialists sought links with the Muslim north.

Before mid-century much economic exchange was peaceful and of limited scale. After mid-century, large parties of traders and raiders, supported by formal or informal ties with northern Muslim states or commercial enterprises, came south seeking ivory and ever greater numbers of slaves. Their impact was correspondingly more disruptive. Although the transfer of slaves to Muslim traders was often peaceful, violence was necessary for their procurement. Thus, even when Muslims did not raid for captives themselves, their demands frequently created conflict among local societies. As time passed, Muslims established permanent outposts, often in alliance with local leaders who saw their presence as an opportunity for personal advancement. The result was a widening spiral of violence which eventually drew most societies into its vortex.

The tale is one of movement: flight, forced resettlement, voluntary

89 Burnham, 'Raiders and traders in Adamawa', pp. 52–55.

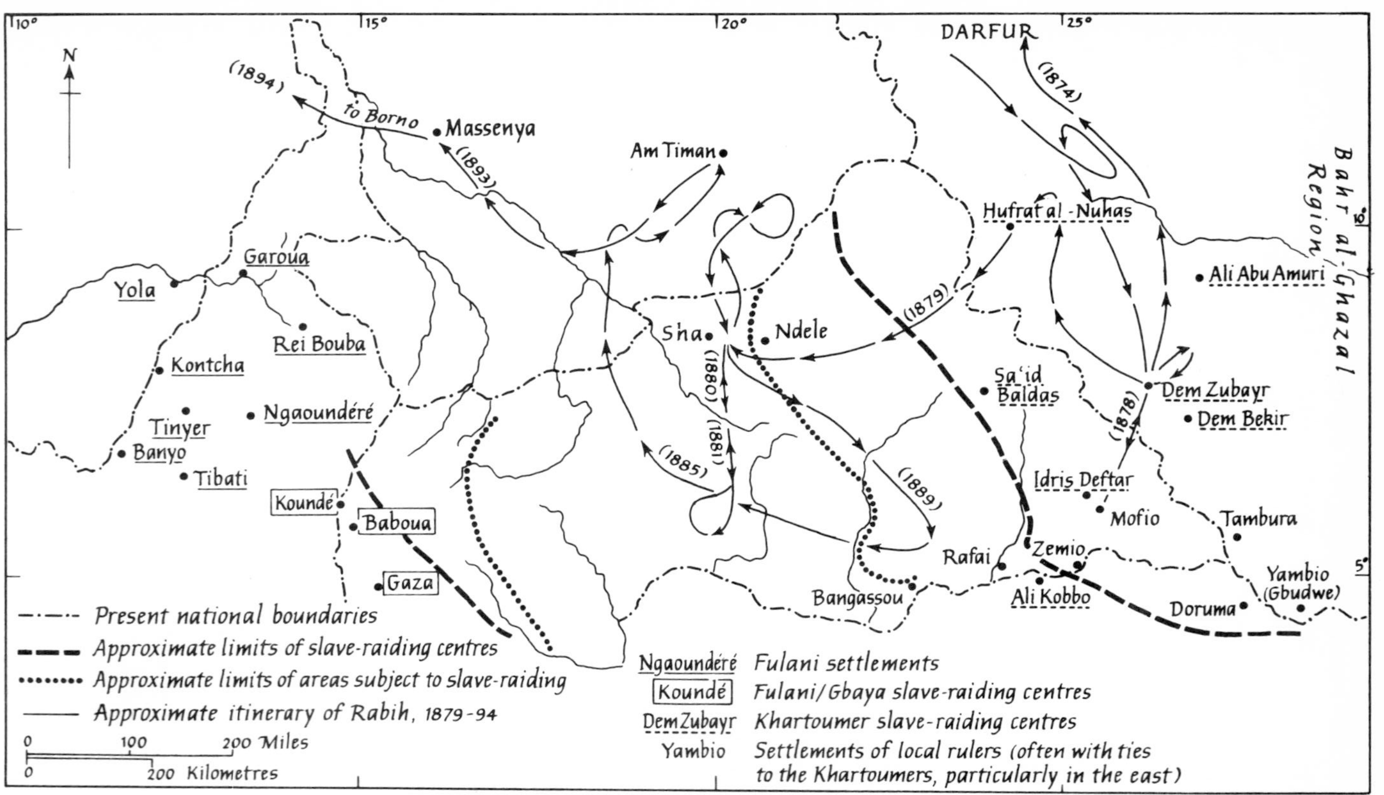

2:5 Muslim slave-raiding and conquest, late nineteenth century

migration. Throughout North-Central Africa, non-Muslim oral traditions tell of migration within the region, most often movement away from the northern borderland. They chronicle attempts to get beyond the reach of the raiders. In the north-east, peoples such as the Kresh were first pushed south by marauders from Dar Fur, then west by slave-raiders from the Nile region, and finally east again by the forces of Muhammad al-Sanusi, ruler of the slave-raiding state of Dar al-Kuti.[90] In the far west, the Gbaya sought to escape Fulani raiding, while in the east the prime perpetrators of violence were the large slave-raiding and slave-trading companies of the 'Khartoumers'.[91]

The history of the Khartoumers is linked with the long series of Egyptian conquests in the Sudan. Between 1821 and 1879, Muhammad ʿAli and his successors carved out an Egyptian empire in black Africa which included the present-day Sudan and north-eastern Zaire. Once established at Khartoum, the Egyptians fostered the economic penetration of lands to the south. Beginning in the 1840s, merchants of diverse nationalities in Khartoum sent their agents beyond the Islamic frontier to join the *jallaba*. These traders mounted ivory- and slave-raiding operations on an unprecedented scale in the southern Sudan during the middle decades of the century.[92] They dominated these areas by combining military power, political alliances and slave incorporation with judicious distribution of long-distance trade goods.

They performed these functions in the context of what has come to be called the *zariba* system.[93] In the 1850s the term referred to the networks of small fortified Khartoumer trading settlements established in the south-western Sudan. In some respects, these outposts resembled earlier *jallaba* colonies. Both grew out of accords between Muslims and non-Muslims, and in each case, cloth, beads and firearms were exchanged for ivory and slaves. Yet there were important distinctions. Whereas the *jallaba* were few in numbers, militarily weak and completely dependent on the favourable disposition of non-Muslims, the Khartoumers arrived in large, well-armed parties, and dominated the lands and peoples around their stations.[94] In addition, the Khartoumer enterprises were larger and better financed than those of their Muslim predecessors.

The Khartoumer companies all asserted their power in similar ways. Usually a merchant party concluded a pact with a non-Muslim authority.

90 Henri Carbou, *La Région du Tchad et du Ouaddai*, Paris, 1912, II, p. 232; Modat, 'Une Tournée en pays Fertyt', 285.

91 Hilberth, *Les Gbaya*, p. 1.

92 Modat, 'Une Tournée en pays Fertyt', 5, 1912, 188, 222; P. M. Holt, 'Egypt and the Nile Valley', in *The Cambridge History of Africa*, V, *c. 1790–c. 1870*, John E. Flint (ed.), Cambridge, 1976, pp. 13–50.

93 Santandrea, *A Tribal History*, pp. 18–19.

94 *Ibid.*, Modat, 'Une Tournée en pays Fertyt', 5, 1912, 188; Wilhelm Junker, *Travels in Africa during the Years 1875 to 1878*, trans. A. H. Keane, London, 1890, p. 367; Evans-Pritchard, *The Azande*, pp. 289–301.

The local leader agreed to supply the station with grain and other staples in return for trade goods and military support. Such an arrangement satisfied the needs of the outpost. It also provided indigenous leaders with external support which could be manipulated to broaden the scope of their authority or extend it over a larger area. The various Khartoumer contingents built *zariba* after *zariba*, and by the late 1860s posts were found every twenty miles. A handful of merchant companies had divided up the region. Each company had its own raiding area controlled from a central *zariba* through a network of smaller stations manned by subordinates. By agreement, a company could not take slaves or ivory in zones delegated to another organisation.[95] Most local leaders and many *jallaba* peddlers attached themselves to these stations.

These events in the Sudan had important implications for North-Central Africa. From the 1850s to the early 1870s, the Khartoumers reigned supreme in the south-western Sudan, but their interests came increasingly into conflict with Egyptian imperial ambitions. Egypt sought direct control of the southern Sudan, and Khedive Isma'il dispatched several expeditions with that aim. The Egyptian ruler ostensibly set out to suppress the slave-trade, a half-hearted policy undertaken largely at the behest of the British. In fact, a major aim of the campaign was to extend Egyptian suzerainty. In either case, it sowed discord between the Khedive's government and the Khartoumers accustomed to ruling the south-western Sudan.[96]

The career of al-Zubayr best illustrates this friction. Originally from the Nile region, he first went to the south-western Sudan in 1856 in the employ of another trader. Over the next decade and a half he built his own network of *zaribas*, and by 1870 had become the district's most prominent merchant-ruler. The Egyptian government did not possess the resources necessary to subdue al-Zubayr, and tried to co-opt him by making him governor. Shortly after taking office, however, the new appointee launched campaigns against Dar Fur, and took over the sultanate in 1874. The victory provided al-Zubayr with a trans-Saharan commercial outlet that avoided the Nile valley and Egypt, and this set the stage for a revolt against Egyptian authority. The Egyptians countered by enticing al-Zubayr to Cairo where he was placed under house arrest. His son Sulayman led a rebellion, but the Egyptian authorities forced him to surrender and immediately executed him.[97] In the wake of this assertion of Egyptian

95 Santandrea, *A Tribal History*, pp. 18–19, 31; Modat, 'Une Tournée en pays Fertyt', 6, 1912, 222–4; Schweinfurth, *The Heart of Africa*, II, pp. 410–32; C. T. Wilson and R. W. Felkin, *Uganda and the Egyptian Sudan*, London, 1882, II, p. 162.

96 Collins, *The Southern Sudan, 1883–1898: a Struggle for Control*, New Haven, Conn., 1962, pp. 14–15.

97 El-Zubeir Pasha, *Black Ivory, or the Story of El-Zubeir Pasha, Slaver and Sultan, as told by Himself*, trans. H. C. Jackson, New York, 1970, pp. 3–89; Modat, 'Une Tournée en pays Fertyt', 6, 1912, 188, 222; Collins, *The Southern Sudan*, pp. 15–17; Collins, 'Sudanese factors', pp. 163–4; O'Fahey and Spaulding, *Kingdoms of the Sudan*, pp. 179–83.

authority, some Khartoumer troops fled west; others joined the government forces.

Nevertheless, Egyptian rule in the south-western Sudan was short-lived. In 1881, two years after Sulayman's death, the Mahdist revolt engulfed the Nile region. Soon after, the Mahdi's forces evicted the Egyptians. The withdrawal isolated Egyptian representatives in the south. At first they resisted the sporadic Mahdist columns sent to the region, but eventually most either fled or surrendered. The Egyptian era thus came to a close.[98]

Because the turmoil on the Nile had disrupted commercial connections with the north, the extensive Khartoumer trading networks did not revive after the Egyptian withdrawal. However, many slave-raiders and their indigenous allies remained in the south-western Sudan. Some had caches of firearms, and were trained in their use, and most knew of the demand for ivory and slaves in the Muslim north. A few individuals mounted their own raiding and trading operations in the 1880s and 1890s; many more moved their headquarters west beyond the Sudan to escape the Mahdists. They also sought better access to the trans-Saharan route from Wadai to the Mediterranean. The *zariba* system was thus reborn west of the Nile–Zaire divide in the heart of North-Central Africa.

The most famous and most important of the new Sudanese raider-traders was Rabih Fadlallah. He left the Sudan in 1879 after the fall of al-Zubayr, his former employer. For the next fourteen years he and his followers sojourned in the eastern part of today's CAR and in the southern Chad basin.[99] Throughout this period, Rabih pressured the surrounding Muslim states, looking for commercial outlets and sources of firearms. He also built an army. When he left Dar Fur, Rabih had a following of only several hundred men, but by 1889, a year before leaving the CAR area definitively, he led a force of more than ten thousand.[100] Rabih's presence affected the entire eastern part of North-Central Africa. He moved his headquarters only a few times, but his bands roamed widely each dry season, once pillaging as far south as the Nzakara, attacking the Banda and Sara with great regularity, and striking as far north as Wadai.

Like other, lesser-known raider-traders such as the Kresh chief, Sa'id Baldas, and the Azande sultan, Zemio, Rabih started with a small, well-armed force, and built his army through slave recruitment. Unlike Middle Eastern rulers who also used this technique, Rabih did not usually purchase

98 Collins, *The Southern Sudan*, pp. 17–42.

99 On Rabih's career up to the Bagirmi conquest, see Cordell, 'Dar al-Kuti', pp. 121–31, 176; Collins, 'Sudanese factors', pp. 163–4; W. K. R. Hallam, 'The itinerary of Rabih Fadl Allah, 1879–1893', *Bulletin de l'institut fondamental de l'Afrique noire*, t. 30, série B, no. 1, 1968, 165–81. Hallam has also written a biography of Rabih: *The Life and Times of Rabih Fadl Allah*, London, 1977.

100 R. A. Adeleye, 'Rabih b. Fadlallah, 1879–93: exploits and impact on political relations in Central Sudan', *Journal of the Historical Society of Nigeria*, v, 2, 1970, 223–42; Hallam, 'The itinerary', 170–8.

his recruits. Because he operated in non-Muslim zones among small-scale societies, his arms and organisation gave him a military advantage over his neighbours. As he raided for slaves, he integrated boys and young men into his detachments, took girls and young women into his followers' households, and offered surplus captives to northern traders in exchange for additional arms and powder.[101]

Rabih's presence in North-Central Africa between 1879 and 1891 had two major repercussions. First, his raids and recruitment policies depopulated many districts. When he arrived in Dar al-Kuti, for example, many Banda moved south between Ndele and Mbres. By the time he moved west, this zone was deserted. His campaigns also pressed heavily on the Muslims of Dar Runga. Earlier in the century, Dar Runga's population was said to have rivalled that of Bagirmi, and the Runga sultan exercised real power over Dar al-Kuti to the south. Following Rabih's raids, many Runga sought shelter with relatives in Dar al-Kuti; others were killed or enslaved. Dar Runga never regained its former power and population.[102]

Secondly, Rabih's presence threatened the spheres of influence of the Sahelian Muslim states. The Wadai reaction is instructive. Sultan Yusuf did not accept with equanimity the presence of a large and growing military force on his southern border. At first Rabih approached the Wadai ruler submissively, asking to be his client and requesting that trading parties with guns and powder be allowed to proceed through Wadai territory to his camps. This tactic failed; the sultan cut off the flow of commerce altogether. Rabih then resorted to violence. Eventually Yusuf permitted caravans to travel to Rabih's camps, but still maintained an embargo on shipments of arms and munitions. The Sudanese raider-trader received a limited supply of weapons through Bagirmi and Borno, but not enough to meet the needs of his growing army. It was in large measure this search for arms and commercial outlets that eventually led him west.[103]

Wadai was not the only state hostile to Rabih. Bagirmi and Borno each opposed him in turn, as indeed did the Hausa-Fulani states of the Sokoto Caliphate still further west. Combined action on the part of these states perhaps might have limited Rabih's power, since they controlled the vital trans-Saharan routes, but rivalries between them prevented concerted

101 Hallam, *Rabih Fadl Allah*, p. 160; Chevalier, *Mission Chari–Lac Tchad*, p. 226; Santandrea, *A Tribal History*, p. 267.

102 Chevalier, *Mission Chari–Lac Tchad*, p. 120; Modat, 'Une Tournée en pays Fertyt', 5, 1912, 196; 6, 1912, 228, 230; 7, 1912, 271; Carbou, *La Région*, II, 223; Casimir Léon Maistre, 'Rapport de la Mission Maistre', *L'Afrique française*, iii, 6, 1893, 6; Martine, 'Essai sur l'histoire du pays Salamat et les moeurs et coutumes de ses habitants', *Bulletin de la société des recherches congolaises*, v, 1924, 23–4.

103 Adeleye, 'Rabih b. Fadlallah', 227–32; Hallam, *Rabih Fadl Allah*, pp. 99–100; Martine, 'Essai sur l'histoire du pays Salamat', 23–4; Modat, 'Une Tournée en pays Fertyt', 6, 1912, 228–30; Archives Nationales du Tchad, W53.9, 'Documents et études historiques sur le Salamat, réunis par Y. Merot: Rabah et Senoussi au Dar Rounga; note au sujet du Rabah au Salamat', Mangueigne, 1950.

action. Bagirmi fell to Rabih's forces in 1893, and Borno followed a year later.

The *zariba* system and Rabih's campaign's established a more permanent and demanding Muslim presence in the east and north of North-Central Africa. Meanwhile, Fulani campaigns in Adamawa expanded Muslim control in the west. Here, too, military conquest and political domination reinforced Muslim commerce. Motivated by the successful *jihads* of Usuman dan Fodio in Hausaland, a Fulani clan called the Wolarbe attacked the non-Muslim peoples of the Adamawa plateau in 1815. The conquerors founded a string of conquest states, nominally under the authority of a Fulani *amir* at Yola. Among the more important of these dependencies was the Mbum state at Ngaoundéré which fell to the Fulani in the 1840s. Over the following decade, Fulani leaders in the area encouraged Fulani immigration. At the same time, they incorporated many Mbum into an elaborate territorial administration.[104]

Events in the Camerounian border region paralleled those along the Nile–Zaire divide for the remainder of the century. From secure positions on the Adamawa plateau, Fulani warriors raided for slaves among non-Muslim peoples. Men and women taken captive were integrated individually into Fulani society; entire non-Muslim settlements were relocated within the Fulani states. In addition, many people were sold for export to Hausaland, where the growing regional economy required labour. Towards the end of the century, the Fulani established permanent settlements in Gbaya country, and formerly non-Muslim centres such as Kounde, Baboua and Gaza became outposts of Fulani slave-raiding. The Fulani also sponsored and protected the Hausa and Borno traders, just as the Khartoumers made clients of the *jallaba* who had traded before them. Gbaya leaders allied with the Muslim intruders as their eastern counterparts had done. They adopted aspects of Muslim culture, and enhanced their power through association with the Muslim economy.[105]

Other non-Muslim states, like those of the Mbum, also became part of the Muslim economy in the late nineteenth century. In the south-east, the Azande and Nzakara allowed large parties of Muslims, mainly traders, to settle within their borders, frequently supplying them with captives. A somewhat different pattern emerged in Dar al-Kuti. In the 1830s, a small community of Muslim teachers and traders from Bagirmi and Dar Runga lived in the region. By the latter part of the century, the Muslims had co-opted their non-Muslim hosts. Dar al-Kuti first became a province of Wadai, and then, with the assistance of Rabih, gained its independence in

104 Burnham, 'Raiders and traders in Adamawa', pp. 44–6; Catherine Coquery-Vidrovitch, 'De Brazza à Gentil: la politique française en Haute-Sangha à la fin du XIXe siécle', *Revue française d'histoire d'outre-mer*, N°. 186, ii, Ier trimestre, 1965, 29–30.
105 Burnham, 'Raiders and traders in Adamawa', pp. 44–7, 52–5; Coquery-Vidrovitch, 'De Brazza à Gentil', 27.

the 1890s. Raiding parties from Dar al-Kuti took up where Rabih had left off. Eventually the sultanate became the last and largest slave-raiding state in North-Central Africa.[106]

Why did the societies of North-Central Africa allow themselves to be drawn into this intensifying spiral of violence, and with what ultimate effect? Although each society responded individually, the answer to this question is simple. They had no choice. Over the course of the late eighteenth and first half of the nineteenth centuries, northern goods became an important, if small, category in local economies. Cloth, beads and other items became prestige goods, along with local products. Among the Banda, for example, bridewealth began to include beads as well as the traditional copper anklets from Hufrat al-Nuhas. Along the Logone, cloth became a desired commodity.

None of these goods, however, was a necessity. Many societies of North-Central Africa received them only intermittently before the late nineteenth century. The big change came with firearms, which began to appear in large quantities after mid-century. Firearms made it easier for raiding parties to take slaves. They were used both by the horse-borne marauders of Wadai, of Bagirmi and of the Adamawa Fulani, and by the foot soldiers of the Khartoumers and of Dar al-Kuti. The use of firearms for offence made them imperative for defence. Even societies that did not engage in raiding searched for arms to protect themselves from more aggressive neighbours. But to procure arms, one had to sell slaves. This led to even greater violence as societies were forced to take captives to ensure their own security. This arms race was first one of quantity, the aim of which was to obtain large supplies of weapons before others could acquire them. It then became one of quality as rifles replaced flintlocks, only to be superseded by repeaters.

These upheavals altered some basic patterns of existence. Individuals and groups began to dominate others to a degree not before possible. The trend towards more centralised leadership continued, although few societies evolved institutions for the peaceful transfer of power. Settlement patterns changed. Under pressure from the Fulani and their Mbum allies, for example, some Gbaya groups adopted the Mbum style of compact villages that brought several clans together, each with its own quarter.[107] Similar threats from Wadai prompted the Sara to build palisades around their villages.

The accumulation of power and wealth encouraged the accumulation of people. Scattered settlement patterns gave way to larger, denser villages. In most cases, raiders took more captives than were exported, and surplus slaves were settled around the raiding centres. This, in turn, brought

106 Cordell, 'Dar al-Kuti', chs 2 and 3.
107 Burnham, *Opportunity*, pp. 58–9.

changes in the relations of production. In subject villages more people than before produced crops for others, and in some places plantations using slave labour appeared. These tribute and labour obligations produced agricultural surpluses which, when accumulated and re-distributed, reinforced central authority. Slaves and surpluses allowed larger quantities of luxury imports. Disparities of wealth reinforced previously marginal social inequalities.

The violence also produced 'voluntary' shifts of settlement, as small groups moved near larger ones for protection. When menaced by raiding, some villages made blood pacts with nearby raider-traders and moved to their headquarters. Alternatively, if a hamlet submitted peacefully to a raiding party, its inhabitants were often allowed to remain together and relocate to the neighbourhood of the raiding centre.

Still other population concentrations appeared. These were refugee settlements. The rock outcroppings found throughout the savannas sheltered large numbers of people. Some settlements united under powerful leaders and fought for their independence. Such was the case at Kazamba in the northern part of present-day CAR where the Manza held off Rabih in 1885, forcing him to veer north. They also repelled repeated attacks by al-Sanusi.[108] The borderlands between different zones of control also afforded refuge. In the first decade of this century, many Banda settled in the cliffs which marked the boundary between Dar al-Kuti and lands under French control.

As slave-raiding intensified, increased flight and denser settlement patterns among both raiders and target populations promoted smallpox epidemics. Outbreaks occurred in Ndele, the capital of Dar al-Kuti, between 1901 and 1906. A major epidemic appeared among the Nzakara in 1905, although its provenance is unknown.[109] Similar episodes undoubtedly occurred elsewhere.

Agriculture also changed significantly. Among the northern Banda, sorghum had long been the major crop. By the end of the nineteenth century, cassava rivalled it in many areas. Sorghums and millets, better adapted to the drier climate of the savanna, did not afford the security of root crops, which needed less care, could be left in the ground until needed and were more easily hidden from raiders.[110] Cassava cultivation also allowed greater freedom of movement. It could be planted and then left

108 Gaud, *Les Mandja*, pp. 95–6; Vergiat, *Moeurs et coutumes des Manjas*, p. 28; Kalck, *Historical Dictionary of the Central African Republic*, trans. Thomas O'Toole, Metuchen, N.J., and London, 1980, p. 74.

109 A. Mesple, 'Mercuri', *Bulletin de la société de géographie d'Alger et d'Afrique du Nord*, 4e semestre, 1902, 634–6; Emile Julien, 'Mohamed-es-Senoussi et ses états', *Bulletin de la société des recherches congolaises*, 9, 1928, 65–6; Dampierre, *Un Ancien Royaume bandia*, pp. 105–33.

110 Renouf-Stefanik, *Animisme et Islam chez les Manza*, p. 50, n.118; Charles Prioul, 'Notes sur la diffusion du manioc dans la partie centrale du territoire centrafricaine', paper circulated at the Ecole nationale d'administration, Bangui, n.d.

relatively untended. Although the plant matured in eighteen months to two years, it could be left in the ground much longer.[111] Thus it served as an insurance crop. It is ironic that cassava, introduced into North-Central Africa as a result of ties with the Atlantic system, helped societies to survive the violence of incorporation into the Muslim economy.

The demographic impact of intensified Muslim raiding in the late nineteenth century was enormous. Available sources all report the depopulation of huge areas. Few, however, distinguish among its causes: flight, death, forced removal to other parts of the region or export. Although no population estimates exist for the whole of North-Central Africa, census information does exist for the south-western Sudan. Adjacent to the Nile–Zaire divide the estimated Bahr al-Ghazal population fell from 1 500 000 in 1882 to 400 000 in 1903, a decline of 74 per cent. A third of the decline was reportedly due to disease, and two-thirds to war.[112] The war casualties resulted from Mahdist expeditions and the increased slave-raiding in the latter decades of the century. These figures are perhaps exaggerated. They do not, for example, take account of the people who simply fled into isolated areas and avoided contact with outsiders, a problem that plagued British colonial administrators in the region well into the present century. Nevertheless, taken together with the qualitative data from the south-western Sudan, these statistics are a convincing indication of a drastic population decline.[113]

All of North-Central Africa, with the exception of the forest margins in the south-west, was ultimately drawn into the Muslim economy. Early French and Belgian colonial expeditions noted the existence of Muslim communities throughout the savanna, from the grasslands of central Cameroun to the Azande states of the Uele. Travellers heading north from Bangui in the 1890s soon began to hear of Muslim traders. Muslim commercial communities were also found in Bangassou, the Nzakara capital, Rafai, Zemio and other Azande states. In the latter region, Muslims from East Africa also established commercial communities.

The long-term effects of Muslim economic expansion might have been the more complete assimilation of North-Central Africa into the Islamic world. The frontier between the Muslim and non-Muslim zones would probably have continued to move southward as it had for more than a millennium. However, another set of outside influences intervened: first by proxy and then directly, the European-dominated Atlantic economy impinged on riverain societies. By the 1880s, Europeans themselves made their way to North-Central Africa. The early expeditions were innocuous,

111 Schweinfurth, *The Heart of Africa*, I, p. 526.
112 Karol J. Krótki, 'La population du Soudan au XIXe siècle et au début du XXe siècle', *Annales de démographie historique* (1979), 172, 176, 178, 194.
113 Santandrea, *A Tribal History, passim.*; Modat, 'Une Tournée en pays Fertyt', 5, 1912, 180, 192, 195; 6, 1912, 235; 7, 1912, 274–5, 278–81.

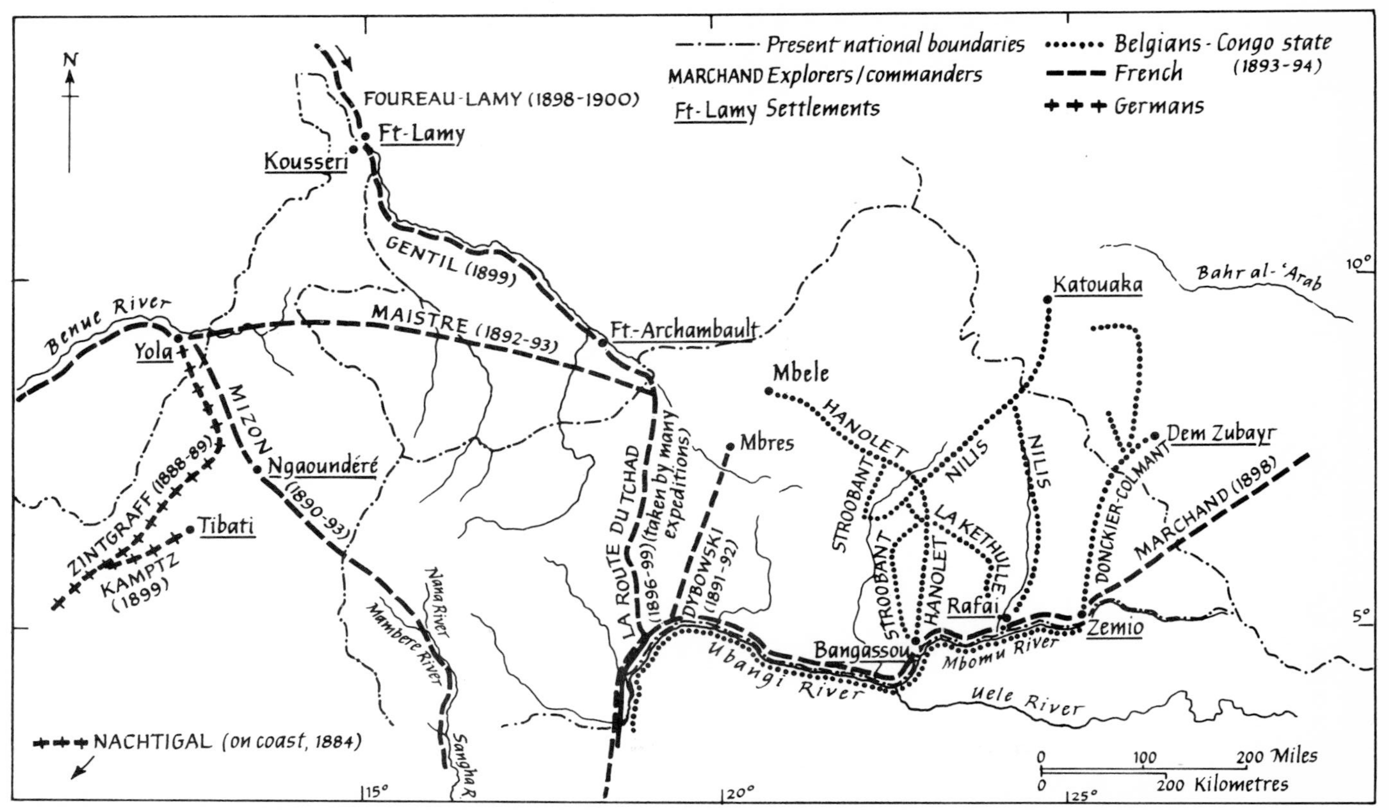

2:6 European exploration and conquest, North-Central Africa

but they gave way to more intensive interference in local affairs. The region was subjected to yet further upheaval as Europeans sought political and economic control for themselves and their clients. Earlier disruption associated with incorporation into the Muslim economy was thus superseded by new violence.

THE EUROPEAN CONQUEST: NORTH-CENTRAL AFRICA BETWEEN TWO ECONOMIC SYSTEMS

Between 1880 and 1910, European intervention in North-Central Africa made the region a still more violent battleground. The Muslim economy of the north and the Atlantic economy of the south-west impinged ever more directly and competed for control. The conflict was aggravated by rivalries within each camp. The Muslim states of Kanem-Borno, Bagirmi, Wadai and Dar Fur had competed for control of non-Muslim regions earlier in the century; Germany, France, Belgium and Great Britain became the new rivals.

Although the European presence on the coast affected the savanna fringes as early as the eighteenth century, direct intervention came only in the 1880s and 1890s.[114] A few years before the foundation of the Congo State in 1885, agents of King Leopold of Belgium made their way up the Zaire and Ubangi rivers, seeking to claim as much territory as possible for their patron and his business associates. They hoped to link up their zone of control with the Upper Nile to the east and with the Muslim states of the Sahel.[115]

During the same decade, competition between the French and British intensified as each moved to control the Upper Nile. For a time in the late 1890s, the eastern part of North-Central Africa became a focal point of this rivalry. French resources were directed primarily at getting the Marchand expedition to the Nile before the British. The confrontation came at Fashoda on the Nile in 1898. The French blinked first, and their dream of an empire stretching from the Niger to the Nile evaporated in the face of British determination to see the Union Jack flying from the Cape to Cairo.[116]

In the west, in present-day Cameroun and Chad, the game of imperialism had yet a fourth European player. Germany first laid formal claim to what would become its colony of Kamerun in 1884 when the explorer Gustav Nachtigal signed treaties with coastal rulers.[117]

114 Coquery-Vidrovitch, 'De Brazza à Gentil', 22–40.

115 R. O. Collins, *King Leopold, England, and the Upper Nile, 1899–1909*, New Haven, Conn., 1968, p.30.

116 *Ibid.*, pp. 1–7, 52–6.

117 Eyongetah and Brain, *A History of the Cameroon*, pp. 65–6, 70–1, 73, 79–81, 84; Jean Suret-Canale, *L'Afrique noire occidentale et centrale*, I: *geographie, civilisations, histoire*, Paris, 1961, p. 226.

Occupation and exploitation followed as the Germans carved out their own sphere of control.

Apart from their rivalries with one another, the European powers were also aware that they had to wrest control from both Muslim and local African interests. Thus the major motive and certainly the major effect of the European conquest was to reorient the region economically. All four European powers tried to monopolise commerce within their zones. This was a major objective on the local level as well as in European capitals. Early patterns of colonial occupation and exploitation reflect this concern. In many instances, European traders preceded government representatives, and their advice greatly influenced the shape of official policy.

The Europeans tried to ensure the profitability of conquest in quite formal ways. Early French treaties almost always included monopoly trade clauses. Along the Ubangi and Mbomu, these provisions were directed more against their European rivals than against Muslim economic interests. In the north, however, French commercial policies aimed at their competitors from the desert edge.

In the end treaties did not suffice. Colonial control ultimately required violence. In Cameroun, the Germans subdued the Fulani by 1902. The French followed their diplomatic defeat at Fashoda in 1898 by re-directing their energies northward. An expedition led by Emile Gentil had marched into the Chad basin in 1897. It claimed the central savanna for France, and even arrived at an accommodation with al-Sanusi, the ruler of Dar al-Kuti. Shortly thereafter, Bagirmi became a French protectorate. In 1900, the French eliminated Rabih in the battle of Kusseri in northern Cameroun. They also manoeuvred to undercut the Sanusiyya Muslim brotherhood. This influential order held together the trans-Saharan network in the eastern desert. Finally, they undermined Wadai, first by promoting internal discontent and then by outright conquest in 1909.[118]

The French then moved to consolidate control. The French resident in Dar al-Kuti assassinated al-Sanusi in 1911 and drove his Muslim followers out of the capital. A year later their formal sphere of control reached as far as the border with the Anglo-Egyptian Sudan, and they began to suppress slave-raiding. During the first decade of the century they also asserted their authority over the rulers of the Azande states of Rafai and Zemio, and placed the Nzakara sultan on the colonial payroll.

What is most apparent looking at the history of North-Central Africa between 1880 and 1910 is how violence engendered by the expansion of the Muslim economy gave way to violence associated with incorporation into the Atlantic economy and the European colonial system. The inequalities in wealth and power accompanying the first were joined by new

118 Suret-Canale, *L'Afrique noire occidentale et centrale,* I, pp. 223, 270, 272: Suret-Canale, *L'Afrique noire occidentale et centrale,* II: *l'ère coloniale (1900–1945),* Paris, 1964, p. 124.

inequalities produced by the second. Some groups dominant in the precolonial era survived the transition. By the 1920s, al-Sanusi's heirs had become the agents of French rule in Dar al-Kuti. The most prominent Syrian merchant in the sultanate married one of the sultan's daughters. In other cases, new individuals seized the initiative.[119] Even though the Muslim economy was eclipsed, many individual Muslim traders adjusted to the new reality. Hausa and Borno merchants became representatives of European commercial houses. At European insistence, a Hausa-Tuareg merchant from Niger became the chief of Fort-Crampel, a major centre in the colony of Ubangi-Shari.[120] And yet it should not be assumed that local societies were but the pawns of these outside forces. Local initiative and resistance altered the impact of colonial rule, just as they had channelled earlier Muslim activities.

119 Accounts of several of these individuals are included in Brian Weinstein, 'Félix Eboué and the chiefs: perceptions of power in early Oubangui-Chari', *JAH*, xi, 1, 1970, 107–26.
120 Pierre Olivier, 'Notes on a conversation with Shéffou, Hausa chief of Fort-Crampel' (my title), handwritten notes taken shortly before Shéffou's death, Crampel (Bandero), CAR, 1966.

CHAPTER 3

The peoples of the forest

JAN VANSINA

> On first entering the great grim twilight regions of the forest you hardly see anything but the vast column-like grey tree stems in their countless thousands around you, and the scarcely vegetated ground beneath. But day by day, as you get trained to your surroundings, you see more and more, and a whole world grows up gradually out of the gloom before your eyes.
>
> Mary Kingsley on the Gabon forest, *Travels in West Africa*, p. 101

The rain-forest is inhabited by peoples who seem on the whole to be very similar in their societies and cultures. Indeed ethnographers usually classify them as a single cultural unit, labelled the Hyläa.[1] They are small-scale societies organised in villages. Their known oral traditions mainly deal with migrations and origins, partly because Europeans did not record other data, partly because this aspect dominates the traditions themselves. The ancestral past of the 9 million or so inhabitants of this area has never been the object of systematic study. A few studies concerning a now-outdated search for origins, and the history of the slave-trade, are all that have been done. And yet theirs has been a lively past, the traces of which can be found in the diffusion of ideas or institutions over large areas. On the whole, these peoples have not formed states. The simple interpretation of these societies as 'segmentary lineage systems' has, as in West Africa,[2] obscured their history; for segmentary lineage systems were seen as fundamentally unchanging structures which mechanically grew and split into segments. It was thought that every man was equal to every other man at his level in the

1 K. Born, 'Nordkongo und Gabun: der Westen', in *Die Völker Afrikas und ihre traditionellen Kulturen*, H. Baumann (ed.), Wiesbaden, 1975, pp. 685–91; H. Baumann and D. Westermann, *Les Peuples et les civilisations de l'Afrique*, Paris, 1948, pp. 90, 191–214.
2 R. Horton, 'Stateless societies in the history of West Africa', in *History of West Africa*, J. F. A. Ajayi and M. Crowder (eds), London, 1971, vol i, pp. 81–104.

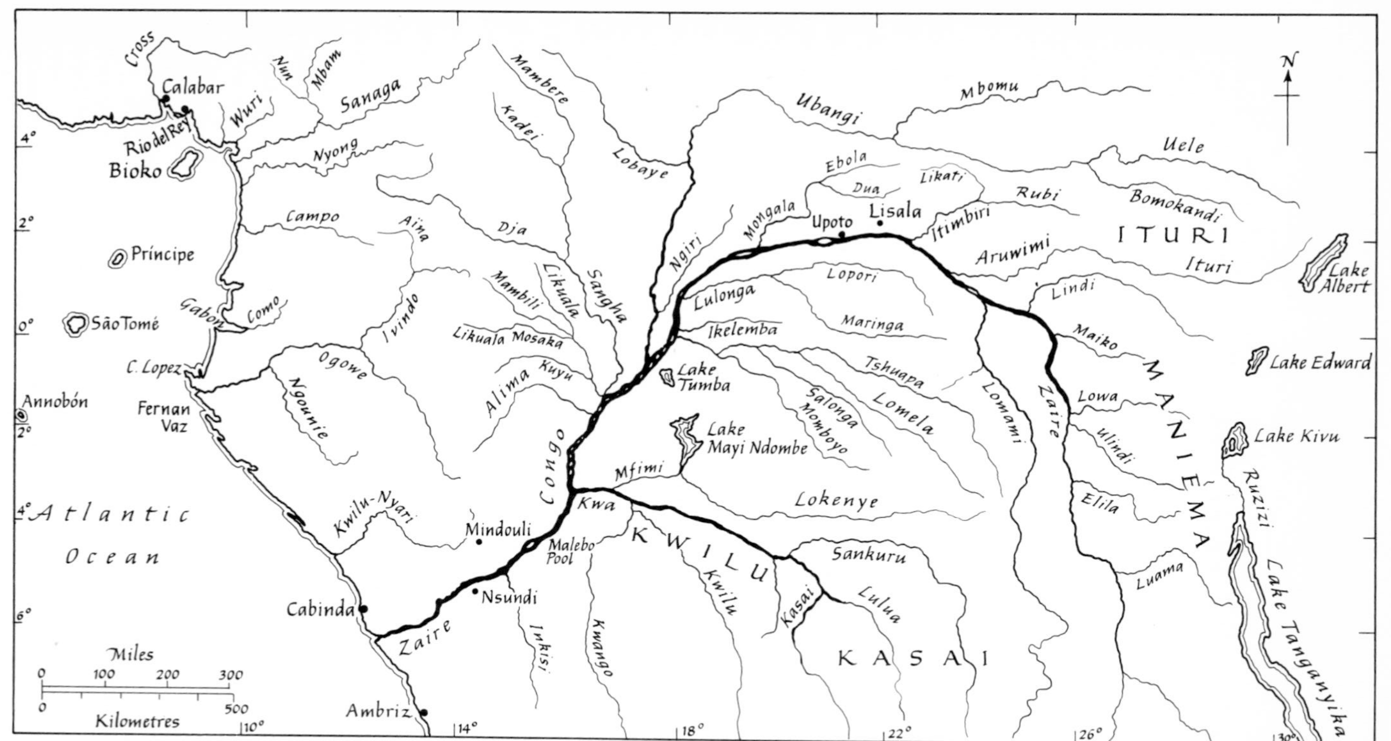

3:1 The forest zone of Central Africa

genealogy; only seniority brought authority and rank. The reality is very different. As a result, most of the history of this area still remains to be studied. For this task, we even lack a well-founded chronology.

What then can be said today? Historical change in the area has been conditioned by two major clusters of variables. One force for change stemmed from internal social dynamics. Neighbouring societies with similar, but not identical, social systems developed their own inherent potentialities; at the same time they interacted with each other continually over many centuries. This development and interaction is the major force that brought about change. The insertion of the region into global trading systems was a later powerful source of change. In the west the Atlantic trading system began to influence some peoples from the sixteenth century. In the north and east it was the Mediterranean and Indian ocean systems which affected the forest peoples, but only after 1860.

THE RAIN-FOREST

Any vegetation map of Africa features a green block of rain-forest straddling the Equator from the Atlantic to the Great Lakes. The world's second largest rain-forest covers an area of nearly 2 million square kilometres and is about the size of the whole farmland of West Africa. This vast expanse seems to cut communications between the savanna and woodlands to the north and south. Yet the rain-forest is not 'impenetrable', as has been believed. It does not bar the flow of people and their cultures; neither is it a single homogeneous mass, as appears on the map.

The forest environment is far more diversified than that of the great deserts. There is inundated forest, there is forest on dry land and there is mountain forest. The large area of inundated forest and marsh stretches 650 kilometres along the Ubangi and Zaire rivers. This heart-shaped area is surrounded by a huge rain-forest on dry soil which stretches from the coastal mangrove swamps in the west to the high-altitude forest in the east.[3]

The dry forest is interspersed with broad rivers. The great bend of the Zaire is 40 kilometres wide and, together with its tributaries, forms its own environment. The forest is also broken by patches of savanna, some of which extend to 2 590 square kilometres and support distinctive fauna and flora. The biggest savanna encroachments are in the southern forest fringes.

3 E. Roche, 'Végétation ancienne et actuelle de l'Afrique centrale', *African Economic History* (*AEH*), vii, 1979, 30–7; A. Aubréville, *Etude sur les forêts de l'Afrique équatoriale française et du Cameroun*. Nogent-sur-Marne, 1948; R. Letouzey, *Etude phytogéographique du Cameroun*, Paris, 1968; G. Caballé, 'Essai phytogéographique sur la forêt dense du Gabon', *Annales de l'université nationale du Gabon* (Sciences), ii, 1978, 87–101; R. Pierlot, *Structure et composition des forêts denses d'Afrique centrale, spécialement celles du Kivu*, Brussels, 1966; J. Lebrun, 'La Forêt équatoriale congolaise', *Bulletin agricole du Congo Belge*, xxvii, 2, 1936, 163–92.

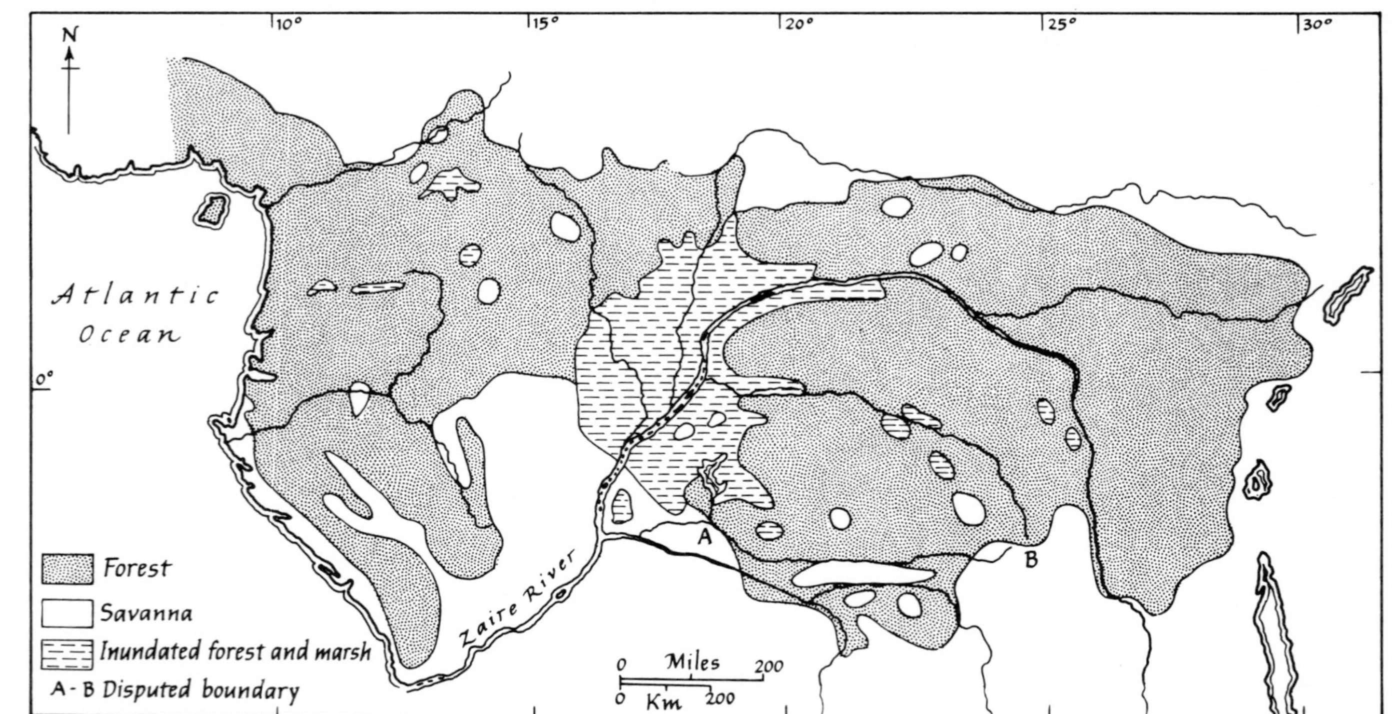

3:2 The rain-forest

Some of the smaller patches may be due to human activity, but the larger ones are very old features in the landscape.[4]

Part of the forest retains primary cover, with sparse undergrowth; it presents great difficulties in clearing. The secondary forest, with luxuriant undergrowth, occupies large areas – for instance, in Rio Muni.[5] Apart from these broad distinctions, vegetation can be finely influenced by soils, by orography and by past botanical history. Most stages of the primary rain-forest contain a bewildering variety of floral species per hectare, while in some climax areas the vegetation primarily consists of a single species over several thousand square kilometres.[6] The people who exploit these environments take full advantage of the ecotones and make even finer distinctions than the botanists. Thus one population differentiates among three environments in 'typical' rain-forest on dry soil.[7] Specialised fishermen live side by side with farmer trappers, and specialised pygmy hunters live in symbiosis with farmers.

POPULATION AND PATTERNS OF SETTLEMENT

The population density of the rain-forest was probably about 3·75 per square kilometre in the 1870s, and it seems to have been low for a very long time.[8] The environment may have been hostile to human occupation, though evidence for this view is lacking.[9] Densities were uneven, with a few nodes of heavy population in a sea of low densities around 2 per square kilometre. The largest node now lies in central Cameroun where densities exceed 50 per square kilometre. Other high densities are reported at the base of the elevated southern plateau, along the fifth parallel in lower Zaire and Kwilu and in pockets such as on the Kukuya plateau, in the land between Bomokandi and Uele and in minor pockets along the great rivers of the central Zaire rain-forest.[10] Nowhere, however, does the almost

4 P. Duvigneaud, 'Les Formations herbeuses (savanes et steppes) du Congo meridional', *Les Naturalistes belges*, xxxiv, 1953, no. 3–4, 66–75; R. Germain, *Les Biotopes alluvionnaires herbeux et les savanes intercalaires du Congo équatorial*, Brussels, 1965; J. Koechlin, *La Végétation des savanes du sud de la République de Congo (capitale Brazzaville)*, Montpellier, 1961; Fontes, 'Les Formations herbeuses du Gabon', *Annales de l'université nationale du Gabon* (Sciences), ii, 1978, 127–53.

5 A. Panyella, *Esquema de etnologia de los Fang Ntumu de la Guinea Equatorial*, Madrid, 1959, 15–16, map 1.

6 Ph. Gérard, *Etude écologique de la forêt dense à Gilbertiodendron dewevrii dans la région de l'Uele*, Brussels, 1960.

7 A. de Calonne Beaufaict, *Les Ababua*, Brussels, 1909, pp. 33–4.

8 G. Sautter, *De l'Atlantique au fleuve Congo*, Paris, 1966, vol. 2, pp. 965–82, 996–9.

9 *Ibid.*, 974–7; J. Maquet, *Les Civilisations noires*, Paris, 1962, p. 116.

10 P. Gourou, *La Densité de la population rurale du Congo Belge et du Ruanda Urundi*, Brussels, 1955; Gourou, *Carte de la densité de la population au Congo Belge et au Ruanda-Urundi*, Brussels, 1951; Sautter, *De l'Atlantique*, maps; E. V. Thevoz, 'Kamerun Eisenbahn–Erkundigungs Expedition', *Mitteilungen aus dem Deutschen Schutzgebieten*, xxxii, 1919, map 3.

empty forest have populations resembling the teeming interlacustrine region to the east.

The modern distribution reflects some very old patterns. This is true for all the striking contrasts, except for the minor pockets which may have formed after 1750 in response to the externally oriented Atlantic trade. A careful study of secondary forests could yield precise knowledge of population distributions over the past several centuries. Until this is done we must be content to note that most of the area has been exploited for many centuries. Only portions of the forest, north of the Ogowe and east of the Ivindo, and in the Ituri and Maniema, contain primary growth near or at its climax. This reflects either a very low density of population or, at the least, an absence of farmers.

In the past individuals often moved from village to village. The social organisation of the forest peoples was attuned to this situation. All forest dwellers lived in villages or in hunting camps,[11] but every free person claimed rights of residence in several villages. The flux of population has been vigorously argued for the hunters of Ituri.[12] It is, however, a general feature of the area, and individual movements were both frequent and far-ranging. A Cameroun pygmy ranged over 50 kilometres during his lifetime,[13] whilst among Ruki farmers women might marry 50 kilometres from their village.[14] Group mobility was also high. Farmers moved more than once a decade, when their soils were exhausted, and hunters shifted camp every month in pursuit of game. Such moves could cover considerable distances. One village that had to flee a quarrelsome neighbour moved 40 kilometres at once, and this was not unique.[15] Fishing villages often remained the most stable. Although fisherfolk would cover great distances when they moved, suitable settlement sites were rare in the inundated forest zone.[16]

The typical population movement in the forest has been a slow drift. Drift occurs when villages begin to move in one direction rather than at random. It is often the consequence of an attraction to a better, but still familiar, environment and of the desire to avoid friction with other settlements under population pressure. The following migration story summarises the main causes given in traditions:

11 Hunting camps like those of the Mbuti are a nucleated form of settlement also.

12 C. Turnbull, *Wayward Servants*, New York, 1965, pp. 81–9.

13 R. Letouzey, *Contribution de la botanique au problème d'une éventuelle langue pygmée*, Paris, 1976, p. 31, fn.15.

14 G. Hulstaert, *Le Mariage des Nkundo*, Brussels, 1938, p. 285; Hulstaert, *Les Mongo*, Tervuren, 1961, p. 16.

15 P. Laburthe-Tolra, *Minlaaba*, Lille, 1977, p. 295, fn.6.

16 R. Harms, 'Competition and Capitalism: the Bobangi Role in Equatorial Africa's Trade Revolution, ca. 1750–1900', Ph.D. thesis, University of Wisconsin, 1978, p. 42; P. Van Leynseele, 'Les Libinza de la Ngiri', Ph.D. thesis, Leiden University, 1979, pp. 26–31, 58–9, 61–2, 102–6.

> They left Selenge when the great famine was at its height. They fled this famine.... Another division occurred at Ikongo because of civil war.... The descendants of Ilonga followed an elephant ... it died ... and the pursuers settled there for good.[17]

A special form of drift, or diaspora, was the spread of fishermen. Between the mid-eighteenth and later nineteenth centuries one group moved down-river from the lower Ubangi. It settled along the banks of the Zaire, creating in the process a new ethnic group. The resulting village colonies formed a 750-kilometre chain among the scattered settlements of local peoples.[18]

In the nineteenth century, massive population movements over rather short distances were reported as groups rivalled one another for better positions near trading routes or shied away from them. In southern Gabon and in Cameroun some large clusters of villages moved 200 kilometres and more in the same fashion and for the same reasons.[19] The distances were not exceptional, but the relative speed of movement and number of villages involved turned drift into migration.

Even movements such as those in Gabon were quite different from the simple 'migration' models of earlier scholars. These old accounts implied movement by hundreds of settlements simultaneously over the same route and covering vast distances. Traditions of shifting villages or of moving families were mistaken for mass migration. Stories of the eighteenth-century movement of the 'Mangbetu' royal family are a case in point. In fact the motion was random, the adventures were limited to a single family and their society was fluid. The tradition sought both to explain the presence of Kere-speakers in the area and to create a 'foundation charter' for the kingdom.[20] Other types of tradition tell of mass migration from the point of origin of mankind to the present place of residence. Migration here is used as cosmological speculation.[21] Epic traditions of migration can easily be misunderstood, yet they movingly portray the drift of villages and individuals.[22] Although these epics can never be taken at face value, they do describe real mobility at some level.

17 M. Isekolong, 'Note historique sur les Nsamba', *Aequatoria*, xxiii, 1960, 2, 57.
18 Harms, 'Competition', pp. 37–80.
19 Laburthe-Tolra, *Minlaaba*, pp. 297–414, map 349; C. Chamberlin, 'The migration of the Fang into Central Gabon during the nineteenth century', *International Journal of African Historical Studies* (*IJAHS*), xi, 1978, 3, 429–56; Cortadellas Amat, *Ngovayang II: un village de Sud-Cameroun*, Paris, 1972, p. 92, map VI and 61.
20 P. Denis, *Histoire des Mangbetu et des Matshaga jusqu'à l'arrivée des Belges*, Tervuren, 1961, pp. 8–18; C. A. Keim, 'Precolonial Mangbetu Rule', Ph.D. thesis, Indiana University, 1979, pp. 38–40; Bertrand, *Les Mangbetu* (MS.), pp. 71–9 – copy in my possession.
21 W. MacGaffey, 'Oral traditions in Central Africa', *IJAHS*, vii, 1974, 417–26 (Kongo); J. Vansina, *The Children of Woot*, Madison, Wisconsin, 1978, pp. 34–40 (Kuba).
22 A. De Rop, *Lianja: l'épopée des Mongo*, Brussels, 1964; J. B. Nsanda, 'Epopée Kiguma: essai d'un genre littéraire lega', Ph.D. thesis, National University of Zaire, 1974.

The case of the so-called 'Fang' migrations illustrates the misuse of such traditions. In the received scholarship many unrelated traditions have been stitched into a single narrative, and false ethnographic 'clues' have been used to derive a people and its culture from some distant area. The traditions of the Fang, Bulu and Beti clusters were thereby fused into a single account of a migration from the middle Sanaga river to the Ogowe river. Since these people use crossbows, as do the inhabitants of the Ubangi bend, they were traced to that area. As some traditions mention lions, the Cameroun savannas were immediately assumed to have been the original environment, despite the fact that Yaoundé had lions as late as 1895. References to horsemen were assumed to refer to Hausa cavalry whose slave raids drove the 'Fang' into the forest. But did these horsemen not gallop into an older tradition as a borrowed marvel?[23] Except in the imagination of the savants, there never were far-flung 'Fang' migrations. The unified mirage vanishes when the accounts of each group are examined individually. The traditions are, in part, cosmological explanations and tales of short-range movements, without a single area of origin.

Elsewhere in Central Africa large-scale reconstructions of migrations arching across the map are merely wanderings of the mind.[24] This is not to deny that population movement occurred. The 'Fang' of northern Gabon really did begin moving towards the coast and the Ogowe from about 1840, assimilating or disrupting the previous inhabitants. By 1900 they occupied roughly the area where they are now found. But it took two solid generations to cover less than 240 kilometres.

To deny mass migration over vast distance is not to deny real mobility and flux in forest societies. The mixture of fluidity and stability is a long-term feature of the past. The flux facilitated the spread of ideas and practices in and across the rain-forest, as shown by the distribution of words, objects, institutions and art styles. The manufacture and use of the double-iron bell spread from north of the forest to the Zambezi before A.D. 1400 and from west to east as far as the Lualaba river. In the realm of belief, convictions about a special type of witchcraft and its associated autopsies occur from the lower Zaire to Lake Albert. In the northern forest beliefs in *jemba* witchcraft occur from Douala to Lake Albert. One type of boy's initiation is found in the Ituri, in Maniema and on the lower Lomami.[25] Such far-

23 Traditions about armour-clad Portuguese among the Kuba travelled from the coast to the Sankuru carried by Imbangala traders. Cf. Vansina, *The Children of Woot*, p. 37.

24 Chamberlin, 'Migration', for a critique of the accepted thesis as stated by P. Alexandre, 'Proto-histoire de groupe Beti–Bulu–Fang: essaie de synthèse provisoire', *Cahiers d'études africaines*, xx, 1965, 403–560.

25 J. Vansina, 'The bells of kings', *JAH*, x, 1969, 2, 187–98; H. Baumann, 'Likundu: die Sektion der Zauberkraft', *Zeitschrift für Ethnologie*, lx, 1928, 73–85; Baumann, 'Die Sambesi–Angola Provinz', *Die Völker Afrikas und Ihre Traditionellen Kulturen*, H. Baumann (ed.), Wiesbaden, 1975, vol. 1, map 633.

flung distribution patterns attest to an almost constant flow of ideas. They are mute witnesses to repeated historical interaction, not to the effects of a few powerful migrations or diffusions.

Population mobility and social plasticity also help to explain profound similarities in the organisation of forest societies, so that all of them, including pygmy communities, appear as variations of a common theme. Certainly the environment was influential, but equally certainly a myriad of contacts helped produce the resulting situation.

THE VILLAGE

The techniques of production required more collaboration by forest-dwellers than was necessary in the savanna. Hence it is no surprise that forest people settled in compact villages which were the basic units of landholding. Village size usually varied from 30 to 250, but hunting camps were rarely more than 50 and farming communities rarely fewer than 100 people. Although forest villages were unequal in size, settlement was nowhere as dispersed as was usual in the northern savanna or in the interlacustrine areas.[26]

The collective character of gaining a livelihood in the forest setting needs to be stressed. Cooperation was necessary to clear primary forest for village sites and for fields. Wealth in land was reckoned as wealth in secondary forest, because this was much less back-breaking to clear.[27] Even so this, too, was a collective endeavour. Hunting, trapping and fishing also involved cooperative efforts. In some parts of the area complex, village-owned trapping systems ran for kilometres, and collective net hunts were common.[28] Community fishing was undertaken in small streams, and on the main rivers specialised fishermen needed not only crews, but also help in canoe-building, setting up weir systems, knotting and repairing nets and gathering the necessary raw materials. Individual effort produced less farmland, less game and less fish than collective endeavour: hence the need to live in villages. Farmers in an open savanna could afford to live in dispersed settlements, but not farmers, trappers, fishermen or hunters in the forest. The direct relationship between the size of a hunting camp and the efficiency of its production of meat has long been recognised.[29] A similar relationship existed between the size of a village and the efficiency of its food production. A village with fewer than 30 members could not subsist

26 A. Cureau, *Les Sociétés primitives de l'Afrique équatoriale*, Paris, 1912; C. Koch, 'Die Stamme des Bezirks Molundu', *Bässler Archiv*, iii, 1913, 286–312.

27 S. Jean, *Les Jachères en Afrique tropicale*, Paris, 1975, 118.

28 For instance in the Makaa group, H. Koch, *Magie et chasse dans la forêt camerounaise*, Paris, 1968, pp. 134–229, esp. pp. 159, 165, 169, 196.

29 Especially with regard to the Mbuti of Ituri. Cf. C. Turnbull, 'The Mbuti pygmies of the Congo', in *Peoples of Africa*, J. L. Gibbs (ed.), 1965, pp. 289–301.

for long. It always lacked manpower. The social organisation had to adapt to this requirement.

Forest history involves understanding social organisation. Villages consisted of corporate groups, which combined features of households, business firms and bands of related and unrelated people. Local people call these groups 'houses'. They consisted of legal kinsmen, collateral kinsmen, wives and other affines of both sexes, clients, 'pawns' given as surety for debt, slaves, adopted persons who acquired their master's kin, pygmy hunters claimed by farmers, blood-brothers and friends.[30]

Each house contained a core 'line'. In most areas lines were patrilineal descent groups headed by a leader. As in New Guinea, the structure of a house was built up around a 'big man'.[31] Most often the leader was succeeded by his brothers or sons. In matrilineal areas brothers, nephews and other members, even slaves, could succeed to the head position. The irregularity of succession was much more striking than the rules later given to colonial administrators. The line provided a backbone to the house in that it ensured continuity beyond the lifetime of its founder. Local ideologies established powerful social charters for the line by reducing the complexity of the house to the notion of a lineage in perpetuity and by vesting legal authority exclusively within the line. Any usurper had to manipulate the genealogy to legitimise his takeover.

Villages could consist of a single house, but often comprised several. The leaders of the houses formed the ruling council. The village headman was often the leader of the strongest house. He represented the village to the outside world, but was only one among his equals in internal affairs. Folk ideology presented this organisation in a genealogical fashion. The core lines were seen as junior lineages branching from a principal lineage and arrayed by seniority. Changes in the relative power of the resident houses forced the readaptation of the genealogies, while the strong corporate character of the village was justified by the claim that it was but a single large lineage. Village ideology reduced a complex reality to an elegant blueprint, and stressed a perpetuity which was far from the truth.

Villages managed a common estate in land and often exercised collective authority over houses of clients or bands of pygmy hunters. Such a strong corporate character was not recognised in kin terms when the village was perceived as a composite group of unrelated lineages. In such cases the founding house governed. In matrilineal societies especially, the composite

30 All forest societies exhibit strong relationships of inequality provided 'pygmies' are seen as part of the society of farmers in their neighbourhood. 'House' is an apt term to designate groups somewhat resembling the early Roman *familia*.

31 J. A. Barnes, 'African models in the New Guinea highlands', *Man*, lxii, 1962, 5–9. Of late several authors have made the same point. For the forest, Van Leynseele, 'Les Libinza de la Ngiri', additional thesis no. 1. In such a line patrifilial succession is common, but does not create a lineage.

house was the rule. Other institutions such as associations or age-grading then developed, in order to provide a corporate character to the village.[32]

In most of the forest, the folk model of social organisation calculated descent in the patrilineal line. In daily life, bilateral links were often as important as the father's line. This was recognised in language and in some legalised customs. Bilateral descent was also important in matrilineal and dual-descent societies such as those south-west of the forest, south of the Ogowe river and in the southern savanna west of the Sankuru. The matrilineal and dual-descent models did affect reality. At the level of the house, the main difference was in justifying a greater degree of individual male mobility. Virilocal residence in a matrilineal society entails male residential instability. At the village level, the difference was more significant. The matrilineal village, unlike the patrilineal one, was often interpreted as a composite group of lineages. It was perceived as a territorial organisation with its own governing principles. Authority was justified by shared territory rather than by shared kinship.

Early scholars were led astray by the folk model which suggested segmentary lineage societies,[33] and therefore missed the main features of house and village organisation. These were inequality and irregularity. Later scholars who elaborated the 'lineage mode of production' aimed at highlighting inequality, but it was much more pronounced, and much more irregularly distributed, than their model implied.[34] The ranking of members by seniority in the core lines was more tentative and more changeable. Rank was more often determined by the fluctuations of power politics than by any lineage structure. Competition among houses was more pronounced and more disorderly than the models imply. The lineage model tended to hide the fact that the full members of the core line were a minority, lording it over clients and pawns, over slaves and women. They competed with one another for the allegiance of collateral kin. Lineage ideology hid the relationship between the production of food, of services and of goods on the one hand, and the structure of society on the other. Collective endeavour required a division of labour according to the hardship involved and the contribution to the common good of the house. The estate was managed by the big man alone.

At the village level the lineage model presented change as an orderly process of fusion and fission. The concept of 'fusion' hid dominance of a big

32 Cf. M. Douglas, *The Lele of Kasai*, London, 1963. More usual is L. Siroto, 'Masks and Social Organization among the Bakwele people of Western Equatorial Africa', Ph.D. thesis, Columbia University, 1969, pp. 80–197.

33 J. Vansina, 'Lignage, idéologie et histoire en Afrique équatoriale', *Enquêtes et documents d'histoire Africaine*, iv, 1980, 1, 133–55, esp. 140–5. For the conventional view, A. Wolfe, *In the Ngombe Tradition: Continuity and Change in the Congo*, Evanston, Ill., 1961, pp. 23–51, 130–5.

34 P. Ph. Rey, *Colonialisme, néocolonialisme et transition au capitalisme*, Paris, 1971, pp. 32–69, 70–216.

house over a small one; 'fission' hid a stalemate in competition between houses. The houses were too unequal in size, too variable in composition, too changeable in both size and power to be real segments of a village lineage. Actual houses and villages behaved in a much more dynamic and unpredictable way than the lineage model allows.

Both the folk model and the reality were mirrored in the religions of the forest peoples. The ideology of descent was expressed in an ancestor cult. The reality crept in through the worship of collateral ancestors and through the belief in nature spirits. Village solidarity was ensured by a common cult of the line's ancestors. In composite villages the common worship of a nature spirit fulfilled this unifying function. Social cohesion within the village was also achieved by common charms or by common ritual associations, such as the *mwiri* cult in central Gabon.[35] Ancestors reflected the ideal model, whereas charms or ritual associations mirrored the reality.[36]

A belief in witchcraft was the most striking evidence that lineages were something less than harmonious groups of equals. This admission of inequality lay at the heart of these beliefs. Witchcraft was held to be at the root of all outstanding achievement, whether for better or for worse. Witchcraft was ambition, hatred or greed. It was a failure to accept equality. In a melancholy way, autopsies of the deceased kept the score and explained real inequality by detecting witch substance.

House and village were both unstable corporations. Over time they could become more or less lineal, more or less territorial, more or less centred on a single big man and more or less long-lived. The potentialities of these institutions for further elaboration in different directions were great. To grasp how these potentialities were realised requires an examination of the relationship among villages.

BEYOND THE VILLAGE

In most of the forest areas villages were autonomous, but they were not equal. Bigger villages dominated smaller ones, sometimes reducing them to subordinate status, sometimes to formal clientship. Villages competed for goods and people. No settlement produced all it needed, so that some goods always had to come from elsewhere. Basic rules of exogamy prohibited village self-sufficiency in women to reproduce its population. So marriage alliances with other settlements were vital. The more affluent a village was in goods and in women, the more people it attracted and the

35 Jean, *Les Jachères*, pp. 101, 107, 108; A. Raponda Walker and R. Sillans, *Rites et croyances des peuples du Gabon*, Paris, 1962, pp. 225–37, esp. pp. 232–5.

36 Thus the term *nkinda* refers to a collective village charm from the coast (Nkomi) to the Kuba and the Ngombe, but the meaning 'ancestor' among the Nkomi becomes 'charm' further east.

stronger it became. Hence competition between villages turned on both goods and people. In many areas this competition led to more permanent alliances between villages so as to lessen insecurity and tension. Alliances are the subject of the next section. One must first understand the general institutions available to regulate contact between villages.

The social division of labour was very pronounced in many parts of the forest. Specialised fishermen relied for most of their supplies of crops on farmers to whom they sold their fish and pots. Many farmers relied on hunters for their supplies of meat. Some villages, located near rich natural deposits, specialised in the production of iron or salt. In extreme environments specialisation went much further. Among the 'water people',[37] some fishermen had no gardens at all. Other neighbouring groups practised intensive agriculture on artificial mounds fertilised by silt. Some specialised craftsmen produced canoes, and others grew palm orchards. Some exclusively raised goats. The existence of a dense network of navigable rivers for the transportation of bulk orders over long distances at low labour costs had stimulated such specialisation over centuries. One consequence was the rise of the trading emporium of Ngombela at Malebo Pool.[38]

Exchange occurred through trade or through reciprocal gift-giving. The first markets may have developed as meetings between fishermen and land dwellers, or between suppliers of ocean salt and consumers. Such contacts began to be institutionalised at an unknown date. Well before 1500 a four-day market week had developed in the south-west, and raffia squares had become a currency. On the great bend of the Zaire, weekly markets used metal currencies.[39]

One other major mechanism for exchange was competitive gift-giving. North of the Ogowe the *bilabi* or *bilaba* pitted rival big men against one another in an exchange of goods from the coast for forest products. Continuity of contact was ensured by a system of credit. Each encounter required that larger gifts be returned at a later date.[40] This institution is described as it operated in the nineteenth century, but the principle was

37 Van Leynseele, 'Les Transformations des systèmes de production et d'échanges des populations ripuaires du Haut-Zaire', *AEH*, vii, 1979, 124–5.

38 H. Van Moorsel, *Atlas de préhistoire de la plaine de Kinshasa*, Kinshasa, 1968, pp. 224–77. For dating (A.D. 1450–1640), cf. P. Demaret, F. Van Noten and D. Cahen, 'Radiocarbon dates from West Central Africa', *JAH*, xviii, 1977, 4, 497.

39 In general, W. Froehlich, 'Das Afrikanische Marktwesen', *Zeitschrift für Ethnologie*, lxxii, 1940, 4–6, 234–8. In the Kwilu–Kwango area the week is linked to trade from Kongo. Cf. J. Vansina, 'Probing the past of the Lower Kwilu peoples (Zaire)', *Paideuma*, xix/xx, 1973/74, 349–53.

40 P. Alexandre and J. Binet, *Le Groupe dit Pahouin (Fang–Boulou–Beti)*, Paris, 1958, pp. 60–61; J. E. Mbot, *Ebughi bifia*, Paris, 1975, pp. 84–7; L. De Heusch, 'Eléments de potlatch chez les Hamba', *Africa*, xxiv, 1954, 337–48 (south-eastern Mongo); G. Dupré, 'Le Commerce entre sociétés lignagères: les Nzabi dans la traite à la fin du 19e siècle (Gabon/Congo)', *Cahiers d'études africaines*, xlviii, 1972, 629.

older. A similar exchange pattern evolved among the people living between the Sankuru and the Lomami rivers who were never drawn into the Atlantic trade system. Houses which had given wives were pitted against houses which had received wives; goods exchanged in competition were those transferred for bridewealth. Trade, or 'potlatch', could lead to partnerships sanctioned by blood-brotherhood. Exchange was not indispensable for the maintenance of inequality within a house.[41] It did, however, reinforce the grip of the trade-partner over his own house, because the link strengthened his control over rare goods and the supply of women.

From time to time competition between villages burst out of the confines of exchange into open hostility. Such fighting was kept in bounds by many restrictions. Village warfare was usually short-lived and involved few casualties. Hostilities were often triggered off by the kidnapping of women and slaves or by murder. Young villagers were quick to clamour for war, but elders preferred negotiation. The young aspired to the respected status of war-leader and hoped for booty. The old feared that war would weaken their leadership and destroy their wealth.[42] Few wars threatened physical annihilation,[43] but the pressure of unrelenting competition accounts for an intensive preoccupation with security. Flight was the favoured option if an enemy was too strong. The search for security sometimes brought third parties into a conflict to limit its duration or severity.[44] Yet, because tight alliances between villages were uncommon, war on a large scale was relatively rare. When such disputes did break out and were not quickly resolved, one of the contesting groups usually conceded defeat or in rare cases migrated away.

In forest societies it was not unusual to marry one's enemies.[45] Marriage was the main mechanism for turning hostility into alliance. Marriage rules forced people to find mates in other villages of the neighbourhood, rather than resort to the settlements that had intermarried before. Thus, alliances were redistributed. Marriage was never restricted to a single form of union, but had several versions.[46] Friends could exchange sisters; women could be

41 Rey, *Colonialisme*, pp. 187–201.

42 Dramatically expressed among the Bekwil by the use of gorilla masks. L. Siroto, 'Gon: a mask used in competition for leadership among the Bakwele', in *African Art and Leadership*, Fraser and H. M. D. Cole (eds), Madison, Wisconsin, pp. 1972, 57–77.

43 At least until slave-raiding developed. For its effects on the 'frontier' in the 1880s on the lower Lobaye, cf. A. Vermeulen, *De ingang der hel*, Amsterdam, 1938, pp. 221–9.

44 H. Bucher, 'The Mpongwe of the Gabon Estuary: a History to 1860', Ph.D. thesis, University of Wisconsin, 1977, pp. 53, 104, fn.57.

45 Mbot, *Ebughi Bifia*, p. 88.

46 *Ibid.*, pp. 88–90 (Fang); Hulstaert, *Le Mariage des Nkundo*, pp. 186–259 (Mongo); W. De Mahieu, 'Les Structures sociales du groupe komo dans leur élaboration symbolique', Ph.D. thesis, University of Leuven, 1975, pp. 376–93, 529–70 (Komo). For the Fang, four main forms of marriage are cited, eight for the Mongo, three for the Komo. These situations were the norm, not the exception.

kidnapped or taken in war; women 'pawns' bore children to their keepers; couples eloped to postpone bridewealth. Several different formulae for bridewealth payments gave a husband differential rights over the woman and her offspring. In the matrilineal south-west, preferential marriages were a significant percentage of all marriages and led to long-term alliances. Leaders received women as a seal to pacts of comradeship. They also loaned women to male clients in order to attract bachelors as followers. The exchange of women thus mirrored the wide range of situations in which competition and alliance occurred. Bridewealth, although important, was only one of the options. Over most of the area it ensured lasting contact between the houses involved and implied continuous payment to wife-givers. Preferred items for bridewealth became a form of money to be used in other transactions.[47] Before 1900 most currencies, especially metal ones, were linked to matrimonial exchanges. Trade and marriage went hand in hand. Hence marriage with bridewealth probably gained in frequency in recent centuries as regional trade developed. Only under colonial conditions did it become the preferred form of marriage.

Marriage was not the only way to create a kinship alliance. This was also done by a claim to common clanship. Clans aligned houses or even whole villages together as equals through the common acceptance of a sign or symbol. Members enjoyed mutual hospitality, which eased the flow of goods and people and also established reciprocal support for leadership. Such clans were not exogamous, they held no estate in common, and they did not constitute corporate groups. That precisely is why they were so successful as lasting mechanisms of alliance. In most matrilineal areas common clanship linked houses from different villages together, but did not link whole villages. In most patrilineal areas, on the other hand, claims to common clanship tied whole settlements together. Clans cut across not only settlements but also whole ethnic groups.[48] They even linked people across patrilineal and matrilineal boundaries. Such relationships were often artificially created. Clan names, clan food avoidance, clan taboos and even clan histories could easily be borrowed. These borrowings created an illusion of unchanging unity rooted in myth and time. Clan charters allayed any suspicion that clans were artificial kin groups. In fact they were pacts of mutual consent, and their composition as well as their characteristics fluctuated with changing regional relationships among houses and among villages.[49]

47 Van Leynseele, *Les Libinza de la Ngiri*, pp. 82–4, 96–8, 126–33 for the relationships between 'money' and 'fundamental exchange', including bridewealth.

48 Bucher, 'The Mpongwe of the Gabon Estuary', p. 30, chart 2, for 'corresponding clans' cutting across the patri–matrilineal boundary in coastal Gabon. Cf. also Rey, *Colonialisme*, p. 80.

49 The close links between 'clan' and general socio-political structures owes much to D. Newbury's work for the western interlacustrine area.

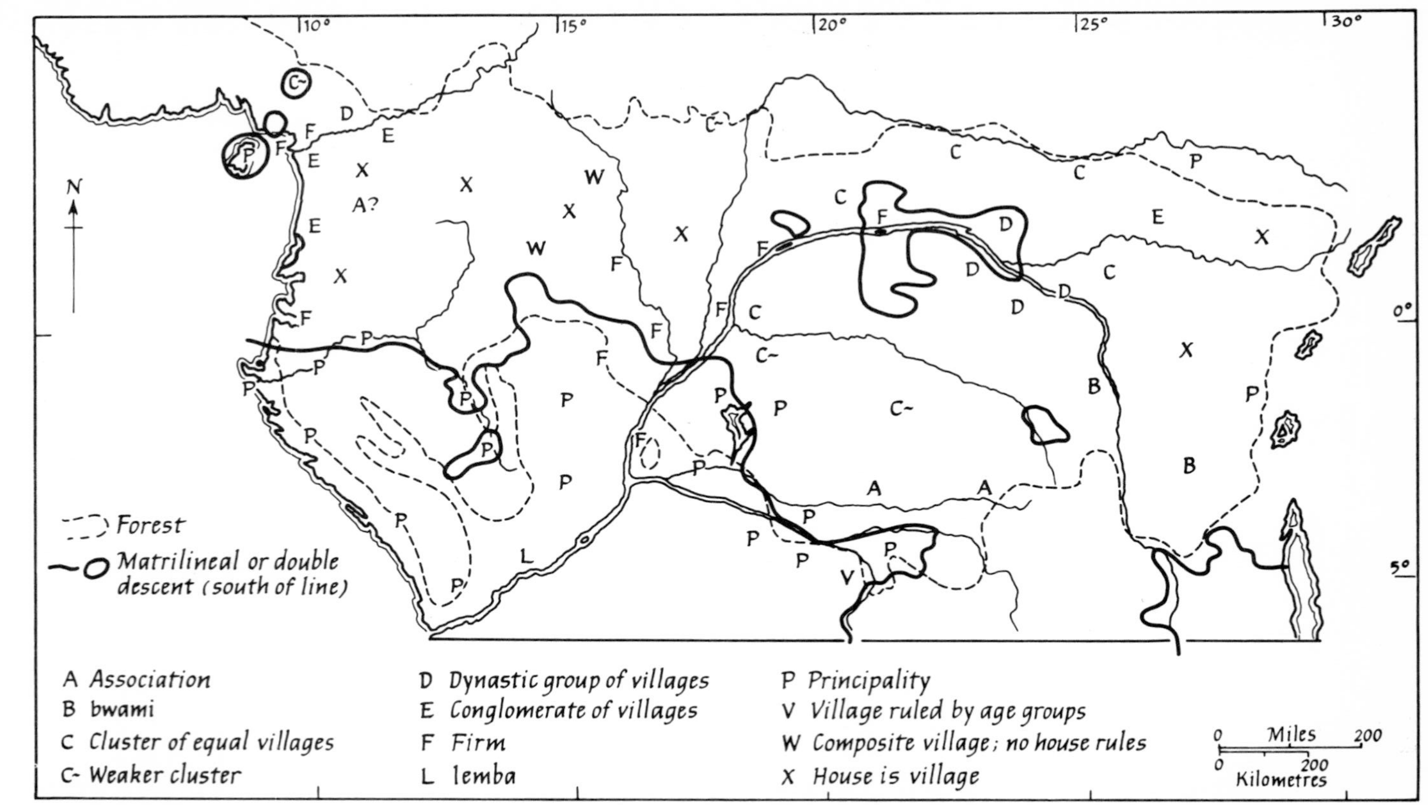

3:3 Political organisation in the forest zone, late nineteenth century

Alliances based on ritual also transcended village boundaries. Often such institutions were associations to initiate boys into manhood. Cults of affliction, a term for rituals of healings, were also common. Although such institutions sometimes functioned like alliances based on kinship, they often did not. They tended to link whole villages rather than individual houses. Associations united villages over long time spans with specific neighbours, thus tending to enlarge the geographic scale of political organisation.

TERRITORIES

The big men of society established ties based on their houses and their villages, and these bonds linked space like the mesh of an unbounded net. In addition to this unbounded network, small groups of villages could establish closer and more stable ties. This created a discrete political space, a territory, often called a chiefdom.

In forest politics the idioms of kinship were regularly used. For example, the villages of the fisherman's diaspora were referred to as mother villages and daughter villages. Such links did not necessarily or even commonly lead to political co-ordination and to the formation of village 'clusters'. Clusters consisted of four or five villages, often of roughly equal size, which established formal alliances bolstered by a fictional account of common descent. Such clusters were well known on the Ubangi, on the Uele, on the Zaire bend and on the Aruwimi river. Villages linked in this way practised much intermarriage and mutual trade. Claims of common descent were expressed as a single, over-arching genealogy, which related to the core of each dominant house in a village. This fiction created inequality among villages by assigning putative seniority. Inequality was sometimes expressed in ritual, as ancestral shrines in a junior village had to be approved by the senior village. One spectacular occasion for expressing ranking among villages concerned the disposal of the remains of a leopard. The leopard's body had to be handed by a junior village to its senior in rank until it reached the most senior village of all, where it was splayed. Its skin and claws became emblems for senior big men.[50] Despite this careful ritual, the ranking was not absolute. Successful houses founded new settlements or dominated old ones by pretext of in-law relationships. Competition for power and rank among big men formed and unformed clusters, so that genealogies were often adjusted to conform to the realities of power.

The 'noble tribute' of a leopard and of other symbolic objects should not

50 G. Le Marinel, 'La Région du Haut-Ubangi et Ubangi-Bornu', *Bulletin de la société royale belge de géographie*, xvii, 1893, 26–8; F. Thonner, *Dans la grande forêt de l'Afrique centrale*, Brussels 1899, pp. 45–6 (district and ethnicity), also pp. 35, 37, 39; de Calonne Beaufaict, *Les Ababua*, pp. 60–8; B. Tanghe, *De Ngbandi naar het leven geschetst*, Brugge, n.d., pp. 3–23, 74–88, 248–51. Wolfe, *In the Ngombe Tradition*, pp. 34–5.

lead to an exaggerated view of subordination among villages in a cluster. Each settlement remained basically autonomous. No village paid tribute to any other; no village depended upon the law court of any other; no village heeded regulations promulgated by the council of any other. The main functional purpose of the cluster was mutual assistance in war. Clusters could and did jointly field armies of warriors. The early colonial period has evidence of such armies: for example, the Yakoma cluster on the Mbomu attacked the first European expedition to reach them with 1 200 men. In another encounter, the Congo State scattered an army which left 1 200 shields and 800 spears on a battlefield. The armies of these northern clusters, helped by the forest environment, enabled local peoples to check the conquering thrusts of mid-nineteenth-century Azande chiefs.[51]

Some clusters were quite stable over time. Districts adopted their names, which then became ethnic labels. Patterns of loyalty gave rise to strongly felt distinctions between 'us' and 'them'. Among the Mondunga-speakers, north of Lisala, four large villages succeeded in keeping themselves so much apart that they preserved their non-Bantu speech in a sea of Bantu neighbours. Other aspects of their culture were nevertheless eroded by assimilation.[52]

Political clusters of villages were not the only form of forest organisation. A second form of political association, a conglomerate, occurred when a successful house grew into a large settlement and defeated its neighbours. Rather than attempt to set its own headmen over the conquered peoples, it merely required tribute payments, which were paid as long as the leading house could enforce its will. Such domination tended to be ephemeral. Large houses implied complex and fragile coalitions between leaders and their allies and followers. Near the end of the eighteenth century, a motley band of Biti house warriors, known as the Mando, allied with the Mapaha house to form a chiefdom south of the upper Uele. When the conglomerate was one generation old it became the nucleus of the Mangbetu kingdom. Similar chiefdoms had risen and fallen in the area but had rarely lasted a full generation. Those that did last acquired an ethnic identity, as did the eighteenth-century Mangbele conglomerate, which gave rise to an ethnic group that survives today.[53] Such conglomerates rarely escaped the ideology of kinship. They also failed to develop stable territorial structures and to solve crises of succession. Conglomerates functioned rather like clusters and, except in a

51 A. Dereine, 'Le soulèvement des Babua', *Africa Tervuren*, x, 1964, 35; A. Vangele, 'L'exploration de l'Oubangi–Doua–Koyou', *Bulletin de la société royale belge de géographie*, xiii, 1889, 30–32; 'De la Mongala', *La Belgique coloniale*, v, 1899, 8b (Budja).

52 F. Thonner, *Dans la grande forêt*, pp. 31–2; G. Van Bulck, *Carte linguistique de Congo Belge et du Ruanda-Urandi*.

53 Keim, 'Precolonial Mangbetu Rule', pp. 45–6; Bertrand, *Les Mangbetu*, pp. 68–81, 151–225, 238 map.

few larger instances, grew to a similar size. The contrast was in the degree of subjection imposed and the consequent instability.

A different situation occurred when the conquering house placed a headman of its own line in the defeated settlement. A dynastic group of villagers was thus created. Corvée labour and tribute payments were required, and the administration was slightly more centralised than in a conglomerate structure. This process occurred, for example, among the fishermen, farmers and trappers of the lands between the Zaire and Itimbiri rivers and near the lower Lomami. The weakest point in this type of structure was the lack of legitimacy where the conquering dynasty failed to create an ideological justification for itself. Many dynasties did not last. One Lomami dynasty extended its sway only after the coming of the Zanzibari traders in 1883. Within twenty years its bid for power had failed. Elsewhere in the Zaire–Itimbiri area longer-established dynasties lasted into colonial times, thanks to a unique exploitation of a system of dual descent.[54]

The process of political consolidation went a stage further when dynastic attempts at overlordship were bolstered by a new ideology. Principalities arose when dynasties claimed legitimacy by right of occupation rather than by right of kinship. A common ancestor cult was replaced by the cult of sacred kings. Supernatural powers and high inequality were equated with rulers. They levied tribute annually. They also possessed a centralised system of justice, developed a rudimentary hierarchy of titled positions, and created an administrative organisation. Above all, they induced strong perceptions of ethnicity. In this they were very different from the looser and more ephemeral political associations.[55]

A celebrated example of the development of 'principalities' comes from the peoples surrounding Lake Mayi Ndombe. The genealogical count suggests that these principalities may have evolved around A.D. 1400. Special recognition was given to big men by the creation of a new role, complete with formal installation, emblems of office, and honorific titles for followers. These big men held privileged links with the supernatural world. Their title was that of *nkum*, or prince. To become *nkum*, a big man had to be wealthy. During his installation, he had to perform miracles to show that the water or forest spirits of the territory had accepted his elevation. The status became hereditary, although a large element of choice by the titleholders in selecting a *nkum* continued to exist, and miracles continued to be required at each installation. The concept of territorial

54 J. Fraessle, *Negerpsyche im Urwald am Lohali*, Freiburg, 1926, pp. 129–38; A. Verbekne, 'Etude sur la peuplade des Bombesa', *Bulletin de la société royale belge de géographie*, lii, 1928, 70–1; H. Sutton-Smith, *Yakusu, the Very Heart of Africa*, London, n.d., 4 (Yawembe); L. Appermans, 15 Oct. 1931, *chefferie Kombe, Registres politiques*, terr. Isangi.

55 N. Van Everbroeck, *Mbomb'ipoku, le seigneur à l'abîme*, Tervuren, 1961, pp. 9–50, 135–60; E. Miller, 'Das Fürstentum bei den Südwest-Mongo, Belgisch Congo', Ph.D. thesis, University of Mainz, 1955.

authority was symbolised by a lump of kaolin ointment and rights over leopards' skins. The *nkum* lived in large capital villages where their households wielded enough strength to overcome opposition. Alliances with other houses were forged through the title system.

The Mayi Ndombe system of principalities spread to other areas in later centuries. The concept of territory, the system of titles and the role of capital villages were adopted by other societies. They spread far to the east, to the upper Lokenye and throughout the Lomela basin. The expansion spawned no fewer than four different political systems in those areas.[56]

The centre from which the concept of principalities spread was the region between the Zaire, Lake Tumba and the northern shores of Lake Mayi Ndombe. The most elaborate form of principality, and the most convincing traditions which identify it as the centre of political innovation, were found in this region, where culturally mixed people had been brought together by conquest. It lay north of an area where kingdoms, such as those of the Tio and Boma, as well as the large chiefdoms of the Kasai, were located. The innovation occurred, therefore, at the northern edge of a large area of centralised political structures which also happened to be matrilineal.

The forest principalities were an unexpected accident of history, but they gradually became a very stable form of political organisation. The crucial innovation was the new political role of the leader, but such roles existed in other places without giving rise to principalities. Sacred kingship was adopted, but elsewhere sacrality did not lead to principalities. The success of the principalities involved the combination of a sacred role, the concept of territorial authority and the ability to translate individual success into a hereditary position. The fact that this happened around Lake Mayi Ndombe may have been related to the need to develop new forms of social organisation when different cultures and societies clashed. The evolving principalities may have been a model for developments further south or, conversely, state formations further south may have been an inspiration for the developments in this area. Apart from these matrilineal south-western forest societies, similar principalities arose only among the matrilineal peoples on the off-shore island of Bioko (Fernando Po). By about 1850 these island principalities had coalesced into a single kingdom.[57]

Political cohesion also evolved on the basis of local associations. The scale of political cooperation often remained limited to the purposes of the association. These could involve boys' initiation, healing clubs or the

56 G. Hulstaert, 'Over de volksstammen der Lomela', *Congo*, 1931, 1, 21, 29, 33, 39, 42; G. van der Kerken, *L'Ethnie mongo*, Brussels, 1944, pp. 336–7, 636–49, 664–70; L. De Heusch, 'Elements de potlatch chez les Hamba', 337–48.

57 A. Aymemní, *Los Bubis en Fernando Poó*, Madrid, 1942; C. C. Gil-Delgado, *Notas para un estudio anthropológico y etnológico del Bubi de Fernando Poó*, Madrid, 1949.

initiation of big men in a club destined to legitimise their authority.[58] In the composite villages of southern Gabon, associations dealing with initiation and cults of affliction were powerful tools of internal government. They limited competition among houses, and created a forum for common external action especially with regard to trade. By the 1880s similar associations had evolved everywhere in the western forest between the Atlantic and the Zaire–Ubangi rivers. Some of the coastal associations were already in existence by 1600.[59]

In the eastern forest, in Maniema, associations were also common. The northern Maniema association practised two levels of initiation, determined by sex, age and status. Clubs of healers and cult groups coexisted with the main initiation groups.[60] In southern and western Maniema a unified association emerged with a complex hierarchy, based on age and wealth. It absorbed all other associations into a single superstructure.[61] The best-known instance is the *bwami* association of southern Maniema, which probably grew out of the merger of different associations of the northern type.[62] However, other internal evolution occurred as well, for the superstructure's appearance was accompanied by startling differences in the corporations based on descent. They were bigger than elsewhere, and controlled more forms of wealth. In less extreme forms the association created a political entity governed collectively by big men ranked according to their status within houses and to their wealth. In its most extreme form, however, a rank was added to the hierarchy of titles, and a single person carried the title of *mwami*. His role was virtually that of a ruler, and the political space governed by his association turned it into a principality. Several chiefdoms developed in this way in the mountains west of the Ruzizi valley. In the eighteenth century or earlier their notion of royalty spread to local states, especially those of Bushi.[63]

There is some evidence that in elaborating the *bwami* associations, some groups were influenced by the political organisation of their southern savanna neighbours, whose system was known as *luhuna* after the chair which was its main political emblem. Here chieftaincy was elective, and

58 A. Poupon, 'Etude ethnographique de la tribu Kouyou', *L'Anthropologie*, xxix, 1918/19, 53–88, 297–335.
59 Walker and Sillans, *Rites et croyances*, pp. 99–293; A. Battell, *The Strange Adventures of Andrew Battell of Leigh*, E. G. Ravenstein (ed.), London, 1901, pp. 56–8.
60 De Mahieu, 'Les Structures sociales du groupe Komo dans leur élaboration symbolique', pp. 156–260.
61 D. Biebuyck, *Lega Culture*, Berkeley, Ca., 1973, pp. 17–19, 66–141.
62 By providing an object for corporate rights. P. C. Lloyd, *The Political Development of Yoruba Kingdoms in the Eighteenth and Nineteenth Centuries*, London, 1971, esp. pp. 50–1, proved this in the Yoruba case.
63 Mulyumba wa Mamba, 'Aperçu sur la structure politique des Balega–Basile', *Les Cahiers du Centre d'Etudes de Documentation Africaine*, 1978, 1, 23–50, 55–60; Mulyumba wa Mamba, 'La Structure sociale des Balega–Basile', Ph.D. thesis, Université Libre de Bruxelles, 2 vols, 1977; Biebuyck, *Lega Culture*, pp. 69–71, 233; R. Sigwalt, 'The Early History of Bushi', Ph.D. thesis, University of Wisconsin, 1975, pp. 79–117.

restricted to a limited term so that all big men of a territory ruled in turn.[64] The chair as supreme emblem was adopted by some of the *bwami* associations along with other hierarchical features. The main difference between government by the *bwami* and *luhuna* associations was that in the latter a single position of authority rotated among big men, whereas in the former authority remained collectively in the hands of a few.[65] The formation of the *mwami* kingship, which probably developed later, was even more of an accident than the western developments around Lake Mayi Ndombe. In both cases, however, the interaction of different cultures seems to have provided the crucial element of inspiration.

KINGDOMS

Kingdoms are principalities so large that the ruler can no longer govern his villages directly and commands chiefs to do so. Kingdoms usually grew out of principalities. Sometimes, as in the Mangbetu case in north-eastern Zaire, they arose directly out of conglomerates created by a single leader. Among the Mangbetu, Manziga created the Mabiti political order. It was rumoured that he himself had risen from the rank of slave. His son, Nabiembali, succeeded to office about 1815. He defeated the Mangbele and other conglomerates, fought off Azande invaders and founded the Mangbetu kingdom. It differed in scale from the earlier conglomerates, and encompassed peoples with very distinct languages and markedly different ethnic allegiances.

Nabiembali concluded marriage alliances with the prominent big men in his domains, and appointed his sons born from such unions to rule their mothers' groups. He tied other groups to himself by sending women from his kinfolk to them in marriage. Tribute was levied when needed in the guise of kinship gifts between brothers-in-law and between maternal relatives. A fictional family seniority also evolved within the central groups. Nabiembali claimed to be the eldest son by a new, all-embracing genealogy. This became the political charter of the kingdom and gave it a name, derived from the ancestor, Ngbetu, Mangbetu. Thus, the new royal ideology still relied on the idiom of descent and kinship.

The political system constantly faced the danger of falling apart. In about 1860 Nabiembali's eldest son ousted his father, but one of the old man's

64 A. Moeller, *Les Grandes Lignes des migrations des Bantous de la province orientale du Congo Belge*, Brussels, 1936, pp. 510–41; Bulaimu Abemba, 'Le Mode de production lignager face à la traite arabe et à la colonisation: le cas des collectivités locales du Maniema', *Les Cahiers du CEDAF*, 1979, 6, 14–20.

65 Biebuyck, *Lega Culture*, p. 83, notes that all other Lega obtained initiation into the higher *kindi* grade from the Babongolo, a southern group (p. 10), and they in turn had been influenced by the Bangubangu and Binja south (p. 233) among whom *luhuna* type associations were known (p. 18), as in Moeller, *Grandes Lignes*, pp. 533–9, and Abemba, Bulaimu, 'La Mode de production', 14–20.

most trusted allies, together with other sons, rose in revolt. In less than a decade the kingdom had shrunk dramatically, while an equally impressive new polity, that of the Matshaga, rose to compete with it, and other Mangbetu princes expanded to the south and east on their own account. Azande pressure continued to threaten the north and west. Soon after 1865 bands of armed traders from Khartoum helped to precipitate the collapse of the Mangbetu kingdom. Mbunza, the last great king, was killed in 1873 or 1874, and the Matshaga became the major power in the area. Structural weakness had brought the downfall of the kingdom. It was never more than an overblown conglomerate.[66] By some kind of miracle, however, a diminutive Mangbetu kingdom survived the Egyptian occupation of 1881, the Zanzibari raids of 1887 and the 1891 invasion by the Congo State.

Far away to the south another kingdom developed on the Sankuru river. The Kuba kingdom grew out of many tiny principalities, each one having a capital village surrounded by hamlets. Their *nkum* leaders were immigrants who had crossed the Sankuru in a slow drift to the south. The authority of each *nkum* was balanced by that of his councillors. In some chiefdoms the *nkum* prevailed, in others the councillors did. Two chiefdoms developed particularly strong leadership. One expelled all the aboriginal inhabitants of the area; the other assimilated local populations as subjects. The second group defeated the first one around 1600. However, a generation later the vanquished rallied round an immigrant from the west who founded a kingdom among them. The kingdom overcame the competing principalities between 1625 and 1680 and organised an effective administration based on a title system. By the early eighteenth century stable government had been provided by a complex system of checks and balances among the royal family, aristocrats, senior councillors, tax officials and judges. This administration coerced people to increase the production of agricultural surplus, reorganised the division of labour between men and women and adopted the new American food crops. Increasing surplus allowed the development of additional specialisation of labour. This in turn created more state revenue to support additional full-time artisans and title-holders. Economic growth furthered the development of trade. The Kuba began to export luxury cloth and ivory, and to import slaves, copper, beads and salt.

By 1900 the unchallenged Kuba state had become the hub of trade routes leading to Angola, to Shaba and to the lands east of the Sankuru and north of the Lokenye. Social stratification had become very pronounced. As a by-product of this process the arts, patronised by the privileged social classes, flourished because patricians vied one with the other in conspicuous consumption.[67] The Kuba kingdom arose out of principalities of the Mayi

66 Denis, *Histoire des Mangbetu*; Keim, 'Precolonial Mangbetu Rule'; Bertrand, *Les Mangbetu*.
67 Vansina, *The Children of Woot*.

Ndombe type, although later inputs of crops from America, and perhaps a distant connection with the Atlantic trading system, played crucial roles in its development.

In the far south-west, between the ocean and Malebo Pool, kingdoms arose at an earlier date, perhaps before the fourteenth century, on the fringe of the forest and the savanna. It is not really known how these kingdoms developed. By the early sixteenth century, the main kingdom on the Atlantic was Loango. The adjacent southern principalities of Kakongo and Ngoyo, were then either dependent on Loango or had not yet come into existence.[68] Another principality was Bungu, the cradle of the dynasty which founded the kingdom of Kongo in about the fourteenth century. Bungu was destroyed about 1620 by immigrant warriors from Kongo.[69]

Loango was rumoured to have been founded by a house of smiths, the Buvanji, who became the first ruling dynasty. They came from the area of Ngoyo in the south, where tradition links them to the shrine of Buunzi.[70] Two economic factors affected first the rise of the principalities and then of the kingdom of Loango: one was the development of copper-mining in northern Kongo, especially around Mindouli; the other was a local trade in fish, in ocean salt, and in palm products. These were exchanged for minerals from the inland forest. Commercial demands drove leaders of coastal communities to forge closer ties both among themselves and with the interior. In the process of commercial growth clanship, associations and principalities developed. The kingdom of Loango resulted from the fusion of several principalities by processes yet little known.

In the region east of the Loango coast another extensive kingdom developed, that of the Tio, which occupied the plateaux north of Malebo Pool. The founder king was said to have come from the north and was bound by a ritual tie to a petty ruler far away on the Alima. Although its later strength owed much to its closeness to the iron and copper mines of Mindouli and to the markets of Malebo Pool, the Tio kingdom arose far from these economic resources. The Tio plateaux were very lightly settled, the population was unusually mobile and led by 'Masters of the Land', whose authority was linked to the shrines of nature spirits. Conquest played little role, and the great Tio lords, like those of Loango, were the scions of former principalities.[71]

68 D. Pacheco Pereira, *De Esmeraldo de Situ Orbis*, D. Kimble (ed.), London, 1937, book 3, chap. 2, item 2, p. 171) mentions Panzalungo (Mbanza Loango); *Correspondance de Dom Afonso roi du Congo 1506–1543*, L. Jadin and M. Dicorato (eds), Brussels, 1974, 205, for mention in 1539 of 'Cacongo', 'Ngoyo', 'Pamzu alumbu' (Mbanza Lumbu-Loango) and 'Ibungu' (Bungu). Similar terminology of 1535 in A. Brásio, *Monumenta Missionária Africana*, Lisbon, 1953, vol. 2, 38 (doc. 14).

69 Vansina, 'Notes sur l'origine du royaume du Congo', *JAH*, iv, 1963, 34–6.

70 P. M. Martin, *The External Trade of the Loango Coast*, Oxford, 1972, p. 8; P. Hagenbucher-Sacripanti, *Les Fondements spirituels de pouvoir au royaume de Loango*, Paris, 1973, pp. 22–8.

East of the Tio and north of the Kwa river, the small but tightly knit Boma kingdom was first mentioned in the seventeenth century. The rulers claimed to hail from south of the Kasai and to have found well-organised principalities, where attempts at further centralisation developed. The newcomers were but one of several would-be founders of states in the area. In the end they overcame all their rivals except the Nunu principality, composed of fishermen and traders, and the Dia principality, whose leaders seem to have made shrewd use of their salt resources. These principalities probably shared political innovations with their northern *nkum* neighbours.[72]

Significant differences existed in the organisation of the three main kingdoms of the south-west forest. By 1600 Loango consisted of the capital and seven provinces. Its succession was matrilineal, the king could not be easily deposed except perhaps after military defeat, and presumptive successors were appointed to four provincial governorships ranked by title and residence, the senior heir living closest to the capital. The Loango ruler's power was great. Both his titled officials and appointed officials collected tribute, waged war, supervised trade, carried messages and performed rituals. One of them served as a prime minister and ruled during interregna. The king's power derived from his support in the capital and was exercised by a small royal guard. His legitimacy, linked to his sacred status, derived from the Buunzi shrine. At each royal installation the priest had to be present and to exchange gifts and counter-gifts with the king. The aristocracy, or chiefs of the land, may have provided recruits for the position of provincial governor. Even around 1600, however, when centralisation in the state was strong, there are hints that the aristocrats had power of their own. They may already have formed a crown council to install kings. In the mid-eighteenth century, when the ruling line died out, the Loango aristocracy created a new régime of its own.[73]

The Tio kingdom was hardly a state when compared to Loango. The king was a religious figure. The density of population was so low that there was probably no centralised institution in the whole realm, except occasional tribute-giving to the king. Local lords officiated at the installation of the king and thereby legitimised their titles. Their political role was confined to levying tribute and holding court in competition with rival lords. Local peoples had much leeway in choosing the lord to whom they would owe their fickle allegiance. As big men, some lords did accumulate the military force to drive out hostile groups. In the seventeenth century instances of forced emigration did occur. It is likely, however, that the poverty of the country, the scarcity of water and shortages of food were the major factors behind such migrations.[74]

71 Vansina, *The Tio Kingdom of the Middle Congo*, London, 1972, pp. 439–43.

72 R. Tonnoir, *Giribuma: contribution à l'histoire et à la petite histoire du Congo équatorial*, Tervuren, 1970, pp. 48–58.

73 Martin, *The External Trade*, pp. 10–29; Hagenbucher-Sacripanti, *Fondements*, pp. 61–87.

74 Vansina, *The Tio Kingdom*, pp. 313–407, 443–4, 451–6.

The Boma kingdom was different again. Landholdings were governed by an aristocracy older than the ruling dynasty. These aristocrats collected tribute and dispensed justice. Where landholdings had not been taken over by political powers, the old 'chiefs of the land' still exercised those rights. The king and his council could override these prerogatives only in cases of necessity. Boma social stratification was rigid, ascriptive and accompanied by a detailed terminology of social ranking. The ruling dynasty married into the aristocracy and so found officials among close male kin. As in Loango, succession was regulated by the appointment of heirs-presumptive to a hierarchy of titles tied to a hierarchy of residences.[75]

The Central African rain-forest has been the scene of a dynamic and complex political history. It is one that did not normally turn to political centralisation and the creation of kingdoms. The basic social corporation was the house, and the territorial unit was the village. Competition between houses and villages furthered autonomy and decentralisation. Clusters overcame this to create more security; some houses enjoyed ephemeral success in building conglomerates such as that which temporarily underpinned the Mangbetu kingdom. Social organisation, revolving around big men, developed along many paths but was generally inimical to the growth of kingdoms, and yet some stable principalities arose and some of them became kingdoms. However, this was so unlikely that it seems to have happened independently only twice or thrice. One example was on the island of Bioko, another near Lake Mayi Ndombe and a third in the lower Zaire area. The last two regions may have been in contact with each other and therefore may not be independent centres of kingdom formation.

INTERCONTINENTAL TRADE

In 1472 Portuguese caravels sighted Bioko. A decade later they anchored in the estuary of the Zaire river.[76] The first Europeans probed the coasts of Central Africa in search of areas where African trading partners were numerous and organised.[77] By 1500 a stable organisation had begun to take shape. The first tentative occupation of São Tomé in 1485 was renewed about 1500.[78] The island soon became a pivot in the trading system as well

75 Tonnoir, *Giribuma*, pp. 261–312.

76 A. Galvão, *Tratado dos descobrimentos*, Porto, 1944, p. 129; F. Bontinck (ed.), 'Histoire du royaume du Congo (1624)', *Etudes d'histoire africaine*, iv, 1972, 90, n.1.

77 E. Ardener, 'Documentary and linguistic evidence for the rise of the trading polities between Rio del Rey and Cameroons 1500–1650', in *History and Social Anthropology*, I. M. Lewis (ed.), London, 1968, pp. 81–126.

78 A. Ryder, *Benin and the Europeans, 1485–1897*, London, 1969, p. 26 n.4; L. I. Ferraz, *The Creole of São Tomé*, Johannesburg, 1979, pp. 9, 15–17; R. Garfield, 'A history of São Tomé Island, 1470–1655', Ph.D. thesis, Northwestern University, 1971, pp. 1–32.

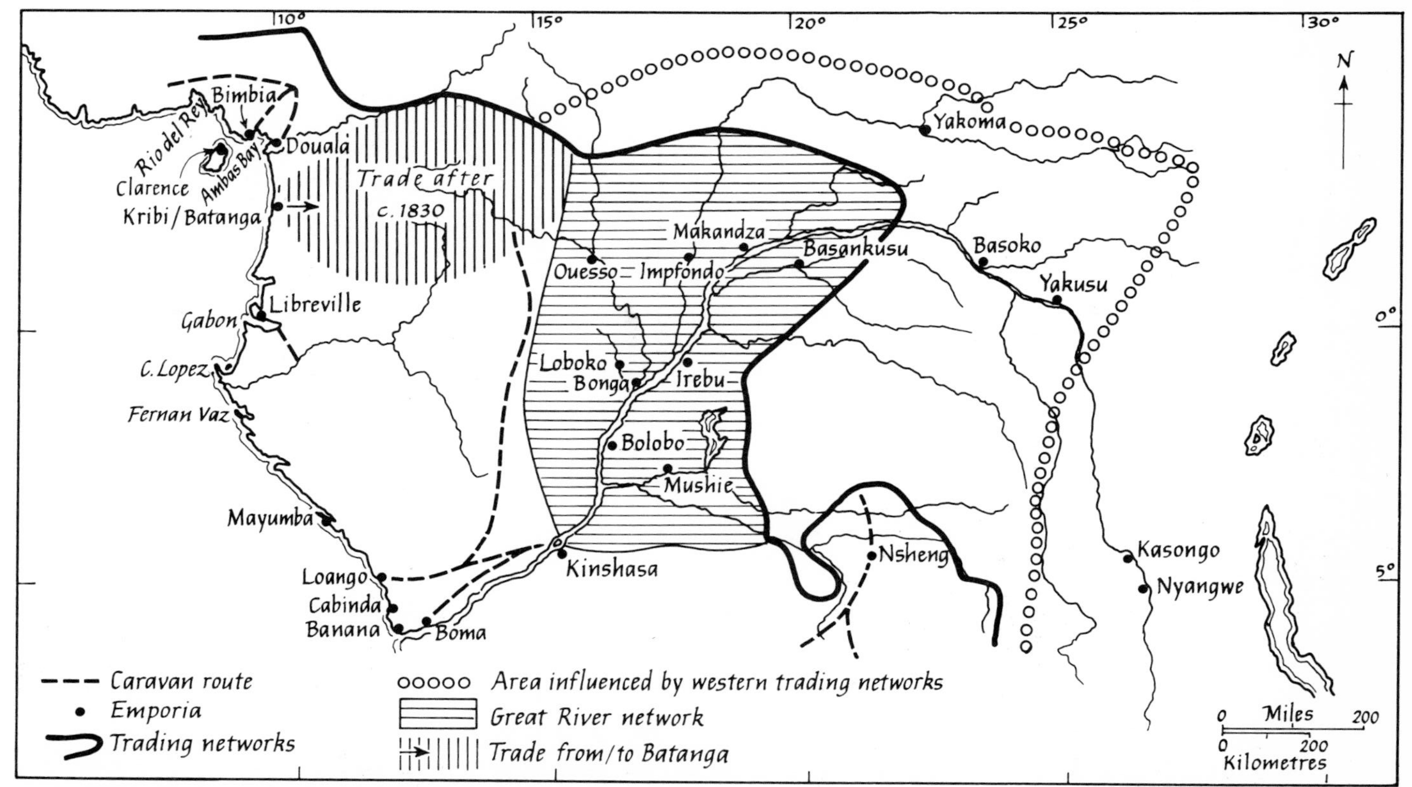

3:4 The Atlantic trade, c. 1875

as a sugar-producing colony. Atlantic traders found the kingdom of Kongo to be the best-organised African trading partner. The forested coast of the north was neglected. By 1514 Kongo had been induced to export slaves, and soon the old trading network of the Zaire river began to provide slaves from above Malebo Pool.[79] The impact of the slave-trade was thus felt in the interior of the forest before it influenced the coastal peoples. One coastal landing point was Cape Lopez, where ships took on water and wood before crossing the Atlantic. The cape had no ready-made African trading concern and therefore never became a centre for trade.[80] In Loango, the royal capital was the hub of trade in local goods. The town's integration into the Atlantic system was rather slow. From about 1576 a trade in ivory, redwood and raffia cloth developed, to be followed by a modest trade in slaves. The scale of trading was such that some of the products came from regions halfway to Malebo Pool and as far north as the Ogowe bend.[81] At about the same time, São Tomé declined. Slave imports had become so numerous that major revolts broke out from 1574. They could not be quelled, and sugar-cane plantations were destroyed. The uprising of 1586 forced many Portuguese settlers off the island. Nevertheless Portugal did not completely abandon São Tomé. This was in contrast to Annobon, where similar developments led to the evacuation of all planters. The island was left to develop a maroon society, the only one in Africa.[82]

Dutch ships arrived on the Central African coast in 1594. They began a regular trade in ivory and tropical wood in the Gabon estuary. The Dutch almost ousted the Portuguese from the Loango trade and sacked the surviving São Tomé settlement. Far to the north, Calabar displaced the Rio del Rey as a major market. In about 1650 a small settlement, founded by a single house at Douala, became the new outlet for trade from the Cameroun rivers.[83] Until the 1660s, however, the Dutch traded very little in slaves. They left that market to the Portuguese.

In the 1660s an era of massive slave-trading began on the Loango coast. A generation later the trade spread further north. At the same period French and British traders began to arrive. France and Britain became the main trading nations for the next century, but no European power ever succeeded in establishing a slave monopoly, even at single harbours. Thus, English attempts in 1721–3, and Portuguese attempts in 1783–4, failed to fortify Cabinda on the Ngoyo coast. As competition increased, slave prices rose. By 1750 imports of guns and powder, previously outlawed by the

79 Vansina, *Kingdoms of the Savanna*, Madison, Wisconsin, 1966, pp. 52–3.
80 K. D. Patterson, *The Northern Gabon Coast to 1875*, Oxford, 1975, pp. 7–9, and fn.71.
81 Martin, *The External Trade*, pp. 33–42, 126; Battell, *The Strange Adventures*, pp. 52–4, 58–9.
82 Garfield, 'History of São Tomé', pp. 1–145.
83 Ardener, 'Trading polities', pp. 107–12.

Portuguese, rose to an impressive total of 50 000 guns per year on the Loango coast.[84]

From the mid-eighteenth century the Douala trade expanded to handle slaves from the Cameroun grasslands, then ravaged by invaders.[85] The Gabon estuary became the outlet for two routes. The northern ones brought ivory that passed from hand to hand from as far away as central and southern Cameroun. The southern route relayed slaves from the middle Ogowe through middlemen. By 1700, Gabon slaves were also on sale in the Ogowe delta, where the Orungu and Nkomi kingdoms were constituted. Further south, Mayumba became an outlet for local exports.[86] In the late seventeenth century the kingdom of Kongo declined and Loango became the outlet for long-distance caravans from Malebo Pool and from southern Kongo. Soon, however, rival harbours began to compete. The centre of gravity of the slave-trade shifted southwards towards the Zaire estuary during the eighteenth and early nineteenth centuries. Markets flourished even further south at Ambriz in the 1760s and 1770s, thus accelerating Loango's serious decline. There was a slight recovery at Loango after the Napoleonic wars, but it was the Zaire estuary that gained most of the business.[87]

During the nineteenth century, trading patterns became quite different. A trade in ivory and raw agricultural materials developed alongside the continuing slave-trade. Slaving was increasingly hampered by naval squadrons sent to suppress it. Both these trends led to the multiplication of points of contact between Europeans and Africans along the coast. While slavers sought hidden creeks in which to build barracoons to hold their captives until shipment, legitimate traders sought to cut out intermediaries, to find new markets and to shorten the distances between the sources of bulk supply and points of shipment. By the 1850s the whole forest coast from Banana in the south to Rio del Rey in the north was dotted with new

84 P. M. Martin, 'The trade of Loango in the seventeenth and eighteenth centuries', in *Pre-Colonial African Trade*, R. Gray and D. Birmingham (eds), London, 1970, pp. 149, 153; Martin, *The External Trade*, pp. 33–92.

85 R. Austen and K. Jacob, 'Dutch trading voyages to Cameroun, 1721–1759; European documents and African history', *Annales de la Faculté des Lettres et des sciences humaines*, Yaoundé, vi, 1974, 1–27; A. Wirz, 'La "Rivière de Cameroun": commerce pré-colonial et controle du pouvoir en société lignagère', *Revue française d'histoire d'outre-mer*, xl, 1973, 219, 172–95.

86 Bucher, 'The Mpongwe of the Gabon Estuary', pp. 120–39, 160–94; Bucher, 'The settlement of the Mpongwe clans in the Gabon estuary: an historical synthesis', *Revue française d'histoire d'outre-mer*, lxiv, 235, 1977, 149–75; Bucher, 'Mpongwe origins; historiographical perspectives', *History in Africa*, ii, 1975, 59–89; Patterson, *The Northern Gabon Coast*, pp. 9–33, 68–76; E. Ardener, *Coastal Bantu of the Cameroons*, London, 1956, pp. 17–31; Ardener, 'Trading polities', pp. 100–13; Austen and Jacobs, 'Dutch trading voyages', 24; H. Deschamps, *Traditions orales et archives au Gabon*, Paris, 1962, p. 113; F. Gaulme, 'L'Ancien Pays de Cama', Ph.D. thesis, University of Paris, 1975; J. A. Avaro, *Un Peuple gabonais à l'aube de la colonisation*, Paris, 1981.

87 Martin, *The External Trade*, pp. 93–7, 136–41.

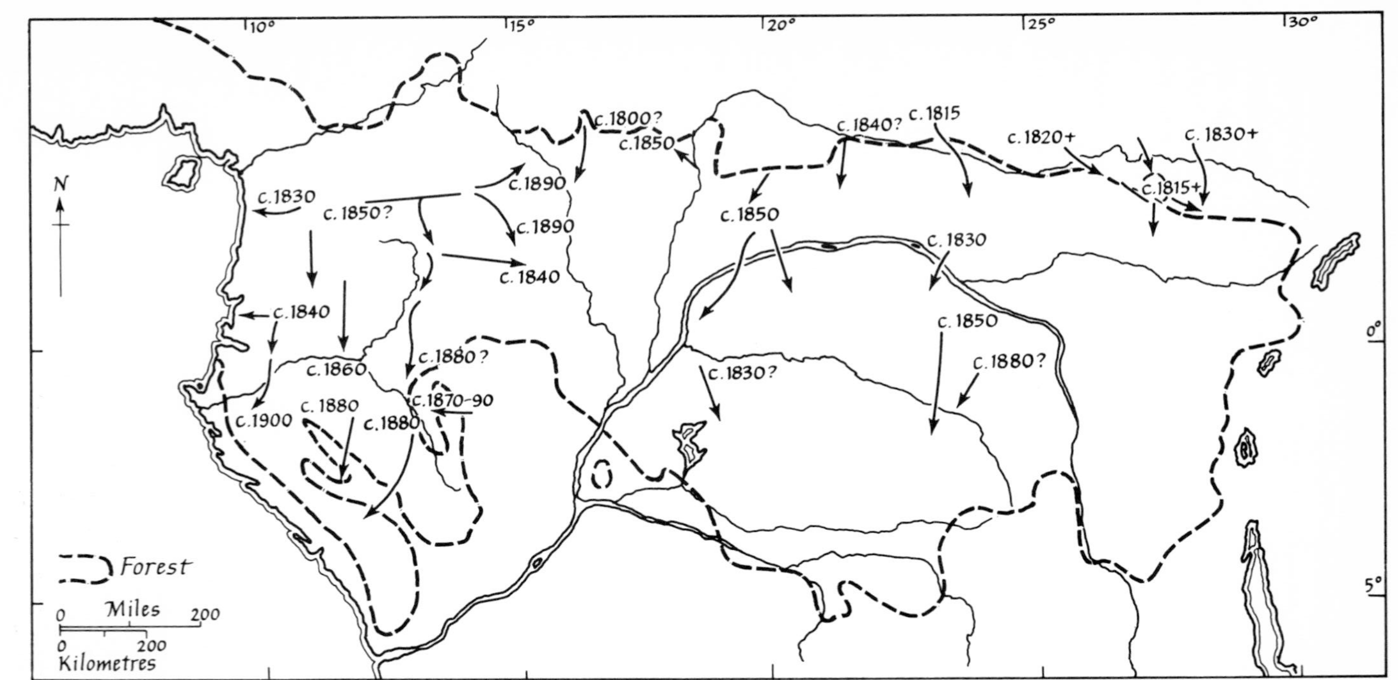

3:5 War and population movements, c. 1800–1880
Note: Most movements are related either to the expansion of the Atlantic trade or to the Zande expansion.

posts. In 1828 an important new trading station opened at Batanga to tap the whole interior of the southern Cameroun.[88]

The spread of commercial stations was accompanied by the establishment of British and French naval stations at Clarence in 1827,[89] and at Libreville in 1839. At the same period mission posts were founded. European traders and hunters began to move inland from the Gabon coast in the 1850s. By 1880 de Brazza had arrived on the shores of Malebo Pool. His Makoko treaty with the Tio signalled the scramble for this portion of Africa.[90]

The Atlantic trading frontier expanded into Central Africa over four centuries. By the late eighteenth century river-borne expansion had reached the lower Ubangi and overland expansion had reached the upper Ogowe from the south. In the north, the upper Wuri, the Mungo and the Cross river basins, the Douala interior and the Cameroun grasslands had all been tapped. A century later the whole western forest as far as the lower Aruwimi and the Sankuru had been drawn into the system. Even beyond those limits people participated indirectly in trans-continental trade.

As the frontier advanced, ever-widening areas were drawn into turmoil. Communities near the line of advance fought their neighbours to gain access to the developing trading routes. Others fought to flee from the new dangers. The most spectacular upheavals occurred in southern Cameroun and northern Gabon. Before 1830 this vast area had been relatively sheltered from the impact of trade. Ports were far away, and informal trade through gift-giving prevailed.[91] The opening of Batanga and the settlement of French Libreville triggered large-scale population movements, some towards the trading posts and some away to the deep interior. Populations who acquired guns attempted to subject their neighbours. These movements lasted fifty years and affected people between the coast and the Zaire basin. They are usually associated with the so-called 'Fang

88 A. Wirz, *Vom Sklavenhandel zum Kolonialen Handel*, Zurich, 1972, pp. 96–9; B. Schnapper, *La Politique et le commerce français dans le golfe de Guinée de 1838 à 1871*, Paris, 1961; A. J. Wauters, *L'Etat indépendant du Congo*, Brussels, 1899, p. 386; R. Austen, 'Slavery among Coastal Middlemen: The Duala of Cameroon', in *Slavery in Africa*, S. Miers and I. Kopytoff (eds), Madison, Wisconsin, 1977, pp. 317–18; C. Chamberlin, 'Competition and Conflict: the Development of the Bulk Export Trade in Central Gabon during the Nineteenth Century', Ph.D. thesis, University of California at Los Angeles, 1977.

89 A. de Unzueta Y. Yuste, *Guinea continental española*, Madrid, 1944, pp. 16–22; Gil-Delgado, *Notas*, pp. 170–80.

90 H. Deschamps, *Quinze ans de Gabon: 1839–1853*, Paris, 1965; H. Brunschwig, *Brazza explorateur: les traités Makoko 1880–1882*, Paris, 1972.

91 O. Lenz, *Skizzen aus West Afrika*, Berlin, 1878, pp. 280–2; Alexandre and Binet, *Le Groupe dit Pahouin*, pp. 33, 60–1; P. Laburthe-Tolra, *Minlaaba*, pp. 836–7; C. Zoll'owambe, 'Visage africain d'une coutume indienne et mélanésienne', *Bulletin de la société d'etudes camerounaises*, xix–xx, 1947, 55–60.

migrations'.[92] In the Zaire basin, some frontier communities became highly militarised. The ensuing strife stretched upstream from the Ubangi to the upper Uele, where Azande expansion and Mediterranean traders added to the disruption.

Behind the trading frontier a new spatial organisation took shape as a novel economic order emerged. Different regions began to specialise in different products and services. Some specialised in producing raffia cloth, or tobacco, or groundnuts, or salt, or pottery, or ironware, or canoes, or foodstuffs for traders, or even sugar-cane, wine or goats. Specialised communities of carriers sprang up along the rivers. Caravan routes were organised overland. Specialised slave-raiders, and even specialised pirates, appeared. These developments did not occur just in one place but over and over again. Pirates, for example, were reported from the coast near Mount Cameroun, from the Alima delta and from the islands in the bend of the Zaire.[93] Such a profound restructuring of economic relationships obviously made a deep impact on local society.

The eastern half of the forest was brought within the orbit of intercontinental trade at a late date but with extreme speed. The first traders from the Zanzibar coast appeared on the upper Zaire in the 1860s. A generation later these merchants of slaves and ivory had reached the Sankuru and the Aruwimi, where they met competitors from the Mediterranean commercial world. The latter reached the Uele river about 1867 and for two decades afflicted the north-western rain-forest.[94] So swift was their appearance that one tale presents it as if a single trader had arrived with a bag. He let loose an army out of it and the country was overrun.[95] The shock was greater than in the west, because trade remained firmly in the hands of foreigners and was not linked to local African enterprise. The foreign traders travelled with their own well-armed caravans. They often raided and looted more than they traded. In the south-east near the forest margin they recruited local allies, who were used to life in the forest and enabled the traders to set up a patron–client network of big men.[96] Whole

92 Laburthe-Tolra, *Minlaaba*, pp. 327–49; V. T. Levine, *The Cameroons from Mandate to Independence*, Berkeley, Ca., 1964, p. 18; L. Siroto, 'Masks and Social Organization among the Bakwele People' pp. 66–70; Chamberlin, 'Competition and Conflict', pp. 439, 449–50; also Lenz, *Skissen aus West Afrika*, fn.95; J. Leighton Wilson, *Western Africa*, New York, 1856, pp. 302–3.

93 L. Z. Elango, 'Britain and Bimbia in the nineteenth century, 1833–1878: a study in Anglo-Bimbian Trade and Diplomatic Relations', Ph.D. thesis, Boston Univeristy, 1975, pp. 31–3; G. Mazenot, *La Likouala-Mossaka: histoire de la pénétration du Haut Congo (1878–1920)*, Paris, 1970, pp. 150, n.2 (Iboa), 173.

94 G. Schweinfurth, *The Heart of Africa*, London, 1874, vol. 2, pp. 33–4; P. Ceulemans, *La Question arabe et le Congo (1883–1892)*, Brussels, 1959, pp. 41–4.

95 A. S. Clarke, 'The Warega', *Man*, xxix, 1930, 66–8.

96 A. Droogers, *The Dangerous Journey*, The Hague, 1980, p. 49; Mahieu, *Structures sociales*, pp. xxx–xxxiii, 182–4; E. Rzewuski, '*Asili ya Bangwana*: Origine des Bangwana', *Africana Bulletin*, xxi, 1974, 117–46; O. Baumann, 'Ausflug nach Siwa-siwa's Dorf', *Mitteilungen de* *(continued overleaf)*

areas underwent a generation of large-scale fighting. Colonial occupation came in the wake of this disruption and resulted in even greater disorder.

THE AGRICULTURAL REVOLUTION AFTER 1600

One early effect of the Atlantic trading system was the importation of new crops to equatorial Africa. These crops became the staple food of many areas. Their diffusion was faster than the movement of the trading frontier. Already by 1850 the whole region, east as well as west, was affected by the new agriculture. Such a change was tantamount to a revolution in the farming way of life.

Before 1600 the banana was the staple crop of the forest and sorghum or millet were staples in the grasslands and in the savanna patches of the forest. Secondary crops, especially tree crops, were important too, but the calendar of crop rotation revolved around the staple crops. The gradual replacement of these staples by maize, and later cassava, revolutionised the farming calendar. It influenced the whole daily round of agricultural life. The new crops also created greater food surpluses, which bolstered trade and especially the trade in slaves.

The transformation began with the arrival of maize from America. By 1608 both cassava and tobacco were reported to be growing on the Loango coast.[97] At the same time ground-nuts, beans and numerous American vegetables and peppers arrived. The European cabbage followed later. The last major crop innovation was the introduction of *macabo*, cocoyam, from Jamaica to Bioko in 1842. It later also found a home in the Cameroun forests.[98] The diffusion of new crops over such a wide area dramatically demonstrates the ability of farmers, especially women, to adopt innovations.

The new crops were at first planted in little plots near the houses where women could watch their growth. Some then reached the status of staple crops, and were introduced into the fields. New crop rotations and work patterns were devised. In this process the Nzabi, for example, invented two separate systems of crop rotation with the proper associations and fallows. One related to cassava and the other to ground-nuts. Each had effects on the social division of labour and on land tenure.[99] Although such drastic social changes take time, the American complex of crops swept through the area

(96 *continued*)
K.u.K. Geografische Gesellschaft zu Wien, 1887, 167–70 (Komo village in 'Arab' times); G. A. Graf von Götzen, *Durch Afrika von Ost nach West*, Berlin, 1899, pp. 268–98 (Komo country just after the defeat of the Zanzibari).

97 F. Pigafetta and D. Lopes, *Description du royaume de Congo et des contrées environnantes (1591)*, Louvain, 1965, W. Bal (ed.), p. 76 (maize); Vansina, 'Finding food and the history of precolonial Africa: a plea', *AEH*, vii, 1979, 11–12.

98 Ardener, *Coastal Bantu of the Cameroons*, p. 45.

99 Jean, *Les Jachères*, pp. 110, 123–7.

in only two and a half centuries. Even in the east, maize and cassava had been established before the colonial conquest. The speed of this spread, and the profound changes which it wrought, were truly revolutionary.

Cassava was the most successful crop. It spread faster than the others – even faster than tobacco, which was introduced about the same time. By 1698 cassava was already a staple crop of long standing at Malebo Pool. At that time tobacco, which 150 years later dominated the district's exports, was still scarce.[100] The differential spread was due to the relative advantage of each crop. Cassava was highly valued, because its yield was so much greater than that of the yams it replaced. It was well adapted to the forest and a better hedge against famine. The root could be left in the field for up to two years. It offered security against short-term climatic disaster. Since the cassava root did not have to be harvested at a fixed date, it offered flexibility. This contrasted favourably with cereal cultivation, which could lead to famine if war or other disturbance interrupted harvesting. The expansion of long-distance trade increased the market demand for food. Traders, porters and slaves all had to be fed. Cassava was an ideal food for this purpose. A special preparation of sour *kwange*, cassava 'bread', was developed, and could be preserved for up to six months. *Kwange* became the staff of life in the great river trade. Some districts became great exporters of cassava.[101] In addition to the root starch, cassava leaves provided a useful vegetable. The crop's advantages outweighed its liabilities: it probably exhausted the soil more than yams; it was also less nutritious than yams or bananas; and it required more work by women in its preparation as a food. Despite these drawbacks cassava replaced yams everywhere. By contrast it displaced bananas as a staple food only on the Loango slave routes and along the Zaire and its tributaries above the Pool to the Ubangi and the Aruwimi. The link between cassava and the slave-trade is very clear.[102]

Of the other American crops maize, tobacco, ground-nuts and beans became the most prominent. Farmers came to prefer maize to sorghum because of its better adaptation to high humidity. It eventually replaced sorghum and millet everywhere, even on the northern forest fringe. Beans and ground-nuts soon came to be linked with it in crop rotations that would conclude with cassava. Nitrogen-fixing beans were important, not only for their nutritional value, but also because they retarded the exhaustion of the soil. This was clearly understood, and legend tells how war was waged when people refused to share bean seeds.[103] In the high-

100 Vansina, *The Tio Kingdom*, pp. 266, 280, 450.

101 Harms, 'Competition and Capitalism', pp. 118–21; Vansina, *The Tio Kingdom*, pp. 296–7; Sautter, *De l'Atlantique*, 272–4.

102 M. Miracle, *Agriculture in the Congo Basin*, Madison, Wisconsin, 1967, 11, map 107, for the situation about 1950.

103 Ayom Awak, 'Histoire de l'évolution de la société Mbuun de l'entre-Kwilu-Lubwe du XVIIe au XXe siècle', Ph.D. thesis, University of Paris, 1975, pp. 33, 47.

altitude forest and the lakes area of the east, beans came to compete with the banana as a staple crop.

The effects of this new agriculture were deep. Since cassava demanded more female labour, the division of labour shifted to the disadvantage of women. The social division of labour was also altered by the new systems of crop rotation. Nzabi men who abandoned agriculture for trade left their 'pygmies' to clear the forest and their women to process cassava.[104] Among the Kuba, changes in the division of labour and in the choice of crop doubled the output of farming families and provided a surplus for the development of the state.[105] The production of food crops for caravans probably led to an increased local use of slave labour. Without cassava, forest agriculture might not have supported the eighteenth- and nineteenth-century volume of slave traffic and general trade. The new crops also emphasised regional specialisation. The nineteenth-century Nzabi country exported ground-nuts; Malebo Pool and its northern plateau exported tobacco; and the plantations of the upper Alima, Ikelemba and Lulonga exported cassava.[106] All were American crops. The impact of the new crops on demography is difficult to assess. More food became available, but cassava was less nutritious. Farm clearings increased, but so did the habitat of the mosquito, bringing a presumed rise in diseases such as malaria and yellow fever. Harder work by women led to higher rates of miscarriage and perhaps of abortion.[107] Finally the role of agriculture in the whole food-producing complex probably grew in importance, to the detriment of gathering and hunting.

The Europeans on the coast also introduced some domestic animals to the farming scene. Pigs may or may not have been raised in the forest before the arrival of the Portuguese.[108] Pig-farming certainly spread during these centuries. Pigs became a substitute for warthogs, wild game so desirable that in 1867 the Mangbetu were trying to domesticate it.[109] Ducks, domestic doves, the occasional house cat and even forest sheep were raised in the 1880s.[110] None of the domestic animals became staple foods,

104 Rey, 'Articulation des modes de dépendance et des modes de reproduction dans deux sociétés lignagères (Punu et Kunyi du Congo-Brazzaville)', *Cahiers d'études africaines*, xxxv, 1969, 429–33; Rey, *Colonialisme*, pp. 98–9, 236.
105 Vansina, 'La Hache et la houe', *Problèmes de l'enseignement supérieur et de développement en Afrique centrale*, Paris, 1975, pp. 205–20.
106 G. Dupré, 'Le Commerce entre sociétés lignagères: les Nzabi dans la traite à la fin du XIXe siècle (Gabon-Congo)', *Cahiers d'études africaines*, xii, no. 48, 1972, 626. For cassava see fn.106. For tobacco see Vansina, *The Tio Kingdom*, pp. 266–7, 280.
107 Harms, 'Competition and Capitalism', pp. 208–11.
108 First mentioned by Pigafetta and Lopes, *Description*, p. 76.
109 Schweinfurth, 'Das Volk der Monbuttu in Central Afrika', *Zeitschrift für Ethnologie*, 1873, 5–6.
110 Sheep were unknown in most forest communities, which is to be expected, given their grazing requirements. Terms for sheep indicate a spread from the coast of Cameroun and Gabon south-eastwards. Cf. C. Ehret, 'Sheep and Central Sudanic Peoples in southern Africa', *JAH*, ix, 1968, 2, 216–17.

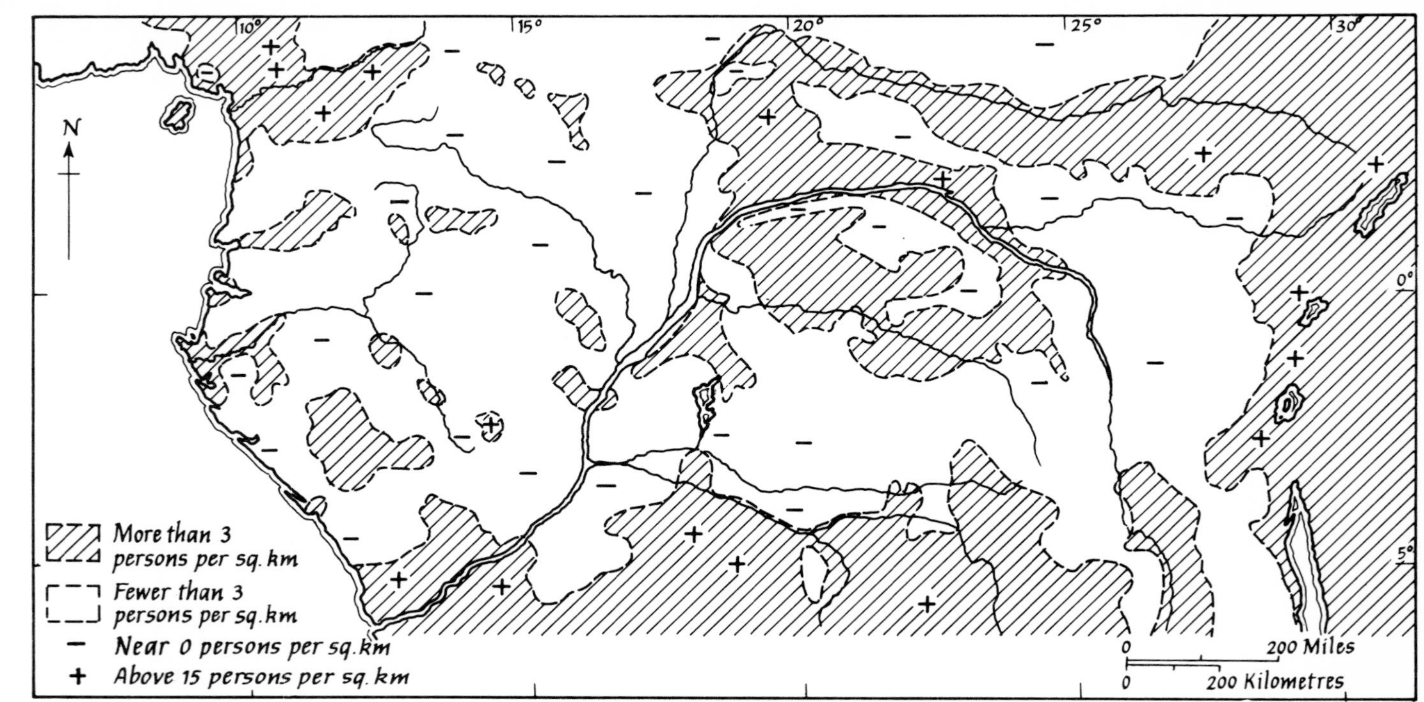

3:6 Estimated rural population in the forest zone, c. 1880

however, and in contrast to the situation with staple crops the innovation remained marginal.

THE SOCIAL IMPACT OF INTERCONTINENTAL TRADE

The Atlantic trade had first taken root in those places where large-scale political organisation existed to meet the demands of foreign traders. On the coast, Kongo and Loango were the only large states. Where such organisation was lacking, new structures developed in time. North of Loango, and no doubt inspired by its example, small kingdoms came into being. In the Gabon and the Wuri estuaries, polities developed directly out of the 'house'. They evolved in relative isolation from their hinterland. In contrast, commerce along the Zaire and its tributaries did not lead to larger political organisations. Instead, the house was transformed into a firm and later into an alliance of firms. In the east, the irruption of Zanzibari traders brought a very different transformation. Patron–client ties linked immigrant firms to local house networks. The successful clients of such firms later acquired dependent houses of their own.

Most equatorial African traders dealt in slaves. This had the effect of changing the status of slaves. The slave stratum of society split into two; those to be exported, and those who were to serve local masters. At the other end of the spectrum, splits began to occur in the upper ranks of the kingdoms as well. Merchant princes who had built up their own houses could act in concert to limit or even destroy central authority. Major reorganisations followed, and the number of social strata continued to increase. Fine distinctions between social levels became more patent. Outside the old kingdoms, the existing social stratification also changed as a higher percentage of the population became unfree. Membership of the top stratum became less bound by ascriptive criteria and more open to successful entrepreneurs. This implied increased social distance between strata, greater tension within communities and potential turmoil. In Gabon and Douala social disorder constantly threatened. The possibility of anarchy was less likely on the Zaire river because defence needs kept the nineteenth-century townships together. In smaller communities disruption and a lack of legitimacy undermined stability. Thus, in different ways, all the peoples of the forest were facing radical social transformation on the eve of the European invasion. These changes need to be examined in each of the different social settings.

When, by the 1580s, trade in Loango became more intensive, a caravan system developed. Early caravans were assembled by clan leaders who ensured safe passage by alliances with clan sections inland. At first Loango traders did not go beyond the Kwilu-Nyari river.[111] As the trade grew in

111 Rey, *Colonialisme*, pp. 220–4; Hagenbucher-Sacripanti, *Fondements*, p. 20.

frequency, volume and distance, the old alliances ceased to suffice. A ritual organisation, *lemba*, evolved to regulate markets, ensure safe passage and guarantee law and order. The *lemba* was controlled by assemblies of big men or by judges from surrounding communities. By the mid-seventeenth century the *lemba* association was well established in Loango. It eventually affected all the decentralised communities as far as the Pool. At the same time, a new influence penetrated into the area. When the Kongo kingdom collapsed, several Kongo nobles created principalities north of the Zaire, most successfully in Nsundi. With them came farmers who gradually encroached on Tio lands, assimilating local people in the process. The Kongo eventually took over the mining district of Mindouli, without provoking any known reaction from the Tio kingdom. The movement of *lemba*, of immigrant farmers, and of Kongo nobles was accompanied by increased economic diversification. Trade grew and transformed the whole social landscape.[112]

In the kingdom of Loango major political upheavals began to unfold after 1750. Merchant princes from the founding clans had gained wealth, prestige and independence by organising caravans. The crisis came to a head when a king died without an obvious heir. Twenty-seven clans of local aristocrats, organised in six factions and led by the wealthiest leaders with the largest slave retinue, disputed the royal claim. The stalemate was broken by the Buunzi priest of Ngoyo, who supported Mwe Pwati, a claimant unrelated to any of the factions. These grudgingly accepted the nomination, but acted rapidly to establish their own domination over the state. They moved the capital to the town where their representatives lived, and strengthened the crown council with powers to elect or depose kings. In the provinces local aristocrats gained the upper hand over court nominees. The newly-established royal line quickly split into two factions, and the balance between royalty and aristocrats was never redressed. Princes were barred from accumulating wealth, and aristocrats converted their shrines into treasuries. When Mwe Pwati died in 1766 the struggle between the royal and merchant capitals was resolved in favour of the latter. By the time his successor was installed in 1773 the new order had become the 'tradition'. After 1787 no further king was installed for almost a century, and the power of the merchants was unrestrained. In the process, however, decentralisation went further, as these men found themselves undercut by the best-placed and ablest leaders along the caravan trails.[113]

In the eighteenth century Loango's territory shrank. Before 1770, its eastern hinterland had become a set of independent principalities and the northern Mayumba coast became autonomous. Other provinces seceded or disintegrated, and by the 1780s the old state of Ngoyo had become a

112 J. Janzen, *Lemba, 1650–1930: the Regional History of an African Drum of Affliction*, in press.
113 F. Hagenbucher-Sacripanti, *Fondements*, pp. 61–4, 70, 72, 75–6, 78–99; Rey, *Colonialisme*, pp. 255–9, 514; Martin, *The External Trade*, p. 169.

larger kingdom than Loango. The vacuum was filled by a mixture of *lemba* leaders and local leaders with Kongo pretensions. In the north the Bumwele clan, fired by trade success, vainly sought to develop its own kingship.[114]

In the interior, the Tio kingship was also challenged by its merchant lords in the mid-eighteenth century. They had developed an ideology of legitimacy based on *nkobi*, or portable shrines. The ideology had been borrowed from their north-western neighbours. The new shrines helped ambitious provincial lords to carve out domains for themselves[115] and to cast off allegiance to the king. The resulting struggle ended in compromise by about 1830. The king bolstered his own status by acquiring some shrines. Northern Tio lords who competed with the river trade through their overland contacts with Loango saw their shrines legitimised in return for general allegiance. They were given a prominent voice in the conduct of central politics. This reconciliation between north and south led to a short period of increased royal authority. By the 1860s, however, the strain between the competing regions once again weakened the kingship. Separate coalitions had appeared, and northern and southern lords had become almost autonomous.[116]

Away to the north, the Ogowe area also saw a period of kingdom-building during the eighteenth century. It began with the formation of the Orungu kingdom in the delta and the Nkomi kingdom in Fernan Vaz. This region of Cape Lopez seems to have borrowed inspiration freely from Loango, and even Kongo, in creating a political structure. By about 1750 these examples were followed by several other groups up-river. By 1840, however, the Orungu kings were unable to maintain control over the dispersed slave-trade, and the monarchy began to dissolve. It was finally ruined by the establishment in the 1860s of European trading posts up-stream.[117]

When the Dutch arrived in the Gabon estuary, they found the political arena largely dominated by a single group, whose leader they termed 'king'. Small houses had united in order to keep the estuary free from interlopers. They did not quite succeed, and rival coalitions survived. In the seventeenth century some Gabonese houses actually bought slaves from the

114 Martin, *The External Trade*, pp. 168–9; Rey, *Colonialisme*, pp. 196–9, 266, 514; Janzen, *Lemba*, ch. 2, 'The Nsundi Systems'.

115 I. Löffler, *Beiträge zur Ethnologie der Tege*, Mainz, 1975, pp. 78–80; M–C Dupré, *La Dualité du pouvoir politique chez les Téké de l'ouest: pouvoir tsaayi et pouvoir nzinéké*, 23; Vansina, *The Tio Kingdom*, p. 332; P. Bonnafé, personal communication of field-notes: 'Histoire du plateau Kukuya', pp. 28–31 (Me lo kima).

116 Vansina, *The Tio Kingdom*, pp. 456–63 and map 455.

117 Patterson, *The northern Gabon Coast*, pp. 68–76; Chamberlin, 'Competition and Conflict', pp. 17, 145–6, but cf. O. Lenz, 'Reise auf dem Okande in Westafrika', *Verein der Gesellschaft für Erdkunde*, 1875, pp. 251–2; and Lenz, *Skizzen aus West Afrika*, pp. 194–5; Walker, *Notes d'histoire du Gabon*, Brazzaville, 1960, pp. 62–89; F. Gaulme, 'Cama', pp. 102–251; Avaro, *Peuple gabonais*, pp. 127–260.

Dutch, to strengthen their power. The increased manpower was put to work on fields while free men went to sea on trading expeditions. This 'trading' involved long-distance raids by people of the estuary as far away as Cape Lopez and the Rio del Rey. By 1698 this order fell apart. The dominant clan lost its hegemony and split. New immigrants arrived, and the estuary lost its relative unity as groups of houses competed to secure the trade. No clear victor had emerged before the French arrived in 1839. This event polarised two factions, and the ultimate victory went to the French-backed group. Once again Mpongwe society had become a single system. Now it was highly stratified and contained every class from resident European to export slave. Class consciousness was reinforced by outward signs, by conspicuous consumption and by expressions such as *le grand monde* and *le petit monde*. A place was found in this scheme of social inequality for trading partners from the interior. Marriage transactions paid special attention to class.[118] Although the Gabon class structure may have been more extremely stratified than that of Douala, it was not radically different.

The Cameroun port of Douala, which began as a single house, grew after 1750 as clients flocked to it with their slaves. The port was at the head of several separate trading networks, along the Mungo, the Wuri, the Kwakwa and the Dibamba rivers. This growth led about 1775 to a split among the rulers. An offshoot of the ruling house founded a rival establishment near Mount Cameroun. As the town grew, slaves became a large portion within it. In the 1840s an association called *jengu* was established to control and even to terrorise them. Another association, called *epanga*, united junior free men and others who ran away from Douala to the lesser settlements. Commercial competition led to tension among the big men who headed the Duala houses. The Duala 'kings' and their legitimising genealogy no longer had the power to keep order among the 'houses' in the town. Even after the creation of local courts of equity in 1856, fission and strife continued. By 1880 the Duala leaders were calling for a European protectorate. The old notion of government no longer functioned.[119]

In the nineteenth century trade settlements along the Zaire river successfully transformed the notion of 'house' into that of a business firm. A successful trader acquired junior kin, wives, clients and slaves, and founded a town. The preferred strategic location was opposite the mouth of a tributary. The best locations attracted several house-firms. By the 1850s

118 Bucher, 'The Mpongwe of the Gabon Estuary', *passim*, esp. pp. 44–60, 80–7; Patterson, *The Northern Gabon Coast*, pp. 48–143; N. Metegue N'Nah, *Economies et sociétés au Gabon dans la première moitié du XIX*[e] siècle, Paris, 1979.

119 A. Wirz, 'La "Rivière de Cameroun"', 172–95; Austen, 'Slavery among Coastal Middlemen', pp. 305–33; Elango, 'Britain and Bimbia', *passim*, esp. pp. 25–33; 'Der Epangabund', *Deutsche Kolonialzeitung*, xv, 46, 17 Nov. 1898, 414–15; E. Mveng, *Histoire du Cameroun*, Paris, 1963, pp. 171–81; C. Dikoume, *Elog Mpoo*, pp. 114, fn.6, 211, 212.

places such as Bolobo, Mushie, Bonga, Irebu, Makandza, Upoto and Basoko each had populations of more than 10 000 people grouped in ten or twelve firms. Several smaller towns had more than 5 000 people. Given the low over-all density of population, such urban agglomerations profoundly altered population distribution. The whole scale and nature of social and political organisation were also affected. Above all, however, the ownership of slaves increased dramatically. In many towns two-thirds or more of the inhabitants were technically slaves.

The river towns were governed by coalitions of the wealthiest leaders. Their structure was fairly unstable, and the organisation of the core lines varied. Some towns down-stream were matrilineal, whereas their up-stream kin were patrilineal. The intense interaction along the Zaire nevertheless produced great cultural homogeneity. This was reinforced by a common way of life in all the communities. Fashions, customs, charms and laws, all travelled with the traders. The movement of wives who wed in distant places spread common usage among river-bank societies, as did the mobility of slaves. Continual movement and flexibility of business organisation produced a very dynamic culture.

Along the river there reigned an unfettered spirit of competition for fixed capital. It was unhampered by aristocratic pretences or state-building schemes. The business ideology sharpened notions of witchcraft and sorcery, of competition, inequality and success. Individuality was heightened by belief in guardian spirits taking the shape of hippopotamuses or crocodiles who travelled with their protégés. The new economy profoundly affected demographic trends by furthering abortion and relying on foreign women and young male slaves to reproduce the system and society itself.[120]

The Atlantic system brought other less well-documented transformations. These included both the destabilisation of river village organisations[121] and the opposing growth of large houses where military threat forced people to unite. Many of the clusters that have been discussed may have been formed to provide security in this aggressive climate. In some societies military leadership challenged authority established by wealth and marriage. Even if power was not usurped, martial ability forced leaders to grant titles and emblems.

In the eastern half of the forest the irruption of Swahili traders led to very different forms of organisation. Caravans from Zanzibar settled at Nyangwe and Kasongo in the late 1860s. These forest-margin towns were first administered by a coalition of leaders. Very soon senior patrons such as Tippu Tip gained commercial domination over their rivals. In 1878, when

120 Harms, 'Competition and Capitalism', pp. 149–66, 192–249.
121 L. Siroto, 'Masks and Social Organization', esp. pp. 294–314 for the 'destabilisation' of the eastern Bekwil.

expansion into the forest began, local allies were invaluable. They knew the environment, they knew its constraints and they knew its produce. They moved with the caravans, and some of them soon became leaders themselves. As clients of Zanzibari patrons, they adopted much of the east-coast culture. The new traders created a territorial organisation. They appointed headmen all the way to the mouth of the Lomami, calling them *mokota*, a title common near Nyangwe. In northern Maniema they came across local big men whom they called *sultani*. The office was soon transferred, however, from the older leaders to younger people who could best provide the ivory. The original clients of the Zanzibari turned these headmen into their own junior clients. The patterns of clientship were never united, and the territory controlled by the Zanzibari remained profoundly decentralised. Only the most important leaders such as Tippu Tip or Mwene Dugumbi were allowed to compete. Lesser men were loyal to their patrons, but when a patron grew weak they knew when to shift to a new protector. The impact of a mixed east-coast and Nyangwe culture was very profound. The system was dismantled only very slowly. In 1894 the Congo State won the 'Arab war', but the local Zanzibari leaders survived, as did the chains of clientship. The leaders adopted the new administrators as their patrons. In communities far away from the rivers the Zanzibari system was dismantled only during the 1920s.[122]

CONCLUSION

This chapter is the story of transformations undergone by houses and villages in forest societies. Because these structures were the fundamental corporations responsible for social life and its continuation, this has been a generalised account of social history, showing how the composition of these structures, and the nature of their leadership, allowed them to adapt to changing conditions. Even the challenge posed by the Atlantic trading system was met. Only in the one exceptional case of the Duala was structural failure evident as the society drifted into anarchy.

There exists a deep continuity in the social history of the forest peoples. It runs from the days when they developed the house and the village, probably more than a thousand years ago, down to the European conquest. This intrusion finally destroyed their nature and autonomy between about 1870 and 1910. Before this the intercontinental trade in slaves had led to profound social change. Inequality of status always had existed, but with the advent of intercontinental trade, space had to be organised on an ever-widening scale. The trade led to increasingly rigorous social stratification through larger geographic arenas, leading to the widespread formation of social classes. This was a transformation deeper than anything that had

122 Vansina, *Kingdoms of the Savanna*, pp. 236–41.

occurred before. In its effects it was more important than the emergence of kingdoms in the south-west.

The main outlines of this history are beginning to emerge, though more field research and archival work will sharpen the perspective. At the level of detailed history almost nothing has yet been done. Research in the past has been deflected by unwarranted attention to 'migrations' and by the static analysis of 'lineage' systems. Ideologies have been structuralised, cosmologies reified and actual realities neglected. The recovery of the past will also require new approaches towards historical sources. Meanwhile this presentation must suffice. In a minority of situations historical research exists and the ground is firm. In the majority of cases, however, the ground remains as treacherous as the marshes of the great Zaire river itself.

CHAPTER 4

The paradoxes of impoverishment in the Atlantic zone

JOSEPH C. MILLER

The people of savanna-woodland, highland and semi-arid south-west Central Africa involved themselves intensely with European foreigners from beyond the Atlantic shores between the fifteenth and nineteenth centuries. For Europeans, the objective was to explore and exploit this 'treasure trove' of tropical riches. The Portuguese came first, in search of souls to save for the Christian God and precious minerals for their Iberian monarchs. They were joined in the seventeenth and eighteenth centuries by Dutch, English and French competitors. All discovered that the real wealth of West-Central Africa was its human population. Each year they bought African captives by the tens of thousands and sent them across the Atlantic to work as slaves in the mines, plantations and cities of the Americas. This trans-Atlantic trade in slaves dominated European activities along the coast until the middle of the nineteenth century. After 1830, British cruisers suppressed the maritime slave-trade, and a new generation of foreign merchants bought wax, ivory and red rubber to supply factories and cities in distant Europe.

The Portuguese officers imposed only a marginal military and administrative presence along the Atlantic coast of Central Africa before the last decades of the nineteenth century. However, African commitment to the trade flowing from the Atlantic intensified over a much larger area. Within this 'Atlantic zone' of externally-oriented commerce and culture, Africans adopted preferences for foreign goods, and they competed for access to markets in ways that set the stage for an expansive burst of European military conquest after 1880. That conquest converted the old Portuguese coastal toe-hold to the full-blown modern colony of Angola. It coincided with a similar imposition of military rule elsewhere in Central Africa under the flags of France, Britain, Germany and the Congo State.

The African side of these events centres on the rivalries and ambitions which wracked the varied peoples caught up in the dramatic expansion of the Atlantic zone. Some fought against it, and others fled. Many others, however, welcomed the change. The complex relationships among differing African interests propelled the Atlantic zone into the heart of Central Africa.

The history of the peoples of West-Central Africa is dominated by competition. Even people who spoke the same language vied with one another for personal advancement and, on occasion, even for survival. The urgency of their competition might seem to reflect a background of fundamental scarcities.[1] Such an assumption of dearth may be no more directly verifiable than the assumption of plenty which underlay the European myth of a 'tropical treasure trove'. Yet shortages of land and food help to explain many historical developments in West-Central Africa. Populations did not necessarily increase with regularity in the era before slaving, nor was good, usable land readily available even when the slave-trade reduced population. Harvests sometimes matured dependably and bountifully, but at other times they withered in drought and fell prey to pests. Land, rainfall and female fertility were therefore key issues in West-Central Africa. Scarcities, though not constant nor present in all places, provoked conflict, although West-Central Africans often lived in peace and harmony as well. People who lived close to the soil and relied on the sun, the land and the rains for crops and rangelands were, of course, vulnerable to changing ecological conditions.

Against these constraints, the history of West-Central Africans presents a double paradox in the years between the coming of the first Europeans and the temporary end of African political independence. People of every category turned new opportunities flowing from the Atlantic zone to old ends. They thus embraced foreign fashions and adopted imported weapons as they attempted to defend their own ways of gaining power and wealth. Fear of defeat by local rivals drove men and women to welcome traders and risk dealing with strangers. Those who accepted Christianity and obtained flint-lock muskets achieved short-term gains. Many of their descendants, however, suffered immense losses in the long run. At one time or another, farmers, stock-raisers, priests, traders, soldiers, aristocrats and monarchs all sought advantage for themselves and their kin and allies through contacts with the overseas market for African labour and produce. The unexpected cost of such commitments created new conflicts and further appeals to outsiders for help. By the end of the nineteenth century, local power and prestige depended widely on imported goods and weapons. New

1 For the general significance of scarcity of resources, see John Tosh, 'The cash-crop revolution in tropical Africa: an agricultural reappraisal', *African Affairs*, lxxix, 314, 1980, 79–94; Philip D. Curtin, *Economic Change in Pre-colonial Africa*, Madison, Wisconsin, 1975, pp. 22–3; Joseph C. Miller, 'Lineages, ideology, and the history of slavery in Western Central Africa', in *Slavery and Ideology in Africa*, Paul E. Lovejoy (ed.), Beverly Hills, California, 1981, pp. 40–71, and 'The significance of drought, disease and famine in the agriculturally marginal zones of Western Central Africa', *Journal of African History* (*JAH*), xxiii, 1, 1982, 17–61.

economic forces from beyond the ocean had taken over. Nineteenth-century West-Central Africans could no more influence these than their ancestors could control the earlier scourges of irregular rain and ambitious rivals.

A no less incessant dialectic lent similarly dramatic qualities to the history of the Europeans in the Atlantic zone before the colonial period. Conflict, inability to foresee the future and failure to learn from the past drove successive groups of Portuguese to thrust into Central Africa between 1480 and 1880. They came from a society in Europe no less divided than the

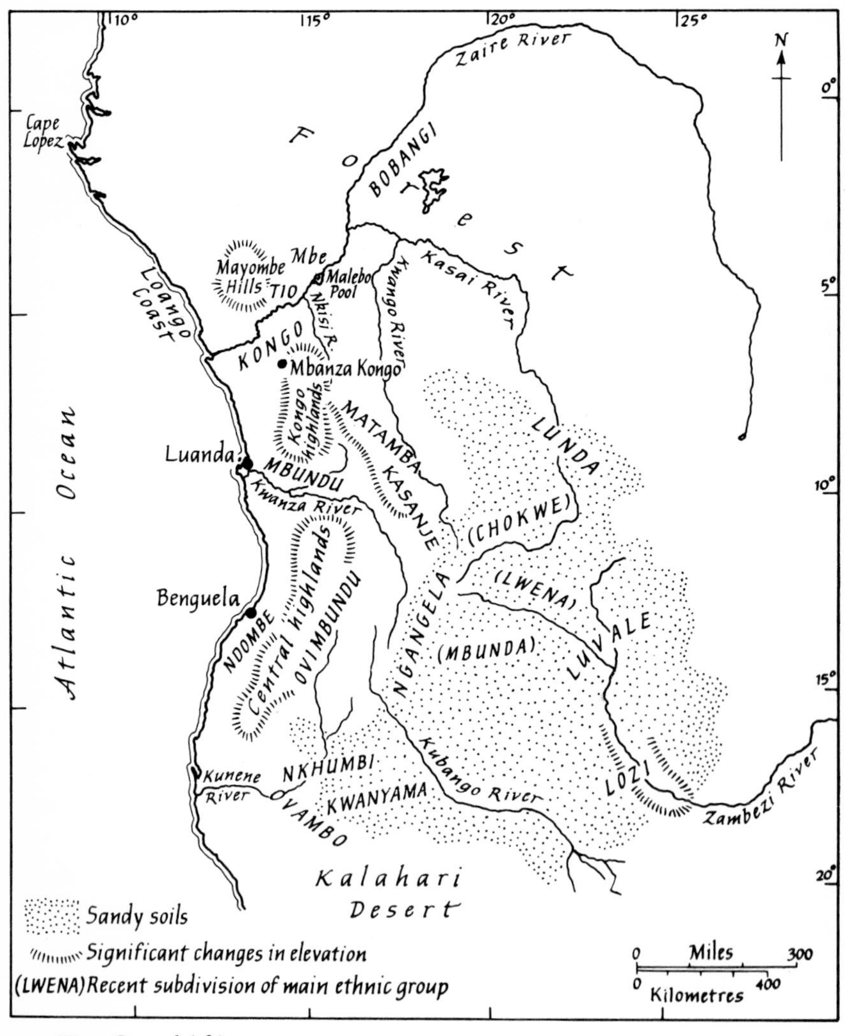

4:1 West-Central Africa

societies of the Africans. Relative economic weakness at home drove many to search for wealth and power in the imagined paradise of Africa. The late-nineteenth-century generation of these fortune-hunters carried the effort to the point of artificially partitioning colonies in Africa. They hoped that political rule would allow them to tap the tropical cornucopia that had eluded their predecessors for four hundred years. Ironically, they succeeded only in spreading ruin, so that the West-Central Africans they conquered were even less capable of satisfying their hopes than their ancestors had been.

PEOPLE AND AGRICULTURE IN THE FIFTEENTH CENTURY

The Atlantic zone expanded haltingly from sheltered bays and river mouths along the coast. The strong, cold Benguela current swept sand from these streams into long, narrow islands and created ideal anchorages for European ocean-going vessels. The best bays were those of Benguela, Luanda and the Loango coast north of the Zaire river. Africans found them attractive also for their molluscs, their good fishing waters and their natural marine salt pans.

The Atlantic zone already extended a hundred kilometres inland by the fifteenth century. African traders distributed salt, shells and dried fish from the bays to people in the mountains behind the coast and to the farmers of the savanna woodlands beyond. The northern coastal settlements were outposts of economic and political systems centred in the wetter and more populous highlands of the hinterland. Toward the more arid coastal lowlands of the south, the river mouths were settled by relatively autonomous small populations who remained distinct from the more numerous peoples of the central plateau.

By 1400, the farming populations of the interior savannas had spread outward from their earliest nodes of settlement in well-watered river valleys to cultivate the higher and drier lands along the watersheds.[2] Agricultural settlement in such marginal zones was precarious, since the staples of those times, sorghum and millet, suffered setbacks from drought nearly every decade. Widespread failure of the rains forced farmers to forage in the woods in order to survive. About once every century such droughts became nearly universal catastrophes of five to ten years' duration. Entire communities collapsed then, as the young, the old and the

2 The notion of oases as population centres may be found in Steven Feierman, *The Shambaa Kingdom*, Madison, Wisconsin, 1974, pp. 22–31, and 'Economy, society and language in early East Africa', in Philip D. Curtin *et al.*, *African History*, Boston, 1979, pp. 117–46. For West-Central Africa, Jean-Luc Vellut, 'Les Grands Tournants dans l'histoire de l'Est du Kwanza au XIXe siècle', *Revista do Departamento de Biblioteconomia e Historia* (Rio Grande, Brazil), i, 2, 1979, 93, 96 and *passim*; also Miller, 'Lineages, ideology, and the history of slavery'.

weak succumbed to malnutrition and disease. Stronger individuals took refuge with more fortunate relatives, and the most daring pillaged the lowlands where ground-water still supported crops and life.

Scarcities of this intermittent sort drove the people of West-Central Africa to concentrate in a few extensive areas of superior rainfall and adequate ground-water from an early time. It was in these centres of persistently dense population that the major ethnolinguistic communities took shape. Near the arid southern coast, the lower river valleys undoubtedly carried people through times of want. Towards the interior, river basins that broadened into flood plains became agricultural oases inhabited by permanent populations. From these nodes, people might expand into the surrounding hills in times of plentiful rains, but they retreated back into the valleys in times of drought.[3]

The Nkisi valley near the Zaire river and the middle Kwango were such population centres.[4] The Kunene ran through two nodes of dense habitation; one where the upper river flowed off the central highlands, and another in the broad flats on the edges of the Kalahari.[5] The lower Kubango and upper Zambezi flood plains provided similar stability in drought-prone areas to the east.[6] The affluents of the Kasai formed other small habitable pockets of alluvial soils.[7] On the edge of the central Zaire basin valleys widened, soils were firmer and the flora and fauna more diversified. This forest mosaic and the superior rainfall there offered a particularly propitious environment for dense farming populations.[8] For a

3 W. Gervase Clarence-Smith has pioneered climate history in southern Angola: 'Drought in Southern Angola and Northern Namibia, 1837 to 1945', unpublished seminar paper, Institute of Commonwealth Studies, 1974. For the nineteenth century, see Jill R. Dias, 'Famine and disease in the history of Angola, c. 1830–1930', *JAH*, xxii, 3, 1981, 349–78.

4 Anne Wilson, 'The Kongo Kingdom to the Mid-Seventeenth Century', Ph.D. thesis, University of London, 1977, p. 41; Joseph C. Miller, *Kings and Kinsmen: Early Mbundu States in Angola*, Oxford, 1976, pp. 70–3 ff.

5 Gladwyn Murray Childs, *Kinship and Character of the Ovimbundu*, London, 1949, reprinted 1969, pp. 174–6, and 'The chronology of the Ovimbundu kingdoms', *JAH*, xi, 2, 1970, 241; W. G. Clarence-Smith and Richard Moorsom, 'Underdevelopment and class formation in Ovamboland, 1845–1915', *JAH*, xvi, 3, 1975, 365–82; reprinted in *The Roots of Rural Poverty in Central and Southern Africa*, Neil Parsons and Robin Palmer (eds), London, 1977, pp. 96–112.

6 W. G. Clarence-Smith, 'Climatic Variations and Natural Disasters in Barotseland, 1847–1907', unpublished paper, University of Zambia, School of Education, History Staff Seminars, 1976–7; Robert J. Papstein, 'The Upper Zambezi: a History of the Luvale People, 1000–1900', Ph.D. thesis, University of California at Los Angeles, 1978, pp. 6, 7, 83; Thomas J. Larson, 'The Hambukushu migrations to Ngamiland', *African Social Research*, ix, 1971, 27–49; Gwyn Prins, *The Hidden Hippopotamus: Re-appraisal in African History: the Early Colonial Experience in Western Zambia*, Cambridge, 1980, pp. 19–21.

7 J. Jeffrey Hoover, 'The Seduction of Ruwej: Reconstructing Ruund History (The Nuclear Lunda: Zaire, Angola, Zambia)', Ph.D. thesis, Yale University, 1978, pp. 3–6.

8 Muzong Wanda Kodi, 'A Pre-colonial History of the Pende People (Republic of Zaire)', Ph.D. thesis, Northwestern University, 1976, 2 vols., vol. 1, pp. 71–5; H. Nicolaï, *Le Kwilu*, Brussels, 1963.

long time, the farmers of all these centres lived without reference to the remote Atlantic zone or its trade.

Not all settlement strategies emphasised agricultural potential, particularly on the margins of the Kalahari. Early settlers there took up cattle-herding. In the flood plains they could combine pastoralism with cultivation. These agro-pastoralists spread fields up the smaller western streams of the lower Kunene and grazed their herds up to the limit of the sweet grass on the southern slopes of the central highlands. Transhumant grazing systems along the streams of the southern escarpment reached north to the steppes of Benguela. During the short rainy season, herds dispersed over the surrounding hill country, to return each dry season to the home valleys.[9]

Elsewhere, security ranked high among the priorities of people who occupied inaccessible but viable corners of the region. Montane forest from the Zaire to the Kwanza concealed small plateaux where lowland peoples could retreat in search of safety.[10] The granite boulders of the middle Kwanza and nearby caves and islands offered similar protection.[11] The inselbergs and the western escarpment of the central highlands also secured people from raiders.[12]

A growing sense of community evolved within each of these relatively isolated demographic nodes, whatever the nature of its attraction. Shared concerns, shared languages based on three or four ancestral Bantu tongues, and shared techniques of production emerged. Farmers circulated women as wives within their valleys and came to consider nearly everyone as kin. The herders' feelings of community were anchored in their grazing circuits. Joint defensive efforts welded refugees in the rocky highlands even more closely to one another.

The communities formed by these long-term processes of interaction had already created the main ethno-linguistic identities of today by the fifteenth century. Inhabitants of both banks of the lower Zaire and the adjacent Nkisi valley shared a Kongo language and culture. The lower Lukala and middle Kwanza peoples behaved in recognisably distinctive

9 Joseph C. Miller, 'Central and southern Angola to ca. 1840', in *The Formation of Angolan Society*, Franz-Wilhelm Heimer (ed.), forthcoming. See also Alvin W. Urquhart, *Patterns of Settlement and Subsistence in Southwestern Angola*, Washington, D.C., 1963; Mário Maestri Filho, *A agricultura Africana nos séculos XVI e XVII no litoral angolano*, Porto Alegre, 1978.

10 For example, John K. Thornton, 'The kingdom of Kongo in the era of the civil wars, 1641–1718', Ph.D. thesis, University of California at Los Angeles, 1979, pp. 28–9, 40–1; Beatrix Heintze, 'Unbekanntes Angola: der Staat Ndongo im 16. Jahrhundert', *Anthropos*, lxxii, 1977, 763–74.

11 In general, David Birmingham, *Trade and Conflict in Angola*, Oxford, 1966, pp. 88, 92, 93–4, 95, 125–6; for the island Mbola na Kasashe, Miller, *Kings and Kinsmen*, pp. 93, 104, 169, 171.

12 W. G. Clarence-Smith, *Slaves, Peasants and Capitalists in Southern Angola*, London, 1979, pp. 84–8, discusses later refugees in these mountains as 'social bandits'; Miller, 'Central and southern Angola'.

ways, which the Kongo acknowledged by terming them 'Mbundu'. The same Kongo term, given a southern prefix, became 'Ovimbundu' when applied to still different inhabitants of the central plateau. In the valley of the middle Kwango people called themselves 'Pende' at that early date.[13]

People in the southern regions tended to distinguish themselves according to whether they emphasised farming or herding. The predominantly agricultural folk near the mouth of the Kaporolo took the name 'Ndombe'. Herders south of them often bore names identifying them with the rivers on which they centred their transhumant cycles. The concentration of agro-pastoralists in the Kunene–Kuvelai flood plain acquired the designation of 'Nkhumbi'. The most southerly people in the flood plain distinguished themselves as 'Ovambo', and the people east of them acquired the name of 'Kwanyama'.[14]

The tendency toward clearly defined population groups emerged more strongly in the semi-arid south and west than in the moister east or in the forest margin. Farmers raising millet and sorghum in the sandy plains of the east must have lived in dispersed, small village communities. They probably had a shifting kaleidoscope of collective terms for themselves. Westerners indiscriminately labelled them 'Ngangela'.[15] People in the diverse and rich lands of the Kasai region moved about with relative freedom. The constant movement of villages and individuals led people there to define their social identities in terms of widespread and diffuse clan links. Local clan segments often became the primary units of cooperation among kin, and village identities grew at the expense of kinship. A multiplicity of other organisational and political principles blurred even these community boundaries.[16] The modern ethnic diversity and weak sense of ethnic identity of the forest fringe peoples testify to a history rather different from that of the clearly-defined clusters of the west and south.

Even though the history of large population groups, isolated by geography and hence inward-looking, produced distinctive languages and habits, broad 'tribal' identities explain little about the past. Local inequalities between elders and juniors, between men and women,

13 Cf. Wilson, 'Kongo Kingdom', pp. 17 ff.; Miller, *Kings and Kinsmen*, pp. 56, 60, 70–3; G. L. Haveaux, *La Tradition historique des Bapende orientaux*, Brussels, 1954.

14 Miller, 'Central and southern Angola'. General ethnography of southern Angola in Carlos Estermann, *Etnografia do sudoeste de Angola*, Lisbon, 1960–61, 3 vols. (translated as *The Ethnography of Southwestern Angola*, Gordon D. Gibson (ed.), New York, 1976–7, vols. 1 and 2, and as *Ethnographie de sud-ouest de l'Angola*, Paris, 1977, 2 vols.)

15 For example, João António Cavazzi de Montecuccolo, *Descrição histórica dos três reinos do Congo, Matamba e Angola*, P. Graciano Maria de Luguzzano (trans. and ed.), Lisbon, 1965, 2 vols, vol. 1, p. 214. On the ethnography of the eastern regions, Merran McCulloch, *The Southern Lunda and Related Peoples (Northern Rhodesia, Angola, Belgian Congo)*, London, 1951, and sources cited.

16 Jan Vansina, *Kingdoms of the Savanna*, Madison, Wisconsin, 1966, pp. 110–16. Also his *Introduction à l'ethnographie du Congo*, Kinshasa, 1966, pp. 129–59, and 'Probing the past of the lower Kwilu peoples (Zaire)', *Paideuma*, xix–xx, 1973–4, 332–64.

between weak and strong, and between refugees and host populations overshadowed such cultural unities.

In farming regions, small communities of locally-born male relatives tended to control the absolute necessities of agricultural societies, land and the labour to work it. People there conceived of social relations in terms of 'segmentary' kinship. Close kinship, generally calculated through female links, ideally united brothers and nephews who lived together on the lands of their ancestors and who shared concern for the fertility of both land and women. In practice, this ideal also divided them. Old men controlled their sisters and nieces in order to live in luxurious ease from the agricultural exertions of female labour. They exchanged women among themselves as marriage partners and commanded the respect and services of unmarried men by offering or withdrawing the prospect of a future wife. Wealthy and powerful older men thus dominated their junior kinsmen.

Ancestry also emphasised parochialism by favouring local descent over foreign ancestry. This preference generally favoured men, whether old or young. Women were born among in-laws at the homes of their fathers, and they later moved to live with their husbands in villages where they had no kin. As outsiders there, they had few ways of marshalling supporters against overbearing husbands with rich local connections. Their lot, however powerless, was preferable to that of refugees from marginal lands who sought protection and sustenance in those same villages during times of drought. These helpless new arrivals joined war captives in disadvantaged groups of kinless residents constituting a despised lower stratum of society similar to 'slaves' in western societies.

The egalitarian ideology of these communities, termed 'lineages', emphasised the co-residence of closely related kin. In practice, villages contained only a small core of locally-born relatives, who enjoyed status superior to the large number of dependent wives, clients and visitors without strong kin ties. Elders emphasised the distinctiveness of their respective communities, and this stress on parochial unities partially hid the real divisions within each local unit. Only in areas of sparse and recent settlement did kinship in fact coincide with residence, as open lands allowed the discontented to spread outwards in groups of close relatives. By the fifteenth century, such conditions remained only in agriculturally marginal zones recently vacated in time of drought. The Ngangela, east of the Kwanza and Kunene, exemplify such a population separated into lineages defined in the classic terms of ancestry and residence. Few wider loyalties diluted their parochialism.

Farmers in more densely-inhabited regions lived in more complex societies but retained some of the kin structures inherited from earlier days of lower population. First arrivals sometimes retained descent as a way of distinguishing their permanent rights of residence from the 'guest' status of more recent arrivals. They thus became more powerful landowners.

Farmers displaced by drought or war fled into these areas in their times of need. They probably formed more numerous groups of slaves, clients and dependents of other sorts. Descent rules continued to prevail, because outsiders, slaves, clients and guests could never gain full rights to lands owned by local ancestors so long as lineage ideology remained at the core of social and political thought.[17] Such localism formed a deep-rooted barrier to wider ties, even when inter-regional contact became frequent.

THE INITIAL GROWTH OF THE ATLANTIC ZONE

Ecological differentiation was the first factor which led to regular trading contacts in West-Central Africa. Peaceful commerce regularly cut across major boundaries between wetter and drier areas. In time of crisis, however, such contacts could turn to violent conflict. A belt of such recurrent fighting developed on the western and southern fringes of the central highlands. In time of drought, farming populations descended from the plateau to steal cattle from stock-raisers below the western scarp. They also raided fields that survived along the lower rivers after their own crops of sorghum had withered and died. Other raiders descended from the northern slopes to the tributary valleys of the Kwanza.[18] Such conflicts increased in intensity toward the west and south, where agriculture was more precarious and drought more frequent, but they were also known elsewhere.

Persistent conflict unified the people who escaped such violence by withdrawing to natural rock fortresses. Although people in every local region intermittently occupied such defensive sites, they congregated permanently in a few such refugee centres. War leaders there organised residents and strangers alike in centralised political institutions. A shared need for protection encouraged submission to the most able commanders in a common defensive effort. These warlords in turn concentrated power in their own hands, and delegated authority by personal appointment rather than by honouring prestige or power derived from other sources. By this process the isolated and spacious plateau of Humpata became the highland kingdom of Huila.[19] Mountain fastnesses on the central plateau sheltered the redoubts of the powerful lords of Kulembe.[20] Chiefs entitled '*ndembu*' gathered followers among rugged mountains and forests in southern Kongo.[21] In times of trouble, the isolated stand of granite boulders at Pungo Andongo on the middle Kwanza became a strategic

17 Sources for the general interpretation in Miller, 'Lineages, ideology, and the history of slavery'.
18 Miller, 'Central and southern Angola'.
19 Miller, 'Central and southern Angola'.
20 Miller, *Kings and Kinsmen*, pp. 89–90, and 'Central and southern Angola'.
21 Thornton, 'Kingdom of Kongo', pp. 28–9, 40–1.

centre around which the politics of the entire Mbundu region came to revolve.[22]

Defensive needs in the fertile zones also promoted temporary war leaders to permanent political office. There was, however, a difference. Centralisation among farmers tended to preserve the local lineage communities from which the larger entities emerged. The earliest recognised rulers of this sort commanded territories defined by river basins, because they depended on agricultural production to a greater extent than did the warlords. The power of valley kings therefore often centred on their claimed ability to bring adequate rains. Such early kings as Feti and Coya on the plateau,[23] the *kitome* lords of Kongo,[24] and the *malunga* chiefs of the Kwango[25] achieved only this incipient stage of political centralisation. The simultaneous growth of a central authority specialising in rain-making or war-leadership, together with the maintenance of lineage identities, produced political systems characterised as 'segmentary states'.[26]

Early segmentary polities emerged also at sites of raw materials critical to later Iron Age civilisations. Farmers prized the purer and tastier salts from the few superior salt pans and springs – for example, in the middle Kwango valley – in their heavily starchy diets. They also required iron for implements and weapons, and copper for ornaments and for storage of wealth. Four outcrops of copper provided much of the valuable metal for decoration and currency in West-Central Africa. Mining, manufacturing and distribution generally lay in the hands of owners famous for their power and wealth.[27] Smiths with a superior iron technology had entered the Kongo region from the north-east. By the sixteenth century, their descendants used a piece of iron called *ngola* as a symbol of political authority in the Mbundu region.[28]

Where production required little technical skill or coordination, as with salt, centralisation grew around resource centres while preserving lineage loyalties. Masters of the salt pans functioned primarily as market police and as keepers of the peace among the strangers who congregated to produce salt for themselves. They invested their profits in marriage networks which spread their influence throughout nearby descent groups. Centralisation

22 Miller, *Kings and Kinsmen*, pp. 41, 95–6. Compare, Joseph C. Miller, 'The formation and transformation of the Mbundu states from the sixteenth to the eighteenth centuries', in *Formation of Angolan Society*, Heimer (ed.), forthcoming.
23 Childs, *Kinship and Character*, pp. 174–6.
24 Wilson, 'Kongo Kingdom', pp. 25–9.
25 Miller, *Kings and Kinsmen*, pp. 59–63, 80, 86.
26 See Aidan Southall, *Alur Society*, Cambridge, 1956, and development of the notion in Feierman, 'Economy, society, and language'.
27 For example, the *mbuta* chiefs in Wilson, 'Kongo Kingdom', pp. 24–5; also Miller, *Kings and Kinsmen*.
28 Miller, *Kings and Kinsmen*, pp. 63–73 ff.

thus grew paradoxically by strengthening the existing descent-based institutions of the elders. Copper or iron production favoured only slightly less segmentary forms of authority. Smelting and refining demanded technological skills not commonly found among ordinary farmers. Hence embryonic monarchies arose among widely scattered villages but did not overcome the segmentary basis of their polities.

Political centralisation based on inter-regional trade also retained its segmentary character. Much of this trade moved between the coast and the interior. In the early seventeenth century maritime fishing, shell-gathering and salt production all supplied nearby highland markets. Salt from Benguela went to both the southern and the central highlands in exchange for copper and feathers.[29] Salt both from the Kisama mines and from coastal pans reached the Mbundu and the lower Kwanza.[30] Fleets of fishing canoes supplied inland markets with dried fish.[31] These trade routes brought maritime riches to the emergent polities of the inland farmers before 1600.

The most far-reaching growth of the Atlantic zone took place in the Kongo region, where east–west trading routes crossed others linking northern forests to southern grasslands. The early kings of Kongo had ample opportunity to organise and profit from this trade. They used their commercial wealth to spread centralised authority over older lords in a wide region along the lower Zaire river. On the fertile plain of Vunda these lords of Kongo, entitled *mani* Kongo, built a large population of slaves and other followers.[32] They extended their influence over the surrounding population centres by dispatching loyal emissaries and relatives to settle there, by concluding marriage contracts with the aristocratic families in the provinces and by working out alliances with the warlords of the local mountain redoubts. They thus created a complex and fragile polity. Like many African states, it was more extensive in its theoretical than in its practical reach. The king's word was heard only faintly beyond the slave and client population of the capital district. The symbols of the ultimate maritime sources of royal wealth were small *nzimbu* shells from the bay at Luanda. These circulated as the currency of the realm. Although fifteenth-century Kongo kings probably had carried centralisation as far as any rulers in West-Central Africa at that time, they supervised only a feeble commercial linkage of the Atlantic zone and the forest basin. They still

29 Miller, 'Central and southern Angola'.

30 Beatrix Heintze, 'Beiträge zur Geschichte und Kultur der Kisama (Angola)', *Paideuma*, xvi, 1970, 159–86; and 'Historical notes on the Kisama of Angola', *JAH*, xiii, 3, 1972, 407–18.

31 Ralph Delgado, *O reino de Benguela (do descobrimento à criação do governo subalterno)*, Lisbon, 1945, pp. 307–17.

32 Emphasis on slaves at the Kongo court, especially in Thornton, 'Kingdom of Kongo', ch. 5.

ruled their domains through older noble families whose elders enjoyed a greater antiquity than their own.[33]

CONTENDING INTERESTS IN THE ATLANTIC ZONE

The first Portuguese caravels probed West-Central African waters as the Kongo state coalesced in the later fifteenth century. They thus connected the region to other parts of Africa, to Europe and eventually to Asia and the Americas. In so doing, they suddenly expanded the opportunities for profit available to Kongo rulers. Local lords also increased their hitherto limited power by casting their lot with the strangers from beyond the seas. Just as those Africans welcomed the Portuguese in hoping to catapult themselves past local rivals, so many Portuguese who stepped ashore in Africa came in search of fortune that eluded them at home. From this union of the weak, both sides derived new forms of strength.

The Portuguese explorers who dropped anchor in the Zaire estuary in 1483 came from a small kingdom on the periphery of a Mediterranean commercial system that was drawing vital African gold from below the Sahara.[34] Largely excluded from the central Mediterranean core of this trade by their remote western location, the Portuguese held advantages over the dominant Italians only with respect to maritime technology. Their superior naval instrumentation and rigging had allowed them to explore the open oceans off north-western Africa.[35]

The leaders of these overseas initiatives were relatively weak in the internal politics of the Portuguese monarchy. The first adventurers set out to enrich struggling members of the royal house in alliance with lower nobles ambitious to emulate the powerful landed aristocracy. Their efforts hardly constituted a powerful or consistent initiative on a fifteenth-century world scale, even though they did assume some significance in the confines of West-Central Africa. These coasts never became a major attraction for metropolitan Portuguese before 1880.[36] Struggling and under-financed competitors came, out of desperation, to try to make quick fortunes. Royal attention in Lisbon was focused on the Gold Coast as Europe's single largest source of the precious metal,[37] and within twenty years of Diogo Cão's

33 For the fifteenth-century background and sixteenth-century Kongo, see Wilson, 'Kongo Kingdom'. But cf. John K. Thornton, 'The Kingdom of Kongo, 1390–1678: the development of an African social formation', *Cahiers d'études africaines*, forthcoming, and 'Early Kongo-Portuguese relations: a new interpretation', *History in Africa*, viii, 1981, 183–204.

34 John Day, 'The great bullion famine of the fifteenth century', *Past and Present*, lxxix, 1980, 3–54.

35 A. de Oliveira Marques, *History of Portugal*, 2nd ed., New York, 1976, pp. 133–39; Charles R. Boxer, *The Portuguese Seaborne Empire, 1415–1825*, New York, 1969.

36 For this emphasis, Oliveira Marques, *History of Portugal*, p. 247.

37 John Vogt, *Portuguese Rule on the Gold Coast, 1469–1682*, Athens, Ga., 1979, pp. ix, 59–92 (esp. 65, 77–9, 87–92), 152–3, 207–9, and Appendix C, 217–20.

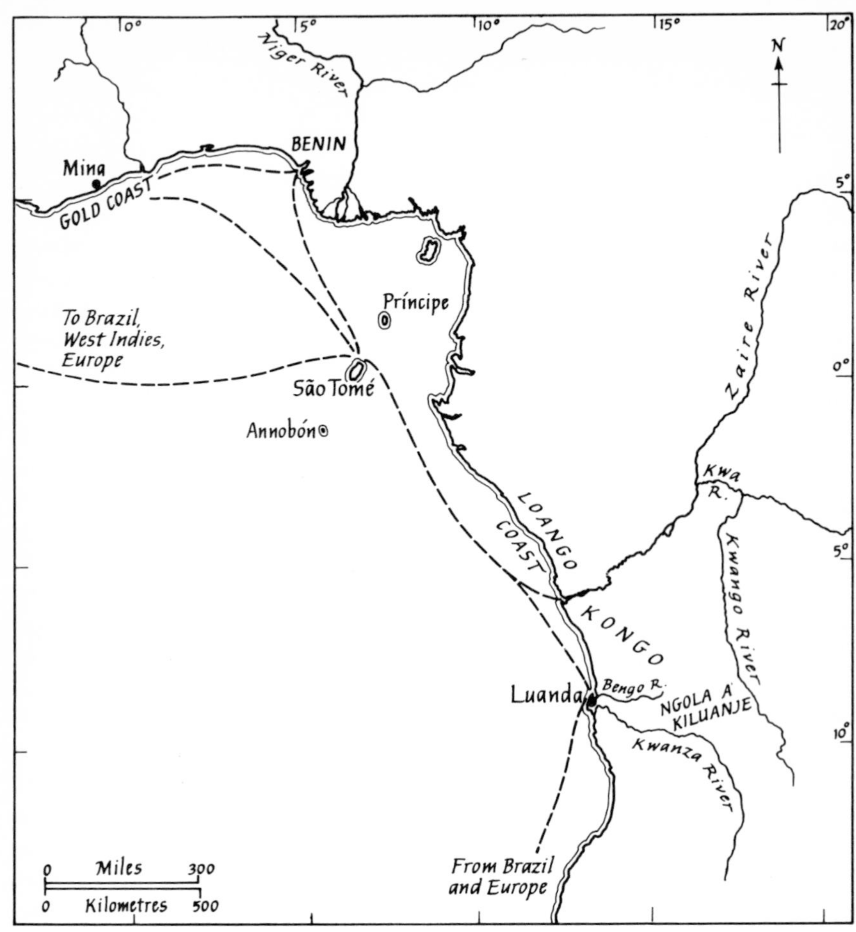

4:2 The Gulf of Guinea in the sixteenth century

arrival in Kongo, another Portuguese explorer, Vasco da Gama, redirected the attention of the monarchy to the riches of India and the East.[38] Kongo and adjoining regions thus remained a backwater of empire. They were eventually to be over-shadowed yet again by the sugar, the gold, the diamonds, the cotton and the coffee of 'the Brazils' in Portuguese America.

The also-rans who came to West-Central Africa – lower nobility, younger sons, foreign mission orders, merchants without capital and criminals – set a tone of commercial recklessness and ruthlessness that became hallmarks of the expanding Atlantic zone. The renegades who did well in Africa earned their modest successes by turning their backs on the

38 Boxer, *Portuguese Seaborne Empire*, pp. 39–64.

metropole that despised them. The Portuguese Crown and the established metropolitan bourgeoisie repeatedly failed to gain control over these Portuguese in Africa. The colonists meanwhile built connections through marriage and political influence at African courts, engaged in local forms of commerce and production, and employed local slave labour to enrich themselves. The institutions they created in Africa remained Portuguese in name, but they owed more to Africa than to Europe.

In the early sixteenth century, weak African–European contact resulted in an extension of mainland African influence to the coast and nearby islands, principally São Tomé and Príncipe in the Gulf of Guinea. In comparison, the extension of European influence to Africa was more limited. The Portuguese monarchy never widened its goals much beyond an initial fruitless search for precious metals, and the dominant tone of the European connection remained diplomatic and religious. A halting exchange of Kongo hostages and Portuguese royal emissaries initiated diplomatic relations in the 1490s. Portuguese kings followed this by sending missionaries, craftsmen, soldiers, artisans and diplomats. Trade was not significant, particularly after an early commerce in copper failed to attain significant proportions.[39]

The most important early commercial success linked Kongo with São Tomé and Príncipe. The two uninhabited equatorial islands were awarded by Portuguese kings to independently-minded captains, who settled them with slaves from the mainland. They soon pioneered a regional trading system that connected African markets around the Gulf of Guinea from Luanda to the Gold Coast by trading labour, cattle, salt and cloth.[40]

This early interest in slaves set lasting precedents. On the mainland it channelled the expansion of the Atlantic zone through the rulers of the segmentary African states. The first slaves came from the great African lords with whom the Portuguese had established diplomatic contact, the kings of Benin near the lower Niger and of Kongo in West-Central Africa. Such kings were in strong positions to benefit from the trade. They not only held a formal monopoly over dealings with foreigners but also controlled the circulation of labour in their domains. Slaves from the royal African courts, particularly Kongo after Benin shut down its slave market in 1516, propelled São Tomé into a sugar boom that lasted until the opening of new sugar regions in Brazil in the 1570s. Sugar made wealthy landed planters in São Tomé out of the lowly Portuguese immigrants. Some became influential in African society, marrying into the Kongo nobility[41] or serving as mercenaries for Kongo kings. Their children grew

39 For the 'old Kongo kingdom', in addition to Wilson, 'Kongo Kingdom', see W. G. L. Randles, *L'Ancien Royaume du Congo des origines à la fin du XIXe siècle*, Paris, 1968.

40 Robert Garfield, 'A History of São Tomé Island, 1470–1655', Ph.D. thesis, Northwestern University, 1971.

41 Thornton, 'Early Kongo-Portuguese relations', 191–2. On Benin, A. F. C. Ryder, *Benin and the Europeans, 1485–1897*, New York, 1969, pp. 24–75.

up to create the first creole community of Euro-African culture and descent in West-Central Africa.

In 1526 João III of Portugal attempted to reassert personal command over the sugar revenues of São Tomé by terminating the captaincy system and appointing a royal governor. He also reined in the Euro-Africans of both São Tomé and Kongo. The Euro-African planters of the island countered by establishing a new slave-buying station at Luanda,[42] and their complex commercial circuits continued to thrive between the 1520s and the 1570s. They sold sugar to Portuguese merchants at São Tomé for European textiles, metalwares, wine and beads, which they distributed through Kongo markets. They also traded in African products from north of the Zaire, in salt and *nzimbu* shells from Luanda, and in cattle and other goods from the south coasts.[43] Meanwhile, the royal factors in Kongo pursued the distinct metropolitan search for Christian allies, precious metals, and taxes payable on the local commerce in slaves.

Royal authority returned again to the Gulf of Guinea only in the 1560s and 1570s, when Dutch pressures restricted Portugal's interests in the East and when gold dust from Mina diminished. The Crown intensified its search for new mineral riches, both to the gold-fields of Mutapa and to mythical silver mines near the Kwanza. The royal initiative on the mainland arrived in the person of another weak contestant whose proposed civilising mission turned out to establish precedents of violence and destruction. Portugal's crusading king Sebastião authorised an impecunious minor noble, Paulo Dias de Novaes, to lead the search for silver in the lands of the Mbundu. In a complex agreement, the Crown kept for itself only rights to all precious metals that might be found; it entrusted the souls of the people to the Jesuits. Resident African labour was allocated to Novaes to develop the country economically and recoup the cost of his undertaking. Both the Euro-African slavers and the Jesuits opposed the Novaes charter and forced limits on his privileges. The faltering Novaes then sought to recover his costs by direct military conquest. Insufficient backing from Lisbon and weakness relative to the established traders forced Novaes to resort to violence to retrieve his failing venture. Later venturers from the metropolis of an equally precarious financial standing, repeatedly resorted to violence, as had Novaes, in order to attempt to recover their losses.

42 On the early stages of Portuguese activities in and around Luanda: Beatrix Heintze, 'Das alte "Königreich Angola" und der Beginn des portugiesischen Engagements, 1500–1800', *Internationales Afrikaforum*, xii, 1, 1976, 67–74; 'The Portuguese in Angola, from the arrival of Diogo Cão until the end of the Atlantic slave trade', in *Formation of Angolan Society*, Heimer (ed.), forthcoming; 'Der portugiesisch-afrikanische Vasallenvertrag in Angola im 17. Jahrhundert', *Paideuma*, xxv, 1979, 195–223; 'Die portugiesische Besiedlungs- und Wirtschaftspolitik in Angola 1570–1607', *Portugiesische Forschungen der Görresgesellschaft* (Reihe I: Aufsätze zur Portugiesischen Kulturgeschichte), xvii, 1980, forthcoming.

43 David Birmingham, 'Early African trade in Angola and its hinterland', in *Pre-Colonial African Trade*, Richard Gray and David Birmingham (eds), London, 1970, pp. 163–73.

The outbreak of large-scale hostilities between Novaes and the main Mbundu kingdom of Ngola a Kiluanje occurred in 1579 and contributed to the establishment of a resident community of Euro-Africans at Luanda. The African forces initially drove the Portuguese out of the highlands and down to the tide-waters of the Kwanza and the Bengo. The desperate Novaes generated immediate revenues by awarding his followers grants of land along the river valleys. The Jesuits reaped the principal benefit from these awards and formed an ecclesiastical, landed establishment. Other associates of Novaes became a local landed gentry, whose autonomy and prosperity subsequently ran counter to the centralising intentions of the Crown.[44] The Novaes land grants thus extended to the mainland the contest between Portuguese centralising tendencies and local slave merchants and landowners. Their struggle became a permanent feature of Portuguese society in the Atlantic zone.

Two contending, loose alliances had thus formed within the Portuguese sphere. A community of Euro-Africans, descended from São Tomé planter families, Portuguese immigrants in Kongo, and Novaes's henchmen, was centred on Luanda. They often made common cause with Jesuits, who shared their commitment to landholding, to local trade and to slaving by peaceful arrangements with African authorities. The rival faction consisted of recent immigrants with direct connections with Europe. These external interests, initially represented by Crown-appointed mercantile firms and officials, set out to expand the flow of slaves to Brazil and to increase the African market for manufactures. The mainland Euro-Africans put their slaves to work on local plantations and supplied captives to the sugar estates of São Tomé. They traded Kongo and Loango palm cloths, copper, cattle, shells and salt in exchange for people. The immigrant traders offered imported substitutes for these African products: Indian cottons, Portuguese wine, Brazilian sugar brandies (the infamous *agoardente* or fire-water) and northern European metalwares. The struggle between the two sets of traders repeatedly drove one party or the other to seek allies among nearby African powers. As they did so, they brought more African participants into the fray and enlarged the area of the Atlantic zone.

After the union of the Portuguese and Spanish thrones in 1580, violence east of Luanda grew with the arrival of new Spanish Habsburg officers. The Novaes privileges terminated with his death in 1589, and royal governors imposed direct control. These were military men, and they were unable to exert commercial control over the Euro-Africans and their African trading partners. Their weakness led them to favour armed conquest as a means of gaining access to the trade.

Metropolitan Portuguese merchants joined in the effort to restore direct European influence at Luanda at the end of the sixteenth century. The

44 Heintze, 'Portugiesische Besiedlungspolitik'.

Crown supported their trade in European and Asian wares, from which it gleaned tax revenues. In return, merchants obtained the privilege of selling their goods in Angola under royal contract. They also assumed responsibility for collecting the royal tax on slave exports. Since the Crown received only a pre-arranged, fixed amount from their receipts, the traders had every reason to increase the volume of slaving beyond that foreseen during negotiations over the contract price. These expansionary strategies led to abuses for which slave contractors became infamous. They introduced large quantities of foreign goods on credit, thereby creating a dependency of indebtedness. They also undertook military expeditions with African mercenaries whom they paid with imported wines and textiles.

The pre-eminence of immigrant firms and officials at Luanda continued to grow. The local creole families withdrew to the north and south, thus extending the dispersal established earlier when São Tomé people had fled royal officials in Kongo to settle at Luanda. Some Euro-Africans retreated from Luanda to Benguela, where they opened a slave market about 1615. Others fled to settle beyond the reach of Portuguese justice in the interior. There they continued the practice of marrying into African noble families. They often became locally powerful, particularly at Ambaca and Pungo Andongo east of Luanda and at Caconda in the central highlands. These Euro-African renegades bore Christian names, spoke a modest amount of Portuguese, and often appeared in government records as Portuguese subjects indistinguishable from new immigrants. In reality they formed a distinct, and in many ways very African, community.[45] In the nineteenth century these groups became well known as 'Ambakistas' in the Luanda hinterland and as 'Ovimbali' in Caconda.

Repeated metropolitan interventions over the next two centuries continued to drive the Euro-Africans to the inland fringes of the Atlantic zone. Portuguese merchants could consolidate their hold over only a small area near Luanda. In the 1640s the metropolitan initiative passed formally to the Dutch, who escalated their harassment of Portuguese holdings in Africa in order to seize Luanda and Benguela. Brazilian colonials intervened in 1648 and drove out the Dutch from the ports and restored nominal Portuguese rule.[46] They encouraged governors of the later seventeenth century to become bellicose raiders on behalf of Brazilian

45 For comparable developments in Mozambique, Allen Isaacman, *Mozambique: the Africanization of a European Institution – The Zambezi Prazos, 1750–1902*, Madison, Wisconsin, 1972; and for Upper Guinea, George E. Brooks, 'Luso-African Commerce and Settlement in the Gambia and Guinea-Bissau region', Boston University, African Studies Center Working Paper no. 24, 1980.

46 Birmingham, *Trade and Conflict*, pp. 104–13; Phyllis M. Martin, *The External Trade of the Loango Coast 1576–1870*, Oxford, 1972, pp. 33–72; Charles R. Boxer, *The Dutch Seaborne Empire, 1600–1800*, London, 1965, and *Salvador de Sá and the Struggle for Brazil and Angola 1602–1686*, London, 1952.

interests, which desperately needed Angolan slaves. However, the Brazilians lacked both the European goods of the Lisbon merchants and the local connections of the Euro-Africans, so they could not acquire slaves by peaceful means. Judicial officers and royal factors at Luanda favoured Lisbon merchants over Brazilians and Angolans, but even so the metropolitan merchant houses regained their influence only in the 1730s. The Brazilians then retreated to Benguela. The Euro-Africans co-operated with anyone they could, trading with Brazilian slavers at the southern seaport and smuggling in British and French imported goods all along the coast. Each European competitor tried to overcome the others with new infusions of commercial credit. These credits collectively contributed to the eastward extension of the Atlantic zone.

AFRICAN GAINS AND LOSSES

The infusion of new wealth from the Atlantic trade heightened competitive pressures within African societies, where people became involved with the religion, weapons, trade goods, and politics of the Portuguese factions. Recurrent drought and the contradictions of segmentary politics continued to cast people loose from their social moorings and to leave them exposed to capture or enslavement. However, foreign contacts accelerated political consolidation and change in the ideology of kingship in Kongo and among the Mbundu. Political violence flared from its normal endemic state into prolonged epidemics of warfare. With kidnapping and man-stealing, a sense of insecurity spread. Judicial systems incorporated new methods of generating slaves. Decisions to exchange people for imports or for political support from Europeans thus followed the rhythm of climatic and political change in Africa, as well as pulsations in the expansion of the Atlantic zone.

The pace of political consolidation quickened first in the kingdom of Kongo. The *mani* Kongo, like other rulers facing well-entrenched local aristocracies, exerted his personal power by dispersing enemies. In the 1480s, the king Nzinga a Nkuwu must have recognised in the arriving Portuguese several possible strengths that he might apply to consolidating his tenuous power. The Portuguese had no connections with his powerful domestic rivals, from whose ranks kings usually had to draw their followers. They brought with them prestige goods that a monarch could distribute to encourage loyalty from less wealthy relatives and appointees. In addition, the Christian cult promised to build bridges of shared religious faith across gulfs of regionalism and descent. Nzinga a Nkuwu thus converted briefly to Christianity in his initial *rapprochement* with the Portuguese, but soon he reverted to the local respect for royal ancestors, perhaps because of domestic opposition. He died in 1506 without having fully exploited the potential of the new alliance.

His son, Mbemba Nzinga, baptised as Afonso I, ruled from 1506 to 1543. He implemented more fully the partnership with the Portuguese. The value of the alliance was evident in the extraordinary length of his forty-year reign. He temporarily restrained the segmentary tendencies of the Kongo state and undertook major territorial expansion. He consolidated his hold on the royal title by excluding all collateral lines of royalty from future claims to the kingship. Effective use of Portuguese musketeers enabled him to clear the main commercial route up the lower Zaire of regional intermediaries. He made direct contact with Tio traders at Malebo Pool. By establishing Christianity as a pre-eminent royal cult, he freed himself from interference by the priests and councillors of local interests. All of these benefits he obtained by nurturing the diplomatic and mineral

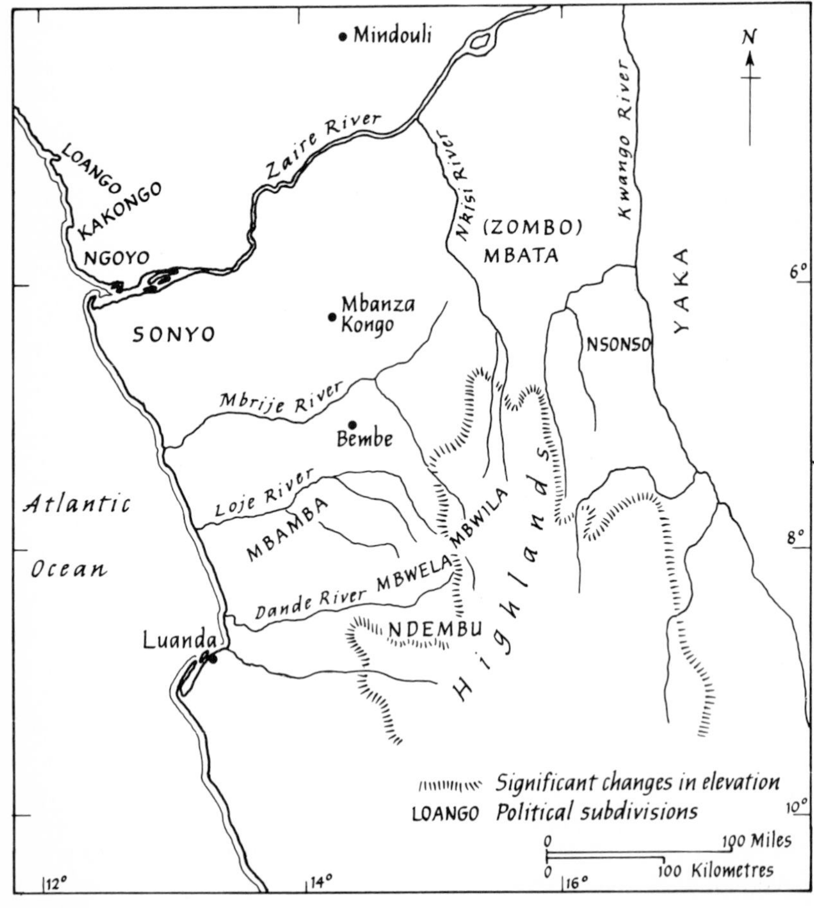

4:3 Kongo and adjoining regions
Source: Adapted from J. K. Thornton, 'The Kingdom of Kongo in the Era of the Civil Wars, 1641–1718', Ph.D. thesis, University of California, Los Angeles, 1979.

interests of the Portuguese monarchs in Europe. From them he obtained the priests, advisers, soldiers and goods that his policy of domestic centralisation required.

Afonso I strengthened his rule principally by freeing himself from obligations to the regional nobility. However, in the process he fell into a new dependency on unreliable, weak, distant and ill-informed support from beyond the sea. The new dependence later spread throughout the kingdom, as his domestic rivals sought to recover their eroded eminence with similar foreign support. The provincial nobility and minor royalty of Kongo fought back by enlisting willing allies among the Euro-Africans of São Tomé. In return, the São Tomé traders required slaves from Kongo. They could acquire only limited numbers from Afonso's wars of conquest and from his trade contacts with the interior basin of the Zaire. As foreign demand for slaves rose in the 1520s and 1530s, the São Tomé traders, in search of war captives, supported movements for regional autonomy. They purchased refugees from civil wars directly, without waiting for them to pass as tribute to the royal court and enrich the kings.

Afonso's centralising policies began to falter in the 1540s, when royal Portuguese support for the *mani* Kongo weakened. In 1543 he died. His royal faction had grown isolated from regional politics, even as increased slaving and direct trading to the coast strengthened western provincial lords in Sonyo and Mbamba. The scramble for Kongo slaves had spread kidnapping and pervasive unrest, and none of Afonso's immediate heirs could restore security or reaffirm the royal power. The period of dynastic instability came to an end only after 1568. In that year, an assault by mysterious cannibal 'Jagas' drove a new king, Alvaro I, and his court from *mbanza* Kongo.[47] A full-scale Portuguese military intervention, led by the governor of São Tomé and supported by island planters, restored Alvaro I to the Kongo monarchy in the early 1570s. Alvaro I ruled for nineteen years, and his successor, Alvaro II, from 1587 to 1614.[48]

The long reigns of these two *mani* Kongo indicated the effectiveness of the foreign military intervention that finally established monarchs friendly to the São Tomé slaving interests at the Kongo capital. The Kongo kings' power henceforth rested on Euro-African trade, and foreigners became the key to the delicate balance of domestic power in the kingdom.

47 On this vexed question, see Jan Vansina, 'The foundation of the kingdom of Kasanje', *JAH*, iv, 3, 1963, 355–74; David Birmingham, 'The date and significance of the Imbangala invasion of Angola', *JAH*, vi, 2, 1965, 143–52; Jan Vansina, 'More on the invasions of Kongo and Angola by the Jaga and the Lunda', *JAH*, vii, 3, 1966, 421–29; Joseph C. Miller, 'Requiem for the "Jaga"', *Cahiers d'études africaines*, xiii, 1, 1973, 121–49; John K. Thornton, 'A resurrection for the Jaga', *Cahiers d'études africaines*, xviii, 1–2, 1979, 223–27; Joseph C. Miller, 'Thanatopsis', *Cahiers d'études africaines*, xviii, 1–2, 1979, 229–31; Anne Wilson Hilton, 'The Jaga reconsidered', *JAH*, xxii, 2, 1981, 191–202.

48 For sixteenth-century Kongo generally, Wilson, 'Kongo Kingdom'. Compare Thornton, 'Kingdom of Kongo', and 'Early Kongo-Portuguese relations'.

Nevertheless, the ironies of such dependence became clear almost at once. The São Tomé traders settled with their Kongo protégés just when they lost economic power to Paulo Dias de Novaes and to the royal Portuguese interests at Luanda.

Slaving through Luanda, like that from Kongo, at first grew with increasing centralisation of Mbundu political power. One holder of the Mbundu *ngola* emblem of authority commanded trade routes and economic resources similar to those which had brought power and wealth to Kongo kings in the early sixteenth century. These Ngola a Kiluanje, or 'conquering Ngola', dominated the iron deposits above the lower Lukala river and controlled commercial routes that carried Kisama salt to interior plateaux. In the 1520s, forty years after establishing relations with Kongo, Portuguese emissaries made diplomatic contact with this Ngola. However, Lisbon deferred to Afonso I when the Kongo ruler insisted that they should approach the Ngola only through *mbanza* Kongo. The slavers of São Tomé

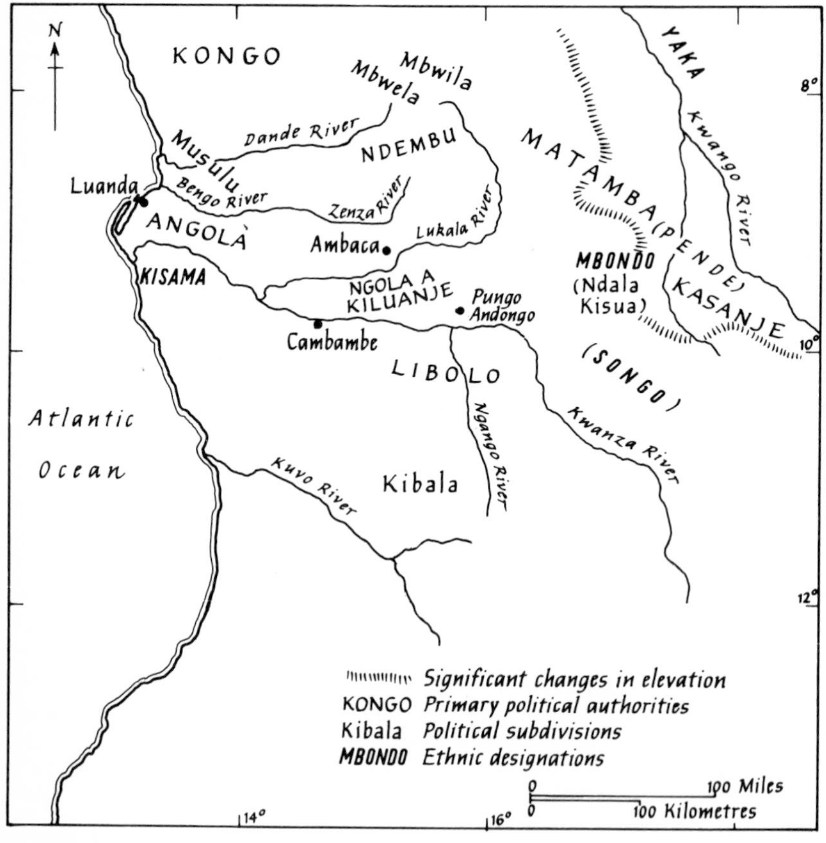

4:4 The Mbundu region

were thus left free to move into Mbundu lands.[49] With their support, the Mbundu kings mounted military conquests that brought Ngola armies to the southern borders of Kongo. They also overran parts of the populous middle Kwango valley and advanced south of the Kwanza. By the 1560s, the Ngola a Kiluanje had created a major Mbundu kingdom. The flow of captives probably intensified during a period of drought in the 1560s[50] and supplied thousands of hands to the São Tomé sugar estates. These slaves, and rumours of silver mines in the vicinity, attracted the attention of the Crown in Portugal.

Paulo Dias de Novaes arrived in the 1560s to negotiate a greater measure of metropolitan participation in this trade. The Mbundu kings may have faced regional tensions in their greatly enlarged domain and initially welcomed the Portuguese support. However, the provincial parties prevailed and sent armies to defeat Novaes in 1579. The victorious Mbundu rebels then proceeded to sell captives to the São Tomé slavers for a full generation, mostly on their own terms.

As warfare and slaving spread among the Mbundu, they generated resistance on all sides. In particular, they gave birth to bands of refugees who undermined the Ngola kingdom. Chieftains leading dangerous bands of warriors appeared in about the last third of the sixteenth century. *Ndembu* lords held out in the mountains between Kongo and Mbundu. The *ndala kisua* lords consolidated a defensive Mbondo polity on the cliffs above the middle Kwango. Previously uncentralised Ngangela near the upper Kwanza defended themselves by taking up a warrior cult centred on a political title of Lunda origin, '*kinguri*', borrowed from the east.[51] Other great lords took up positions on defensible rocky outcrops bordering the central highlands.[52]

With tensions rising, failure of the rains in this drought-prone region could only accelerate widespread disorder. The rains failed frequently in the last third of the sixteenth century.[53] Bands of cannibal marauders usually known as Imbangala, but called 'Jaga' by the Portuguese, ravaged the lower valleys and the coast south of the Kwanza. Their total disdain for agriculture, their anthropophagy and their assaults on better-watered land all suggested that they were fugitives from hunger in the highlands. Their mobile bands of predators were organised militarily to a degree that made them virtually invincible to either African or Portuguese armies. In 1611, one band of Imbangala formed a temporary alliance with the Portuguese

49 See Heintze essays cited in fn. 42 above. Also Miller, *Kings and Kinsmen*, pp. 73–86, and 'Formation and transformation'.
50 Miller, 'Significance of drought, disease, and famine', 20, 33–4.
51 Miller, *Kings and Kinsmen*, pp. 128–75; compare 'Formation and transformation', 'Central and southern Angola' and 'Significance of drought, disease, and famine', 25–8.
52 Miller, 'Central and southern Angola'. See also Beatrix Heintze, 'Wer war der "König von Banguela"?' in *In Memoriam Jorge Dias*, Lisbon, 1974, pp. 185–202.
53 Miller, 'Significance of drought, disease, and famine', 34–40.

governor. He and his successors in Luanda found them effective allies against the Ngola a Kiluanje and used them as mercenaries to strengthen royal control of the Luanda slave-trade at the expense of the Euro-Africans. Renewed drought in 1614–1615 swelled Imbangala ranks with desperate men who helped the Portuguese to devastate the Ngola state. They also dealt a blow to Kongo military power. By 1619, the drought had grown so severe and the destruction so extensive that even the Imbangala lords abandoned the coastal waste-lands and retreated to the oasis of the middle Kwango. Behind them they left a flow of some 10 000 captives a year directed toward the ships of their allies, the Portuguese royal governors. The São Tomé slave-trade had meanwhile declined, leaving the Euro-African slavers on Luanda island with only the trade in Kongo raffia cloths and the agriculture of the coastal valleys.

The final crisis for the Ngola a Kiluanje kings came with still another recurrence of drought in the 1620s. The new, determined and able royal governor, Fernão de Sousa, lacking his predecessors' alliance with the vanished Imbangala, struck a bargain with the palace entourage of slaves and clients around the Ngola's court. These courtiers formed the core of royal power in any African segmentary state. They had become a strong and coherent factor in the politics of the Ngola kingdom during two generations of military victories. However, the preceding decade of defeat and drought must have discredited them. Some of them were willing to accept external support from the Portuguese in the early 1620s.

In a gesture doubtless well-established by precedent, the court faction dispatched a woman as emissary and potential wife to seal the pending arrangement with the Portuguese governor.[54] This woman was the talented and ambitious Nzinga, a slave-born half-sister of the last Ngola a Kiluanje.[55] She plotted a palace *coup* with the slave faction by arranging the death of the legitimate heir-apparent to the Ngola title. She proved unable, however, to consolidate her control over the regional parties beyond the royal capital. Fernão de Sousa then turned to collaboration with a faction of the legitimate Mbundu royalty and nobility. Nzinga took the side of the Imbangala. These young warriors, impatient with agriculture and old lineage politicians, were again resurgent during another drought, that of 1626–1628. Nzinga and her Imbangala allies fought the Portuguese expeditions sent to restore the line of impotent Ngola kings at the core of

54 For this tendency generally: George E. Brooks, 'The *Signares* of Saint-Louis and Gorée; women entrepreneurs in eighteenth-century Senegal', in *Women in Africa: Studies in Social and Economic Change*, Nancy J. Hafkin and Edna G. Bay (eds), Stanford, Ca., 1976, pp. 19–44; Robert Stein, *The French Slave Trade in the Eighteenth Century: an Old Regime Business*, Madison, Wisconsin, 1979, p. 123. For Angola, Joseph C. Miller, *Way of Death: the Angolan Slave Trade, 1730–1830*, in preparation; Thornton, 'Early Kongo-Portuguese relations', 191–2.

55 Joseph C. Miller, 'Nzinga of Matamba in a new perspective', *JAH*, xvi, 2, 1975, 201–16; compare 'Formation and transformation'.

the dissolving kingdom. These Portuguese armies created the military zone between the lower Kwanza and the Dande that became known as Angola.[56]

The small area of Portuguese military government east of Luanda became the centre of the expanded slave-trade.[57] After 1630, growing involvement with the Atlantic zone enabled local lords to create centralised states modelled on the kingdoms of Kongo and Ngola a Kiluanje. Refugees from their assaults regrouped around war leaders for protection and went on the offensive as one means of maintaining a stout defence. The mid-seventeenth century thus saw two sorts of African slaving kingdom arise on the periphery of the Portuguese zone of conquest. In the northern refugee zones *ndembu* lords resisted, sometimes successfully, military sweeps in search of slaves. Repeated Portuguese attacks defeated the more exposed groups south of the Kwanza. In the better-populated areas, Imbangala-style leaders imposed themselves as lords who organised resident farming populations. The two most successful of these leaders consolidated their authority over the populous middle Kwango valley. Nzinga claimed the area of Matamba in the north-west, and Imbangala lords created a state to the south later called Kasanje.

Once settled in the Kwango valley, both immigrant political élites faced the classic dilemma of central rulers in segmentary states as they sought to come to terms with long-established regional nobles and lineage communities. Nzinga postponed the day of reckoning by reviving her still-born alliance with the Portuguese in 1655. Christian missionaries and European traders at her court helped her to control Matamba until her death in 1663. The Imbangala in Kasanje drove out the old Pende chiefs and then recruited support from the remaining local descent groups by opening the royal title to candidates from their ranks. They also accepted refugees from Nzinga's more exclusive régime in Matamba and welcomed other fleeing Imbangala leaders. They distributed noble titles to co-operative members of all these groups and established a succession system in which the central title rotated among all of them. Only in the 1650s did the Kasanje kings accept foreign slavers as allies. Thereafter they became a major source of slaves for governors at Luanda for nearly two centuries.

Consolidation of Matamba under Nzinga and of Kasanje under the Imbangala advanced slaving beyond the Kwango. The armies of the two states also fought each other for dominance within the valley in the later seventeenth century. Local slaving and warfare continued in Kasanje on the occasion of succession struggles for the royal title, but kings increasingly acquired more slaves from the Lunda and others in the east. The regional lords in Matamba restored a similarly segmentary polity in 1680 at the

56 Heintze, 'Portugiesisch-afrikanische Vasallenvertrag'.
57 Birmingham, *Trade and Conflict*, pp. 113–32.

expense of Nzinga's chosen heirs. They expelled Portuguese merchants and directed slaves north-west to the *ndembu* rather than to Luanda. Incumbent kings in both mature Kwango valley states owed their power to the sale of slaves, but they faced constant challenges from regional nobles heading

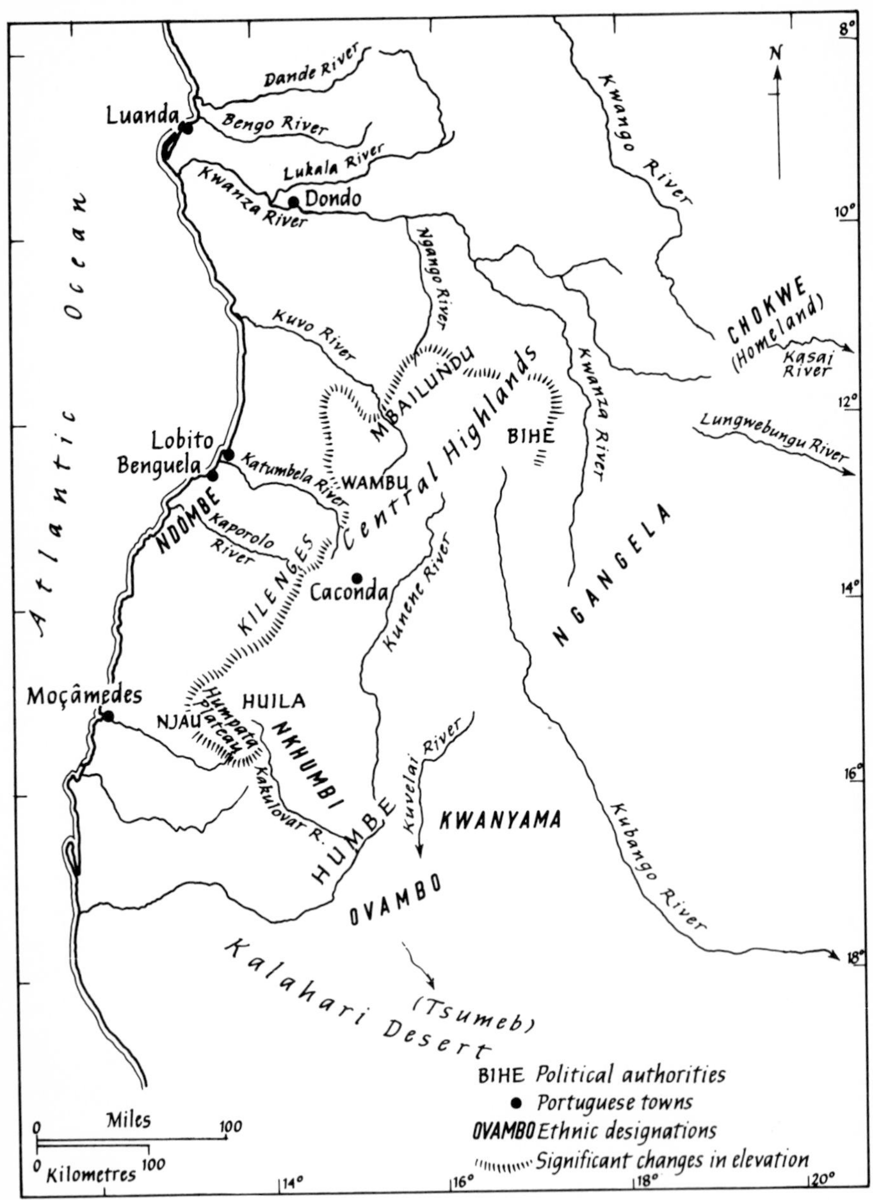

4:5 Central and southern Angola

alliances of kinsmen. Their wars pushed eastward the Atlantic zone, by this time indistinguishable from the zone of slaving.[58]

The Atlantic zone also advanced eastward from a second port at Benguela. From there Euro-Africans, joined by an assortment of immigrant renegades from Lisbon and Luanda, often settled on the higher elevations leading to the interior plateau. They married into the emerging élites of neighbouring African states, surrounded themselves with retinues of slaves and became commercial brokers. Slave-raiding soon drew these Euro-African traders eastward to the upper Kunene. Royal officials at Luanda exercised no effective control over Benguela, let alone over the highlands to the east. A pathetically weak garrison was stationed at Caconda, but it had no impact on the highlands beyond. Warfare spread over the central plateau during the 1720s and 1730s, as farmers regrouped for defence under the warlords of Wambu, Mbailundu and other kingdoms. During some forty years of internecine warfare these lords raided one another's followers for captives. The losers were sold for firearms and other imports, which preserved the power of the victors. The plateau population entered the Atlantic zone directly at the stage of civil wars, without ever passing through the preliminary centralising phase evident in Kongo and among the Mbundu. Only in times of severe drought did the highland kings unite temporarily to attack Portuguese trading posts and coastal valleys.[59]

In the seventeenth century Kongo kings attempted to stem the drift toward decentralisation that followed the spread of slaving, but fragmentation had already proceeded too far to be reversed. São Tomé merchants extended the Atlantic zone eastward to slave markets and centres of palm-cloth production in the lower Kwango valley.[60] A rival palm-cloth market developed in the south-western Kongo province of Mbamba, giving the local lords there influence as kingmakers at *mbanza* Kongo. In the 1620s the rise of uncrowned rulers in Mbamba marked the first step in consolidating the long-term fragmentation of real political power in Kongo. Later monarchs at *mbanza* Kongo and its Christian see, São Salvador, reigned more as high priests of a royal Christian cult than as the powerful kings of old. Politically they became creatures of great provincial slaving lords. The rulers of Mbamba and of a half-dozen other ancient provinces effectively reasserted their autonomy. They vied incessantly with one another, selling slaves they captured in civil wars and competing to install protégés at the Christian cult centre. The dukes of Sonyo province became particularly rich and powerful in the 1630s and 1640s after Dutch buyers of Kongo slaves arrived along the Zaire banks of their domain. Thereafter Sonyo rulers might participate occasionally in

58 Miller, 'Formation and transformation'.
59 Miller, 'Central and southern Angola'.
60 Wilson, 'Kongo Kingdom', pp. 121–53.

Kongo royal politics, but in fact they became virtually autonomous rulers of a distinct eighteenth-century Sonyo state.

The idea of the old Kongo kingdom died hard. The greatest of the seventeenth-century *mani* Kongo, Garcia II (1641–61) and Antonio I (1661–5), tried courageously to restore the real power of their predecessors. Christianity became closely associated with the lost greatness of the kingdom. Both kings attempted to stem growing intrusions from the Portuguese government at Luanda over the economy and over the Christian cult at the heart of Kongo royal legitimacy. In 1665, their resistance overflowed into open hostilities that culminated in a mortal confrontation at the *ndembu* stronghold at Mbwila. The grandeur of the ancient kingdom erupted in a last, crusading quest for salvation. The *mani* Kongo, Antonio I, and his principal lieutenants all perished. With them fell the lingering illusion that Kongo monarchs could again exercise real power.[61]

Antonio's defeat at Mbwila confirmed the power of the regional slaving lords. The two most powerful *ndembu* redoubts, Mbwila and Mbwela, commanded much of southern Kongo and controlled the Kwango commercial routes along which slave caravans passed. The most important consolidation of regional political power occurred further east, when Yaka on the farther bank of the Kwango began receiving slaves from sources as far inland as the Lunda and selling them to the Kongo. In the north the Mbata people in the Nkisi valley also developed as specialist slave-buyers and -sellers. Under the new ethnic name of Zombo they, too, spread their commercial contacts beyond the Kwango.[62]

Three broker principalities along the Loango coast north of the Zaire estuary also drew slaves from the Kongo region after the mid-seventeenth century. The restoration of Portuguese authority at Luanda in 1648 forced the Dutch to concentrate their purchasing of African captives in the north. Loango supplied their demand by direct commercial contact with the Tio plateau and the Zaire basin. The two southerly states of Kakongo and Ngoyo looked across the Zaire valley to Kongo for their sources of slaves. When English and French slavers joined the Dutch in the eighteenth century, the Vili of Loango extended their trading diaspora south through Kongo to Mbwila. On the coast small launches picked up slaves at bays and estuaries virtually within range of the Portuguese cannon at Luanda. Small Kongo merchant principalities emerged as brokers on each trading beach. Slaves came directly west from the commercial focal points of the interior

61 Thornton, 'Kingdom of Kongo'; compare Anne Hilton, 'Political and social change in the kingdom of Kongo to the late nineteenth century', in *Formation of Angolan Society*, Heimer (ed.), forthcoming. Also on the important late-seventeenth-century Christian revival of the Kongo state ideal known as Antonianism, António Custódio Gonçalves, *La Symbolisation politique; le 'prophétisme' kongo au XVIIIe siècle*, Munich, 1980.
62 Vansina, *Kingdoms of the Savanna*, pp. 203–7. See also Nicolăi, *Kwilu*; M. Plancquaert, *Les Yaka: essai d'histoire*, Brussels, 1971; Hilton, 'Political and social change'.

at Mbwila and Mbwela. Ngoyo became the principal outlet for the western Kongo slaving system centred on independent Sonyo.[63]

The growth of small broker states along the coast, the persistence of warlords in the mountains and central highlands and the consolidation of merchant princes in the populous regions completed a full cycle of revolution and warfare in the Atlantic zone by the end of the seventeenth century. The successive tiers of ports, polities and trading posts acquired a momentum of their own, beyond their ultimate dependence on trade with the world economy. In port towns from Loango to Benguela, life virtually revolved around huge ships that disgorged imports and took on slaves. Euro-African planters and military commanders in the hinterland of such ports employed slaves to grow provisions for the towns. They also imposed a heavy-handed military rule on surrounding homesteads. Their Euro-African kinfolk ranged eastward in a thinning net of trading settlements, supported by occasional military reconnaissance missions whenever trails came under attack from bandits or rebellious lords. Older kings of the population centres, who based their rule on agricultural tribute and regional trade in locally-produced goods, fell to military challengers who surrounded themselves with slave retinues and sold captives to Atlantic-oriented trading partners.

The nature of African political power had thus changed. This great transformation tended to follow a single, characteristic pattern. Initial contact linked foreign slavers to established African kings with small numbers of people to sell. Luxury goods for royal courts were exchanged for the modest numbers of slaves obtainable through existing institutions of coercion. When demand for slaves soared, it exacerbated segmentary conflicts in these partially centralised African political structures. Dynasties turned to violent foreign conquest to save themselves and for a generation or so pursued political centralisation, but war became endemic as regional lords rose up to defend their ancient privileges. Refugees fled to seek protection in warlord states that in turn threatened the old kingdoms and themselves became committed to further slaving. If drought intervened to intensify these struggles, major polities could succumb to famine and banditry. Local depopulation, exhaustion and social disintegration finally brought the conflicts to an end. The lords of the most favoured areas, such as the Kwango valley, then set about repopulating their domains by brokering the trade in slaves from new, inland war zones to the Atlantic coast. The western populations thus restored themselves by importing women and raising their offspring. Their commerce with foreigners flourished as never before under the guidance of the new centralising merchant princes.

63 Martin, *External Trade*, pp. 73–135, and 'The making of Cabindan society, seventeenth to nineteenth centuries', in *Formation of Angolan Society*, Heimer (ed.), forthcoming; Miller, *Way of Death*.

For the time being, small Ngangela lineage communities survived almost untouched by warrior lords beyond the Kwango and the upper Kunene. To the south, slave-trading had also hardly reached the Ovambo and other peoples of the lower Kunene. For ordinary farmers and herders in those regions of the far interior, life continued largely unaffected by the Atlantic zone. Failure of the rains created a few slaves from the waves of refugees seeking food in times of famine. A few of these poor folk fell into the hands of minor notables, who sold them to visiting traders from far in the west. These local notables received prestige goods in return and strengthened the marginal power they were able to exercise over their neighbours. Few of them could have anticipated the long-range consequences already evident nearer the coast of the apparently innocent bargain they had struck.

EIGHTEENTH-CENTURY EXPANSION OF THE ATLANTIC ZONE

In the eighteenth century, an ever larger demand for African slave labour beyond the Atlantic drove the trading frontier deeper into the interior. New Portuguese merchants introduced an unprecedented quantity of cheap goods at Luanda. At the same time, agents of British and then French industrialists dispersed slaving from the few major arteries of Luanda, Benguela and Loango to a whole series of small capillaries along the coast. These traders threw the Euro-African community at Luanda into a century-long crisis. Their plentiful financial resources also overheated the seventeenth-century African political systems in the Kwango valley, on the Loango coast and across the central highlands. In many areas new groups seized the commercial initiative in a century-long repetition of the earlier dissolution of centralised power in the west. This revolution once again increased slave exports from the economies of the new societies.

At Luanda, huge ships from Lisbon unleashed a flood of wares on credit which factors principally offered to poorer and weaker people in and around the port in the 1730s. These ruffians – immigrant sailors, political exiles and criminals rusticated from Portugal – were neither integrated into the established 'peaceful' trading system of the Euro-Africans nor into the mercantile aristocracies of African kingdoms. Their new role helped to further the commercial and political revolutions under way. Lisbon merchants at Luanda hid behind the privileges of the royal slave contract to consolidate their position. The slave contract gave tax farmers priority under the bankruptcy laws of the empire in collecting debts on imported goods. The contractors manipulated these powers like a vice to squeeze Euro-African traders who failed to repay debts on the huge credits awarded to them. The cheap European and Asian textiles spread widely through the interior and became the major eighteenth-century trade currency of the

Atlantic zone, replacing palm cloths and salt previously controlled by the Euro-Africans.

At Benguela, the influx of new wealth came indirectly through Rio de Janeiro rather than directly from Lisbon. As a result, it continued to flow through the hands of the resident Euro-Africans rather than immigrant Portuguese. The Brazilian connection supported Benguela's efforts to increase its administrative autonomy from metropolitan-dominated Luanda. The Brazilians principally offered the cheap *agoardente* that 'lubricated' trading transactions along the coast. These arrangements expanded the officially taxed slave-trade from Benguela from minor proportions until it nearly equalled the flow from Luanda in the 1780s and 1790s.

Slaving increased elsewhere south of Luanda even faster than the spectacular rise of legal exports from Benguela. The French became major buyers all along the south-west African coast after 1763. They were regarded as smugglers by Luanda officials and traders bent on defending Lisbon interests, but they violated the ineffective Portuguese trading monopoly with impunity. The French developed new sources of slaves, particularly from the northern slopes of the central highlands, at the mouth of the Kuvo and in the far south at the Kunene estuary. They enjoyed particular success along the Loango coast, where their African trading partners spoke fluent French by the 1780s.[64]

Within the politics of the Portuguese colony, metropolitan traders again clashed with resident Euro-Africans between 1730 and 1790. The conflict was especially bitter due to the helplessness of Lisbon firms faced with northern European competition. The metropolitan immigrants in Luanda found themselves caught between low-cost French and British goods on the one hand and Euro-African trading expertise on the other.

The local creoles manipulated their connections with middle-level military, ecclesiastical and administrative institutions of the colony to harass the outsiders. The Euro-Africans were particularly strong throughout the interior, where immigrants direct from Europe died with predictable frequency. They held a critical grip on the provisioning of food and water for slave cargoes. They charged high prices for filthy Bengo river water, monopolised supplies of foodstuffs during droughts, obstructed the boarding of the ships with bureaucratic requirements and generally raised the costs of slaving for their metropolitan competitors. The

64 Joseph C. Miller, 'The slave trade in Congo and Angola,' in *The African Diaspora: Interpretive Essays*, Martin L. Kilson and Robert I. Rotberg (eds), Cambridge, Mass., 1976, pp. 75–113; 'Some aspects of the commercial organization of slaving at Luanda, Angola – 1760–1830', in *The Uncommon Market: Essays in the Economic History of the Atlantic Slave Trade*, Henry A. Gemery and Jan S. Hogendorn (eds), New York, 1979, pp. 77–106; 'Portuguese slaving from Angola – some preliminary indications of volume and direction, 1760–1830', *Revue française d'histoire d'outre-mer*, lxii, 1–2, 1975, 135–76; *Way of Death*.

tragedy of these delaying tactics was the death of starving, sick and weakened slaves awaiting embarkation.[65]

The metropolitan slavers fought back against the Euro-Africans by using their superior financial resources. They repeated the old tricks of slave contractors in loaning goods and then foreclosing on debts not repaid by unlucky borrowers. They also transferred the risk of slave mortality to colonials by forcing them to retain ownership of slaves through the peak stages of slave mortality on interior trails, in Luanda and on the Middle Passage. A general economic depression in Brazil after 1760 lowered the prices which Euro-Africans received for their slaves. It was thus Euro-Africans, not the Lisbon merchants, who suffered the loss from slave deaths.[66] A succession of strong governors – in particular, Governor Francisco Innocencio de Sousa Coutinho from 1764 to 1772 – supported the metropolitan firms. Sousa Coutinho attempted to throttle the Euro-African inland trade and condemned their flourishing coastal culture. He expelled the Jesuits with whom they worked closely. He also favoured ships from Lisbon at the expense of those from Brazil and added political and administrative pressures to the economic hardships the Euro-Africans were then suffering.[67]

The resulting economic hardships worked their way down through the layers of merchants to rest finally on the shoulders of ordinary Africans trapped in the zone of military administration east of Luanda. Euro-Africans in the colonial army used their arbitrary power to recover their rising costs by exploiting local slaves and conscripting free Africans. They carried on barely-veiled robbery in the name of tax-collecting. Others manipulated the local salt currency to combat the imported textile moneys, at the expense of African consumers. Euro-African smuggling to the British and French partially relieved the pressure, but many Africans still fled Portuguese Angola. The hard times thus finally contributed to yet another eastward extension of the Atlantic zone. The hard-pressed Euro-African traders sought new sources of low-cost slaves beyond the Kwanza and Kunene, through the violent slaving revolution building up among the Ngangela.

A simultaneous revolution in European military technology made cheaper and more plentiful fire-arms widely available in the early eighteenth century.[68] The flood of new arms contributed to decentralisation in the African states nearest the Portuguese territories. The well-

65 Miller, 'Some aspects of commercial organization', 91–4; *Way of Death.*

66 Joseph C. Miller, 'Mortality in the Atlantic slave trade: statistical evidence on causality', *Journal of Interdisciplinary History*, xi, 3, 1981, 385–423; also *Way of Death.*

67 Ralph Delgado, 'O governo de Sousa Coutinho em Angola', *Studia*, vi, 1960, 19–56; vii, 1961, 49–86; x, 1962, 7–47.

68 W. A. Richards, 'The import of firearms into West Africa in the eighteenth century', *JAH*, xxi, 1, 1980, 43–60.

established kings of Kasanje (see Map 4:1) remained attached to the governors and metropolitan merchants at Luanda, whose economic interests they represented. They consequently suffered from intermittent official Portuguese efforts to restrict the sale of powder and guns. However, fire-arms reached the middle Kwango through the Vili trade with the British and French at Loango. The weapons passed into the hands of regional lords in Kasanje as well as to the Luanda-oriented kings. Wars, almost certainly linked to the influx of guns in the 1720s and 1730s, disturbed the middle Kwango valley in the 1740s.[69] In the following decade, provincial nobles at the head of lineage coalitions seized control of the Kasanje kingship from the court factions, which were descended from the original Imbangala founders.[70]

The warlords of the central highlands suffered a similar decline in the later eighteenth century. In the 1730s they had waxed powerful as English and French traders introduced fire-arms along the coasts south of the Kwanza. Mbailundu, the largest plateau kingdom, dealt with the French at the Kuvo in complete disregard for Portuguese claims to control trade. The jealousy of Lisbon merchants eventually provoked military intervention from Luanda in the early 1770s.[71] This Portuguese expedition, probably the largest of the eighteenth century, displaced the old warrior lords on the central plateau and installed merchant princes willing to sell slaves to the Portuguese in Wambu and other highland states near Caconda. The long-term beneficiaries, however, were the Benguela Euro-Africans. In the 1760s, they had opened a major trade route across the fertile and populous watershed toward new sources of slaves beyond the upper Kwanza. This trading frontier reached the upper Zambezi before the end of the eighteenth century. Along the route, a new dynasty of merchant princes arose in the eastern highland kingdom of Bihe. By the 1780s, the Wambu and Bihe nobility were intermarrying with Euro-African trading families and accepting nominal Christianity and alien advisers at their courts.

The commercial expansion of highland Euro-Africans only peripherally touched the southern population centres in Humbe and the Humpata plateau. Local polities there retained considerable autonomy, owing to their independent access to the Atlantic zone. French trading up the Kunene left the remote Humbe political institutions relatively unaffected. However, Huila passed into its phase of dissolution with the boom of French slaving in the 1770s and 1780s at the bay later named Moçâmedes.

69 Birmingham, *Trade and Conflict*, pp. 139, 142–5.
70 On eighteenth-century Kasanje: Miller, 'Formation and transformation'; Jean-Luc Vellut, 'Le royaume de Cassange et les réseaux africaines', *Cahiers d'études africaines*, xv, 1, 1975, 117–35, and 'Relations internationales du Moyen-Kwango et de l'Angola dans le deuxième moitié du XVIIIe siècle', *Etudes d'histoire africaine*, i, 1970, 75–135.
71 On this campaign, especially Elias Alexandre da Silva Correa, *História de Angola*, Lisbon, 1937, 2 vols., vol. 2, pp. 47–68.

One minor western noble on the Humpata plateau broke away on the strength of his direct contacts with the French and became a powerful lord known as Njau. The lords of Njau overshadowed the older Huila kings by the 1790s.[72]

Recurrent drought contributed to the surge in Benguela slave exports in the late eighteenth century. The most severe rainfall shortage of the entire century, a ten-year dearth between about 1785 and 1794, forced starving people into the hands of those with food, who then sold them as captives. Intensified slaving based on ecological crisis had long-term multiplier effects. Famished and weakened slaves who left under such circumstances died in much greater numbers than people taken in better times.[73] American efforts to replace those who died kept demand in the New World higher than if healthier and hardier labourers had been shipped.

The revolutionary sequence of political change that recurred in the expanding Atlantic zone caused the slaving frontier to roll eastward like a wave. Behind the wave, merchant princes accumulated slaves from the disturbed areas. They also took others in tribute from their own population by less overtly violent means. The process started on the coast in the mid-sixteenth century, crossed the Kwango and upper Kwanza in the eighteenth century, and reached the innermost parts of Central Africa in the late nineteenth century.

Slaves coming from Central Africa thus varied in the circumstances of their enslavement. Some were swept up ahead of the wave, and others were dragged along behind its advancing crest of violence. East of the frontier, drought, judicial condemnation and political conflict in segmentary kingdoms produced slaves, but with less serious demographic consequences. Where the wave of violence crested and broke, slaves came in growing numbers from territorial conquests on the edges of centralising monarchies. Capture, exile and flight caused temporary local depopulation. Civil strife reduced the areas of safety and compressed survivors into communities of refugees. Border raids, wars of conquest, and civil strife on the slaving frontier disturbed only the limited regions in the frontier zone. The slaving frontier moved sufficiently rapidly over the centuries to restrict its maximum violence in any single region to little more than a generation or two.

The violent advance of the slaving frontier of the Atlantic zone condemned many people to capture and sale, but the restoration of a tense peace in its wake sent no fewer poor and hungry people to the Americas. Most slaves in the area of capitalist credit originated from innumerable small incidents of kidnapping, personal betrayal and financial crisis. Inability to repay debts became the new factor most distinctive of the

72 Miller, 'Central and Southern Angola'.
73 Miller, 'Legal Portuguese slaving'; 'Significance of drought, disease, and famine'.

Atlantic zone. By the late eighteenth century, infusions of European credit left many Africans with debts in trade goods that they could not cover. Men borrowed to buy additional wives, only to be forced later to sell their children.

It is far from certain that slave exports alone produced disastrous long-term demographic losses. Most export slaves were young males. Their departure left a fertile population numerically dominated by females in the age cohorts of greatest fertility. These women could have borne children at rates capable of replacing the people lost to slavery.[74] However, conditions worsened in other ways for those who remained behind. Survivors driven into cramped, defensible sites strained the capacity of battle-torn lands to support them. Such artificial shortages of land exacerbated the hardships of drought and enlarged the number of hungry refugees vulnerable to capture and sale. Captors might rationalise their enslavement as a last-ditch escape from death by starvation. The remaining population of slaving zones created extra people in order to survive and then came to survive by exporting its surplus members. If exports ceased, people had to devise alternative demographic strategies.

MATURATION OF THE ATLANTIC ZONE IN THE NINETEENTH CENTURY

The nineteenth century saw the Atlantic zone expand to the heart of Central Africa and then enter an era of population growth and ecological strain. The drain of slaves to the Americas regained its late eighteenth-century peak in the 1820s and in the 1840s and then dropped sharply and finally after 1850. Political and commercial systems based on slaving continued to generate captives, however. These became a reservoir of cheap slave labour for new patrons and owners within the Atlantic zone. African lords of the old mercantile trading states and Euro-Africans of the territories of the Portuguese conquest at first grew stronger from their control of these people. In the long run they had to admit defeat as new men challenged their power. Control of labour remained the crux of the struggle, even after slave exporting officially ended. Slaves remained the basis of wealth in Africa. The reality did not change when imperialism arrived, cloaked in a humanitarian crusade to end slave-trading. The ending of the Atlantic slave-trade transferred slavery from America back to Africa.

At the same time, a feverish export trade in commodities exhausted the commercially exploitable natural resources of West-Central Africa. Resource depletion and population pressure led to an economic and ecological crisis which coincided, at the end of the century, with European

74 On demography: John K. Thornton, 'Demography and history in the Kingdom of Kongo, 1550–1750', *JAH*, xviii, 4, 1977, 507–30, and 'The slave trade in eighteenth-century Angola', *Canadian Journal of African Studies*, xiv, 3, 1980, 417–27.

military conquest. Greater quantities of imported textiles and manufactures, particularly fire-arms, intensified the struggle between rich and poor, powerful and weak. The area of conflict extended into the equatorial forests and across the Zambezi by mid-century.

Early nineteenth-century changes in the patterns of trans-Atlantic slaving began the transition from exporting people to the Americas to retaining them as slaves in Africa. The regions from which most captives came shifted generally northward in the period between 1800 and 1850 to draw from the more populous, wetter savannas and the forest fringe. The old Brazilian slave-trade at Benguela declined gradually from the first decade of the century. However, a new group of British-backed Brazilian merchants carried on active slaving near Luanda through the 1840s. They also extended their operations north to the old English sources of captives near the mouth of the Zaire river and along the Loango coast. Simultaneously, the British government in London expanded its famous campaign to restrict the Atlantic slave-trade to the seas south of the Equator. They forced the Brazilians to outlaw maritime slaving in an empty gesture in 1830 and brought subsequent illegal slaving to an effective end just after 1850. Meanwhile, British suppliers of manufactured goods ventured directly to African shores north of Luanda to satisfy African consumer desires for cheap imports in return for such 'legitimate' exports as vegetable oils, dye-stuffs, ivory, wax, exotic woods and feathers.[75]

The merchants of metropolitan Portugal, having failed to establish their economic sway in Angola during the eighteenth century, found themselves on the sidelines for nearly forty years, from the Napoleonic wars of the 1790s through the Portuguese monarchy's exile in Brazil from 1808 to 1822. They lost not only to the British but also to the Euro-Africans of Angola. Between 1810 and 1870 the creoles enjoyed the most prosperous period in their history since the sixteenth century. Wealthy Luanda families supplied Brazilian slavers and invested their profits in slave retainers, in commercial networks, in bush trading posts and in a resplendent and distinctive style of living.[76] The thriving, illegal slave-trade could not be controlled by governors, and the Euro-Africans prospered from their continued freedom from metropolitan constraints. In the central highlands,

75 For the early nineteenth century, Manuel dos Anjos da Silva Rebelo, *Relações entre Angola e Brasil, 1808–1830*, Lisbon, 1970; Leslie M. Bethell, *The Abolition of the Brazilian Slave Trade: Britain, Brazil, and the Slave Trade Question, 1807–1860*, Cambridge, 1970; David Eltis, 'The Transatlantic Slave Trade, 1821–1843', Ph.D. thesis, University of Rochester, N.Y., 1978, esp. pp. 280–8.

76 Jill R. Dias, 'Changing patterns of power in the Luanda hinterland: the impact of trade and colonisation on the Mbundu, c. 1845–1920', in *Formation of Angolan Society*, Heimer (ed.), forthcoming; Douglas Wheeler, 'Portuguese in Angola, 1836–1891', Ph.D. thesis, Boston University, 1963; Douglas Wheeler and René Pélissier, *Angola*, London, 1970, pp. 51–108; W. G. Clarence-Smith, 'The political economy of Portuguese colonial expansion in Angola in the nineteenth and the early twentieth century', in *Formation of Angolan Society*, Heimer (ed.), forthcoming.

around the government outpost at Caconda and in the eastern kingdom of Bihe, their prosperity was based more on sales of wax and ivory than of slaves.

The Portuguese bourgeoisie, resurgent behind the new liberal government after 1825, mounted a campaign to regain access to Central African markets. Traders, shippers and bankers found themselves excluded from Brazil, which became independent from Portugal in 1822, and turned to consolidate their European ties with Britain. Their old-fashioned methods in trading, agriculture and industry prevented them from selling elsewhere in Europe. Instead, they followed in the steps of their ancestors and sailed for West-Central Africa in a renewed, faltering, but determined quest for tropical riches.[77] Tariff reforms favoured metropolitan wines at the expense of the familiar *agoardente*. The national assembly in Lisbon passed labour codes between 1834 and 1872 which limited Euro-African slaver control of African labour in the colony. They disguised the measures as liberal reform, but the forced labour systems they created were only a moderate improvement on the old system of slavery. The Euro-Africans continued to buy captives from beyond the Kwango as 'freed' or 'servant' workers until the twentieth century.[78]

The new credits from Europe flowed into the hands of ambitious African upstarts who once again seized the opportunity to make gains at the expense of the old nobilities and royalties. They brought yet another social and political revolution to the region in the second half of the nineteenth century. They built up slave followings and patron-client systems with their new wealth[79] and employed their retinues to produce new commodities for British legitimate trade. Others sent their dependents out as head-bearers in caravans that carried bulky wax and ivory westward in the 1840s and 1850s. After 1870, they added rubber to the inventory of commodities they collected and processed for shipment to the coast. Their new revolution carried one step further the tendency towards decentralisation already begun wherever the slaving cycle had passed.

The shift from slave exports to the employment of slaves occurred first in the central highlands. The decline of Benguela and its Brazilian slaving

77 Wheeler, 'Portuguese in Angola'; Richard Hammond, *Portugal and Africa, 1815–1910: a Study in Uneconomic Imperialism*, Stanford, Ca., 1966. Clarence-Smith, *Slaves, Peasants, and Capitalists*, p. 13, presents the metropolitan perspective, which dates the entry of major capital to the 1870s.

78 James Duffy, *A Question of Slavery: Labour Policies in Portuguese Africa and the British Protest, 1850–1920*, Oxford, 1967; for a slightly later period, Jill R. Dias, 'Black chiefs, white traders, and colonial policy near the Kwanza: Kabuku Kambilo and the Portuguese, 1873–1896', *JAH*, xvii, 2, 1976, 276–90; David Birmingham, 'The coffee barons of Cazengo', *JAH*, xix, 4, 1978, 523–38; W. Gervase Clarence-Smith, 'Slavery in coastal southern Angola, 1875–1913', *Journal of Southern African Studies*, ii, 2, 1976, 214–23, and *Slaves, Peasants and Capitalists*.

79 Joseph C. Miller, 'Slaves, slavers, and social change in nineteenth century Kasanje', in *Social Change in Angola*, Franz-Wilhelm Heimer (ed.), Munich, 1973, pp. 9–29.

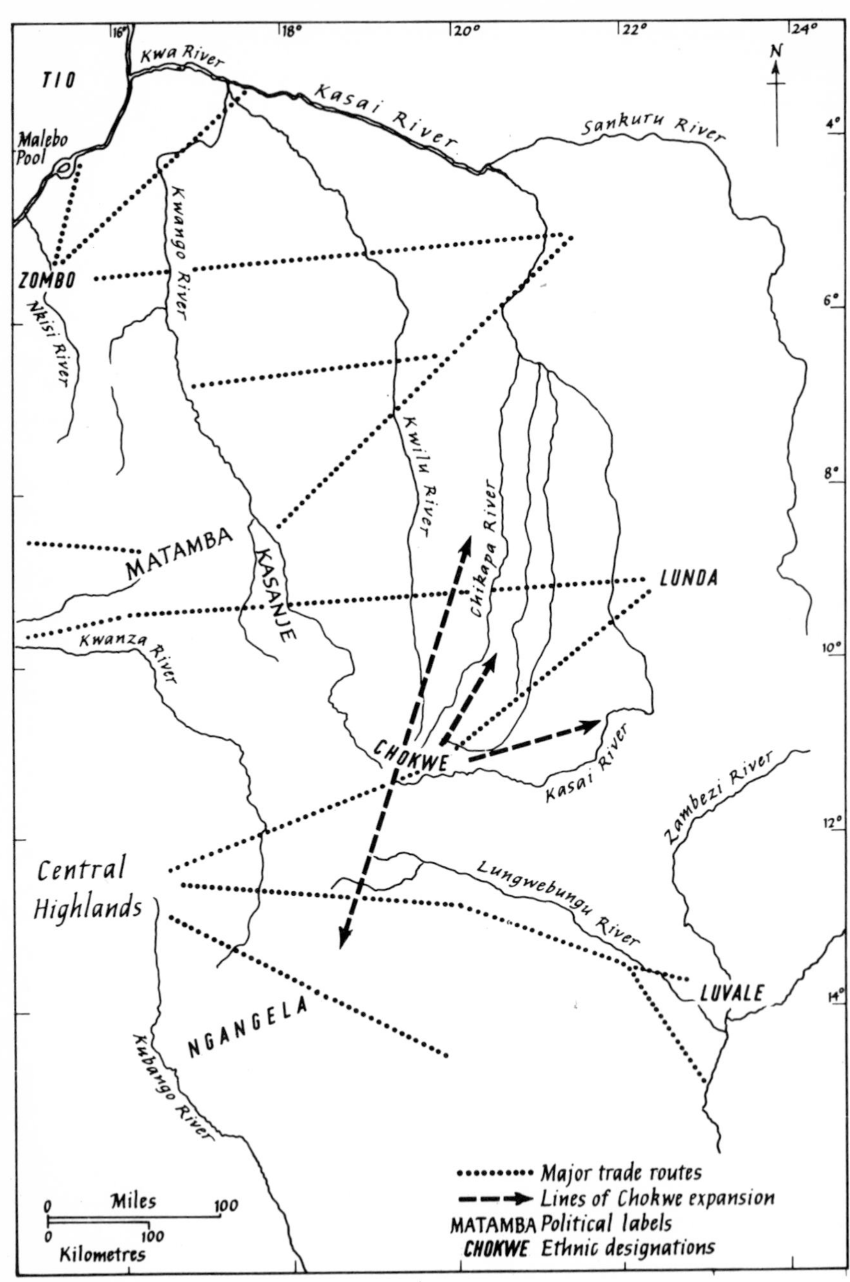

4:6 East of the Kwango and the Kwanza rivers, nineteenth century

encouraged the rise of a new generation of commoner merchants in place of the old trading aristocracies. Portuguese immigrants and residents of Euro-African descent also prospered. Together, they organised huge Ovimbundu caravans on the trans-Kwanza routes. Slaves for local employment, ivory, wax and a few captives for shipment to the coast flowed back to the west. When elephant herds dwindled and the ivory supply declined, the immigrant Portuguese retreated to the coast in the late 1870s. Local merchants were then left poised to prosper from the rubber boom that followed in the 1880s. The European immigrants who later flocked back to the plateau to take advantage of new opportunities found themselves in need of armed protection from the colonial government in Angola. The threat of military conquest thus loomed at the end of the nineteenth century.[80]

The new commercial system radiating from the central highlands reached the upper Zambezi flood plain and the heart of the Lunda empire beyond the Kasai river. It also brought wax and hides to the plateau from the southern agro-pastoralists.[81] A sharp rise in ivory prices during the 1830s further intensified the ivory trade in the eastern regions. By the 1840s, the kings and merchants of the central highlands had brought the full impact of the Atlantic zone to the sparse populations beyond the upper Kasai, where wax and elephants abounded.

In the mid-nineteenth century, a group of refugees whose ancestors had hidden from slaving in the forested hills at the source of the Kasai became important. These Chokwe applied their hunting and woodsmen's skills to producing wax and ivory for export. Restricting their imports to fire-arms, and spending little on unproductive ostentation, these hardy highlanders produced most of the wax and ivory exported through Benguela by the 1850s. They invested most of their profits in captive women bought from passing slave caravans. Within a generation, the Chokwe elders had put these women and their children to work processing raw wax into exportable cakes. Further profits brought more guns and more women under their control.

The Chokwe patrons kept their demographic and economic bubble growing for the remainder of the century. The severe drought of 1873–1876[82] drove many of them north down the river valleys. As they advanced they exploited fresh wax and ivory resources. Plentiful supplies

80 W. Gervase Clarence-Smith, 'Class formation in the central highlands of Angola, 1840s to 1910s', in *Formation of Angolan Society*, Heimer (ed.), forthcoming; Jean-Luc Vellut, 'Diversification de l'économie de cueillette: miel et cire dans les sociétés de la forêt claire d'Afrique centrale (c. 1750–1950)', *African Economic History*, vii, 1979, 93–112; Childs, *Kinship and Character*; Miller, 'Central and southern Angola'.

81 Clarence-Smith and Moorsom, 'Underdevelopment and Class formation', pp. 370–1; see also W. G. Clarence-Smith, 'The penetration of the capitalist mode of production in the agropastoral societies of southern Angola from 1844 to 1920', in *Formation of Angolan Society*, Heimer (ed.), forthcoming.

82 Dias, 'Famine and disease', 361, 368.

of female labour allowed them to dominate the rubber boom in the 1880s. The pursuit of creepers and bushes containing latex sap propelled Chokwe expansion to the Kalahari border by 1890. They absorbed most of the population from the Kwango to the Kubango and Kunene rivers through marriage and conquest.[83]

The Chokwe expansion was also a victory of rough frontiersmen over previously dominant Lunda lords with their highly urbane culture.[84] The Chokwe arrived in Lunda territory when political tensions within the empire were high. There the violent phase of slaving had pushed the state past its peak of centralisation into a period when wealthy regional lords fought over the Lunda royal title. The western Lunda contenders for power found themselves on the path of the advancing Chokwe. They saw their chance to benefit from the ivory and wax boom by enlisting Chokwe to cull these commodities from the woodlands of their domains. These same lords then engaged proficient Chokwe warriors to promote their political cause in the Lunda succession struggles of the 1870s. They swept eastward to the very heartland of the empire. In the ensuing war the Lunda lost control of their mercenaries, and saw their imperial capital fall in 1886 to enormous caravans and armies of Chokwe. These attacks dissolved the Lunda empire in a series of events that bore some resemblance to the 'Jaga' invasion of Kongo in 1568 and to the Imbangala assaults on the Mbundu during the 1610s and 1620s.

Trading caravans from the western regions joined those of the Chokwe in the Lunda area. The immigrants became the major political and military force east of the upper Kunene and Kwanza for a full generation between about 1870 and 1900. The Chokwe, the merchant princes from the central highlands, traders from Kasanje, and others from the middle Kwango mounted trading and raiding parties a thousand muskets strong. Wives and children accompanied these slow-moving armies of occupation. Leaders functioned as both military commanders and commercial envoys seeking latex, wax, elephants and people. Their razzias led to the capture of slaves, whom they sent to their homelands.[85] Their military power represented the fruit of investment in slaves and guns after trans-Atlantic slave exports had ended in the early 1850s. The terms of trade in the world economy had moved temporarily in Africa's favour to permit such accumulation.[86]

83 Joseph C. Miller, 'Cokwe trade and conquest', in *Pre-Colonial African Trade*, Gray and Birmingham (eds), pp. 175–201; J. J. Hoover, 'The Seduction of Ruwej', pp. 303–16; Edouard Ndua (Solol Kanampumb), 'L'Installation des tutshokwé dans l'empire Lunda, 1850–1903', Mémoire de licence, Université Lovanium, Kinshasa, 1971; Jean-Luc Vellut, 'Le Lunda et la frontière luso-africaine', *Etudes d'histoire africaine*, iii, 1972, 61–166.

84 Hoover, 'The Seduction of Ruwej'.

85 See also Robert J. Papstein, 'The historical evolution of the Societies of Eastern Angola, with special attention to the nineteenth century', in *Formation of Angolan Society*, Heimer (ed.), forthcoming.

86 A. G. Hopkins, *An Economic History of West Africa*, London, 1973, pp. 124–66; J. Forbes Munro, *Africa and the International Economy, 1800–1960*, London, 1976, pp. 64–86.

Eastern Kongo built up a similar prosperity by converting profits from export of forest products, ivory and rubber into slaves. The north-eastern Kongo, or Zombo, linked the thriving river trade of the lower Zaire and the Kwa to the ocean. North of the lower Zaire, the Vili and other Loango coast traders became contacts for plateau-dwellers who hauled exports overland to avoid expensive charges levied at the great market of Malebo Pool.[87]

The old royal tradition of central Kongo retained only a faded eminence and a much-altered Christian cult. Baptism, the right to burial in one of the ruined churches in São Salvador, investiture in the old medieval Portuguese Order of Christ, and other Christian rituals and customs marked the few people there who could claim ancient local roots in a land long since awash in a sea of foreign slaves. Descendants of sixteenth-century royalty clung to Christianity as a signal distinction not taken from them by the changing times. They thus fought over a powerless Christian kingship dominated by regional chiefs. The *mani* Kongo, hardly more than a chief priest, derived his modest revenues from conducting Christian rituals.[88]

The eclipse of the kings was widespread. The Kasanje central political title was disputed among great trading leaders of the kingdom in the 1840s. The people of the valley united to repel military intervention by Portuguese and Euro-African traders in the 1860s, but by the 1880s they were divided again into antagonistic commercial coalitions. Unable to cooperate to stave off greater external intrusions, they grew increasingly vulnerable to Portuguese military aggression.[89]

The high cost of dependence on imported fire-arms made even powerful rulers vulnerable in the nineteenth century. In the south, imported weapons threatened the security of the Kunene flood plain. Incessant Nama cattle-raiding, and a damaging Portuguese military expedition from 1859 to 1863, forced the Nkhumbi and Ovambo to arm themselves in self-defence. To do so, they sold increased amounts of ivory and hides in the 1860s and 1870s. By the 1880s, however, the herds of elephant had been decimated, and the Ovambo were left exposed to external threats from African and European neighbours alike. Lacking the means to replenish

87 Hilton, 'Political and social change'; Susan Herlin Broadhead, 'Trade and Politics on the Congo coast, 1770–1870', Ph.D. thesis, Boston University, 1971; Jan Vansina, *The Tio Kingdom of the Middle Congo 1880–1892*, Madison, Wisconsin, 1973, pp. 247–312, 445–51, and *The Children of Woot: a History of the Kuba Peoples*, Madison, 1978, pp. 186–95; Martin, 'Making of Cabindan society'.

88 Hilton, 'Political and social change'; Susan Broadhead, 'Beyond decline: the kingdom of the Kongo in the 18th and 19th centuries', *International Journal of African Historical Studies*, xii, 4, 1979, 615–50; Douglas Wheeler, 'A nineteenth-century African protest in Angola: Prince Nicolau of Kongo', *African Historical Studies*, i, 1, 1968, 40–59; François Bontinck, 'Notes complémentaires sur Dom Nicolau Agua Rosada e Sardonia', *African Historical Studies*, ii, 1, 1969, 101–19.

89 Miller, 'Slaves, slavers, and social change'; René Pélissier, *Les Guerres grises: résistance et révoltes en Angola (1856–1961)*, Orgeval, 1977, pp. 84–97.

their arsenals by direct sales of ivory to foreign merchants, they turned to raiding cattle and kidnapping people from the southern slopes of the agricultural highlands. These raids eventually escalated the conflict on both sides and imposed ever more expensive burdens on the Ovambo. At the same time, their aggressiveness inevitably invited retaliation from the newly-powerful European government of Angola.[90]

The intensified exploitation of ivory and rubber after 1850 planted the seeds of future collapse. The Chokwe advanced outward from their original home because they, like the Ovambo, had exterminated the diminishing herds of elephant. Rubber production grew in the 1880s on the basis of destructive techniques of gathering latex, as the creepers were cut down and the bushes uprooted without provision for regeneration or replacement. The advancing Chokwe typified the fragmented organisation of the Atlantic zone's export sector. Nearly everyone attempted to get into the game. Groups greater than a few neighbouring villages rarely united, and any single party which failed to extract the maximum available ivory or rubber in the shortest possible time would permanently lose the opportunity to others who would exercise no such restraint. The Chokwe and others had committed themselves to a spiralling expansion that would lead inevitably to economic disaster and political defeat.[91]

Ecological deterioration also loomed. The massive new slave population removed tree cover and exhausted fragile soils. It did not require much degradation to spell disaster in a region that had always proved sensitive to drought. Few could pursue the geographical expansion that had solved the Chokwe dilemma of overpopulation in the early 1870s. Climatic fluctuations threatened greater instability as the century wore on. Already in the 1870s, precariously balanced populations had to sell children as slaves to Europeans who had seized the fertile valleys of the coastal rivers.[92] Prolonged dryness would threaten famine and epidemics at the very time when military pressures from Europe intensified.

The pressure from Portuguese Angola on its African neighbours stemmed from the efforts of the metropolitan bourgeoisie to find the same African Eldorado that had eluded all their predecessors. Commercial interests from Lisbon and Porto had tried to seize the colonial economy from Euro-African slavers in the 1830s with their well-publicised campaign to 'end the slave-trade'. They wanted instead to plant cotton for the textile mills of Portugal. They also introduced sugar cane and coffee to replace their lost Brazil. Sugar production allowed Euro-African planters to distil a local variant of Brazilian *agoardente* and thus cut imports of

90 Clarence-Smith and Moorsom, 'Class formation'; Clarence-Smith, *Slaves, Peasants and Capitalists*, ch. 5.

91 Compare the later similar effects in the Congo, Robert W. Harms, 'The end of red rubber: a reassessment', *JAH*, xvi, 1, 1975, 73–88.

92 Dias, 'Famine and disease', 370.

Portuguese wines. Coffee and cotton also tended to fall into the hands of local African and Euro-African landowners and holders of slave labour, excluding metropolitan financial capital. A small colony of Portuguese, mostly loyalists from Pernambuco in Brazil, settled in the 1840s on the southern bay of Moçâmedes. Metropolitan planners wanted a beach-head to penetrate the arable Humpata plateau and exploit the Nkhumbi of the eastern rivers, but the settlers failed to make significant advances into the interior before the 1870s.[93] Metropolitan attempts to enter the Euro-African world of nineteenth-century Angola intensified in the 1870s with the world recession.[94] European creditors experienced an urgent need to collect the funds they had invested. It was the familiar situation of financial stringency in which earlier metropolitan Portuguese had repeatedly turned to armed intervention. On this occasion, new military technology and a weakened African population allowed the invasion to succeed.

CONCLUSION

Despite the diversity of experience in West-Central Africa, the single paradox of increased opportunity and intensified struggle runs through the rise of slaving and the shift to 'legitimate' trade. Kings pursued the quite conventional end of greater political centralisation. Regional lords fought back to retain the autonomy traditional in African segmentary states. The struggle touched nearly everyone. These developments interacted with underlying tendencies toward demographic growth. Population pressures contributed to violence and slaving, even as slaving maintained the fertility of a female-dominated population. Long-term pressure of people on the environment reached its critical stage in the late nineteenth century and early colonial period. Although the attendant deprivations were new in their intensity, they were very old in their precedents. Droughts and famines had afflicted West-Central Africans since the first farmers had settled near the Atlantic.

93 Clarence-Smith, *Slaves, Peasants and Capitalists*; Pélissier, *Guerres grises*, pp. 23–159; Dias, 'Changing patterns of power'.

94 W. G. Clarence-Smith, 'Mossamedes and its Hinterland, 1876–1915', Ph.D. thesis, University of London, 1975.

CHAPTER 5

The societies of the eastern savanna

THOMAS Q. REEFE

The vast eastern savanna and woodland zone of Central Africa lies between the rain-forest in the north and the Zambezi river in the south. It is bordered on the east by Lakes Tanganyika and Malawi and is open on the west towards the Kasai river. The zone divides naturally east and west along the Copperbelt and the Zaire–Zambezi watershed. The Zaire and its many tributaries flow north, whereas the Zambezi and its tributaries flow south and then east.

LANDSCAPE AND WATERSCAPE: PEDESTRIANS AND PADDLERS

Ecology has shaped history here. Water-flow and rainfall have influenced the course of human movement and settlement. Streams and rivers often serve as convenient landmarks in inter-village territorial disputes. They have marked the boundaries of expansion for both major and minor states. Wide, deep rivers and large lakes form natural barriers; land corridors have been important. Strong men, be they elders, warlords or kings, have fought for control of strategic fords and river crossings. The role of ferryman, of paddle and of dug-out canoe is almost as important in oral traditions as the role of warrior, of spear and of war-knife.

Streams are fed by an increasingly ungenerous rainfall as one travels from north-west to south-east. The moisture-laden air mass hovering over the Zaire basin moves south-east each year to start off the wet season. The rains begin in late August along the forest fringe and reach the middle Zambezi, over 1 300 kilometres away, a good three months later. Annual rainfall drops from an average of 150 centimetres or more in the north-west to below 70 centimetres on the middle Zambezi, and the reliability of rainfall declines on the same axis.[1] Regional droughts are a reality in the

1 *Atlas de la République du Zaïre*, Paris, 1978, pp. 15–19; Andrew D. Roberts, *A History of Zambia*, London, 1976, pp. 6–7.

south, and, as one drought-stricken group says, 'when the rain falls, God falls'.[2]

Farmers and fisherfolk, pedestrians and paddlers, have had to master or compromise with a harsh environment characterised by thin soils and scarce natural resources. A dominant reality has been the ability of peoples to manipulate and exploit the land and waterscape available to them. The Iron Age subsistence agriculturalists of the past 1 500 years have supplemented their diet of Sudanic cereals and Malayasian food crops with protein from game and fish. Since the second half of the seventeenth century New World food crops like maize, ground-nuts and cassava have been adopted. The rainfall axis is matched on the ground by a north-west to south-east ecological gradient. The mixed forest-savanna borderland gives way to an increasingly open grasslands environment interspersed with light woodland on the plains and more densely wooded areas along the banks of streams. Groups and individuals willing to move across this gradient have been able to enjoy a better life by exchanging the special products of one ecozone for the products of another.

The interaction between dense riverain and lakeside populations, and dispersed dry-land settlements, has been one of the basic dynamics of history in this part of Central Africa. The region's average population density has always been low; unreliable rainfall and rapid water run-off have done little to encourage the even settlement of savanna and woodland. By contrast, the fertile catchment basins and the shorelines of lakes, perennial streams and rivers have been oases attracting human population. Many of the streams flowing from the Zaire–Zambezi watershed pass through small, shallow depressions called *dambos*, which slowly release the waters of the rainy season. The marshes and pools or *dambos* serve as local sources of fish and game. Their thin strips of fertile, alluvial soils have supported small concentrations of agriculturalists for centuries.[3]

On a much grander scale, major rivers flow into large depressions and basins at widely separated locations. Extensive permanent swamps are found where drainage of floodwaters is not assured by topography. A rise of only a few feet in the water level of broad, shallow Lake Bangweulu can lead to the submersion of extended stretches of land for a decade or more. Agriculture is then restricted, food supplies diminish and famine can occur. This can be overcome only by migration or by increased bartering of foodstuffs from dry-land farmers.[4]

2 Edwin W. Smith and Andrew M. Dale, *The Ila-Speaking Peoples of Northern Rhodesia*, 1920, reprint ed., Hyde Park, N.Y., 1968, vol. 2, p. 204.

3 Swanzie Agnew, 'Environment and history: the Malawian setting', in *The Early History of Malawi*, B. Pachai (ed.), Evanston, Ill., 1972, p. 39 and n.9; Roberts, *History of Zambia*, pp. 7–8.

4 W. V. Brelsford, *Fishermen of the Bangweulu Swamps, a Study of the Fishing Activities of the Unga Tribe*, Rhodes-Livingstone Papers no. 25, Livingstone, Rhodes-Livingstone Institute, 1946, pp. 20–29, 117.

Elsewhere, man has been offered greater opportunities when a better balance is achieved between water trapment and drainage. There are major flood plains that first catch seasonal run-off and then gradually release the waters down-stream in an annual cycle. The flow and ebb of floodwaters can be matched by patterns of transhumance. Four basins have played a particularly important role in the past: the Upemba depression of the upper Zaire; the lower Luapula river at the south end of Lake Mweru; the flood plain of the upper Zambezi; and the flats of the middle Kafue. These flood plains have attracted substantial human settlement throughout the second millennium A.D. Visitors to the Upemba depression have been struck by its hospitable environment:

> all along the river and on the flooded plains are deposited sandy-clay alluvial soils which are enriched by decomposing papyrus or by floating

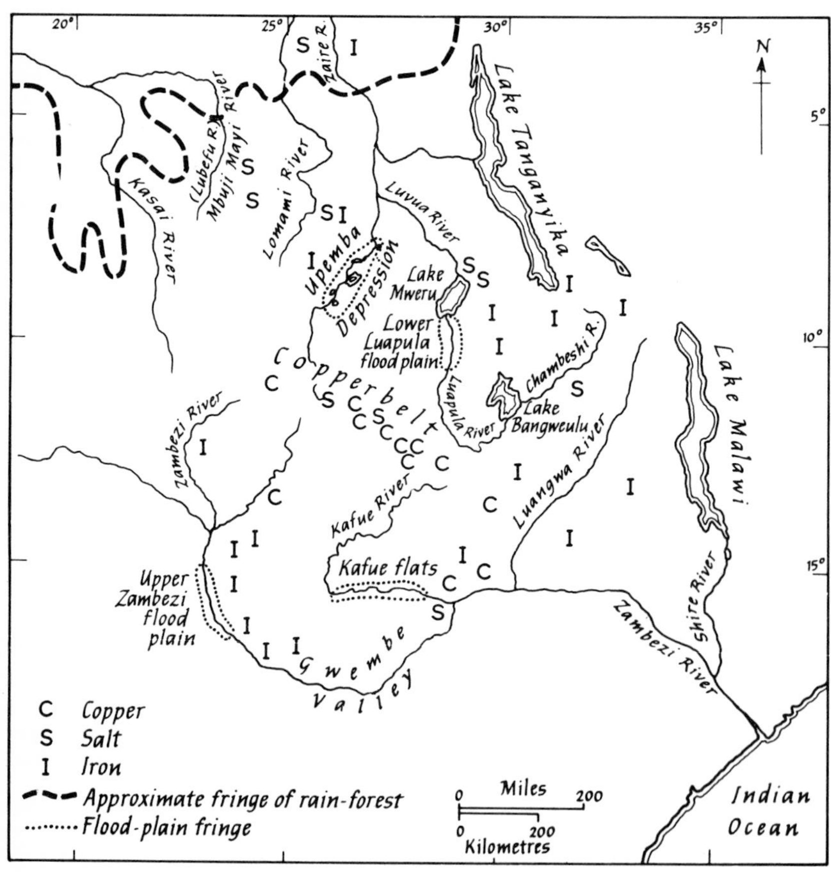

5:1 The eastern savanna: flood plains and natural resources

vegetable debris carried on the current. Along the river shore, these soils form a belt of varying width upon which villages are built and where people do their farming.

The earth is very rich, very light and excessively fertile, thanks to the silt left behind each year by the floods.[5]

All the rivers, lakes, plains, and swamps, as far as we can see, are just teeming with life. Animal, reptile, bird, fish, insect and human life all find their place, since water always attracts life. Elephants, letchwe and lions roam the plains; hippo's, croc's, and fish swarm the lakes and rivers; swamp bucks . . ., pythons and monkeys fill the marshes. Herons, cranes, ducks, storks, fish-eagles and hundreds of other birds of all descriptions and colours turn those waterways into a little paradise.[6]

The largest quantities of game on the plains, and the fish in the lakes, lagoons and marshes, have served as a source of protein both to be consumed locally and to be exported over long distances to hungry, dry-land farmers.

Flood-plain fishermen rather than savanna farmers may have been the first people forced to experiment with forms of social and political life which extended beyond the hamlet and village level. Dense populations had to compete for the few stretches of land not inundated during the annual flood; they staked out claims to the best dry land along the fringes of the basin. Competition had to be regulated lest it lead to violence and the disruption of life on the flood plain. Groups have had to be mobilised for public works projects, Central African style, to manipulate the flood. For centuries channels have been cleared and maintained through the morass of floating papyrus islands and vegetable debris in the Upemba depression so that people could then move in their dug-out canoes and successfully exploit their natural environment. In order to expose shore lines for agriculture, the water level of some lakes was controlled by dams. The right of fishermen to enter or leave lakes and lagoons through drainage channels was governed by hereditary channel priests and their political overlords.[7] Kingdoms have been centred on some flood plains, while the dense populations in other plains and river valleys have been the target of raids and conquests by large-scale dynastic states.

Centuries of slash-and-burn agriculture have altered the relationship between savanna and woodland in many areas. The tsetse fly, carrier of trypanosomiasis, animal sleeping sickness, has survived in shifting belts of

5 Havard Duclos, 'Monographie de la chefferie de Kikondja', *Terre Air Mer*, lix, 4, 1933, 268–9. Translation by the author.

6 E(dmund) Hodgson, *Fishing for Congo Fisher Folk*, London [1934], p. 13.

7 Verney L. Cameron, *Across Africa*, London, 1877, vol. 2, pp. 84–5; Emile Francqui and Jules Cornet, 'L'Exploration du Lualaba depuis ses sources jusqu'au Lac Kabele', *Le Mouvement géographique*, x, 24, 1893, 102; Thomas Q. Reefe, *The Rainbow and the Kings: History of the Luba Empire to 1891*, Berkeley and Los Angeles, 1981, pp. 68–71.

forest and undergrowth. This has limited pastoralism to well-defined fly-free zones in central and western Zambia; the areas of greatest cattle concentrations have been the upper Zambezi flood plain and the Kafue flats. Human experience is as much about constancy as it is about change, and the affection of a keeper for his cattle seems to be a universal feature of pastoralism. The cattle-keepers of the Kafue flats loved and valued their cattle,

> above all their possessions, above kith and kin, wife or child. ... It is stated that the origins of the practice of knocking out their front teeth was in order to resemble their cattle. Horns that hang down and swing, or that are otherwise distorted, excite high admiration, and an ox or cow is bought for its beautiful voice. Nor is their admiration merely verbal. The writers have known a large but ugly ox exchanged for one shapelier, though smaller. To render an admired beast still handsomer, it is decked with ruffs, necklaces, or bells. A high compliment to a friend or wife or lover is to name an animal after them, and it is considered an act of discourtesy to part with this particular beast.[8]

Central Africa is a region well-known for its plethora of ethnicities. Earlier views about the pre-colonial past of the eastern savanna have been shaped and misshaped by issues of contemporary ethnicity. The pre-colonial past is not, however, best explained as ethno-history. Ethnicity is a concept to be used with caution, for the nouns, nicknames and pejorative epithets by which groups identified one another constantly changed before the European conquest. Only in the late nineteenth century were people locked into formal ethnic identity and conflict by colonial agents. There is, however, another reason to reject ethnicity: it over-emphasises difference. A more striking historical feature has been the continuity and similarity of the cultural tradition that has prevailed for so long across this vast area of open savanna and woodland with its scattered population.

It is therefore wiser to identify peoples by geographical location, for they are known in relation to the land and the resources they used. The conventional names of pre-colonial states, which should not be confused with contemporary ethnicities, may be cautiously used in their political sense. Such caution may appear confusing to those who already know the history of savanna peoples through their present-day ethnic markers, but reference to the conventional ethnic terms will be found in the footnotes.

THE EASTERN SAVANNA, 1400–1700

One must travel a thousand miles either west or east from middle Africa to reach a sea coast, and written eyewitness descriptions of the peoples of the savanna and woodland date only from the late eighteenth century. It was

8 Smith and Dale, *Ila-Speaking Peoples*, vol. 1, pp. 127–8.

not until the nineteenth century that traders, explorers and missionaries regularly walked across the area. For history one must turn to stories of mythical origin which seem to describe an earlier period. These traditions and myths of genesis do present problems of analysis, however, and individual tales yield only an occasional, tantalising glimpse of what happened before about A.D. 1700. Archaeology has begun to help, but it is still difficult to establish a chronology for the eastern savanna before the beginning of the eighteenth century.

The most striking feature of the middle African past has been the persistence of small-scale polities. Life has been lived at the local level. Low population density and dependence on foot transport has preserved the primacy of hamlet clusters and villages. Even the recent history of such societies is difficult to unravel from oral tradition; where the small society has given way to centralising political rule, all history is lost. Traditions about chieftainship atrophy quickly to little more than lineage or clan genealogies. Although the agricultural population of the grasslands has been geographically stable since well before the fifteenth century, individuals and small groups have moved easily across the landscape, selectively borrowing ideas and institutions from neighbours and adapting them to local circumstance. This pattern of drift has led to the emergence of conflicting and diffuse migration legends. These, together with the history of cultural exchanges among close neighbours, give an unwarranted sense of movement to savanna history. If history is about change, it is also about that which endures, and widespread patterns of cultural continuity and homogeneity survive at the grassroots. Pervasive historical patterns show striking correlations between that which endured among small polities and village clusters and that which was created in the eighteenth and nineteenth centuries.

Widely-known proverbs are deeply embedded in cultural traditions. The wisdom they express is built upon ancient associations. 'A counsellorship is like an axe: among strangers one should take it out of its handle.' This proverb, which warns that you may demand deference at home, but should not stand on your dignity among strangers, emphasises that the axe has been an important symbol of political authority in the savanna.[9] Political symbols like ornamental axes and clapperless bells excavated by archaeologists demonstrate that savanna peoples did not lack for political leadership in this millennium.[10] On the other hand, there was

9 William F. P. Burton, 'Proverbs of the Baluba. Proverbes des Baluba', *Bulletin des juridictions indigènes du droit coutumier congolais*, xxiii, no.5, 1955, 129.

10 Pierre de Maret, 'Chronologie de l'Age du Fer dans la Dépression de l'Upemba en République du Zaïre', Ph.D. thesis, Free University of Brussels, 1977–8, vol. 2, pp. 347–50; de Maret, 'Sanga: new excavations, more data, and some related problems', *Journal of African History (JAH)*, xviii, 3, 1977, 333–4; Brian M. Fagan, D. W. Phillipson and S. G. H. Daniels, *Iron Age Cultures in Zambia (Dambwa, Ingombe Ilede and the Tonga)*, vol. 2, London, 1969, pp. 92–4.

great variety in leadership among elders and village strong men. No single, homogeneous political authority operated among widely separated groups. Although large-scale dynastic states evolved from older, local political patterns, they only began to draw neighbouring polities into their spheres in the eighteenth century. The older historical processes did not deal with kingdoms and empires. This negative point is worth emphasising because the received versions of savanna history dwell on ancient, and unproven, imperial tradition. Before 1700 the well-springs of change did not lie in political centralisation and expansion. They lay elsewhere.

The eastern savanna is the central section of a wide matrilineal belt of peoples extending south of the rain-forest. Matrilineal clans, identified by sacred animals, were important in the south-eastern savanna. These exogamous clans based on male residence dispersed rapidly to create a loose sense of belonging among widely separated settlements. As clan allegiances gave way to territorial ties, kinship systems changed. By the middle of the second millennium, people living between the Luapula river basin and Lake Malawi were organised into matrilineages which claimed ancestral rights to land.[11]

The management of inequality is an important theme in the history of the savanna. Matrilineal descent rules work against the accumulation of wealth and the concentration of authority in the hands of ambitious men. The fecundity of sisters and the productivity of their children had to be shared with their husbands. This equalising pressure was overcome, however, by the realities of savanna scarcities and by the necessity to compensate descent groups for serious social wrongs. Opportunities did arise for men to transcend matrilineal constraints and gain access to the labour of others without reciprocity. Pervasive practices of female 'pawnship' enabled men to enjoy rights to the labour and offspring of women outside the competitive channels which regulated behaviour between husband and brother-in-law.[12]

Pawnship and slavery evolved in a continuum of servile institutions. Ambitious men manipulated these institutions to create personal followings and new kinship groupings. The peoples of the Zambezi and Kafue valleys and adjacent plateaux developed complex systems of pawnship and slavery well before the long-distance slave-trade to the East African coast was introduced in the nineteenth century. The most common method of enslavement in this often parched land was the offering of an individual to a prosperous farmer during time of famine in exchange for

11 Roberts, *History of Zambia*, pp. 72–4; Jan Vansina, *Introduction à l'ethnographie du Congo*, Kinshasa [1967], pp. 191–3.

12 Mary Douglas, 'Matriliny and pawnship in Central Africa', *Africa*, xxxiv, 4, 1964, 301–13; Audrey I. Richards, 'Some types of family structure amongst the central Bantu', in *African Systems of Kinship and Marriage*, A. R. Radcliffe-Brown and Daryll Forde (eds), London, 1950, pp. 207–51.

food. Slaves served many important functions. In cases of disputed succession a respected slave might preserve continuity and centralisation in the descent group. Among the pastoralists of the Kafue flats, wealth produced by slaves was used to buy cattle. This enabled wealth to be accumulated and stored in cattle, and a prosperous cattle-owner became a strong man in the society, figuratively 'a bull'.[13] There was wide variety in the rights and obligations that existed between masters and slaves, but it would be naïve to overstate the humanity of the institution in the hierarchical societies of the savanna. Slaves were often targets for ritual murder and other abuses.[14]

Patrilineal descent is practised in two areas of the savanna. The peoples of the Tanganyika–Malawi corridor practise the patrilineal descent of their Tanzanian neighbours.[15] More important is a separate culture zone of patrilineal peoples in the upper Zaire valley.[16] Here, rules of matrilineal descent slowly gave way to those of patrilineal descent. This particular culture zone was characterised by patterns of intense, localised political experimentation and innovation. Strong men competed for power and attempted to perpetuate their rule through their children. After 1700 many peoples of this zone became incorporated into large-scale states. Despite the fundamental changes, many matrilineal vestiges remained to mark the important competitive realities which endured. For example, sister's sons and maternal uncles continued to mobilise supporters in royal succession disputes, although the candidates in both chiefships and kingships came from the royal male line.[17]

The hiving off of dissatisfied villagers, of disaffected lineage segments and of those seeking a more generous land- and water-scape was among the most common causes of human movement in middle Africa. It had major implications for change among the segmentary matrilineal societies of the savanna and woodland. Short-range migrations were most commonly directed toward zones with abundant natural resources and hospitable ecological environments. Despite the dispersed settlement pattern, there was no such thing as vacant territory, and land not under cultivation was claimed for hunting and gathering. Migrants and refugees wishing to settle beyond the sphere of their close kin had to conquer, or reach an

13 Robin J. Fielder, 'Economic spheres in pre-colonial Ila society, *African Social Research*, no. 28, 1979, 620–23, 629; Timothy I. Matthews, 'The Historical Tradition of the Peoples of the Gwembe Valley, Middle Zambezi', Ph.D. thesis, University of London, 1976, pp. 392–7.

14 *Ibid.*, p. 394, n.2.

15 Roberts, *History of Zambia*, p. 73.

16 George P. Murdock, *Africa, Its Peoples and Their Culture History*, New York, 1959, pp. 28, 272; Vansina, *Introduction à l'ethnographie du Congo*, pp. 165–7.

17 Stephen A. Lucas, 'L'Etat traditionnel Luba', *Problèmes sociaux congolais*, no. 79, 1967, 105; Jan Vansina, *The Children of Woot, a History of the Kuba Peoples*, Madison, Wisconsin, 1978, p. 101.

accommodation with, people already on the land.[18] The search for land provided leaders who possessed it with opportunities to increase their human capital by attracting refugees as settlers. The point is made in the oral lore of Mwanza, a small polity in the Upemba hills, which once allowed refugees to settle along the nearby shore of the upper Zaire river.

> The more powerful the stranger group, the more favourable were the terms it gained from its new hosts. Hence the good spirit between Nkulu (run-aways from the West), and the Mwanza people who give Nkulu refuge. The newcomers were nearly as numerous as the Mwanza folk among whom they found themselves, so that they demanded respect. Had they been fewer they would certainly have been regarded as slaves. Even at the most favourable estimate, the stigma rests on their name, though many generations have passed. 'You were runaways, we had to give you refuge. You are virtual slaves.'[19]

Conflict and competition over rights in land and water are part of the essence of village life. The task of minimising conflict, allocating resources and dealing with newcomers resulted in the pervasive influence of the earth priest. Although terms for earth priest vary among groups, it is most commonly translated as 'lord of the earth'. Savanna and woodland dwellers made no clear-cut distinction between the living and the dead, and the ancestors were believed to affect directly the fortunes of the living. Among many peoples of the upper Zaire river and its tributaries the earth priest was the leader of the lineage which founded the village on its lands. Earth priests propitiated the founding ancestral spirits to ensure the fertility of the land and the bounty of the hunt. Earth priests did little to control selection of field and garden sites on the open savanna where cultivable land was plentiful. Rather, they fulfilled well-defined regulatory roles where there was competition for specific territory and limited resources. In regions of plentiful rainfall, earth priests had few rain-making functions. Instead, they supervised the hereditary rights of lineage heads to regulate access to hunting land, to fishing streams and to wild fruit trees.[20] Among the often drought-stricken pastoralists of the Kafue valley, earth priests placated ancestral pool spirits before people could fish. Similar institutions existed

18 Argument adapted from Robin Horton, 'Stateless societies in the history of West Africa', in *History of West Africa*, vol. 1, edited by J. F. A. Ajayi and Michael Crowder, New York, 1972, pp. 93–6; see also N'Dua Solol Kanampumb, 'Histoire ancienne des populations Luba et Lunda du plateau du Haut-Lubilash, des origines au début du XXe siècle (Bena Nsamba, Inimpimin et Tuwudi)', Ph.D. thesis, National University of Zaire at Lubumbashi, 1978, vol. 1, pp. 92–127, 219–21.

19 William F. P. Burton, *Luba Religion and Magic in Custom and Belief*, Sciences Humaines no. 35, Tervuren, 1961, 63.

20 J. Jeffrey Hoover, 'The Seduction of Ruwej: Reconstructing Ruund History (The Nuclear Lunda; Zaire, Angola, Zambia)', Ph.D. thesis, Yale University, 1978, vol. 1, pp. 101–2; Thomas Q. Reefe, 'A History of the Luba Empire to c. 1885', Ph.D. thesis, University of California at Berkeley, 1975, pp. 124–6.

among fishing peoples of the Bangweulu swamps, where the 'lord of the weir', who was descended from the person who originally built the weir, determined which people could help him repair and maintain it and share in its fish catches.[21]

In some cases earth priests took on political functions to rule more effectively over a village or hamlet cluster. In other cases newcomers established their rule over a village, and the political pretensions of the earth priest were modified or suppressed. A 'lord of the people', a political chief, then came to dwell alongside the earth priest to represent the interests of the immigrants. The varieties of chieftainship in this part of middle Africa were often an expression of arrangements worked out between political chiefs and earth priests at a very local level. They were less often the result of migrants travelling long distances to impose their political culture upon subject populations. There are few signs of clear-cut, long-distance borrowing of political systems and inventories.[22] Tribute exchange was one of the essential lubricants of the political process. In order to garner tribute, political chiefs had to reach accommodations with earth priests who regulated access to the products of the land. These accommodations gave way to normalised relations expressed in ritual. In the patrilineal zone of the upper Zaire an earth priest often presented a political chief with sacred regalia during formal investiture ceremonies. It was also known for an earth priest to marry symbolically a political chief in special rites.[23] Much local history has been about the manipulation of lineage ideology by strong men, by 'bulls', and the transformation of these strong men into more permanent 'lords of the people'.

Other important processes have occurred at the intersection between local interests and more extensive religious patterns. This is the heart of Bantu Africa, and variety is the result of interplay from a common cultural baseline. For centuries people have believed in a High God who is a creator removed from the affairs of men. In the west, extending into Angola, the god is known as Nzambi or Nyambe. In the east he is known as Leza, and in the south-east as far as Mozambique he is known as M'Bona.[24] The commonly held faith in the supernatural power of ancestral spirits and of

21 Brelsford, *Fishermen of the Bangweulu Swamps*, p. 72; Smith and Dale, *Ila-Speaking Peoples*, vol. 1, pp. 388–9.

22 Hoover, 'Seduction of Ruwej', vol. 1, chaps 6–7; Thomas Q. Reefe, 'Traditions of genesis and the Luba diaspora', *History in Africa*, iv, 1977, 183–206.

23 Hoover, 'Seduction of Ruwej', vol. 1, pp. 103–4; Theodore Theuws, 'Outline of Luba culture', *Cahiers économiques et sociaux*, ii, 1, 1964, 9.

24 Merran McCulloch, *The Southern Lunda and Related Peoples (Northern Rhodesia, Belgian Congo, Angola)*, Ethnographic Survey of Africa, West Central Africa, Part I, London [1951], pp. 72–3; Roberts, *History of Zambia*, p. 73; J. M. Schoffeleers, 'Cult idioms and the dialectics of a region', in *Regional Cults*, R. P. Werbner (ed.), Association of Social Anthropologists Monograph 16, London, 1977, pp. 219–39; Ernest van Avermaet, *Dictionnaire Kiluba–Français*, Sciences de l'Homme, Linguistique vol. 7, Tervuren, 1954.

High Gods accounts for the clusters of similar cults found all the way from the rain-forest to the Zimbabwe plateau. It is difficult to draw lines between types of cult, for specialists often overlapped in function and penetrated one another's organisations. Ancestor cults, territorial cults and cults of afflictions were all-important to the life and death of savanna peoples. Shared faith in the supernatural power of a cult and its priests was often more likely to bring people together from widely scattered locations than was the ephemeral charisma or personal authority of a local 'lord of the people'.

For centuries peoples of the upper Zaire have journeyed to sacred pools, caves and groves where famous ancestral spirits dwelt in order to consult diviners and mediums about their human concerns.[25] Faith was renewable, even aggressively so, and the power of these spirits was believed to reach out and spontaneously possess an unwilling subject.

> This possession is quite an arbitrary affair on the part of the spirit. Frequently the one possessed strongly resents the intrusion, though he cannot throw it off. It may make him thin and weak, or even kill him. Cases are not uncommon where mediums have literally prophesied themselves to death.

Possession may have been a misfortune for the individual, but it was welcomed by the community.

> ... The rest of the village is delighted with these seizures. Natives look on from a respectful distance, remark with awe a 'vidye' has come to our village. We are blessed. Now we can consult with the spirit-world.[26]

In the south, cult priests and prophets were obsessed with a single issue: rain. The pattern of rainfall and water-flow and their failure often encouraged neighbours to meet and interact. The role of the rain-maker was important along the 230-mile Gwembe valley on the middle Zambezi. The valley peoples traded with, and were raided by, states to the south, and provided sanctuary to refugees. They did not themselves develop a tradition of strong political centralisation.[27] The meaningful spatial concept was the ritual territory of the rain-maker, not the tributary domain of the chief. Earth priests performed the necessary rites at local rain-shrines. Their limited political authority was an extension of their ritual authority. On the Gwembe alluvial flood plains failure of the flood was a serious matter, and portions of the dense riverine populations had to move to the

25 Burton, *Luba Religion and Magic*, 50–59; Van Avermaet, *Dictionnaire Kiluba–Français*.
26 Burton, *Luba Religion and Magic*, 51–2.
27 Chet S. Lancaster, 'Ethnic identity, history and "Tribe" in the middle Zambezi valley', *American Ethnologist*, i, 4, 1974, 712–13; T. I. Matthews, 'Portuguese, Chikunda, and peoples of the Gwembe valley: the impact of the 'lower Zambezi complex' on southern Zambia', *JAH*, xxii, 1, 1981, 25–26.

surrounding uplands and plateaux.[28] Under these circumstances prophets possessed by rain-spirits were a common phenomenon. The compound of a prophet became a cult centre which continued to attract the faithful from considerable distances long after his death. Cult priests and supplicants from the lower rainfall regions of the valley floor travelled up-hill to consult with, and seek inspiration at, famous cult centres along the northern escarpment where rainfall was more generous and reliable.[29] This traffic between cult centres brought the peoples of two ecological zones into intimate contact.

In regions where small-scale polities were created and consolidated, strong men had to compromise with the resident specialists at the cult centres of the deep religious substratum. Chiefs who ruled small village clusters in the hills west of Upemba received ritual symbols in exchange for payments and gifts. The mediums and diviners to whom the gifts were sent lived at the sacred pool of an ancestral spirit whose supernatural aura and power extended over their several political dominions.[30] A similar situation arose in the south-east, where the people of the Shire river valley believed in the High God called M'Bona. Local strong men competed with M'Bona cult priests for the allegiances of valley subjects. M'Bona was believed to control the rains, so that competition between priests and chiefs was most intense during periods of human desperation triggered off by prolonged droughts. In the sixteenth century a local warlord named Lundu succeeded in consolidating the small-scale polities of the Shire valley. Oral traditions say that during a time when the rains were withheld Lundu killed M'Bona in an epic struggle. In fact, Lundu executed M'Bona's cult priest and destroyed his cult centre in the hills above the valley. From other sources it is known that there was a generalised drought in this part of Africa in the 1560s, but despite its severity, the entire M'Bona cult could not be eradicated; it was too powerful. A compromise was finally arrived at in which M'Bona cult priests cooperated with Lundu and his successors and legitimised their rule. Oral traditions say that M'Bona's spirit did not allow the rains to return until Lundu had rebuilt M'Bona's cult centre in the valley where, not incidentally, Lundu's power was strongest.[31]

28 Matthews, 'Historical Tradition of the Peoples of the Gwembe Valley', pp. 24–31, 46–7; Thayer Scudder, *The Ecology of the Gwembe Tonga*, Kariba Studies, vol. 2, Manchester, 1962, pp. 111–29.
29 Richard P. Werbner, 'Introduction', in *Regional Cults*, Richard P. Werbner (ed.), pp. xvi–xvii.
30 Reefe, 'History of the Luba Empire', pp. 113–14; Reefe, *Rainbow and the Kings*, pp. 88–9; Theodore Theuws, *De Luba-Mens*, Sciences Humaines no. 38, Tervuren, 1962, pp. 221–32.
31 Matthew Schoffeleers, 'The history and political role of the M'Bona cult among the Mang'anja', in *The Historical Study of African Religion*, T. O. Ranger and I. N. Kimambo (eds), 1972; reprint, Berkeley and Los Angeles, 1976, pp. 73–9; J. B. Webster, 'Drought and Migration: the Lake Malawi Littoral as a Region of Refuge', in *Proceedings of the Symposium on Drought in Botswana*, Madalon T. Hinchey (ed.), The Botswana Society in collaboration with Clark University Press, 1978, p. 153.

Thus was the will of the High God shaped to the political needs of the warlord.

Trade had real vitality among the societies of the eastern savanna. Extensive regional trade in indigenous produce and prestige goods is one of the characteristics of the developed phase of the Later Iron Age in middle Africa. This trade grew out of an older system of inter-village exchanges that dates back to the Early Iron Age.[32] Subsidiary exchanges met specific local needs.[33] Durable goods like iron hoes and axes, salt blocks and copper ingots were common units of exchange. Their value in relation to other goods was based on local conditions of supply and demand. Short-falls could be made up through trade. Raw materials were imported to manufacture finished products. Populous flood plains and centres of natural resources became emporia which acted as magnets, drawing in goods from hundreds of kilometres away. Key links were established between flood-plain canoe paddlers and savanna pedestrians. Dried and smoked fish were usually the most important flood-plain export, and people would travel long distances to barter quantities of this tasty protein. Packets of dried fish were exchanged for iron tools, dug-out canoes, tough fibres for making nets and baskets, and other dry-land products.[34] Salt was an important exchange commodity. Villagers flocked to the pans near Lake Mweru and the Luvua river for salt, as there were few districts like this where blocks of cake salt could be obtained from distilled brine in sufficient quantity to meet the needs of savanna peoples.[35] Rarer still were districts where metal and salt could be produced side by side. The Copperbelt became a nexus of trade, because salt marshes and pans were interspersed among the copper diggings.[36]

Customs embedded in the fabric of societies west of the Upemba depression convey a sense of the cultural richness of the trading experience. Villagers travelled in informal bands of five to twenty people, carrying the raw material of their locality or the products of their artisans. Naturally, the

32 Brian M. Fagan, 'Early trade and raw materials in South Central Africa', in *Pre-Colonial African Trade, Essays on Trade in Central and Eastern Africa before 1900*, Richard Gray and David Birmingham (eds), London, 1970, pp. 24–38.

33 Fielder, 'Economic spheres in pre-colonial Ila society', 622; Marvin P. Miracle, 'Aboriginal trade among the Senga and Nsenga of Northern Rhodesia', *Ethnology*, i, 2, 1962, 212–22; Miracle, 'Plateau Tonga entrepreneurs in historical inter-regional trade', *Rhodes-Livingstone Journal*, no. 26, 1960, 34–47.

34 Brelsford, *Fisherman of the Bangweulu Swamps*, pp. 46–51, 117–22; Max Gluckman, 'The Lozi of Barotseland in North-Western Rhodesia', in *Seven Tribes of British Central Africa*, Elizabeth Colson and Max Gluckman (eds), 1951; reprint ed., Manchester, 1959, pp. 10–11.

35 Burton, *Luba Religion and Magic*, pp. 47, 76; R. J. Moore, 'Industry and trade on the shores of Lake Mweru', *Africa*, x, 2, 1937, 138–46; Georges Van Der Kerken, *Les Sociétés bantoues du Congo Belge et les problèmes de la politique indigène*, Brussels, 1920, pp. 21, 179, 317.

36 Fernand Grevisse, 'Salines et saliniers indigènes du Haut-Katanga', *Problèmes sociaux congolais*, 11, 1950, 7–85; Burkhart Waldecker, *Salines du Katanga, notamment de Mwanshya*, Collection de Mémoires, vol. 26, Lubumbashi, Centre d'Etudes des Problèmes Sociaux Indigènes, 1968, parts 2, 3.

counsel and protection of ancestral spirits was sought prior to departure and along the way. Nkambo Kayembe was a presiding protective spirit over the Luvua salt industry. Traders came to have such faith in his supernatural power that they evoked his spirit through ritual during periods of bartering at a salt market 500 miles away on the Lomami.[37] Travellers everywhere preferred not to journey at night. They gained extra moments of daylight with a special 'Holding Up the Sun' ceremony performed along the trail; three small termite mounds, of the type used to support a cooking pot, were placed in the fork of a tree to catch and hold the late afternoon sun.[38] Trading sometimes led to raiding, and travel was not without its risks. This was particularly true for those involved in the copper trade. People rejoiced when traders returned from a dangerous journey to the copper diggings in the Mutumba mountains at the western end of the Copperbelt. This rejoicing was ritually commemorated when a boy returned from the supernatural danger of the circumcision camp. The village chanted, 'He went to Mutumba! Rejoice! He returns.'[39]

The copper trade was a key indicator in a slow-changing political economy. Whereas iron was smelted and re-worked primarily into tools and weapons, copper was used almost exclusively as an ornamental or prestige good in Central Africa. Copper bracelets were used in the north as political insignia. The metal was wrapped around royal canes and drawn into fine, thin wire for ankle coils and the adornment of people of high social and political status. It was produced at malachite outcroppings on the Copperbelt and at scattered mines south of there. Small, delicate, H-shaped ingots 7 to 25 millimetres in length were the norm before 1700. In recent centuries smiths poured molten copper into rough, cross-shaped moulds, producing ingots of 2 kilogrammes or more.[40] The first Angolan traders to visit the malachite pits found that the earth priests of the Copperbelt were also the master blacksmiths who transformed copper bars into political power with the aid of their kin and slaves.

> ... we travelled across ... valleys and hills, and saw on the summit of the hills, stones which appear true (green?), and where they dig the copper; in the midst of this country is where they make the bars. There are two proprietors of the 'Senzalas'; the first is named after the land Muiro and the other is called Canbembe. Those owners are the head smiths, who order the bars to be made by their 'sons' and their own 'macotas' (slaves).

37 Burton, *Luba Religion and Magic*, p. 76.

38 Author's field research among the Luba people of Zaire, 1972–3.

39 O. Nennen, 'La Circoncision chez les Samba (Baluba)', *Congo*, ii, 3, 1927, 375.

40 Frederick S. Arnot, *Garenganze, or, Seven Years' Pioneer Mission Work in Central Africa*, 1889; reprint, London, 1969, pp. 238–9; Michael S. Bisson, 'Copper currency in central Africa: the archaeological evidence', *World Archaeology*, vi, 3, 1975, 276–92; Oscar Michaux, *Au Congo, carnet de campagne, épisodes et impressions de 1889 à 1897*, Namur, 1913, p. 339.

> ... These two proprietors were also at one time sovereigns of the lands, as well as owners of the mines left them by their predecessors.[41]

The scale of extended regional trade increased in the fifteenth century. A shift in the quantity of copper produced and traded points to an economic take-off. Copper-smelting began at isolated sites in the fifth century, and continued at low levels until about the thirteenth century. Production rose sharply after 1400, and at one site about 130 metric tons of copper were smelted between the fifteenth and seventeenth centuries.[42] The rise in production was matched by a rise in the quantity of ingots arriving as trade goods among the peoples of the Upemba depression.[43] By the eighteenth century, regional trade networks had interlocked across the entire eastern savanna, and the Copperbelt had become the meeting point of two great regional trading systems.[44] One ran north to the fringes of the rain-forest. Cloth strips woven from raffia palm fibre were the export speciality of the better-watered north, and raffia cloth reached the Copperbelt along a thousand kilometres of twisting paths.[45] A second network radiated south from the Copperbelt diggings towards the Zambezi. By 1400 a trading centre for copper, beads and other prestige goods had developed at Ingombe Ilede, in the Gwembe valley, and linked Zambian trade with the Zimbabwe trading system.[46]

Extended regional trading systems were creatures of the Central African interior. It was not until 1750 that they began to come into direct contact with the continent's coasts and the world mercantilist economy. Even then an indigenous trading class does not seem to have developed until the late eighteenth century, and specialised, long-distance traders did not begin to arrive from west and east until the following century. It was the cult specialists and the local strong men, along with their lineages, who retained the surpluses from both production and trade. Members of this privileged 'class' converted their surpluses into political capital according to local principles of reciprocity and redistribution. Greed was also at work. The increase in the quantity of copper traded was an indicator of growing patterns of inequality between villagers and élites. Copper output increased

41 Richard F. Burton (ed.), *The Lands of Cazembe*, London, 1873, p. 222. For the most likely date for this observation (1808), see François Bontinck, 'Le Voyage des pombeiros: essai de réinterprétation', *Cultures au Zaïre et en Afrique*, v, 1974, 51–67.

42 Michael S. Bisson, 'The Prehistoric Coppermines of Zambia', Ph.D. thesis, University of California at Santa Barbara, 1976, pp. 421–8; 'Prehistoric copper mining in Northwestern Zambia', *Archaeology*, xxvii, 4, 1974, 242–7.

43 De Maret, 'Chronologie de l'Age du Fer', vol. 2, pp. 354–7; de Maret, 'Sanga: new excavations', 334.

44 Vansina, 'Long-distance trade-routes in Central Africa', *JAH*, iii, 3, 1962, 387.

45 Richard Burton, *Lands of Cazembe*, p. 223; Reefe, *Rainbow and the Kings*, pp. 95–6.

46 Fagan, Phillipson and Daniels, *Iron Age Cultures in Zambia*, vol. 2, pp. 102–5, 139; D. W. Phillipson and Brian M. Fagan, 'The date of the Ingombe Ilede burials', *JAH*, x, 2, 1969, 199–204.

as the appetite for precious metal rose. Trade links began to interconnect, and the demands of élites further afield were fed into the copper-smelting villages.

Although extended regional trade was a symptom of change, it was not the sole cause of change. Increases in commerce could not radically transform local patterns of human domination. If evidence from more recent centuries is any indication, leaders and spiritual guides often did live better than others. They had more subordinate kin, more pawns and more slaves. They had more leisure time, but their consumption of expensive prestige goods dissipated accumulation of wealth that might have been turned to long-term aggrandisement.[47] They also used copper bars and ornaments for bridewealth and other social expenditures. Bridewealth became more important as the quantity and variety of goods available for payment increased through trade. Although competition for resources remained intense, these social payments diffused material possessions downwards. Thus the regional political economy of the savanna was initially one in which trade helped to disperse more efficiently scarce resources among a scattered savanna population.

It was only much later, during the seventeenth century, when extended regional trade reached the upper limits of its carrying capacity, that the political economy of the savanna began to be transformed. Even then political change was not regionally extensive. It spread outward from discrete centres. During this epoch, savanna kingdoms, expansive dynastic states, began to emerge in widely separated regions. Some kingdoms developed along the major lines of regional trade. At the same time segmentary societies and small-scale polities tended to persist in areas least affected by trade. Nevertheless, large-scale state formation was not inevitable where trade was intense. Rather, extended regional trade interacted with other dynamics at very specific locations, and for specific local reasons, to promote the survival and success of a few initial kingdoms in the savanna. It is necessary to stress that these kingdoms developed from an older stratum of small-scale polities. It is possible to trace the history of the ones that came to dominate villages across the most extensive stretches of savanna and woodlands. They thrived from before 1700 until the middle decades of the nineteenth century.

KINGDOMS OF THE SAVANNA: AN OVERVIEW, 1700–1850

Measured against the sheer territorial magnitude of the eastern savanna and the long-term continuity of its historical traditions, the development of large-scale states was the exception, not the rule. Few of the new kingdoms came into direct and meaningful contact one with another until the

47 Fielder, 'Economic spheres in pre-colonial Ila society', 630–1, 641.

nineteenth century. None the less, their impact was significant. Territorially extensive spheres of political overrule were created where none had existed before. Institutions invented or modified by royal dynasties were exported to expanding peripheries. These large-scale states also inspired experimentation and innovation among the petty polities on their frontiers. Ambitious leaders on the periphery frequently sought to gain prestige by associating themselves with a neighbouring big power. In opposite cases, exiles and refugees from the larger states imposed their own will among their hosts. The fame of big states spread rapidly. Petty ruling lineages claimed fictional ancestry from royal dynasties to enhance their legitimacy. The names of several kingdoms stand out: the Lunda empire, the Luba empire and the Lozi kingdom. Many famous satellite and border states also developed after 1700: the Kanyok and Mutombo Mukulu kingdoms, between the Luba and Lunda empires; the Kanongesha polity

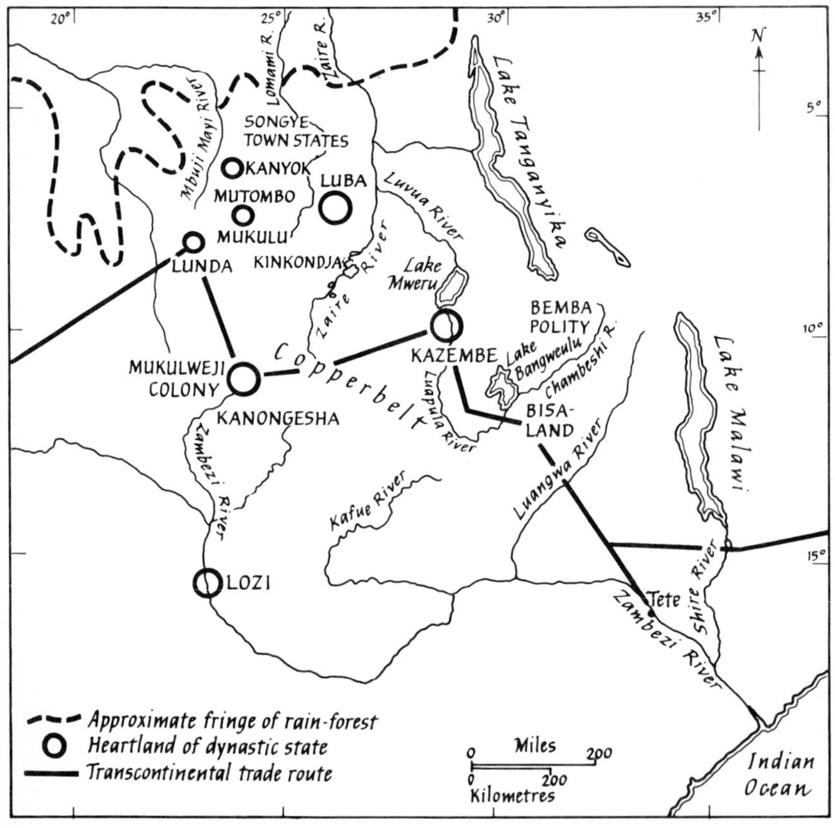

5:2 Kingdoms of the savanna, 1700–1850

and the Kazembe kingdom which was derived to some degree from the Lunda system. The dispersed Bemba polity and the Songye town-states were independent developments.

Major states expanded outward from the well-defined territorial core of an ancestral polity in order to conquer, absorb or mediate with neighbours. Royal authority was strongest in the heartland. In small states leaders were vulnerable to the supernatural aura of local spirits and the demands of their autonomous ritual specialists. In the heartland of large states the old worship of ancestral spirits was manipulated by the dynasties. Priest-guardians of Lozi royal graves were the men who coaxed rain from the clouds.[48] Antiquity legitimises in Africa, and royal graves were important institutional symbols of dynastic power. In the Lunda empire and the Kazembe kingdom they clustered near a capital, while in the Luba empire royal graves were scattered across the heartland. Lozi and Bemba graves served as mnemonic markers to the longevity of the royal line.[49] Antiquity could be manipulated. The royal dynasty of the Luba empire co-opted to its kinglist non-royal ancestral spirits whose names were venerated in the heartland. The old centres where these spirits were worshipped came to be accepted as royal graves.[50]

In societies where villages of a few hundred people were the norm, royal courts were among the largest urban groupings on the savanna. Court populations numbered in the thousands, and sometimes in the tens of thousands.[51] Life could be comfortable for those at the top. Women, slaves and refugees grew crops in extensive plantations around the court, and neighbouring villages were also expected to deliver foodstuffs regularly. Demands could be excessive, and villagers sometimes resisted the establishment of a royal court in their neighbourhood or fled once the court was built.[52] Courts pulled in resources at rates not previously seen. Kings could do on an extensive territorial scale what strong men could do only locally. Rulers were tribute-mongers of prestige goods, and royal courts became vital consumption and redistribution centres for iron, salt, copper and beads. The Lozi court was the institution through which finished iron

48 Gwyn Prins, *The Hidden Hippopotamus, Reappraisal in African History: the Early Colonial Experience in Western Zambia*, Cambridge, 1980, p. 128.

49 Cameron, *Across Africa*, vol. 2, pp. 66–7; A. C. Pedroso Gamitto, *King Kazembe and the Marave, Cheva, Bisa, Bemba, Lunda, and Other Peoples of Southern Africa*, trans. Ian Cunnison. Lisbon, 1960, vol. 2, pp. 12–13, 116–17, 123, 126; Andrew D. Roberts, *A History of the Bemba: Political Growth and Change in North-Eastern Zambia before 1900*, London. 1973, p. 14; Victor W. Turner, *The Lozi Peoples of North-Western Rhodesia*, Ethnographic Survey of Africa, West Central Africa, part III, London, 1952, pp. 34, 50.

50 Reefe, *Rainbow and the Kings*, pp. 57–8.

51 Jean-Luc Vellut, 'Notes sur le Lunda et la frontière luso-africaine (1700–1900)', *Etudes d'histoire africaine*, iii, 1972, 74.

52 Gamitto, *King Kazembe*, vol. 2, p. 115; Reefe, *Rainbow and the Kings*, p. 146.

products passed.[53] Salt and copper circulated widely in the Lunda and Kazembe tribute networks along with goods brought in through long-distance trade with the east and west coasts of Africa.[54]

Court life was energised by the comings and goings of tribute bearers. Kings expressed their pleasure or displeasure with subordinates by the type and quantity of prestige goods they passed out. Much of court gossip was inspired by the complaints of those who felt they had received inadequate payments from their monarch. Infants sometimes lay across the knees of their seated parents asleep. A king could recite a proverb of forbearance about the backbiting of tributaries using this common domestic image: 'They speak; they speak of me. I am great. I hold their problems on my knees.'[55]

The handful of kingdoms that developed into very extensive territorial states possessed institutions and customs that cut across the parochial interests of the subordinate lineages over which they ruled. Key structures of these states were adapted from ancient and widespread cultural patterns. The symbolic idioms used at court were descended from traditions predating the eighteenth century. Court organisation and ritual shared features found in zones far more extensive than any individual state. The ancient process of local borrowing and widespread cultural diffusion went on.

The residential organisation at the Lunda royal court was modelled on the land tortoise, a sacred animal among many people of the savanna. The 'People of the Eyes' lived in front of the king's enclosure, and the 'People of the Tail' at the rear. These images fed into the metaphors of courtly life. In Angola the gait of the tortoise evoked a sense of chiefly majesty. At the Luba court the 'People of the Tail' were, appropriately enough, the slaves and refugees who lived under the king's protection, behind the royal enclosure. The battle order of state armies mirrored the residential organisation of royal courts.[56] The warrior tradition was deeply embedded in political symbolism. *Musumba*, the common word for 'war camp', was also a widespread term for 'royal court' or 'royal enclosure'. The hunter and warrior *kutomboka* dance was performed at royal investitures in the north and during male puberty rites in the west.[57]

Most royal dynasties claimed origins from fictional wandering hunters and warriors. Epic genesis myths accounted for the beginnings of all things political. Each myth was unique to the régime which it legitimised and, in a

53 Prins, *Hidden Hippotamus*, pp. 107–8.

54 Vellut, 'Notes sur le Lunda', 82–90.

55 Author's field research among the Luba people of Zaire, 1972–3.

56 Henrique A. Dias de Carvalho, *Ethnographia e história tradicional dos povos da Lunda*, Lisbon, 1890, pp. 64, 215 and map facing p. 226; Hoover, 'Seduction of Ruwej', vol. 1, pp. 107–9, 129; Reefe, *Rainbow and the Kings*, pp. 109, 224–25, n.3; Harold Womersley, 'Legends and History of the Baluba', unpublished manuscript, map entitled 'Layout of Capital (Dipata) of Kabongo Kumwimba Nshimbu at Lubiai Town, Kabongo'.

57 Hoover, 'Seduction of Ruwej', vol. 2, pp. 567, n.126, 572, n.150.

series of episodes, accounted for the arrival of the essential sacral kingship of the ruling dynasty. When taken as a whole, what is most distinctive about the genesis myths is that they seem struck from a common mould, although adapted in their form and symbolic expression to specific political environments and geographical locations.

The savanna myths were actually elements of a distinguished tradition of genesis, integral to the intellectual history of Central Africa, whose roots go back to the first settlement of Bantu-speaking peoples. Borrowing has been continuous among near neighbours, and it is difficult, if not impossible, to tell where local intellectual innovation ended and the diffusion of ideas began. Generations of kings and oral historians who sang their praises borrowed, assembled, combined and tooled existing myth episodes, motifs and symbols to meet their own needs. The elements of myth were drawn selectively from other traditions which did not serve political aims, but explained man's fundamental relationship to nature and the universe. In this sense dynastic genesis myths have preserved for us glimpses of a matrix of thought which is of considerable antiquity.[58] Unfortunately, the elements of the genesis tradition are not yet sufficiently understood and researched to present a fully coherent intellectual history of savanna peoples.

In the myths one character, Nkongolo, from the Luba genesis, represents an example of how widespread elements were combined over time to create complex and highly evocative images attached to the land and re-enacted in ritual. Red, white and black, the primary colours of royal myth, are potent symbols expressing cosmological concepts and moral norms throughout Central and Eastern Africa.[59] Colours were wedded to images of power and danger which sprang from commonly shared life experiences. In societies of barefoot pedestrians every child is taught about the danger of venomous snakes, and the sinister appearance, movement and power of this reptile has captured the imagination of many African groups. The 'Snake-Destroyer' who kills people and changes the course of rivers is evoked in belief systems and myths from Luba westward. 'Nkongolo' is the word for the rainbow, believed to be created by the coupling of two serpents in the sky.[60] In myth he was characterised as the autochthonous chief whose red or lighter skin tone was closely associated with the cruelty and malevolence of an older and more barbaric political order. People today can trace the Red Way of Nkongolo as the path of red soils that leads from the former heartland of the Luba empire to the point where Nkongolo is believed to have ordered his followers to divert the course of the Lomami

58 Luc de Heusch, *Le Roi ivre ou l'origine de l'état*, Paris, 1972, pp. 10–11, 298.
59 Victor W. Turner, *The Forest of Symbols, Aspects of Ndembu Ritual*, Ithaca, 1967, chap. 3; Auguste Verbeken, 'La Signification mystique des couleurs chez les Bantous', *Zaire*, i, 1947, 1139–44.
60 Hoover, 'Seduction of Ruwej', vol. 1, p. 235 and n.62.

river in order to build a fortified island. It was to this location that Nkongolo was pursued by the hunter Mbidi Kiluwe, a truly black-skinned culture hero who was believed to have brought with him new and refined practices of sacral kingship. This wandering hunter impregnated one of Nkongolo's sisters, who gave birth to the warrior Kalala Ilunga, a black-skinned son and putative founder of the royal dynasty of Luba.[61] The extremes and contrasts of life and environment are stark on the savanna and easily reduced to symbolic statement. One interpretation of this myth sees the 'Snake-Rainbow' as the symbol of sterility, the dry land and the dry season. Nkongolo is the man of heat in contradistinction to Mbidi Kiluwe, a celestial hunter-hero symbolic of fertility and the rainy season. Myth and ritual came to overlap, for the epic struggles and larger-than-life actions of the three heroes were re-enacted in the investiture rituals of kings, reaffirming at the same time the enduring relationship between man and nature.[62]

Expansive kingdoms were distinctive in that their rulers found systematic ways to contain centrifugal tendencies. Innovation gave certain states and dynasties a competitive edge. Succession disputes within the heartland did not tear the centre apart. Large dynastic states were held together by a political ideology, often expressed in the genesis myth, that dictated competition for a single sacral kingship. Royal males and their supporters fought one another to gain access to the resources of the centre. The worst that seems to have happened was that the expansion of the state was hindered for a time by succession struggles. Dynasties which endured, through innovative structures or simple good fortune, for two generations without a major succession crisis were able to direct their attention and resources away from the centre and toward the expanding frontiers.

Big powers were born out of competition for both material and human resources. Some states were centred upon populous flood plains, although political centralisation elsewhere in middle Africa often originated in areas possessing unique resources like salt, iron and copper.[63] Seasonal visitors came to produce or barter goods, and their activities had to be monitored, controlled or exploited by local leaders. These visitors might even become permanent immigrants, increasing the human base available to leaders of resource centres. Migration played a role in the development of large states as it did in the emergence of small-scale polities and local patterns of dominance. Space was something to be overcome on the lightly populated savanna, and expansive surges of kingdoms and empires were often

61 Reefe, *Rainbow and the Kings*, chap. 3; Harold Womersley, *In the Glow of the Log Fire*, London, 1974, pp. 17–62.

62 Luc de Heusch, 'What shall we do with the drunken king?', *Africa*, xlv, 4, 1975, 364–5; de Heusch, *Le Roi ivre*, chap. 2; Reefe, *Rainbow and the Kings*, pp. 43–4.

63 Joseph C. Miller, *Equatorial Africa*, Pamphlet no. 518, American Historical Association, Washington, D.C., 1976, p. 14.

directed towards distant areas containing extensive natural and human resources.

As with elders and strong men before them, kings and their minions sought direct access to human production and reproduction through the manipulation of servile institutions. The Lozi king had many slaves. They served him at court and fulfilled his needs in the heartland. Slaves became as important a set of living symbols of the Lozi king's wealth and status as did his cattle herds tended by slaves.[64] Slaves were distinctive for their powerlessness. The reality was expressed in a proverb: 'A slave is like dry bark which softens when placed in water.'[65] The most pliable slaves were those brought back to the centre of a kingdom as prisoners captured during conflict along distant peripheries. Prisoners were sacrificed at royal graves following successful completion of Kazembe military campaigns.[66] Many villages in the heartland of the Luba empire were stocked with prisoners of war. Here the slave's lament was, 'They insult me, I eat; if I am angry and leave, I will not be able to find the paths to return to my home, to my kin.'[67]

These political offspring of locally competitive processes were equally creatures of overt violence. Military conquest was fundamental. Flood-plain polities often defended themselves from landward attack by withdrawing behind their aquatic frontiers. In the Upemba depression people could survive for extended periods by living in villages built upon floating papyrus islands anchored in the middle of lakes and streams. The savanna analogue to the collective public works projects of the flood plains was the building of elaborate, palisaded enclosures. Fortifications were built to protect villages during extended periods of raiding and general insecurity. Larger ones encompassed cultivable land. Such heartland enclosures in Luba and Lunda date to a time before the eighteenth century, and two immense enclosures were built in the Kanyok kingdom at the end of that century.[68] The outlines of earthwork ruins can still be seen on the ground, and the Kanyok ones measure 6 and 11 kilometres around. These fortifications are described today by oral historians.

> The [enclosure] consisted of a deep circular trench with a wall on the inside. This wall, made of branches and mud, had peepholes at the level of a man's knees, chest and head. Thus, standing, kneeling, or lying the

64 Eugene L. Hermitte, 'An Economic History of Barotseland, 1800–1940', Ph.D. thesis, Northwestern University, 1974, pp. 130–32.

65 Prins, *Hidden Hippopotamus*, p. 73.

66 Gamitto, *King Kazembe*, vol. 2, p. 117.

67 Reefe, *Rainbow and the Kings*, pp. 153–4.

68 Hoover, 'Seduction of Ruwej', vol. 1, pp. 345–6; Jason Sendwe, 'Traditions et coutumes ancestrales des Baluba', *Problèmes sociaux congolais*, no. 24, 1954, 113; Womersley, 'Legends and History of the Baluba', pp. 6–7.

> Kanyok warriors on the inside could shoot through the holes and stop an attacker. The attackers, on the other hand, could see no one and their arrows and lances would plunge harmlessly into the mud wall.[69]

Trenches were about 5.5 metres wide by 3.5 metres deep, and it has been estimated that between 10 000 and 15 000 hoe agriculturalists had to be mobilised over the course of several dry seasons to excavate some 325 000 cubic metres of earth for the 17 kilometres of dry moat surrounding both enclosures.[70]

Terror was used by aggressive dynasties both at the centre and toward the periphery. Intrigue, poisonings, witchcraft accusations and the like were potentially disruptive features of daily political life, and rulers had to rely upon more than the supernatural aura of their sacral kingship to maintain order among the competing factions at the royal court. Executioners were dreaded court officials, for they were prepared to dismember title-holders who displeased the king.[71] At the Kazembe court the 'Cutter of Ears' was a royal executioner.[72] 'If an order or speech of the Kazembe is not promptly understood (he often asks who has not heard him, if he is in bad humor, as he frequently is) this is enough to make him order the immediate cutting off of the malcreant's ears "In order to hear better." '[73] Mutilations were also carried out among frontier populations. In the mid-nineteenth century, when the Luba empire reached its greatest territorial extent, large numbers of mutilated prisoners were pushed in front of warriors to terrorise opponents on the battlefield.[74]

Historical process and individual personality combined to create the strong, innovative leadership that was a necessary ingredient to the growth of kingdoms. The message of dynastic oral traditions is that kingdoms and empires were led by capable and ruthless leaders. There is no reason to believe that such was not the case. Epithets of royal strength and power were derived from ancient, symbolic layers. Thus, the ruler of the Lunda empire was called 'Lord of the Viper'.[75]

Kings and counsellors were skilled in the art of lineage politics. Skills were transferred to the periphery, where expansion often occurred by power-brokering among local lineages and strong men. These factors interacted among different peoples in different ways. It was the actions of

69 John C. Yoder, 'A People on the Edge of Empires: History of the Kanyok of Central Zaire', Ph.D. thesis, Northwestern University, 1977, p. 164.
70 *Ibid.*, p. 169.
71 Cameron, *Across Africa*, vol. 2, pp. 68–70, 148–9; Roberts, *History of the Bemba*, p. 167.
72 Gamitto, *King Kazembe*, vol. 2, p. 113.
73 *Ibid.*, pp. 88–9.
74 François Bontinck (ed.), *L'Autobiographie de Hamed ben Mohammed el-Murjebi Tippo Tip (ca. 1840–1905)*, Brussels, 1974, section 160; Cameron, *Across Africa*, vol. 2, p. 128.
75 Hoover, 'Seduction of Ruwej', vol. 2, pp. 541–2, n.26.

rulers and dynasties, of counsellors and clients, that gave texture to the historical experiences of the individual kingdoms that are to be described.

KINGDOMS OF THE SAVANNA: LOZI, LUBA, LUNDA

The upper Zambezi flood plain was the heartland of the Lozi kingdom. It measures some 175 kilometres long, averages about 50 kilometres in width and extends over an area in excess of 8 000 square kilometres. Rains and floods have failed from time to time, leading to occasional crises, but an account of 1853 gives a more typical characterisation. 'The soil is extremely fertile, and the people are never in want of grain, for, by taking advantage of the moisture of the inundation, they can take two crops a year. The Barotse (Lozi) are strongly attached to this fertile valley; they say, "Here hunger is not known".'[76] Lozi kingship was a creature of the plain. In an old proverb the king was likened to a hidden hippopotamus who sought the protection of the deep waters of the Zambezi: 'The bull hippopotamus who leads the herd swirls the deepest waters of the river, [because] the white sands of the shallows betray him.'[77] A twist on this proverb emphasises the symbiotic relationship between ruler and ruled: 'The hippopotamus is child of the herd, he dives to the deepest waters, [because] the white sands of the shallows betray him.'[78]

Villages were built on man-made mounds that rose just above the floodwaters. Each village guarded its mound, and protected its ancestral claims to nearby weirs and dams where large quantities of fish were caught. Identity with mound village and surrounding territory was strong.[79] People were divided into descent groups led by local flood-plain strong men who increased their human capital by attracting migrants and refugees to their spheres. By the seventeenth century a Lozi proto-kingdom existed at the plain's northern end.[80] During the earliest phases of state growth, a patchwork of relationships developed between the king and strong men. The king controlled the redistribution of iron, and subordination was expressed by receiving clapperless iron 'Bells of Kings' as symbols of delegated royal authority. The patchwork took on uniformity as the followers of individual bell-holders were organised into distinctive military and service units of the state.[81] Membership in a unit was hereditary. As lineage members broke away to resettle elsewhere, participation in a specific unit lost its association with local spheres of

76 David Livingstone, *Missionary Travels and Researches in South Africa*, New York, 1858, p. 235.
77 Prins, *Hidden Hippopotamus*, p. 119.
78 *Ibid.*, p. 120.
79 Gluckman, 'Lozi of Barotseland', pp. 8–9.
80 Mutumba Mainga, *Bulozi under the Luyana Kings: Political Evolution and State Formation in Pre-colonial Zambia*, London, 1973, p. 214.
81 Prins, *Hidden Hippopotamus*, pp. 97–105.

power. Centralisation occurred as leadership of these units was consolidated among title-holders at the king's court. The process was well under way by the reign of Yeta I, the third ruler of the Lozi kinglist, for after him kings were the only royals who could create new units. As political overrule was extended, mound-building and other public works projects using the corvée labour of these military and service units became widespread. By the nineteenth century the flood plain was dotted with mounds marking the locations of former capitals of Lozi kings as well as the capital mounds of the living king and his territorial chiefs.[82]

Transhumance came to be regulated by rituals of kingship. As the flood began, the king in his royal barge led a fleet of dug-out canoes filled with royalty and retainers away from his capital on the plain in a ritual that started the annual migration of his people to the dry land. Months later, after the waters subsided, the king's return to his capital in the heartland signalled the reoccupation of the plain by his subjects. The royal barge was the technological wonder of the state; it was also the perfect symbol of unity. In the early nineteenth century a royal barge required twenty paddlers. It was 40 to 50 feet in length and a bit under 10 feet at the beam. Construction was a royal affair, conducted behind screens at the capital, and the wood, cloth and ropes used to make it came from all over the kingdom.[83]

Lozi rule was distinctive for the innovative methods used to create hegemony. Ngalama, the fifth ruler on the kinglist, extended his domain from north to south and brought the entire flood plain under dynastic control. Ngombala, his successor, founded a southern capital, dividing the plain into two spheres of dynastic influence. The southern capital was ruled by a royal male, and not infrequently it was this male who succeeded to the central kingship of the north.[84] An appointive bureaucracy was created as rulers chose non-royals to hold the important advisory and administrative titles at court. This bureaucracy grew larger as the state expanded and new administrative categories and groupings were created by successive kings. The bureaucracy came to have its own vested interests, and it was becoming a personnel bloc that competed with royalty for resources and influence by the end of the eighteenth century.[85] Competition did not lead to schism and civil war. There was plenty for all at the top, because expansion under King Ngombala and his successors gave the dynasty access to new natural and human resources.

Armies and raiding parties struck out from the flood plain in the

82 Hermitte, 'Economic History of Barotseland', pp. 40–44, 137–8; Mainga, *Bulozi under the Luyana Kings*, pp. 36–9.

83 Gluckman, 'Lozi of Barotseland', pp. 11–13; Prins, *Hidden Hippopotamus*, pp. 117–18, 277, n.17.

84 Gluckman, 'Lozi of Barotseland', pp. 23–9; Mainga, *Bulozi under the Luyana Kings*, pp. 54–8.

85 Mainga, *Bulozi under the Luyana Kings*, pp. 39–54, 62–4.

eighteenth century, incorporating nearby groups as tributaries while harassing more distant peoples for booty, prisoners and cattle. Tribute overseers were settled among woodland fringe groups which had previously traded with the peoples of the Zambezi plain. Woodland tributaries were expected to dispatch cohorts of young men and women periodically to serve as slaves of the Lozi king. About 1800, groups from the north-western periphery of the state were relocated along the eastern marches of the plain, where they served as military allies. The immigrants introduced cassava and other crops from Angola, and their agricultural techniques were well suited to cultivating unexploited sections of the eastern marches of the flood plain.[86]

The Lozi kingdom was a dynamic state in the seventeenth and eighteenth centuries. Kings and their subordinates experimented with new institutional forms, while power relationships shifted between royals and bureaucrats. Prestige goods were consumed by a flood-plain aristocracy famous for its life style. Callouses were the symbol of labour. Long finger nails became the symbol of leisure among even minor Lozi chiefs: 'Like all chiefs, Sewisha lets his finger nails grow as long as possible to show that he is a chief and does no manual labour.'[87] Oral traditions say that an eighteenth-century Lozi queen bathed in milk and was called 'She Who Lacks Nothing'.[88]

The Lozi state was the creation of the flood plain. The Luba empire was a creation of the grassland. The longevity and stability of the Luba empire was built upon prosaic processes of resource manipulation, for its savanna heartland in the Lomami valley contained contiguous zones of generous salt and iron deposits. Genesis myth and court ritual were enriched by a matrix of symbols about salt and iron-making, many of which date to a time before the creation of the empire. For example, the blacksmith's anvil has been an important symbol among the peoples of the eastern savanna for a thousand years. In more recent times rulers of the empire underwent a special 'Striking the Anvil' ceremony in order to establish intimate ties with a sacred iron-producing district in the heartland that was associated with an heroic figure in myth.[89]

A small dynastic state was created in the salt and iron zones before 1600. The expropriation and redistribution of natural resources were combined with the availability of human resources. The heartland was located just a few dozen kilometres north-west of the populous consumer districts of the

86 *Ibid.*, pp. 58–60; Hermitte, 'Economic History of Barotseland', pp. 53–59.
87 J. Stevenson-Hamilton, *The Barotseland Journals of James Stevenson-Hamilton, 1898–1899*, London, 1953, p. 182, quoted in W. G. Clarence-Smith, 'Slaves, commoners and landlords in Bulozi, c. 1875 to 1906', *JAH*, xx, 2, 1979, 225.
88 Mainga, *Bulozi under the Luyana Kings*, p. 61.
89 Cameron, *Across Africa*, vol. 2, pp. 51–3; De Maret, 'Chronologie de l'Age du Fer', vol. 2, pp. 256, 349; Womersley, *Glow of the Log Fire*, pp. 28–30, 68–70, 78, 82–3.

Upemba depression. Inter-lineage struggles for direct control over local producers were undoubtedly part of the formative political process. Eventually, forceful leaders of one extended patrilineage established their right to rule the heartland. They demanded tribute from local villages and from the people who came from near and far to barter for salt cones and iron hoes. By the end of the seventeenth century the power of the rulers of the Luba empire was established among the petty savanna polities west of the upper Zaire and Upemba depression. After about 1700 the influence of the empire's royal dynasty spread north and south along the general axis of extended regional trade running between the rain-forest and the Copperbelt.[90]

Innovation was important. Royal infanticide was legitimised in myth and practised at court in order to reduce the number of male heirs eligible to challenge the kingship.[91] From an early date kings had access to the services of the *bambudye* secret society. Institutions like this were characteristic of people living all the way from the rain-forest to the Bangweulu swamps and beyond to the hills of Malawi.[92] Secret societies were not new, and probably developed first among compact flood-plain and lakeside villages where cross-cutting institutions were necessary to maintain order among competing lineages.[93] How secret societies were manipulated were matters of dynastic and cultural choice which could vary significantly even between close neighbours. On the Lomami the power of chiefly lineages in individual Songye town-states came to be circumscribed by chapters of local, independent, secret societies.[94] Just to the south the same institutional tradition was turned to the single-minded goals of the Luba royal dynasty, and the *bambudye* secret society became a distinctive feature of the dynasty's overrule. The king was the patron of the society, and its members spied for him. Village chapters promoted royal oral propaganda by singing the praises of the dynasty and reciting its genesis myth. Membership in the society became a requirement for holding high office. Affiliation with a chapter offered procedures and mechanisms of interpersonal and interlineage conflict resolution not otherwise available. Eventually the

90 Reefe, *Rainbow and the Kings*, chaps. 7–8.

91 E. d'Orjo de Marchovelette, 'Notes sur les funérailles des chefs Ilunga Kable et Kabongo Kumwimba: historique de la chefferie Kabongo: historique Kongolo: histoire de la chefferie Kongolo', *Bulletin des juridictions indigènes du droit coutumier congolais*, xix, 1, 1951, 9; Womersley, *Glow of the Log Fire*, pp. 63–6.

92 Dugald Campbell, *In the Heart of Bantuland*, 1922; reprint, New York, 1969, chaps. 9–10; Matthew Schoffeleers and Ian Linden, 'The resistance of Nyau societies to the Roman Catholic missions in colonial Malawi', in *The Historical Study of African Religion*, T. O. Ranger and I. N. Kimambo (eds), 1972; reprint, Berkeley and Los Angeles, 1976, pp. 252–73; Vansina, *Introduction à l'ethnographie du Congo*, pp. 170, 193–4.

93 Argument adapted from Horton, 'Stateless societies in the history of West Africa', pp. 99, 101–3, 112–13.

94 Nancy J. Fairley, 'Mianda ya Ben'Ekie: A History of the Ben'Ekie', Ph.D. thesis, State University of New York at Stony Brook, 1978, pp. 38–44, 83–93, 147–54.

society was imposed upon most client polities, and the area of its dispersal was bounded by the empire's most distant tributaries.[95]

The Luba empire became a catalyst for political centralisation among petty client polities. The Kanyok kingdom was created partially in response to Luba domination. Kanyok chiefdoms were incorporated into the empire by the early eighteenth century, and the Luba king became the power-broker among subordinate chiefly lineages. Rival candidates for a chieftainship personally delivered to the Luba king large quantities of gifts as tokens of future tribute payments. He confirmed the successful candidate in office through court ritual. However, Kanyok leaders created their own unified polity about 1800, following a rebellion during the reign of the Luba king Ilunga Sungu.[96] The Kanyok revolt is reported in a scatological oral tradition about Ilunga Sungu's court at Katende.

> The Great Town at Katende began to break up when the King became old. It was so big that 'The Lord of Hygiene' ['Kikoto kya Kaumba', so-called after the 'kikoto' or scavenger beetle] could not, even with the help of his sons and relatives, keep the wide avenues between the various sections of the town cleared of refuse and excrement, even though they worked all day scraping up the dirt with their special long-handled hoes. It is said that the old King himself complained that it was the Bene Kanyoka who were chiefly to blame and should take their dirt home with them, so the people of this western tribe went home in anger and have never paid tribute since. To this day if there is an unclean smell around, men will spit and say, 'This is as bad as when Ilunga Nsungu told the Bene Kanyoka to take their refuse with them!'[97]

Resistance along one periphery was more than matched by conquest and incorporation in other directions. The tributary territories of the Luba empire were doubled between about 1800 and the 1860s.[98] The Kinkondja kingdom, which dominated the northern part of the Upemba depression, was subjugated, and its rulers brought generous tribute payments in fish. Appropriately enough, Kinkondja kings were expected to swim like fish in the dust of the Luba court as an act of obeisance. Expansion often followed the lines of least resistance. It was directed in particular to the small-scale polities and segmentary units north and north-east towards the rain-forest and to the groups lying east and south-east of the Zaire river. Surges of

95 Burton, *Luba Religion and Magic*, pp. 154–67; E. d'Orjo de Marchovelette, 'Quelques Considérations sur les "Bambudie" du Territoire de Kabongo', *Bulletin des juridictions indigènes du droit coutumier congolais*, viii, 10, 1940, 275–89; Reefe, *Rainbow and the Kings*, pp. 46–8.

96 Yoder, 'A People on the Edge of Empires', pp. 56–62, 142–6, 154–64, 187–98.

97 Womersley, 'Legends and History of the Baluba', p. 60; see also, Reefe, *Rainbow and the Kings*, pp. 122–4.

98 Anne Wilson, 'Long distance trade and the Luba Lomami empire', *JAH*, xiii, 4, 1972, 577–9.

expansion were followed by periods of consolidation. Attackers settled amongst newly incorporated populations that often provided recruits for the next phase of expansion. Invariably, permanent tribute-garnering colonies were established in districts where salt, iron and other valuable resources were abundant.

Although the technology of combat could not yield high casualty figures, conquest was still traumatic for the victims. Oral traditions account for defeat at the hands of warriors of the Luba empire in terms of the ritual suicide of local ancestral spirits. Prisoners provided labour and resources for the king. The destinies of ruling lineages changed as Luba rulers sought tractable allies by manipulating the succession in subordinate polities. The charisma of the empire also attracted to its court ambitious lineage leaders and succession contenders from beyond the periphery who sought recognition as clients of the king. They received royal canes, statues and embers from the king's sacred fire and other insignia indicating that they had been permitted to participate in the prestigious sacral kingship of the royal dynasty. By the mid-nineteenth century this gradual expansion was followed by a *pax* Luba. Political overrule, the *bambudye* diaspora and ritual power-brokering tempered regional conflict. Disputes continued, but competition among strong men was regulated by the king's rules.[99] The importance of early nineteenth-century expansion and incorporation is vividly recalled in a praise phrase of Ilunga Sungu, who started the most dynamic phase of the process: 'The kingship of Ilunga Sungu was a *real* kingship; ours today is just the rumbling of distant thunder, a chicken under your arm and dust in your ears.'[100]

Isolated by distance and terrain, the peoples in the very centre of the continent were among the last to feel the abrasive impact of the expanding world capitalist economy. Contact and interchange with the forward edges of this economy began as the eastern savanna was slowly squeezed between two Luso-African frontiers. Long-distance trade pressures were felt from the extreme west by the end of the seventeenth century, and from the far south-east a century later. One frontier was the forward edge of the Atlantic Ocean commercial zone, based in western and central Angola. The other frontier moved slowly inland from Luso-African plantation and trading bases on the lower Zambezi. It was a component of the Indian Ocean commercial zone.

Slaves and ivory were exported from the deep interior. Cloth, weapons, dishes, a wide variety of glass, porcelain, stone and shell beads and other prestige goods were imported in return.[101] At first the exchange patterns

99 Reefe, *Rainbow and the Kings*, chaps. 10–12.
100 Womersley, 'Legends and History of the Baluba', p. 59; see also Reefe, *Rainbow and the Kings*, p. 128.
101 Vellut, 'Notes sur le Lunda', 84.

resembled the older patterns of regional trade. African groups located astride key routes became carriers and middlemen. Products of local African manufacture were transported in both systems. In some cases the prestige goods of extended regional trade, like copper, were also the high-priority goods of long-distance trade.

Power centres developed along trade routes like knots on a string. Local rulers mastered techniques of trade exploitation. Tribute-gathering traditions were automatically appended to commercial exchanges, guaranteeing new economic assets to the politically ambitious. Disruptive processes of slave-raiding and acquisition were quickly diverted inland and away from the bastions of savanna strong men. Thus, the Kasanje kingdom on the middle Kwango river emerged from the seventeenth-century tumult of trade and politics in western Angola. It rapidly became a major power which exploited trade. During the eighteenth century the fair at Kasanje was the main emporium receiving slaves from the eastern savanna for export to the Atlantic coast.[102]

Groups and leaders previously on the fringe of the grassland economy became central actors in new dramas. It was no longer necessary to have direct access to population clusters and resource centres. Dispersed populations located in advance of an expanding Luso-African frontier might be drawn together by the opportunities of long-distance trade. This was the case with the Lunda empire, the eastern savanna trading state *par excellence*. Nevertheless, even in this case state growth evolved from deeply embedded cultural traditions, and local patterns of exchange remained important.

The Lunda empire was an amalgam of colonised peoples. Its roots go back to the creation of a Ruund state in the upper Mbuji Mayi river valley in the seventeenth century. Here the principle of unilineal descent gave way to practices of bilateral descent. As the descent principle changed, lineage ideology was manipulated to the advantage of local strong men. Positional succession and perpetual kinship are closely related concepts used in societies extending from central Angola across the eastern savanna to Malawi. Under rules of positional succession, a successor acquires his predecessor's identity and name, his wives and children, his social roles and responsibilities. By the fifteenth century leaders along the upper Mbuji Mayi were also experimenting with perpetual kinship, whereby a successor acquired the kinship ties of his predecessor. The principle began in the Lunda heartland to define fixed relationships between political titles rather than relationships between individuals holding political office. A superior office became 'father' to a subordinate 'son' office over generations. Perpetual kinship bound titles together in a fixed relationship, which

102 *Ibid.*, 94.

endured regardless of the personal lineage ties of the title-holders.[103] The circulation of an extensive inventory of prestige goods was the bond within this innovative structure, and court title-holders called 'catchers' were dispatched constantly to oversee tribute collection among client polities.[104]

Long-distance trade brought an agricultural revolution to the eastern savanna. Lunda rulers and their subjects were among the first to capitalise on the change. American food crops were introduced from the west as a by-product of the earliest phases of long-distance exchanges. No crop was more important than cassava (manioc), the New World root that can be left in the ground until needed. On the dry grass-lands it became the ideal famine fighter, and in many locations it replaced millet in the staple diet. It was also the foodstuff of long-distance trade. Cassava was being used in Lunda by the mid-seventeenth century. Plantations of cassava were located at intervals along trade routes to sustain caravans.[105] In the Lunda heartland the word for cassava is literally 'food'; other things are simply 'snacks' and only when an individual has consumed cassava can he say that he has truly 'eaten'. The popularity of cassava was such that the subjects of the nearby Mutombo Mukulu kingdom called themselves 'The Cassava People'.[106]

In the eighteenth and early nineteenth centuries the Lunda empire expanded in many directions: west, north, south and south-east. It evolved 'colonial' relationships, so that to become 'Lunda' was to adopt selectively Ruund political titles from the heartland. Ruund colonies were frequently established along ecological frontiers where colonists could exploit the flow of trade between zones of supply and areas of scarcity.[107] The Lunda heartland itself was situated along such a frontier, but the influence of the royal dynasty was neither uniform nor certain even close to the centre.

Just 50 kilometres to the north of the Lunda heartland, on the Mbuji Mayi and adjacent rivers, were congeries of decentralised peoples known as the 'down-river people'. They lived in or near the rain-forest and traded palm-oil and raffia cloth. Their smiths were celebrated for the quality of their iron tools, weapons and ceremonial objects, and their production was the envy of more than one tribute-hungry Lunda king. Invasions were regularly mounted and repelled. Down-river folk were numerous and imbued with a formidable warrior tradition. Naweej I, a famous

103 Ian Cunnison, 'Perpetual kinship: a political institution of the Luapula peoples', *Rhodes-Livingstone Journal*, no. 20, 1956, 28–48; Hoover, 'Seduction of Ruwej, vol. 1, pp. 113–21; Joseph C. Miller, *Kings and Kinsmen: Early Mbundu States in Angola*, Oxford, 1976, pp. 116–17.

104 Hoover, 'Seduction of Ruwej', vol. 2, p. 538, n.12.

105 Richard Burton, *Lands of Cazembe*, pp. 173, 175, 186–8, 219, 222–3; Hoover, 'Seduction of Ruwej', vol. 1, 331–6; Vellut, 'Notes sur le Lunda', 78.

106 Hoover, 'Seduction of Ruwej', vol. 1, p. 331; Edmond Verhulpen, *Baluba et Balubaïsés du Katanga*, Anvers, 1936, p. 231.

107 Hoover, 'Seduction of Ruwej', vol. 1, pp. 336–40.

conqueror of Lunda tradition, died during a campaign against them in the early eighteenth century.[108] These decentralised peoples responded to the Lunda challenge with strategies as diverse as were their matriclan leaders. Some assimilated the full range of Ruund cultural traditions but never paid tribute. Other down-stream warriors were recruited to serve as mercenaries at the Lunda court. In yet other cases, war leaders and their clients continued to resist incursion.[109]

The expansion of Lunda is best seen in the history of its eastern political syncretism and overrule. Forceful subordinates within the heartland could unseat a king or weaken his central authority. These ambitious individuals were commonly sent to the state periphery, where their talents could be used to extend the influence of a royal dynasty. Such a process occurred between about 1670 and 1700, when King Yav a Nawej sent colonists to settle along the Mukulweji river some 400 kilometres south-east of the Lunda heartland. This colony collected tribute from the nearby salt districts on the upper Zaire and the malachite diggings at the western end of the Copperbelt. Local peoples adopted central Lunda political forms, and the colonists learned to speak the Luba language of the indigenous villagers. Local political titles were adopted, and eastern Lunda political tradition emerged from this syncretism.

After 1700 the short-lived Mukulweji colony broke apart during a leadership struggle. A secondary diaspora occurred, which brought Lunda political culture to many peoples of the Zaire–Zambezi watershed.[110] Eastern Lunda norms were imposed upon a region where decentralised polities exercised a loose suzerainty over small and widely scattered populations. Kanongesha was one such polity. The *kanongesha* title-holder was a leader among equal lineage heads. Perpetual kinship was used to link him with titled heads of subordinate lineages. Each title-holder claimed descent from the first holder of the title and possessed a sacred copper bracelet wrapped in human tissue, a key insignia of Lundahood.[111]

Kazembe was a title indigenous to the Mukulweji area, and it became the most prestigious symbol of eastern Lunda expansion. A guardian with this title was established on the upper Zaire to exploit salt resources and to protect a vital river crossing. This became the launching point for an early-

108 Léon Duysters, 'Histoire des Aluunda', *Problèmes d'Afrique Centrale*, xii, 1958, 86–7.
109 Hoover, 'Seduction of Ruwej', vol. 1, pp. 288–303; William F. Pruitt, Jr, 'An Independent People: the Salampasu of Luisa Territory', Ph.D. thesis, Northwestern University, 1974, chap. 4.
110 Hoover, 'Seduction of Ruwej', vol. 1, pp. 249–70; Frank H. Melland, *In Witch-Bound Africa, An Account of the Primitive Kaonde Tribe & Their Beliefs*, London, 1923, pp. 34–9; Mwata Kazembe XIV, *Central Bantu Historical Texts. Volume II. Historical Traditions of the Eastern Lunda*, trans. Ian Cunnison, Lusaka, 1961, chap. 2; Robert E. Schechter, 'History and Historiography on a Frontier of Lunda Expansion: the Origins and Early Development of the Kanongesha', Ph.D. thesis, University of Wisconsin, Madison, 1976, pp. 158–64.
111 Hoover, 'Seduction of Ruwej', vol. 1, pp. 270–77; Schechter, 'History and Historiography', pp. 206, 267; Turner, *Forest of Symbols*, p. 175.

eighteenth-century migration to the east. It was led by Kanyembo I, a scion of the Mukulweji élite. The eastern Lunda moved rapidly across lightly populated terrain subjugating the chiefs of copper diggings and salt pans along the Copperbelt. Kanyembo's 350-kilometre migration reached the dense riverain populations of the lower Luapula flood plain. It was here that the Kazembe kingdom was firmly established about 1740.[112]

Among the southern Lunda of Mukulweji, political forms and practices were the product of assimilation. Such was not the case on the Luapula. The eastern Lunda aristocracy did not depend upon corporate lineage structures to create political linkages. Principles of perpetual kinship and positional succession were rigorously applied to bind together the holders of Lunda 'colonial' titles.[113] Kazembe court structures followed central Lunda models, though the court language was derived from the Luba dialect of the Mukulweji colony.[114] An aristocratic eastern Lunda government was established among riverain matrilineal societies whose own structures were not significantly disturbed.[115]

During the second half of the eighteenth century the Kazembe kingdom became a large-scale dynastic state. It enjoyed good relations with the Lunda empire but was independent. Expansion from the flood plain did not meet strong opposition from small neighbouring polities or scattered populations. Lukwesa I, the third Kazembe, turned his attention from the loyal western copper- and salt-producing tributaries to the east. He was feared and respected. A chief of the dispersed Bemba polity sent generous gifts to avoid confrontation with Lukwesa. Another sought war charms from the Kazembe court. As Kazembe troops raided and pillaged the east, fortified outposts were built to maintain a presence in the conquered territories.[116] Leaders of small local matrilineages had been accustomed to receiving tribute in the form of goats and sheep. After resolving a lineage dispute to his advantage, the king could boast to his court in a praise song:

> I love
> To seize the country by force,
> I who am given lands and people,
> Whereas others are given goats and sheep.[117]

112 Burton, *Lands of Cazembe*, p. 126; Mwata Kazembe XIV, *Central Bantu Historical Texts*, vol. 2, pp. 31–48.
113 Cunnison, 'Perpetual kinship', pp. 28–48; Hoover, 'Seduction of Ruwej', vol. 1, pp. 279–81.
114 Jacques C. Chiwale (ed.), *Central Bantu Historical Texts, III. Royal Praises and Praise Names of the Lunda Kazembe of Northern Rhodesia: their Meaning and Historical Background*, Lusaka, 1962, p. 9.
115 Ian Cunnison, *The Luapula Peoples of Northern Rhodesia*, 1959; reprint, Manchester, 1967, pp. 152, n.2, 156–64; Hoover, 'Seduction of Ruwej', vol. 1, pp. 278–9, 286–7.
116 Mwata Kazembe XIV, *Central Bantu Historical Texts*, vol. 2, pp. 49–50; Roberts, *History of the Bemba*, pp. 96–7, 100.
117 Chiwale, *Central Bantu Historical Texts*, III, p. 16.

By the time Lukwesa died – about 1805 – Kazembe influence extended from the upper Zaire to the Chambeshi river.

Raiding, pillaging and lineage power-brokering were not the only options for aggrandisement. Kazembe received the prestige goods of long-distance trade by way of the Lunda empire in exchange for salt and copper. This westerly route across two-thirds of the continent had inevitable supply problems. Trade along shorter routes to the south-east offered Kazembe kings their greatest opportunities. By the middle of the eighteenth century, African traders were bringing east-coast goods into the savanna by way of the southern end of Lake Malawi. They linked up with Bisa villages east of the Luapula. The eastern Lunda themselves did not engage in lengthy travels to the south-east, but the Bisa were already experienced in regional trade. They quickly adapted to the practice of long-distance trade and became the client traders of Kazembe.

The south-eastern trade link existed by the 1760s.[118] The Copperbelt became the intersection between a new trans-continental trading system and the older north–south regional trade. From the late eighteenth century to the middle of the nineteenth century Kazembe kings jealously guarded their position in these trans-African trading systems. The Portuguese were well aware of Kazembe's role in interior trade. They failed, however, to link the Luso-African frontier of Angola with the Luso-African frontier on the lower Zambezi by way of Kazembe. Explorers and traders representing Portuguese interests lingered for years at Kazembe's court in futile attempts to negotiate a trade pact.[119] The Portuguese could trade with Kazembe, but they could not dominate it. Thwarted Portuguese and Euro-African commercial interests were therefore pushed into the southerly zones of the eastern savanna by way of the middle Zambezi.

The Bisa became expert long-distance traders. They travelled to the south-east coast, to the lower Zambezi and to central Angola. It was said of them: 'the Babisa are great travellers and traders, and, in fact, occupy somewhat the same position in this country as the Greeks do in the Levant'.[120] Their success, however, did not make them strong. They were victims of a tributary political economy. The commercial independence of Bisa chiefs was curtailed by Kazembe kings who drained off the lion's share of trade profits. The Bisa were also vulnerable to external attack in their

118 Edward A. Alpers, *Ivory and Slaves, Changing Patterns of International Trade in East Central Africa to the Late Nineteenth Century*, Berkeley and Los Angeles, 1975, pp. 122–3; Andrew D. Roberts, 'Pre-Colonial trade in Zambia', *African Social Research*, no. 10, 1970, 728–9.

119 Bontinck, 'Voyage des pombeiros', 29–70; Richard Burton, *Lands of Cazembe*; Ian Cunnison, 'Kazembe and the Portuguese 1798–1832', *JAH*, ii, 1, 1961, 61–76; Gamitto, *King Kazembe*, 2 vols; A. Verbeken and M. Walraet (eds), *La Première Traversée du Katanga en 1806, voyage des 'Pombeiros' d'Angola aux Rios de Sena*, Brussels, 1953.

120 David and Charles Livingstone, *Narrative of an Expedition to the Zambesi and Its Tributaries*, New York, 1866, p. 527; Roberts, 'Pre-Colonial trade in Zambia', 729.

homeland. By the 1820s and 1830s these attacks on the Bisa chiefdoms came from the aggressive Bemba polity that had developed on their frontier.[121]

The heartland of the decentralised Bemba polity lay west of the upper Chambeshi. During the middle and late nineteenth century it came to dominate the area between the Luapula and Lake Malawi. The Bemba land was not rich in natural resources, though salt and iron were acquired through regional trade. Because Bemba villages had little to offer in exchange, they often raided for their needs.[122] Their ruthless attacks on the Bisa chiefdoms sought to control trade. The victor's villages were filled with refugees. An eyewitness described one in 1831: 'we reached a big Bemba village. ... The village is large and populous; they say there are many others near. ... [It] has more than 150 huts, there is no stockade, and the people are numerous.'[123] Not far away the countryside was recently deserted, and famine was a reality: 'The land we are in shows many traces of great population. We are told that in these parts there were many battles between Bemba and Bisa, and when the Bemba were victorious they destroyed everything. There are now only the remains of ruined cassava gardens.'[124]

The origins of the Bemba polity belong to the middle of the eighteenth century. A Bemba paramountcy emerged that rotated among the several chiefly lineages in a royal clan. This paramountcy bound separate lineages together by mutual interest.[125] A significant change occurred in the succession pattern of the royal clan between 1770 and 1820. A single shallow lineage established the exclusive right of its male offspring to occupy the kingship. This lineage was able, through intrigue and military muscle, to impose its male scions as territorial chiefs. A body of hereditary councillors became kingmakers in order to prevent succession conflict.

The Bemba continued to raid Kazembe's Bisa clients until the 1850s without prompting Kazembe retaliation. Kazembe–Bemba relations, which had been cordial before the Bisa wars, remained so despite Bemba threats to Kazembe's south-eastern trade route. The reason for Kazembe's passivity was primarily economic. The long-distance trade pattern was beginning to shift towards the north-east where the Bemba were strong. Kazembe had to rely upon Bemba cooperation to open these routes,[126] which brought new merchant-raiders from Tanzania. The change was part of a widespread pattern of invasion that was to alter the whole political and economic landscape of the eastern savanna.

121 Gamitto, *King Kazembe*, vol. 1, p. 165; Stuart A. Marks, 'Settlement history and population of the valley Bisa of Zambia', *Zambia Museums Journal*, iv, 1973, 46–7.
122 Roberts, *History of the Bemba*, p. 182.
123 Gamitto, *King Kazembe*, vol. 1, p. 171.
124 *Ibid.*, p. 186; Roberts, *History of the Bemba*, pp. 114–15.
125 Ibid., p. 297.
126 *Ibid.*, pp. 94–119, 191–4.

TRADERS AND RAIDERS IN THE LATE NINETEENTH CENTURY

During the nineteenth century the peoples and polities of the eastern savanna were subjected to a series of unprecedented invasions from the south, east and west. Indigenous systems of government were dismembered and replaced by distinctive conquest régimes. Opportunism had been the characteristic of lineage and dynastic politics. It remained so but with a new twist. Local strong men freed themselves from the tutelage of kings only to become subservient to new merchant-conquerors and warlords. The spear and war knife were replaced by a new symbol of power: the flint-lock, muzzle-loading gun. Ethnicities were reconstituted, conquerors learned local languages and Swahili became a lingua franca of trade and authority.

Under the new order, older processes persisted with difficulty. Regional trade continued to interact with long-distance trade. Subsistence exchange continued, though travel became more difficult for the average villager.

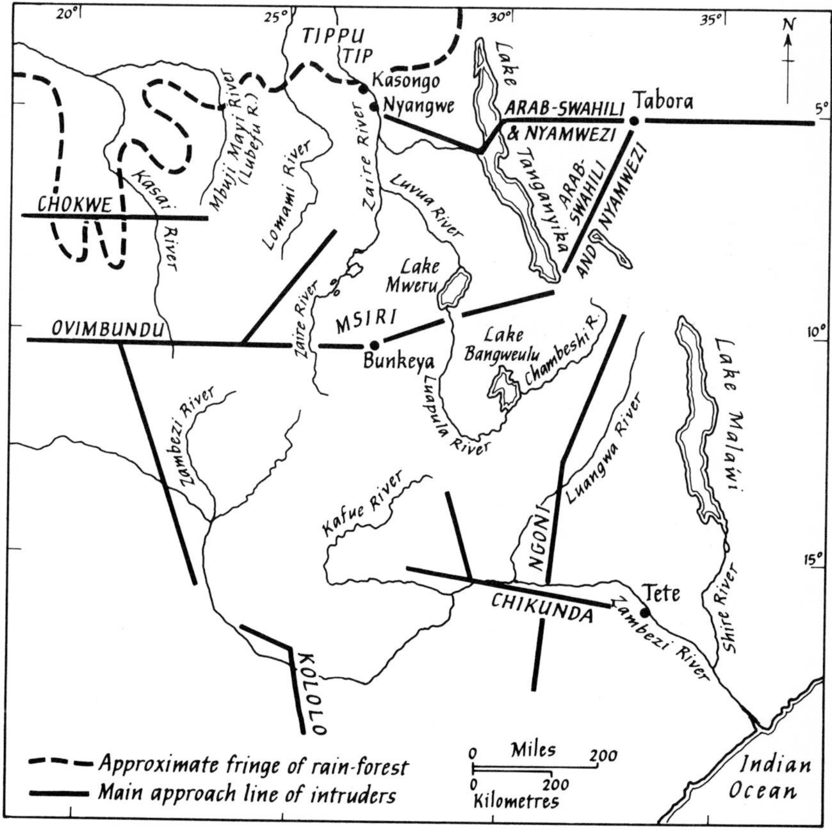

5:3 Traders and raiders of the eastern savanna, 1830s to 1890s

Villages were more frequently overrun by the new lords, and by the 1880s agriculturalists were having to live in stockaded villages. Hamlets were tucked away behind thickets and paths camouflaged in forested river land. In the south cattle-keepers lost their herds, and large areas were depopulated. Short-range migration continued, but movement was more likely to be in the direction of new refugee centres. Genesis myths spoke of wandering culture heroes in antiquity. Ironically, it was during the nineteenth century that rapid human movement and extensive dislocation of population first occurred on a truly epic scale.

Eyewitnesses commented on the horrors of the period. David Livingstone's account of the massacre of market people at Nyangwe on the Zaire is eloquent testimony to the suffering of the era:

> the discharge of two guns in the middle of the crowd told me that slaughter had begun: crowds dashed off from the place, and threw down their wares in confusion, and ran. At the same time that the three opened fire on the mass of people near the upper end of the market-place, volleys were discharged from a party down near the creek on the panic-stricken women, who dashed at the canoes. These, some fifty or more, were jammed in the creek, and the men forgot their paddles in the terror that seized all. The canoes were not to be got out, for the creek was too small for so many: men and women, wounded by the balls, poured into them, leaped and scrambled into the water, shrieking. A long line of heads in the river showed that great numbers struck out for an island a full mile off....
>
> Shot after shot continued to be fired on the helpless and perishing. Some of the long lines of heads disappeared quickly; while other poor creatures threw their arms high, as if appealing to the great Father above, and sank. ... the Arabs themselves estimated the loss of life at between three-hundred-and-thirty and four-hundred souls. The shooting-party near the canoes were so reckless they killed two of their own people....
>
> After the terrible affair in the water, the party of the chief perpetrator, continued to fire on the people there and fire their villages. As I write, I hear the loud wails on the left bank over those who are there slain, ignorant of their many friends now in the depths of [the river].[127]

Life has always been lived on the raw edge in the Central African grassland, probably never more so than during the second half of the last century.

In the 1830s South-Central Africa was invaded by the Ngoni and the Kololo. These two groups had been kicked loose on migratory conquests by the 'Crushing of Peoples', the 1820s' revolution among South African Bantu-speaking peoples caused by the rise of the Zulu military state under

127 David Livingstone, *The Last Journals of David Livingstone in Central Africa*, New York, 1875, pp. 383–4.

Shaka. Soon afterwards, in the 1840s and 1850s, east-coast Arab-Swahili traders, accompanied by Nyamwezi auxiliaries from Tanzania, began visiting East-Central Africa in large numbers. Two of their number created predatory states on the eastern savanna. The Swahili merchant nicknamed Tippu Tip founded his raiding state on the fringe of the rain-forest in the mid-1870s. Meanwhile, the Nyamwezi conqueror Msiri had established his base of operations in the Copperbelt. A third intrusion of Chikunda traders and raiders moved in from Mozambique. The products of their pillage went down-stream on the Zambezi. In the west Ovimbundu traders and Chokwe hunters from Angola had a profound impact. By the 1890s, when the agents of European colonialism first entered the area, these four sets of alien forces had significantly changed the political and economic landscape of the region.

Long-term chaos was promoted by the complex interrelationship between the ivory-trade and the slave-trade. The demand for ivory increased on the international market throughout the nineteenth century. Despite the curtailment of the Atlantic and Indian ocean slave-trades at mid-century, slave demand remained strong on the east coast, along the lower Zambezi and in Angola. The ivory frontier moved rapidly inland as elephant herds were depleted by indiscriminate slaughter. The slave-trade often followed the ivory frontier, and an internal slave and ivory exchange developed.[128]

The internal slave-trade was fuelled, in particular, by local demand for women. Early in the century the Chokwe were an inconsequential cluster of hunters and wax-gatherers on the western fringe of the Lunda empire. By mid-century they were well-armed elephant-hunters who sold ivory for women, whom they absorbed into their porous social structure. Similarly, in the east during the 1880s the Chikunda imported many slaves. Women from Malawi, the Kafue and the Gwembe valley were sold at the rate of one per tusk. Aggressors increased their human capital with slaves, and centralised polities began to develop at the expense of lineage-based relationships.[129] In the south, Lozi soldiers raided their neighbours for cattle and slaves but preferred not to sell prisoners to long-distance traders. The kingdom became an inland slave-buyer, exchanging ivory for slaves imported from as far away as the Luba empire. The upper Zambezi labour system was thereby strengthened. Between one-quarter and one-third of the population were slaves. By the last decade of the century the Lozi king, Lewanika, could direct large numbers of slaves to major canal-building projects for the state.[130]

128 Cameron, *Across Africa*, vol. 2, pp. 323–4.

129 Matthews, 'Portuguese, Chikunda, and peoples of the Gwembe valley', 33–4; Joseph C. Miller, 'Cokwe trade and conquest in the nineteenth century', in *Pre-Colonial African Trade*, Richard Gray and David Birmingham (eds), London, 1970, pp. 174–201.

130 Cameron, *Across Africa*, vol. 2, pp. 141, 217–18; Clarence-Smith, 'Slaves, commoners and landlords in Bulozi', 223–30; Prins, *Hidden Hippopotamus*, p. 73.

Invaders possessed a better military technology and often employed superior infantry tactics. The Ngoni and Kololo had adopted Shaka's battle drill. They were skilled in the use of the stabbing spear and the cow-hide shield. Their fighting units manoeuvred swiftly to encircle the enemy. Other intruders began to make use of flint-locks so quickly that their opponents had little time to adapt to the use of fire-power before being overrun. Invaders also controlled the supply of guns and powder. Where the flint-lock was adopted it sometimes became a symbol of power to replace the copper-bound, wooden staff of chiefly authority.[131] Guns as insignia were encrusted with copper decorations. Warriors 'stood in mute amazement looking at the guns, which mowed them down in large numbers. They thought that muskets were the insignia of chieftainship ... they have no fear of seeing a gun levelled at them.'[132]

The role of weapon technology should not be overemphasised. Trade flint-locks of the era were notoriously inaccurate and had a nasty tendency to blow up. One exploded in the hands of a Luba king, eventually leading to his death.[133] Msiri's warriors bitterly complained about their guns in a fighting verse that starts off with an imitation of the sound made by hammer striking flint: 'Kwarkasa kwasa: Our own flintlocks are slaughtering us.'[134] Eventually many eastern savanna war leaders acquired flint-locks. Although the Swahili were chary of selling guns lest they be turned on themselves, the Ovimbundu were less cautious. One Ovimbundu caravan would arm a local faction, and a second caravan would arm their opponents. The spread of terror generated slaves for sale.[135]

Over time many leaders adapted to the new situation. The spear or poison-arrow ambush proved effective against caravans moving in single file along twisting paths in dense undergrowth.[136] Msiri's dry-land soldiers lost in protracted amphibious warfare with guerrilla leaders in the Upemba depression.[137] One local adventurer, Kasongo Kinyama, learned military

131 Reefe, *Rainbow and the Kings*, pp. 161, 169–71, 199.

132 Livingstone, *Last Journals*, p. 374.

133 D'Orjo de Marchovelette, 'Notes sur les funérailles', *Bulletin des juridictions indigènes du droit coutumier congolais*, xviii, 12, 1950, 365.

134 A. Mwenda Munongo (ed.), 'Chants historiques des Bayeke, Recueillis à Bunkeya et ailleurs', in Collection de Mémoires, vol. 25, Lubumbashi, Centre d'Etudes des Problèmes Sociaux Indigènes, 1967, p. 160. Translation by the author.

135 Reefe, *Rainbow and the Kings*, pp. 183–92.

136 Frederick S. Arnot, *Missionary Travels in Central Africa*, London, 1914, p. 100; Henry M. Stanley, *Through the Dark Continent*, New York, 1878, vol. 2, pp. 103–6; Yoder, 'People on the Edge of Empires', pp. 363–4.

137 H. Capello and R. Ivens, *De Angola á contra-costa*, Lisbon, 1886, pp. 80–90; Antoine Mwenda Munongo, 'Court Aperçu de l'Histoire des Bayeke', 15–17 and trans., 'Lettre de Mwenda II, Mukanda Bantu, à S. M. le Roi Albert à l'époque Prince héritier de Belgique', p. 37, both in Collection de Mémoires, vol. 25, Lubumbashi, Centre d'Etudes des Problèmes Sociaux Indigènes, 1967.

skills during caravan duty with Swahili merchants travelling to Msiri's headquarters, and later bought guns from the Ovimbundu and Chokwe. He then carved a conquest state that terrorised the disintegrating Kanyok kingdom during the late 1870s and 1880s. His gun-toting overseers were called *balungu*, and wore East African conus-shell disc-beads as warrior symbols.[138] The Bemba had a sophisticated military structure which enabled the king to summon rapidly well-organised fighting units when threatened by the Ngoni. Bemba rulers secured their frontiers and continued, unlike many of their grassland contemporaries, to exploit the opportunities of long-distance trade.[139]

Mobility was strategically important to invaders. Resisters had to defend their periphery and ultimately their heartland. Invaders, on the other hand, could choose the path of least resistance. They journeyed along the seams between dynastic states, trading and raiding in segmentary and small-scale societies.[140]

The career of Hamed bin Muhammed el-Murjebi, better known by the caravan name of Tippu Tip, is illustrative. Born about 1840, he was on the trail with his father by the time he was a teenager. He made five long journeys into Central Africa between about 1860 and 1891. His caravans consisted of hundreds and sometimes thousands of Nyamwezi and east-coast porters and gun-bearers. He would stop for weeks, months or even years in an interior region where dense human populations were suitable for raiding or where large elephant herds existed. He negotiated with local rulers whenever possible, but he was not afraid to blast his way out of trouble. He captured hostages, who had to be ransomed with ivory. On his third voyage, from about 1870 to 1882, he established permanent bases of operation on the fringe of the rain-forest in the towns of Nyangwe and Kasongo. His régime was fluid, allowing rapid advancement by loyal individuals. Subordinate warlord régimes were spawned this way.[141] The northern tributary states of the Luba empire were detached from their allegiance. The Songye town-states became ripe targets. Their soldiers had no guns, the towns were populous and ivory was to be had in quantity. The

138 Reefe, *Rainbow and the Kings*, pp. 170–72; A. Van Zandijcke, *Pages de l'histoire du Kasayi*, Namur, 1953, pp. 131–3; Yoder, 'People on the Edge of Empires', pp. 306–14.

139 A. L. Epstein, 'Military organization and the pre-colonial polity of the Bemba of Zambia', *Man*, n.s., x, 1975, 199–217; Roberts, *History of the Bemba*, pp. 119–23, 142–51.

140 For detailed histories of Arab–Swahili trade in this regard, see Andrew D. Roberts, 'Nyamwezi Trade', pp. 39–74, and Christopher St John, 'Kazembe and the Tanganyika–Nyasa Corridor, 1800–1890', pp. 202–30, both in *Pre-Colonial African Trade*, Richard Gray and David Birmingham (eds), London, 1970; Livingstone, *Last Journals*, is a rich primary source.

141 Bontinck, *L'Autobiographie de Hamed ben Mohammed el-Murjebi*; Melvin E. Page, 'The Manyema hordes of Tippu Tip: a case study in social stratification and the slave trade in East Africa', *International Journal of African Historical Studies*, vii, 1, 1974, 69–84; W. H. Whiteley (ed.), *Maisha ya Hamed bin Muhammed el Murjebi yaani Tippu Tip*, supplement to the *East African Swahili Committee Journals*, no. 28/2, 1958, and no. 29/1, 1959.

Songye were devastated, and their unique urban culture never recovered.[142]

Numerous opportunities for subversion were presented to invaders. Where rotating rule was practised, the assistance of invaders was commonly sought by a lineage seeking to establish a permanent royal line.[143] Dynastic states were most vulnerable during succession crises. When the political centre was immobilised by dispute, clients on the periphery became restive. Large states had dominated small ones by arbitrating during succession crises; the same could be done to them. Invaders moved in when succession disputes neutralised unified resistance. Unsuccessful royal contenders sought outside arms supplies and mercenaries, only to become dependent on their new allies. Intruders felt little obligation to maintain the *status quo*. The price of their allegiance was the right to raid villages. They frequently destroyed or restructured political hierarchies. The correlation between succession crisis and invasion was widespread. The Kololo, led by Sebitwane, invaded the Lozi kingdom during a succession dispute in the early 1840s. The Ovimbundu inserted themselves into the Luba heartland in the early 1870s, initiating thirty years of civil war. The Chokwe intervened among the Lunda under similar circumstances. A Kazembe king died in 1862, beginning a civil war that eventually drew in Msiri. Only in the case of the Lozi were the intruders finally driven out, in 1864, by a new royal dynasty.[144]

The eastern savanna became divided into a shifting mosaic of centres from which power radiated out along conquest and trade routes. These power centres were created when invaders established permanent or semi-permanent bases. The most disruptive violence was directed away from the centre towards the expanding frontier. In relation to the harsh times the new conquest capitals were places of peace and order; they were also places of terror. The new towns contained polyglot hostages, refugees, slaves, clients, caravaneers and petty warlords. It was a volatile human population. The merchant-conqueror lived behind his stockade, and maintained order by draconian punishments publicly administered to those who displeased him. One of the largest towns, where routes met from both the east and west, was Bunkeya, Msiri's capital. It was described in the memoirs of a European who visited it in 1891:

142 Fairley, 'Mianda ya Ben'Ekie', pp. 161–75; Alan P. Merriam, *An African World; the Basongye Village of Lupupa Ngye*, Bloomington and London, 1974, pp. 8–24; Hermann von Wissmann, *My Second Journey through Equatorial Africa from the Congo to the Zambesi in the Years 1886 and 1887*, Minna J. Bergmann (trans.), London, 1891, pp. 180–86.

143 Bontinck, *L'Autobiographie de Hamed ben Mohammed el-Murjebi*, secs. 87, 91, 101; Burton, *Luba Religion and Magic*, pp. 17, 21.

144 Duysters, 'Histoire des Aluunda', 92; Mainga, *Bulozi under the Luyana Kings*, pp. 65–104; Mwata Kazembe XIV, *Central Bantu Historical Texts*, vol. 2, pp. 85–105; *Rainbow and the Kings*, pp. 184–8, 192–3.

> Bunkeya was, at that time, a vast agglomeration whose fields extended along a river of the same name. There were about forty villages surrounded by palisades and separated by fields of sorghum, maize, rice, eleusine used to make a good beer, sesame, groundnuts, etc., a few plantations of manioc, sweet potato and yams. . . . M'Siri lived in a large [fortified village] . . . which was [bounded] by a palisade built with posts four meters long, at the base of which had been excavated a deep dry moat. . . . posts were capped with human heads which over time became skulls shining in the sun. The whole circumference of the palisade was decorated this way, and made a most dismal impression upon me.[145]

The new régimes were highly assimilationist. They consisted of a multi-ethnic population held together by concubinage and political syncretism. The backbone of Msiri's power consisted of groups which had come with him from central Tanzania. They called themselves 'The Hunters'.[146] Some were blacksmiths who were taught the art of copper-smelting from the smiths of the Copperbelt, whom they then eclipsed.[147] Msiri's chiefs placed women from their lineages at court both as hostages and representatives of lineage interests. Msiri married the niece of an Angolan trader to cement ties with his Ovimbundu arms suppliers.[148] He sent trusted court personnel and kin, male and female, to distant locations as overseers and garrison heads. Political titles were borrowed from many regions. Some overseers took the eastern Lunda title *kazembe*, while their courtiers bore Nyamwezi titles. Overseers were hailed by the Copperbelt greeting 'Conqueror'.[149]

The conquest states were little more than a shell constantly replenished with new human material. Prisoners were absorbed to maintain or augment a population depleted in battle. The same human reservoir might be tapped more than once. The Ngoni, led by Zwangendaba, crossed the Zambezi in 1835 and assaulted the lower Luangwa valley. Villagers were absorbed and even rose to positions of leadership. Local doctors were co-opted for their expertise in manipulating the supernatural. Almost thirty years later a Ngoni offshoot again returned to the lower Luangwa and

145 Edgard Verdick, *Les Premiers Jours au Katanga (1890–1903)*, Brussels, 1952, p. 33. Translation by the author. See also Guy de Plaen, 'Diplomatie et economie: le système Yeke', *Cultures et Développement*, xi, 1, 1979, 29–31, and Auguste Verbeken, *Msiri, roi du Garenganze, "L'Homme rouge" du Katanga*, Brussels, 1956, pp. 80–89.

146 F. Grevisse, 'Les Yeke', in Collection de Mémoires, vol. 25, Lubumbashi, Centre d'Etudes des Problèmes Sociaux Indigènes, 1967, p. 279; Walter van Dorpe, 'Cadre explicatif de l'établissement Yeke', M.A. thesis, National University of Zaire at Lubumbashi, 1973–4, pp. 7–14.

147 Jean de Hemptinne, 'Les "mangeurs de cuivre" du Katanga', *Congo*, i, 3, 1926, 378.

148 Arnot, *Garenganze*, p. 234; Verbeken, *Msiri*, pp. 89–99; Verdick, *Premiers Jours au Katanga*, pp. 43, 53.

149 Burton, *Luba Religion and Magic*, pp. 30–31; Verbeken, *Msiri*, pp. 101–5.

overwhelmed many stockaded villages. Again captives were taken, but this time the Nsenga language was adopted by the invader.[150]

The conquest states of the eastern savanna traders lacked permanency. Adopted institutions were imposed from on top rather than emerging from a deeply embedded cultural base. Conquest régimes were often built on personal charisma and leadership. When the conqueror died, his sons attempted to seize what there was of a state apparatus or to build their own conquest states. After Zwangendaba's death, in the late 1840s, his state broke apart. Half-a-dozen Ngoni units were scattered around the Lake Malawi basin to create their own assimilationist polities.[151] A dead conqueror's capital was usually abandoned or reduced to the status of a village. Residents became refugees seeking the protection of another warlord or merchant-conqueror. This happened to Bunkeya in 1891 when Msiri was shot by an agent of King Leopold II's new colonial conquest state. Msiri's death was a symbol of the time. The process of migration and conquest was suddenly stopped in the 1890s by the European invasion of the eastern savanna.

CONCLUSION

This has been history on the grand scale, the past of the societies of the eastern savanna for five hundred years. It is part of the pre-colonial heritage of eastern Angola, southern Zaire, Zambia and Malawi. Much of what has been told deals with large polities and extended regional economic phenomena. The available historical data direct this tilt. It is unfortunate. That which is smallest in scale and most local has been significant for the longest time. This should not be surprising in the middle of a continent known for its small-scale societies and localised polities. Traditions of longevity and continuity came from the grassroots, and can be traced from the middle centuries of this millennium and earlier. The lives of canoe-paddlers and head-loading agriculturalists, of hunters and cattle-keepers, have usually been worked out at the village and hamlet level. It is at this level that the pervasive and extensive values can be identified. There exists a deeply embedded cultural baseline left from the ancient diaspora of Bantu-speaking peoples. It has been enriched by centuries of innovation and selective borrowing among close neighbours.

Environment has provided only limited options. Natural resources were

150 Albert J. Williams-Myers, 'The Nsenga of Central Africa: Political and Economic Aspects of Clan History, 1700 to the Late Nineteenth Century', Ph.D. thesis, University of California at Los Angeles, 1978, pp. 234–7, 280–92; see also J. A. Barnes, *Politics in a Changing Society: a Political History of the Fort Jameson Ngoni*, 1954; reprint Manchester, 1967, chap. 2.

151 B. Pachai, 'Ngoni politics and diplomacy in Malawi: 1848–1904', in *The Early History of Malawi*, B. Pachai (ed.), Evanston, Illinois, 1972, pp. 183–5.

unevenly distributed. Those who had iron or copper or salt enjoyed advantages over those who had not. Rainfall was capricious, so that drought and famine were common. Flood plains and lake shores were important sanctuaries, though few and far between. Strong men came and went. The prestige of their titles and the labour of their clients was not sufficient to preserve ascendency for more than a generation or two. For centuries the priests of the rain and the earth were leaders while the ancestors hovered over the villages.

Human relationships were changing and complex: men and women married out; clans dispersed; personal and lineage disputes changed the village; the distressed and the desperate left, though few went far. Migrants and refugees sought the closest protective environment in which to begin their new lives. Short-range migration was the key to savanna displacement up to the eighteenth century, and even persisted in the more recent era of long-range conquest.

The kingdoms of the savanna expanded at the expense of small-scale neighbours. Several kingdoms became the local colonial powers. Dynastic states had a heartland where ancestral institutions and ideologies were developed by invention and borrowing. The symbolic systems of thought and traditions of genesis were shaped to the advantage of a single dynasty. Mechanisms of overrule were imposed upon nearby peoples after conquest, infiltration or mediation. Expansion followed the path of least resistance among small-scale societies. Less innovative neighbours were incapable of protracted resistance, or found the sacral resources of the big states irresistible.

Regional integration was achieved at the economic level, not at the political level. The kingdoms and empires were separated by hundreds of kilometres of sparsely populated savanna. There was little contact between these states before the introduction of long-distance trade from the west and south-east. After about 1700 some of them were drawn into limited competition and cooperation. The shift towards large-scale political units was associated with trans-savanna trading. Regional exchange networks became important during the fifteenth century. For a long time the demand for prestige goods from an ubiquitous 'class' of small-time political and religious élites meant that the political economy remained locally based. By the end of the seventeenth century the networks had interlocked across the whole zone between the forest and the Zambezi. By 1700 a few large-scale states had begun to develop. It is in the three centuries between 1400 and 1700, just beyond the range of reliable dynastic traditions, that research remains to be done.

The fragility of the large states was hard to perceive in 1800. They preyed upon weaker neighbours and did not fight one another. In the absence of dynamic external challengers, the occasional succession dispute did not destroy the state. Systems of overrule were transformed, however, between the 1830s and the 1890s. Invasions by the Ngoni and Kololo and the advent of Swahili, Nyamwezi, Chikunda, Ovimbundu and Chokwe created new power centres. This was a period of great mobility. Centralised and decentralised polities alike were overthrown. Only a few, like Bemba and Lozi, met the challenge. The price of change was paid by savanna villagers. People became the currency in a system of exchange that took a frightful toll. Baptism in the international capitalist economy of the invaders was traumatic. The expanding slave and ivory frontier was brutal. Then, with little warning, these violent conquest régimes were overthrown by better-armed and better-capitalised invaders from Britain and Belgium.

CHAPTER 6

The Indian Ocean zone

ALAN K. SMITH

Between the sixteenth and the later stages of the nineteenth century, the Indian Ocean zone was increasingly drawn into the world capitalist economy. Before 1500, influences both from the surrounding hinterland and from beyond the sea had been factors in the pattern of growth. From the early sixteenth century, however, the involvement of external forces changed significantly as they impinged upon regions that had been only marginally concerned with events beyond their immediate locality. The date at which each group was first required to acknowledge the pressures of an increasingly interdependent world varied considerably. By the nineteenth century, few remained immune and unaffected. Central Africans found that their range of choice, and their opportunities for successful mediation with external forces, became more restricted. As the world capitalist economy matured in the late nineteenth century, it imposed new forms of social relations that were forerunners of the colonial epoch.

The Indian Ocean zone of East-Central Africa can be defined in two ways. Geographically, it is limited to the lowland regions that extend inland from the ocean on either side of the Zambezi river. The geographical entity, however, does not necessarily correspond with the unity of historical experience. From the geographical lowlands, the Indian Ocean zone of influence expanded to include the neighbouring territories in a growing process of historical interrelationship. The boundaries contracted or expanded depending on time, place and interaction.

By 1400, the process of interaction between descendants of early eastern Bantu-speakers and more recent arrivals from the west was well advanced. North of the Zambezi, four main linguistic categories were discernible. The Makonde resided along both banks of the Rovuma river. Their western neighbours were the Yao, who also occupied parts of Tanzania and Mozambique. Both languages were related to clusters spoken further north and were associated with the old movement of Bantu-speakers along the coast. The influence of the Later Iron Age may have penetrated the lands of the Yao and Makonde from the west. Although it is not borne out by linguistic evidence, a number of Makonde traditions refer to a homeland south of Lake Malawi and to a subsequent migration into the Rovuma valley.[1]

Peoples who spoke one of the languages of the Chewa cluster and those who spoke Makua occupied most of the remaining northern territories. Linguistic evidence and traditions suggest that they were heavily

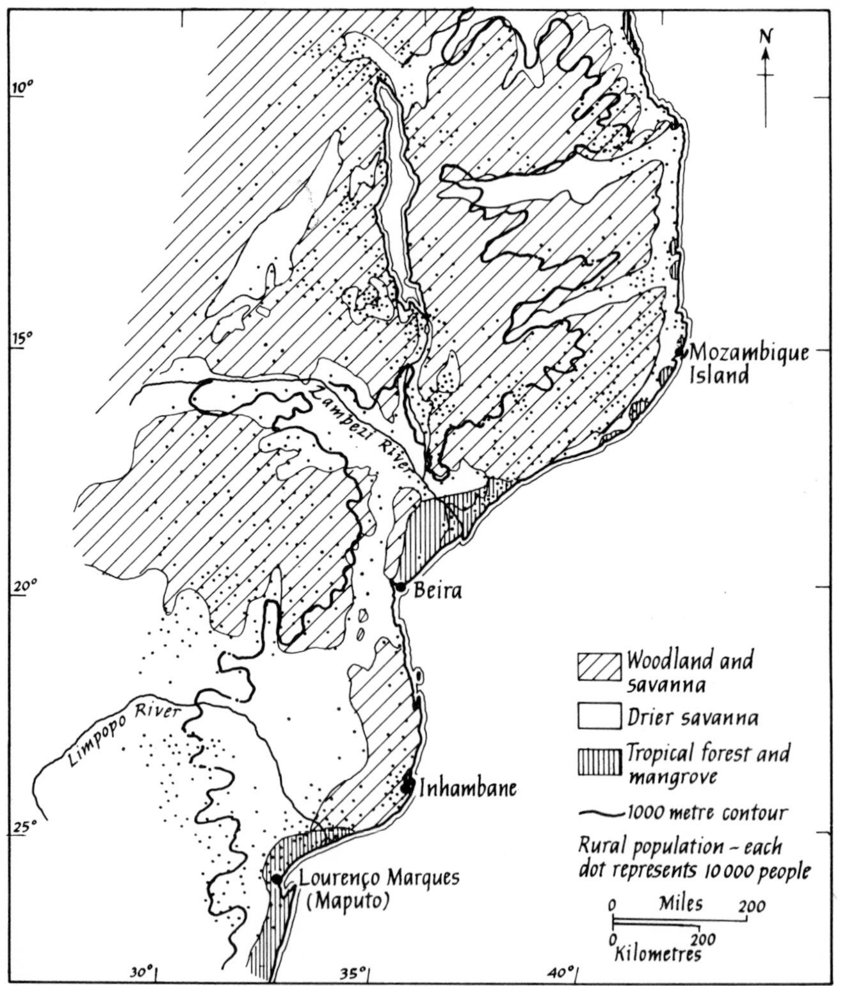

6:1 The Indian Ocean zone

1 Jorge Dias, *Os Macondes de Moçambique*, Lisbon, 1964, vol. 1, p. 73; Yohanna B. Abdallah, *The Yaos*, Zomba, 1918, p. 7; Christopher Ehret, personal communication, 10 Dec. 1975, pp. 2–3.

influenced by western neighbours, and that speakers of both groups of languages had dispersed over a significant area by 1400. Each group recorded traditions that suggested western points of origin. Moreover, the range of dialects within each is sufficiently great that many are mutually unintelligible. The inference is that the dispersal of these peoples began in the distant past.[2]

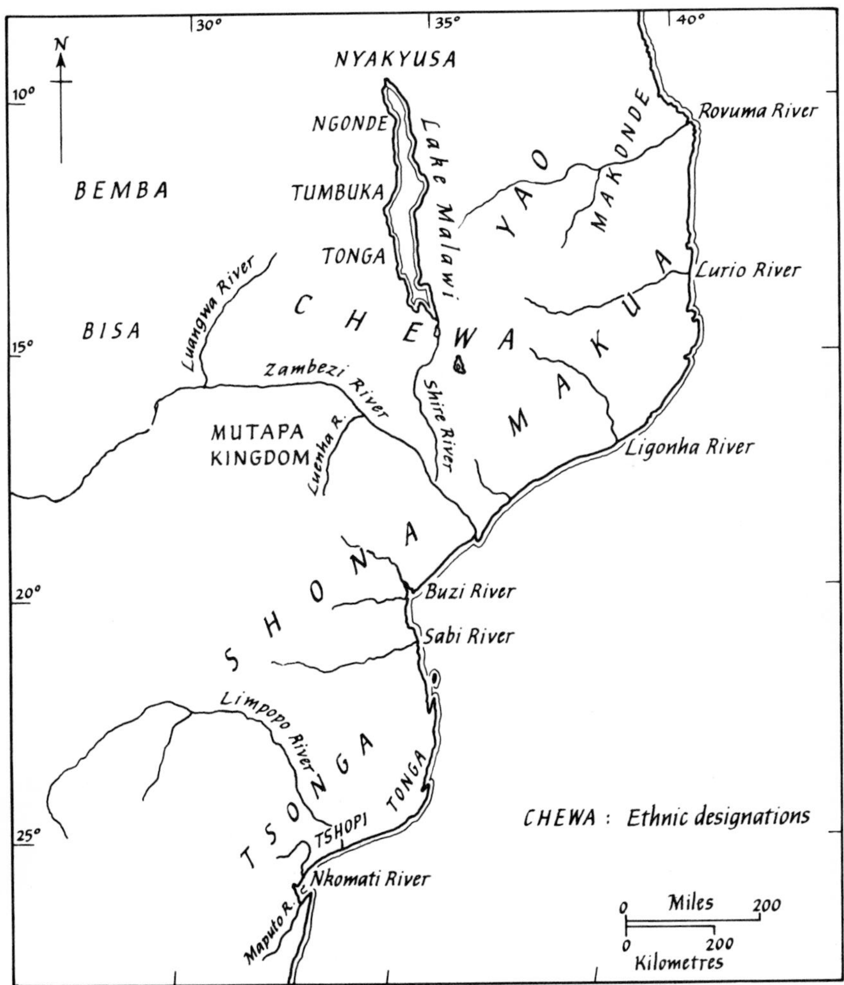

6:2 Ethnographic distribution within the Indian Ocean zone.

2 Soares de Castro, *Os Achirimas*, Lourenço Marques, 1941, pp. 9–13; António Rita-Ferreira, *Agrupamento e Caracterização Étnica dos Indígenas de Moçambique*, Lisbon, 1958, pp. 51–68; J. M. Schoffeleers, 'The meaning and use of the name Malawi in oral traditions and precolonial documents', in *The Early History of Malawi*, Bridglal Pachai (ed.), Evanston, Illinois, 1972, p. 97; Ehret, personal communication, p. 2.

The lands to the south of the Zambezi were occupied by speakers of Tonga, Tsonga and Shona. The Tonga were probably the earliest inhabitants, and at one time may have occupied most of central and southern Mozambique. Subsequently, however, their domains were encroached upon by the other two groups. In the far south, the Tsonga expanded continuously at the expense of the Tonga, a movement that probably began well before 1400. The pattern to the north of the Sabi river was very similar. In that region Shona-speakers from the plateau infiltrated so that few traces of the Tonga remained. This movement also began early in the Later Iron Age and appears to have been complete by 1400.[3]

Much of this interaction of the peoples of the Indian Ocean zone took place in an environment that was harsh and difficult to master. It was dominated by a coastal plain that varied from 20 to 50 miles wide in the north to 200 miles wide in the south. This zone and much of the neighbouring plateau rarely reaches elevations of over 1 500 feet. It presented many problems for human exploitation. Soils, especially in the south, are sandy. Rainfall in the south averages less than 40 inches annually and is both seasonal and unreliable. Over much of the territory, alternative sources of water are few. Moreover, the woodland vegetation often played host to pests that were detrimental to man and beast alike.[4]

Not all of the Indian Ocean zone was inhospitable. There were localised regions where human development of the environment could be more productive. Even the coastal littoral possessed marshes, deltas and semi-permanent areas of water catchment which mitigated some of the uncertainties of rainfall. Elsewhere the river systems that flowed from the plateau provided flood plains, seasonal overflow and water for irrigation that reduced the harshness of the environment. Historically the Zambezi and its tributaries formed the most important system, but others, such as the Maputo, Nkomati, Limpopo, Sabi, Lurio and Rovuma, were ecologically important. In addition, many of the river valleys had fertile soils and the higher regions had fewer pests and diseases.

The total population of the region was probably relatively small. Because data at any time before the twentieth century are inadequate, population estimates for centuries ago are based largely on speculation.[5] It is generally accepted that the area was comparatively underpopulated in the later nineteenth and early twentieth centuries, when Europeans began

3 Alan K. Smith, 'The peoples of southern Mozambique: an historical survey', *Journal of African History (JAH)*, xiv, 4, 1973, 568–80; also see below, chap. 7.

4 Irene S. Van Dongen, 'Physical, human and economic settling' in *Portuguese Africa*, David Abshire and Michael Samuels (eds), New York, 1964, pp. 10–14; *Area Handbook for Mozambique*, Washington, D.C., 1977, pp. 63–79.

5 Thomas Daniel Boston, 'Mozambique: an Interpretation of the Nature, Causes, and Outcomes of the Pre-Colonial Stages of African Economic Development', Ph.D. thesis, Cornell University, 1976.

to record their observations. Although a number of variables might have contributed to the demographic patterns, much of the land was never capable of supporting large numbers of people. Moreover, many of the endemic diseases prevalent in the past probably served as an impediment to population growth.[6]

There was significant regional and localised population variation. Where soils were fertile, concentrations of people often resulted. Between the sixteenth and nineteenth centuries, observers noted that groups of Shona-, Tsonga- and Nguni-speakers lived in dense settlements.[7] Soil fertility and types of cultivation suggest that the Chewa of the Shire valley lived in clusters packed with more than one hundred persons per square mile in the sixteenth century.[8] Densely settled populations also occurred in areas of marginal fertility and inadequate water when surrounding regions were too inhospitable to support cultivation. The contrast between densely settled and unoccupied land was most pronounced in the drier northern and southern extremities of the zone.[9]

THE POLITICAL ECONOMY OF THE LATER IRON AGE

The entire Indian Ocean zone was inhabited by societies whose social relations of production were pre-capitalist. There were, however, significant variations within the respective modes of production. Extremes were found in the material base and in the degree of social stratification. The key variables that governed the nature of a given mode of production were soil fertility, mineral deposits, storable wealth, and the distribution of production within the society. Where the material base was limited, societies tended to be small-scale and relatively undifferentiated internally. When surpluses were available, larger numbers of people tended to congregate in a single political entity, which usually distinguished among different categories of persons. Over time, however, the societies that resulted from a superior material base proved to be unstable. This resulted

6 João dos Santos, 'Ethiopia Oriental', in *Records of South-Eastern Africa* (*RSEA*), George M. Theal (ed.), vii, 256, 319.

7 *Ibid.*, 269; Anonymous, 'Descripcão da Capitania de Monsambique, 1778', in *Relações de Moçambique Setecentista*, António de Andrade (ed.), Lisbon, 1958, p. 402; Senhor Ferrão, 'Account of the Portuguese possessions within the Captaincy of the Rios de Sena', *RSEA*, vii, 375; João Baptista Lavanha, 'Shipwreck of the great ship Santo Alberto', in *Tragic History of the Sea*, C. R. Boxer (ed.), p. 142; Bento Teyxera Feyo, 'Account of the Wreck of the Ships Sacramento and Nossa Senhora de Atalaya ... in the Year 1647', *RSEA*, viii, 340; St Vincent Erskine, 'Journey to the Mouth of the Limpopo', *Proceedings of the Royal Geographical Society*, xiii, 5, 1869, 96.

8 Matthew Schoffeleers, 'A martyr cult as a reflection on changes in production: the case of the Lower Shire Valley, 1590–1622 A.D.', *African Perspectives*, ii, 1978, 27–8.

9 Dias, *Os Macondes*, p. 100; Lavanha, 'Santo Alberto', pp. 142, 146–9.

from their failure to resolve internal structural contradictions that had attended their growth.[10]

Intensive cultivation seems to have taken place over several centuries in the Indian Ocean zone. The first observers at the north end of Lake Malawi, in parts of the Makua heartland and along the Shire valley, noted the sophisticated nature of agricultural production.[11] The same inference might be drawn from the variety of fruits and vegetables spoken of by early travellers. The agricultural techniques and crops of the Tshopi in the 1930s had been present in the area two centuries earlier, suggesting great continuity in production.[12] In the nineteenth century, the agricultural calendar of sowing and planting of some Shona-speaking peoples was divided so as to ensure harvests throughout the year.[13].

Some groups continued to make use of extensive systems of production. Soil fertility rather than ethnic identity would appear to have been a key variable in determining the approach adopted. Thus from an early period, the Makua in the less favoured regions practised bush fallow cultivation, whereas those in more fertile areas cultivated on a more permanent basis.[14] Although long fallow periods required a low human density, they signified neither the absence of horticultural skill and knowledge, nor that yields were inadequate. Some Yao, for example, made use of ridging, fertilisation with ash, and the construction of extensive irrigation and drainage systems.[15] Makonde husbandmen, despite operating on an arid plateau, were able to reduce the period of bush fallow to six years and often to produce a surplus for export.[16] Tsonga cultivators, working in equally

10 A 'social formation' is defined as a geo-political entity. Whereas 'state' connotes something rigid and concrete, 'social formation' 'conveys the idea of a whole composed of heterogeneous components', which also 'implies the idea that given geo-political entities change in terms of their composition and boundaries'. 'Mode of production' is used to refer to the articulation of the forces and relations of production within a designated unit. It is important to note that more than one mode of production may coexist within the same social formation. See, Dominique Legros, Donald Hungerford and Judith Shapiro, 'Economic base, mode of production, and social formation: a discussion of Marx's terminology', *Dialectical Anthropology*, iv, 3, Oct. 1979, 243–8.

11 dos Santos, 'Ethiopia Oriental', 189, 255, 305; Portugal Durão, 'Reconhecimento e occupação dos territórios entre o massangire e Os Picos Namuly', *Boletim da Sociedade de Geografia de Lisboa*, 2ª serie, 7, 1902, 16; David Livingstone, *Missionary Travels and Researches in South Africa*, London, 1857, p. 638; James Elton, *Travels and Researches among the Lakes and Mountains of Eastern and Central Africa*, London, 1878, p. 331; see also Helge Kjekshus, *Ecology Control and Economic Development in East African History*, London, 1977, pp. 26–51.

12 E. Dora Earthy, *Valenge Women*, London, 1933, pp. 29–31; Augusto Cabral, *Raças usos e costumes dos indígenas do Districto de Inhambane*, Lourenço Marques, 1910, p. 17; Bernardo de Castro Soares to António Frões, 1 Aug. 1729, Arquivo Histórico Ultramarino, Documentos Anexos Ás Plantas.

13 Ferrão, 'Account', 380.

14 Saul Dias Rafael, 'Milange e Os Seus Povos', *Moçambique*, lxxxiii, Sept. 1955, 24; Durão, 'Reconhecimento', 16; Eduardo do Couto Lupi, *Angoche*, Lisbon, 1907, p. 91.

15 David Livingstone, *Last Journals*, London, 1874, pp. 57, 73.

16 H. Gillman, 'Bush Fallowing on the Makonde Plateau', *Tanganyika Notes and Records*, xix, June 1945, 37–40; William Allan, *The African Husbandman*, London, 1965, pp. 213–16.

inhospitable places, were nevertheless able to combine extensive fallow with seasonal cultivation of selected crops along river banks, in marshy areas, on the slopes of hills and on top of plateaux. In this manner they augmented production.[17] In the sixteenth century a small number of villages were able to provide all the needs of some 150 Portuguese who unexpectedly sought refuge for several months. These examples attest to the successful agricultural endeavours of most groups in the Indian Ocean zone.[18]

The introduction of maize and cassava from the Americas during later centuries proved to be significant additions to the developing agricultural economies. These crops were soon adopted into the agricultural cycle on a regular basis, and maize became especially important in the southern regions. In the sixteenth and seventeenth centuries, large herds of cattle were common along the south-eastern coast, and it was recorded that the 'people sow but little and live principally by consuming their cattle'.[19] Occasionally millet was hidden from strangers, and other visitors found a scarcity of provisions because the harvest was still to come. After the introduction of maize, which appears to have taken place in the south during the early eighteenth century,[20] cultivation seems to have developed on a firmer foundation. In Zululand and neighbouring areas it became the staple food. Its revolutionary significance can be judged by the fact that the Tsonga came to refer to it as 'king'.[21]

Most of the agricultural labour was done by women, although men often provided assistance. In extensive systems, especially where the clearing of virgin land was required, men were obliged to play a large role in preparing the ground for planting.[22] In some intensive systems, such as those that evolved among groups of Chewa-speakers, men took part in planting, maintenance of crops, and the construction of a variety of irrigation devices.[23] Generally, however, the entire cycle from planting to harvesting remained the responsibility of women, who decided which crops should be sown, the number of fields that should be devoted to each,

17 Henri A. Junod, *The Life of a South African Tribe*, London, 1927, vol. 2, pp. 9–32; David Hedges, 'Trade and Politics in Southern Mozambique and Zululand in the Eighteenth and Early Nineteenth Centuries', Ph.D. thesis, University of London, 1978, chap. 2; Erskine, 'Journey', 96; 'Rapport van Jan van de Capelle aan den Hoog Edelen Heer Maurits Pasques de Chavonnes . . .', *RSEA*, i, 418.

18 Feyo, 'Atalaya', 357–8.

19 'Narrative of the Wreck of the Great Galleon Saint John', *RSEA*, i, 138–9.

20 Manuel Perestrello, 'Narrative of the Wreck of the Ship St Benedict', *RSEA*, i, 236; Francisco Vaz d'Almada, 'Account of the Misfortune that Befell the Ship São João Baptista', *RSEA*, viii, 103; Feyo, 'Atalaya', 348; Jacob Francken, 'Ramspoedige Reize van het O. I. Schip de Naarstigheid', *RSEA*, vi, 492.

21 Junod, *Life*, vol. 2, p. 9; Nathaniel Isaacs, *Travels and Adventures in Eastern Africa*, Capetown, 1937, vol. 1, p. 47; vol. 2, p. 127.

22 Dias, *Os Macondes*, vol. 1, pp. 97–8.

23 H. S. Stannus, 'Notes on Some Tribes of British Central Africa', *Man*, xl, 1910, 323–4; Livingstone, *Missionary Travels*, pp. 122–3.

when planting should begin and how crops should be cared for.[24] Most women developed an expertise that allowed optimum production even without scientific technology.[25]

Men devoted at least a portion of their time to a combination of fishing, hunting, herding of domestic animals, manufacturing or trading, endeavours that played a significant role in enlarging the material base of society. Where there was ready access to rivers, lakes or the ocean, fishing was a major activity. In the inland regions, it was usually undertaken by individuals or in small groups. Along the coast, however, the Makua fished in ocean-braving vessels that held as many as thirty men.[26] The catch was valuable in a variety of ways. The Tonga of Inhambane, for example, preferred eating fish and shell-fish even though many groups possessed adequate supplies of domestic animals.[27] In addition to their value as items of immediate consumption, fish could be smoked and preserved and thus converted into storable wealth.[28] Smoked fish also proved a valuable item of exchange, since most groups were not able to obtain them in any other way.

Hunting, on the other hand, was an endeavour in which almost all men participated. It was especially important among some Yao, Makua and Makonde, who were prevented by tsetse fly from maintaining large herds of domestic animals. Among the Makua, hunting was considered so important that it was undertaken only by secret societies, the members of which specialised in the killing of one specific species.[29] In addition to supplementing food and essential protein, hunting was increasingly undertaken to obtain ivory for exchange in long-distance trade. In many societies the chase of the elephant became such an important economic factor that it was undertaken by large parties of hunters who developed ingenious techniques for slaying their dangerous prey.[30]

Whereas hunting was a widespread activity, the herding of cattle was

24 dos Santos, 'Ethiopia Oriental', 306; Edward A. Alpers, *Ivory and Slaves in East Central Africa*, Berkeley, Ca., 1975, pp. 16–18.

25 Durão, 'Reconhecimento', 16; Director of Agriculture, Nyasaland, quoted in W. E. Morgan, 'The Lower Shire Valley of Nyasaland: a changing system of African agriculture', *The Geographical Journal*, cxix, 4, 1953, 464.

26 dos Santos, 'Ethiopia Oriental', 305; Rafael, 'Milange', 24; John Walters, 'Changing Patterns of Commodity Production in Mozambique District', unpublished paper, University of London, 1977, pp. 2–4.

27 Cabral, *Raças*, pp. 19, 109; André Fernandes to Padre Provinçal da India, 24 June, in *Dos Primeiros Trabalhos dos Portugueses No Monomotapa*, A. P. de Paiva e Pona (ed.), Lisbon, 1892, p. 29.

28 For a discussion of the importance of storable wealth, see Peter Farb, *Man's Rise to Civilization*, New York, 1968.

29 Eugene de Froberville, 'Notes sur les moeurs, coutumes et traditions des Amakoua, sur le commerce et la traite des esclaves dans l'Afrique Orientale', *Bulletin de la Société de Geographie*, 4e Serie, 1852, 322.

30 Adolphe Delagorge, *Voyage dans l'Afrique australe*, Paris, 1847, vol. 1, pp. 489–90, 557–62.

confined to certain areas. These were located south of the Zambezi, in the highlands that bridged the river several hundred miles upstream from its mouth, and extended along the western shore of Lake Malawi into the Lake Tanganyika corridor. In some intensive agricultural systems, such as those of the Nyakusa and Ngonde, the beasts were kept penned and the manure was preserved for use as fertiliser.[31] Whether or not women were allowed to milk the cows varied from group to group, but ultimately responsibility for their procreation, care and consumption belonged to men. Especially in southern societies, cattle played an important social role. They were used to pay *lobola* to the father of the bride, and thus provided sanction to marriage and justification of the husband's control over children. Possession of cattle was also a barometer of wealth, and often allowed an individual or a kin alliance to command service from others. The important social and ritual role ascribed to cattle, however, has often obscured their function in the pattern of consumption. For example, remains at the Shona site at Manekweni reveal a culture that was heavily dependent on the eating of beef.[32] In the sixteenth century the Nguni and Tsonga relied on cattle for sustenance, and were not reluctant to slaughter animals from their vast herds.[33] Cattle thus played a crucial role in the day-to-day existence of many groups.

The degree to which people engaged in manufacturing also differed greatly. Few could match the range of activities practised among the Chewa, who were noted as especially gifted iron-workers, weavers of cotton cloth, manufacturers of salt and practitioners of other skilled undertakings.[34] Elsewhere, perhaps due to limited resources, the scope of production seems to have been more restricted. Moreover, with the probable exception of blacksmiths, who appear to have been prominent wherever sufficient iron could be obtained, craftsmen who possessed specialised skills were rarely full-time specialists.

Mining was another important component of the regional economy. Its purposes fell into two distinct categories. The excavation and smelting of iron ore was undertaken wherever supplies of this crucial metal were available. The entire process was usually the prerogative of a small group of

31 Kjekshus, *Ecology Control*, pp. 36–37.

32 Peter Garlake, 'Pastoralism and *zimbabwe*', *JAH*, xix, 4, 1978, 483; see also R. W. Dickinson, 'The Archaeology of the Sofala Coast', *South African Archaeology Bulletin*, xxx, parts 3 and 4, nos. 119 and 120 (Dec. 1975), 85; dos Santos, 'Ethiopia Oriental', 209; Father Monclaro, 'Account of the Expedition Under Francisco Barreto', *RSEA*, iii, 227.

33 Anonymous, 'Memórias da Costa d'Africa Oriental . . . 1762', in Andrade, *Relações*, p. 189; Anonymous, 'Descripção Sobre o Estado de Sofala . . . Por hum Europeo alli Residente Desde 1824 até 1829', *Arquivo das Colónias*, i, 4, Oct. 1917, 79; Francken, 'Naarstigheid', 492; Lavanha, 'Santo Alberto', pp. 120–22; Feyo, 'Atalaya', 340; van de Capelle, 'Rapport', 418–20.

34 Henry Rowley, *The Story of the Universities Mission to Central Africa*, London, 1866, p. 206; Livingstone, *Missionary Travels*, pp. 111–12; Mary Tew, *The Peoples of the Lake Nyasa Region*, London, 1950, p. 34.

specialists, who often enjoyed a privileged status because of the vital function they played. They produced the essential iron implements for agriculture and the weapons for warfare. The importance of iron was emphasised by the fact that where deposits were either inadequate or non-existent, it was the primary commodity sought elsewhere.[35] The mining of precious metals, on the other hand, served a completely different function. Gold, whose distribution was limited, was used principally as a medium of exchange in overseas trade. Copper, which was more widespread, was an important item of exchange and was also used to make ornaments that distinguished wealthy members of society from those of lower rank.[36]

The availability of surpluses, combined with the fact that different environments provided specialised produce, stimulated a wide network of regional exchange. Foodstuffs comprised the major category of trade items. Livestock, including cattle, goats, sheep and chickens, and items such as dried fish, rice and citrus fruits that could be obtained only in limited areas, provided the bulk of merchandise in transit. Finished iron products, forged by specialist craftsmen, were the most important metal goods that circulated, and the networks often extended over considerable distances. There is evidence that groups with access either to inferior quality ore or inadequate supplies sought out smiths with esteemed reputations.[37] Cloth was yet another major commodity of exchange. It was produced in a number of areas, but the cotton pieces woven along the Zambezi and Shire valleys were most highly regarded.[38] Unfortunately, little is known about the regulation of exchange. It seems reasonable to conclude, however, that by the sixteenth century the regional economy had grown to a level that was significantly more complex than one based on autarkical subsistence production, although it had not achieved the scope of a fully matured market economy.

The regulating principles for the organisation of the relations of production varied considerably. Social scientists have often chosen to categorise societies on the basis of whether matrilineal or patrilineal principles of descent were used to reproduce those relations. Using this

35 Rowley, *Story*, p. 206; Junod, *Life*, vol. 2, p. 138; Rev. John Campbell, *Travels in South Africa ... A Narrative of a Second Journey ...*, London, 1822, pp. 276–7; Will Cooley, 'A memoir on the civilization of the tribes inhabiting the highlands near Delagoa Bay', *Journal of the Royal Geographical Society*, iii, 1833, 312–13.

36 Walter Cline, *Mining and Metallurgy in Negro Africa*, Menasha, Wisconsin, 1937, p. 15; Alan K. Smith, 'The Struggle for Control of Southern Mozambique, 1720–1835', Ph.D. thesis, University of California at Los Angeles, 1970, p. 342; dos Santos, 'Ethiopia Oriental', 206; William White, 'Voyage de Guillaume White de Madras à Colombo et la Baie di Lagoa en 1798', in *Histoire Générale des Voyages*, Charles Walckenaer (ed.), Paris, 1831, xxi, p. 455; 'Mr. Penwell's Account of Delagoa Bay', *RSEA*, ii, 463.

37 Stannus, 'Notes', 331; J. Mackenzie, 'Iron Workers and the Iron Trade in Southern Zambezia', typescript.

38 dos Santos, 'Ethiopia Oriental', 207, 261; Monclaro, 'Account', 229, 234; Manuel Barreto, 'Report Upon the ... Rivers of Cuama', *RSEA*, iii, 481, 505–6; Dickinson, 'Archaeology', 103.

system, the Indian Ocean zone can be divided neatly between the matrilineal peoples to the north of the Zambezi and the patrilineal groups to the south. Thus the Yao, Makua, Chewa and Makonde were all guided by matrilineal rules of descent and shared common notions of clan exogamy, although their ideas on residence patterns and the degree to which lineages were viewed as corporate entities differed.[39] Similarly, the peoples to the south of the Zambezi accepted patrilineal succession and virilocal residence as being the norms. Ideally the polygynous household was more common than among the matrilineal groups; in practice, however, the degree of its incidence varied greatly. Thus, whereas most Tsonga households were polygynous, among the Tonga it was usually only chiefs who were able to marry more than one wife.[40]

Egalitarian notions were prevalent throughout the area. The most important was the shared understanding that land belonged to the people as a whole and thus could not be alienated on a permanent basis. Rather, all members of society were entitled to a piece of ground which would be used for the sustenance of their respective families. Although the process of land allocation varied and sometimes resulted in preferential treatment of some groups, the basic principle of equal access to the means of production was an important ideological underpinning of Indian Ocean zone society.

Egalitarian principles were also operative in the regulation of political affairs in most of the region. The institution of chieftainship was far from universal. Among the matrilineal Makonde, Yao and Makua, for example, a headman was selected from within the bounds of the local residential group. Because lineages did not function as corporate entities, however, the headman could not call on support from beyond the confines of the village. Moreover, even within the village itself his authority was severely limited, partly because residential preference was flexible. This created a situation in which a headman was obliged to compete with his brothers for the loyalty of the kin group. He also had to overcome the natural tension among generational groups that often obliged younger members to establish villages of their own.[41] Polities whose scope of effective action was limited were also prevalent among the Tonga of the Inhambane region. Although patrilineal descent, with its emphasis on lineage cooperation, was the basic means of organisation, the authority of Tonga chiefs only rarely extended beyond their own village.[42] Thus, despite status differentiation within a

39 Dias, *Os Macondes*, vol. 3, pp. 250–53; J. Clyde Mitchell, 'The Yao of Southern Nyasaland', in *Seven Tribes of British Central Africa*, Elizabeth Colson and Max Gluckman (eds), London, 1951, pp. 314–20; Rafael, 'Milange', 34; M. Marwick, 'The kinship basis of Cewa social structure', *South African Journal of Science*, xlviii, March 1948, 260–62.

40 Cabral, *Raças*, p. 83; 'Description of the People of Delago. Bay by Mr Alick Osborne', P.R.O., Adm 1/2269, Cap O, 30a.

41 Mitchell, 'The Yao', pp. 316–26; Rafael, 'Milange', 34; Wilfred Whitely, 'Modern local government among the Makua', *Africa*, xxiv, 4, Oct. 1954, 349–50.

42 Smith, 'The Peoples', 572.

village community, Tonga society was composed of units of equal strength.

Despite the prevalence of egalitarian elements in the institutional and material framework of Indian Ocean zone society, many groups developed mechanisms of social organisation that emphasised distinctions among the body politic. In some cases, special societies were created within a particular group which limited membership in various ways. This was especially prevalent among those who observed matrilineal descent, because the matrilineage did not provide the means of regulating affairs other than those concerning exogamy. The Makua created secret hunting societies, each of which had a distinctive membership and various criteria for gaining entry. Similarly, the Yao banded together in hunting and trading societies whose membership was composed of individuals of different matrilineages. Those who attained ascendancy were able to keep a disproportionate share of the spoils, and thus had the means to attach others to them.[43] The Chewa also had exclusive organisations not based on lineage, one of the most interesting being secret societies whose functions often replicated those of the state.[44] Although membership in these types of societies was theoretically open to all, the fact that such criteria as age, talent or wealth determined admission helped to create and reinforce social distinctions.

Status differentiation was most institutionalised among the Tsonga and the Chewa. In both instances, social distinctions were the mechanisms which extended the minority control over large numbers of people and their land. Among some Tsonga this was achieved because royal lineages were successful in accumulating wealth and, consequently, a disproportionate share of power. Taxation, which was funnelled upwards to the royal lineage, was one source of wealth. Although it often consisted of perishable foodstuffs requiring redistribution, it offered the potential of rewarding those elements of society whose loyalty was most desired. The successful manipulation of the system of *lobola* enabled royal lineages to increase their herds considerably. Ideally the system was one of balanced relationships. On the one hand, a patrilineage surrendered a number of cattle to another in recognition that it had acquired the means of reproducing itself. On the other, the patrilineage that obtained the cattle was provided with the means to pay *lobola* and thus to ensure its continuation. The balanced nature of the system, however, was distorted in the relationship between royal and commoner lineages. Royal lineages invoked the prestige attached to marrying one of their own in order to extort higher payments by commoners. At the same time they used the same justification to acquire women with only minimal compensation. The large herds that accrued to

43 Stannus, 'Notes', 325.
44 M. Schoffeleers, 'A Martyr Cult', 22.

the royal lineage provided it with an additional source of strength that enabled it to maintain its dominance.[45]

The roots of the hierarchical system among the Chewa that resulted in the creation of what came to be known as the Marave state system appear to be more complex. Many traditions ascribe the foundation of these states to a migration from Luba country, which saw immigrants of the Phiri clan establish a number of related states in the lands of the Banda.[46] Within each of the states, lineage affiliation remained important and members were obliged to accept corporate responsibility. The rewards for the royal lineages were significant, because material wealth was based on mining, agriculture, manufacture, and a variety of other resources that were unmatched in South-Central Africa. Through the mechanism of taxation, kings were able to acquire a wide range of commodities that could subsequently be recycled to other lineage heads.[47] Thus the ability of Marave kings to regulate the affairs of their people was greatly facilitated by the wealth at their disposal and their ability to use it for political advantage.

The regulation of international commerce by Tsonga and Marave royal lineages provided an additional mechanism for the growth of status relationships within society. International trade continually spanned and sometimes dominated the history of the Indian Ocean zone. Although many items were exchanged, gold and ivory constituted the principal exports. These items were especially important, because, in the 'blind trade' that long-distance commerce involved, they were ascribed lower value at their source than on the world market.[48] Their production and marketing were controlled and regulated by the few. Special access to these commodities, either as a monopoly or as a regulated portion of the produce, was a right successfully demanded by royal lineages in both Marave and Tsonga society. Through this accumulated wealth they strengthened their domination and extended their rule over large areas.

The diverse patterns of social relations that were evolving in the Indian Ocean zone were thus affected increasingly by contacts with the wider world. By the fifteenth century there was already a long history of international trade. The trade of the Indian Ocean involved many focal points, diverse products and merchants from different lands. Although conflict was not unknown, the general tenor of Indian Ocean commerce was one of peaceful and discretionary exchange. Hindu merchants, who

45 Hedges, 'Trade and Politics', ch. 2, *passim*.

46 Kings Phiri, 'Chewa History in Central Malawi and the Use of Oral Tradition, 1600–1920', Ph.D. thesis, University of Wisconsin, 1975, pp. 47–61.

47 Harry Langworthy, 'Chewa or Malawi Political Organization in the Pre-Colonial Era', in Pachai, *Malawi*, p. 109.

48 For a discussion of blind trade, see Fernand Braudel, *Afterthoughts on Material Civilization and Capitalism*, Baltimore, Md., 1977.

appear to have been in the forefront during the early centuries, gradually relinquished their primacy to Muslims, who subsequently became the leading practitioners of the trade. Muslim trading communities were established to the south of the Rovuma river in the fifteenth century. From their coastal bases, the Muslim Swahili became ever more active, both in penetrating the inland regions and as sailors who traded produce throughout the western portions of the Indian Ocean.[49]

Although international trade encouraged a pattern of growth in the Indian Ocean zone, there were also constraints on the scale that might be achieved. Lineage domination may have effectively regulated the affairs of groups who lived in dispersed territories, but it also produced structural contradictions that posed spatial and temporal limitations on its effectiveness. As generations passed and collateral segments became further removed from the centre of distribution, the incentive for participation in the system decreased. Moreover, within the framework of a polygynous royal lineage, there were those near the apex who wanted a larger share of the spoils. Thus disaffection might take the form of a direct conflict over apical power. Alternatively, highly-placed central individuals or groups who had become genealogically more peripheral might attempt to sever the relationship and to reproduce similar relations without the encumbrance of more senior lineage members. Although there were a variety of ways in which cleavages could be healed, the tendency over time was the extension of lineage domination until it became unwieldy. Segments which successfully severed the bonds of effective control could establish smaller units that began the cycle of growth again.

There also appears to have been a point beyond which increased population density presented problems for some societies in the Indian Ocean zone. The normal pattern for those who functioned under the constraints of pre-industrial technology was for population growth to advance faster than total output. Areas of dense settlement and the transition from extensive to intensive cultivation suggest that this was the case in the Indian Ocean zone. Although there appears to have been a high degree of correlation between population density, intensive agriculture and soil fertility, population density was the crucial variable in such an equation. Soil fertility enables an area to support larger populations, but it is the latter that necessitates changes towards more labour-intensive forms of production.[50] Migration from an area of dense concentration provided

49 Trade in the Indian Ocean is discussed in James Hornell, 'Sea trade in early times', *Antiquity*, xv, 59, Sept. 1941, 239–48; G. F. Hourani, *Arab Seafaring in Ancient and Early Medieval Times*, Princeton, N.J., 1951; Radha Mookeriji, *Indian Shipping: a History of the Seaborne Trade and Maritime Activity of Indians from Earliest Times*, London, 1912; Alan Villiers, *Monsoon Seas: the story of the Indian Ocean*, New York, 1952.

50 Kjekshus, *Ecology Control*, p. 46; Allan, *African Husbandman*, esp. pp. 199–206; for an overview of the continuing debate on this subject, see David Grigg, 'Ester Boserup's theory of agrarian change', *Progress in Human Geography*, iii, 1, 1979, 64–84.

another alternative for those unwilling to adapt to cultivation in an overcrowded area.

Population growth, competition for control of trade and internal conflict all contributed to the need for migration: a continuing cycle of migration was a major theme in Tsonga history. From traditions collected in the eighteenth century, it can be discerned that the flow of migration among the Tsonga was from the interior towards the coast. Apical conflict seems to have been the primary cause of these movements. Oral histories tend to be mono-causal in their interpretation, and the pressure of population should not be overlooked. Indeed, the steadiness and pervasiveness of the movement strongly suggest a motive of more enduring importance than intermittent contests for power. Between the sixteenth and eighteenth centuries, Tonga groups continued the infiltration of the southern hinterland that had begun many centuries before. In the process they incorporated and assimilated the Tonga they encountered and were obliged to make accommodations with the Shona-influenced peoples they met at the mouth of the Limpopo river. As a result, the unique intermixture that came to be known as the Tshopi people was brought into being.[51]

The Yao migrations passed through a number of phases and seem to have been stimulated by a variety of causes. Traditional sources refer to a homeland between the Lujenda and Rovuma rivers from which the Yao radiated in all directions.[52] The initial impulses towards expansion may have resulted from the continuing segmentation of matrilineages. It was generally understood that separating segments should settle as far apart as possible.[53] In the post-1500 period, movement in a south-easterly direction may have predominated. The stimulus was probably a desire to approach the valuable commodities produced by the Marave. Eventually these migrant family groups began to obtain permission to settle among the Chewa-speakers.[54] Subsequently, Yao involvement in procuring ivory and then slaves for the international trade led to a more intensive infiltration. Ephemeral hunting and trading corporations were transformed into tightly-organised chiefdoms. Moreover, as competitiveness in commerce grew and fire-arms were more prevalent, the Yao chiefdoms became more aggressive.[55] By the early nineteenth century, they were poised to take advantage of Chewa weakness.

The cycle of migration and conflict was an essential feature of the Indian Ocean zone social formation. These characteristics were important in determining its articulation with the wider world after 1500. In many

51 Smith, 'The Peoples', 573–9.
52 Abdallah, *The Yaos*, p. 7.
53 J. Clyde Mitchell, *The Yao Village*, Manchester, 1956, pp. 24, 157.
54 Mitchell, 'The Yao', p. 307.
55 Livingstone, *Missionary Travels*, p. 522.

regions, more intense contact with the world economy led to increased exports of selected items and related domestic economic growth. In essence it reinforced the wider material base that underwrote the social formation and provided the means with which to resist attempts at conquest. Since the contradictions that produced the widespread apical conflict negated the emergence of a unified class of potential compradors, the Indian Ocean zone was further buttressed from the full impact of the world economy.[56] The very contradictions that prevented unity at the apex, however, also produced no shortage of opportunists who were willing to grant concessions in return for outside help. Thus the region possessed both strengths and weaknesses that would profoundly influence its relations with the wider world.

INTERACTION WITH EUROPE

Between the sixteenth and the early nineteenth centuries, the Indian Ocean zone became more involved with the wider world. The stepped-up levels of interaction resulted mainly from European initiatives. At the height of their ambition during the seventeenth century, Europeans attempted to subdue various polities in the Indian Ocean zone. Both European weakness and local resilience combined, however, to forestall the incorporation of South-Central Africa into the dependent periphery of the world economy. Rather, the result was a compromise. Although the impact of interaction came to be felt by an ever larger number of people, basic institutional structures were not transformed to suit the needs of the world economy.[57]

Direct involvement with the incipient world economy can be said to have begun at the beginning of the sixteenth century, with the arrival of Vasco da Gama flying the colours of Portugal in the Indian Ocean. This navigational achievement was the culmination of exploration that had begun almost a century earlier and had involved successive voyages southward along the Atlantic coasts of Africa. In most locations the Portuguese attempted to establish trading relations. In those areas, such as Benin and Kongo, where political institutions seemed to resemble their own, attempts were made to convert local peoples to Christianity. Since no document which suggests a long-term outline of Portuguese intentions has been uncovered, it is difficult to determine if there was a mental blueprint which envisaged world-wide expansion or whether these expeditions were

56 For a discussion of the notion 'world economy', see Immanuel Wallerstein, *The Modern World System: Capitalist Agriculture and the Origins of the European World Economy in the Sixteenth Century*, New York, 1974. It will be argued elsewhere that a world economy presupposes a unified class at the apex of peripheral societies that is capable of imposing its will on the majority.

57 Peripheral society in the world economy was characterised by either a slave or a feudal mode of production. Neither came into existence in the Indian Ocean zone.

merely speculative. At any rate, it was not until the 1480s that the first mention was made of possibly circumnavigating Africa and reaching Asia. In 1497, when Vasco da Gama sailed into the Indian Ocean, a new epoch had begun.[58]

From the outset, the Portuguese approach to the Indian Ocean differed from their behaviour in western Africa. Although the carrot was extended to those who were willing to comply with every detail of Portuguese wishes, the stick was reserved for the majority who had the audacity to continue acting in their own best interests. Cities along the entire eastern coast of Africa were intimidated, bombarded and pillaged. Forts were erected at Sofala in 1505 and on Mozambique Island in 1507 respectively, their purposes were to establish a monopoly of the gold trade from the Zambezian plateau and to control the shipping lanes of the western Indian Ocean. These policies remained fairly constant for many centuries, although the ability of the Portuguese to enforce them often fell well below their goals.[59]

Portuguese use of force in the Indian Ocean reflected the differing material bases that supported the conqueror and the conquered. In 1509, the Portuguese defeated a combined fleet of Muslim powers and became masters of the western Indian Ocean. Subsequently, in addition to the important conquests of Goa in 1510 and the Straits of Malacca in 1511, the Portuguese were able to establish a network of more than forty forts and factories that stretched from Sofala to Nagasaki. Their ability to accomplish this feat was based on their use of a developing technology that Europe had often borrowed from other areas of the world and subsequently improved. With its diffusion through late mediaeval Europe, the continent was able for the first time to assume world technological supremacy.[60]

Western Europe, however, also began to need a wide variety of goods that it could neither produce itself, nor obtain by simple mechanisms of exchange.[61] The Indian Ocean trading network on which the Portuguese imposed themselves already involved the circulation of a great quantity of high-quality merchandise. Next to this the products of Europe paled into insignificance.[62] Although gold and silver were desired in the Indian Ocean, an increasingly bullionist Europe was loath to relinquish the

58 C. R. Boxer, *The Portuguese Seaborne Empire*, London, 1973, pp. 15–38.

59 'Account of the Voyage of Vasco da Gama Along the Coast of Mozambique, 1497' in *Documents on the Portuguese in Mozambique and Central Africa, 1497–1840 (DPMCA)*, Lisbon, 1962, vol. 1, p. 25; 'Instructions to Captain-Major D. Franciso de Almeida, 5 March 1505, *DPMCA*, vol. 1, p. 183; Duarte Lemos to King, 30 Sept. 1508, *DPMCA*, vol. 2, p. 291.

60 Carlo Cipolla, *Before the Industrial Revolution: European Society and Economy, 1000–1700*, New York, 1976, pp. 168–74.

61 Europe's needs are discussed in Cipolla, *Before the Industrial Revolution*, Wallerstein, *The Modern World System*, and Braudel, *Afterthoughts*.

62 Wallerstein, *The Modern World System*, pp. 330–34.

commodities that it believed provided the basis of national wealth. Under these circumstances force was the only logical alternative. Even then, however, the Portuguese and their English and Dutch successors were obliged to engage in the local trade and to make their profits by carrying African and Asian goods within the Indian Ocean sphere.[63] In fact, it was not until the nineteenth century, when Europe experienced its industrial revolution and thus began to rewrite the terms of its relations with the rest of the world, that the production of European goods elicited any demand in Asia.

In the Indian Ocean zone the Portuguese attempted to establish a trade monopoly, as they did elsewhere in their empire. They sought to oblige local merchants to deal exclusively with Portuguese factors and to interdict the commerce of those who refused. From the outset, however, they failed in their dual goals. Itinerant merchants who dealt with interior production centres began to bypass Portuguese authorities on the coast and to export their produce along the Zambezi and in its complicated delta. As the Portuguese began to learn more of the intricacies of the inland trade, they decided to move towards the sources of gold, ivory and copper in order to enforce a monopoly. In the 1530s they established settlements along the Zambezi at Sena and Tete.[64] Although the more direct presence of the Portuguese in the interior, which involved the establishment of *feiras* and a more active role by their traders, forced many Muslims either to abandon the trade or to accept a role as Portuguese agents, the Europeans remained dissatisfied. They overestimated the productive capacity of the mining regions, and believed that success would be achieved only by a conquest of the mines themselves.[65]

The policy of conquest and intervention in the interior that was to be pursued between 1569 and the early 1590s was a departure from the general strategy of establishing a monopoly based on the occupation of key locations. The Mwene Mutapa was singled out as the first target of Portuguese aggression. This decision was based largely on the belief that he controlled gold-mines of immeasurable wealth. Dom Sebastião, the young and fanatically religious Portuguese king, also decided that the African ruler must be punished for the slaying of a Portuguese priest. A force of 1 000 fighting men was entrusted to Francisco Barreto, a Portuguese noble-

63 Boxer, *Seaborne Empire*, pp. 39–64.

64 Christovão de Tavora to the king, 20 Sept. 1519, *DPMCA*, vol. 5, p. 203; Francisco de Brito to the king, 8 Aug. 1519, *DPMCA*, vol. 6, pp. 11–13; Alexandre Lobato, *A Expansão Portuguesa em Moçambique*, Lisbon, 1959, vol. 1, pp. 78–112, vol. 2, p. 23; Alexandre Lobato, 'Para a História da Penetração Portuguesa na Africa Central', in Alexandre Lobato, *Colonização Senhorial da Zambézia*, Lisbon, 1962, p. 79; H. H. K. Bhila, 'The Manyika and the Portuguese, 1575–1863', Ph.D. thesis, University of London, 1971, p. 16.

65 José Justino Teixeira Botelho, *História Militar e Política dos Portugueses em Moçambique*, Lisbon, 1934, vol. 1, p. 175; '... the Conditions ... on which war may be made ... especially on the Monomotapa', *RSEA*, iii, 153–6.

man. Poorly led, inadequately provisioned and hopelessly ill-informed, the expedition's strength was dissipated in desultory skirmishes and by illness before it reached its main target. The 200 who remained after several years of fruitless endeavour were finally ambushed and killed to a man.[66] Ignoring the lessons of this fiasco, in the early 1590s the leader of the Portuguese garrison at Sena attempted to interfere in civil strife that was gripping the Marave states. Two expeditions, the first of which suffered heavy casualties, were obliged to leave the field in disarray. Wiser heads prevailed when proposals for subsequent expeditions were mooted. The Portuguese had learnt to respect African resilience when directly confronted by naked force. Thereafter, despite what on paper appeared to be an elaborate bureaucracy, the Portuguese administrative role was limited to themselves. They intervened little in the affairs of neighbouring Central Africans.

During the sixteenth century diverse individuals were attracted to the Zambezi to seek their fortunes. There were Portuguese, Hindus, Muslims, mulattoes, and a variety of Africans from both near and far.[67] Largely self-serving, they were flexible in the way they sought their riches and ambiguous in their loyalties to one another and to the Portuguese Crown. Although the process must have differed from case to case, they appear to have taken an eclectic approach to opportunities. By varying combinations of illicit trade in fire-arms, bribery, mercenary support of one apical interest versus another, divide and conquer techniques and adaptation to the local milieu, they obtained concessions from opportunist groups with whom they dealt. Although the vast majority were probably failures, by the seventeenth century some were able to establish an independent power base from which they reproduced their position in society. Unlike the Portuguese government, these foreigners used force only after cleavages in local social formations had enabled them to lay the foundation for dispensing power.[68]

A struggle for supremacy among the Marave states provided one of the first opportunities for intervention. By the sixteenth century, a number of independent Marave kingdoms had come into existence. They were linked by kinship ties in a hierarchy based on seniority and the relationship of their respective rulers to the founder of the dynasty. As commerce expanded, however, the latent contradictions in the social formation began to surface. The kingdom of Lundu, which was closer to the Zambezi and its trade, attempted to prevent the senior kingdom of Kalonga from direct participation in this commerce. It dispatched armies that subsequently have

66 Monclaro, 'Account', 216–53. See also Chapter 7, p. 258–60, below.
67 Cyril Hromnik, 'Goa and Moçambique: The Participation of Goans in Portuguese Enterprise in the Rios de Cuama, 1501–1772', Ph.D. thesis, Syracuse University, N.Y., 1977, attempts to distinguish among the various ethnic components of the Portuguese sector.
68 Pedro Barreto de Rezende, 'On the State of India', *RSEA*, iv, 418.

been known as Zimba to subjugate the vast territory that extended eastward to the coast and northward from the Zambezi to beyond Mozambique Island. Initially Kalonga sought aid from the Portuguese authorities, but this proved of little avail.[69] Subsequently, however, with the aid of unofficial Portuguese forces, Kalonga overcame Lundu and for nearly a century controlled a huge area. Kalonga's Marave domination left many cultural imprints on conquered Makua subjects.[70] The state became so strong and unified that the Portuguese who had initially supported it were unable to retain much influence and had to be content with occasional gift payments rather than any regular tribute.[71]

The *prazo* (or estate) system that developed along the Zambezi valley and its tributaries represented a more successful infiltration of the social formation of the Indian Ocean zone. Grants of land by an African chief to a *sertanejo*,[72] as reward for a variety of services, subsequently came to include juridical rights. These grants were eventually given the stamp of approval by the Portuguese government representative. The arrangement soon evolved to the point where the *prazero* obtained the right to collect taxes and to exercise certain exclusive prerogatives in trade. At the same time, the people over whom he presided expected some display of largesse, protection from external threats, and non-interference in day-to-day affairs. Most *prazeros* created and maintained slave armies.[73] Like the 'second feudalism' that developed elsewhere the *prazo* system depended on trade, and the success of the *prazero* was linked to his ability as a trader. His responsibility differed, however, from those under other types of feudalism in that he was held accountable both by his slave army for sustenance and by the resident population for the protection of traditional rights. This balance usually proved too difficult to achieve, and the *prazero* was often faced with revolts that he could not quell or an exodus that he could not restrain. The result was that few *prazos* survived for more than one generation, although the system itself continued into the nineteenth century.

The *moradores* (townsmen), who resided in Sena and Tete, were another powerful force in the affairs of the Zambezi. Along with the *prazeros*, they were traders whose influence rested on their ability to exploit conflict among the Shona kingdoms of the south. Over the course of centuries, the growth of multiple collateral lineages attached to the royal household came to threaten the position of various Shona monarchs. Although elaborate devices were concocted to diffuse conflict, outsiders soon realised that

69 Alpers, *Ivory and Slaves*, pp. 47–57.
70 Abel dos Santos, *Monografia Etnográfica Sobre os Macuas*, Lisbon, 1951, p. 18.
71 M. Schoffeleers, 'A Martyr Cult', 27.
72 A *sertanejo* was one who ventured into the interior; see M. D. D. Newitt, *Portuguese Settlement on the Zambesi*, New York, 1973, pp. 34–8.
73 Allen Isaacman, *Mozambique: the Africanization of a European Institution*, Madison, Wisconsin, 1972, pp. 17–43.

power was the sole requisite for continuation in office.[74] Faced with a situation of multiple challenges to his rule, an early seventeenth-century Mwene Mutapa seized the opportunity to stabilise his position by calling on the Portuguese of the Zambezi for help. In return for military assistance, which indeed did consolidate the king's position, the *moradores* received important concessions giving them preferential access to gold-producing regions. Others were soon induced to flock to the area in the hope of obtaining similar concessions. By the time that the next king attempted to close the floodgates and expel the foreigners, it was already too late. The Portuguese, making use of their African retinue, simply deposed him and chose a more pliant successor. With a power derived from additional concessions and from their African following, the merchant adventurers infiltrated the neighbouring gold-producing regions and established similar extractive relations with the respective rulers. Thus opportunism resorted to first by a monarch to solve a specific problem, but subsequently copied by large numbers of the population, created a cycle whereby additional grants could be extorted. For the better part of a century no indigenous agency was able to overturn the process.[75] It was not until the resurgence of the Shona under the Rozwi dynasty at the end of the seventeenth century that *prazero* and *morador* interests were expelled from the southern zone.

North of the Zambezi, the *prazeros* and *moradores* had been prevented from gaining ground by the stability that had returned to the Marave following the victory of Kalonga. By the beginning of the eighteenth century, however, civil strife returned, the Marave state system appeared on the verge of collapse, and the way was laid open for manipulation by outsiders. In a virtual replication of what had occurred in the south, *morador* and *prazero* interests went to the aid of threatened rulers, provided military assistance and extracted concessions in return for their favours. By the middle of the century the concessions provided them with sufficient strength to enable them to impose their will on many of those territories that had not previously succumbed.[76]

In their role as traders, the multi-racial *prazeros* and *moradores* formed one component of an African-dominated export sector that experienced rapid growth. Although gold and other precious metals that had lured the Portuguese and their associates into the interior continued to be traded, it was ivory that emerged as the dominant export. There was an insatiable

74 dos Santos, 'Ethiopia Oriental', 197; D. N. Beach, 'The Rozvi and the Changamire State. The Origins of a Myth: the Historiography of the Rozvi', unpublished paper, International Conference on Southern African History, Maseru, Aug. 1977, p. 21; J. F. Holleman, 'Some "Shona" Tribes of Southern Rhodesia', in Colson and Gluckman, *Seven Tribes*, p. 374.

75 'Treaty of the Portuguese with the Monomotapa', *RSEA*, v, 290–93; Rezende, 'India', 414–15; Baretto, 'Report', 486–7.

76 Newitt, *Portuguese Settlement*, pp. 79–80.

demand by the handicraft industry in India since African ivory was soft and easily worked, whereas Indian ivory was brittle. The trading connection proved especially satisfying to Africans because ivory was considered to have little intrinsic value and was thus easily expendable. Returns from the trade could be viewed as pure profit. As a result, the hunting of elephants

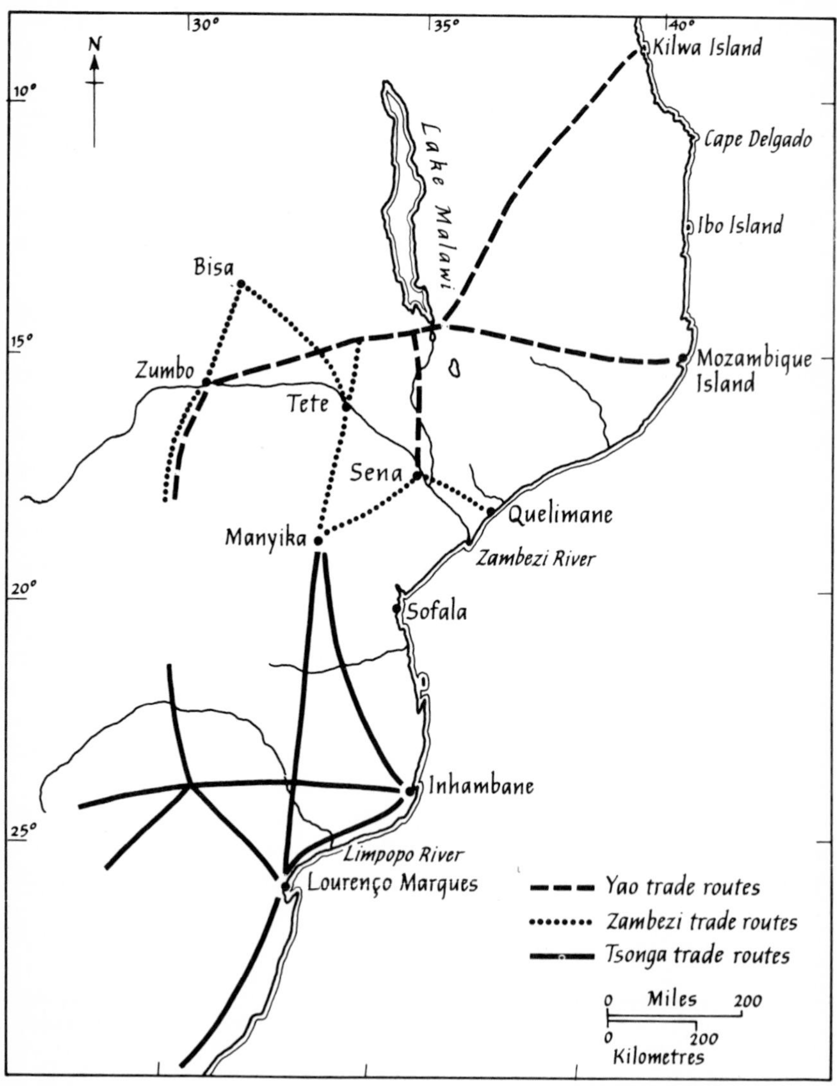

6:3 Eighteenth-century trade routes, Indian Ocean zone.
Source: Adapted and enlarged from Allen Isaacman, *Mozambique: the Africanization of a European Institution*, Madison, Wis., 1972, p. 74.

began to be organised on an unprecedented scale. Adequate data for assessing annual average exports are not available, but at various times each of the major embarkation points reported that vast quantities were shipped to India.[77]

The trade networks that were developed to supply the ivory to the coast, and to the Indian Ocean trading nexus, came to extend over great distances. As the hunting frontier moved steadily towards the interior elephants became virtually extinct in one area after another. No efforts were made to treat elephants as a continuing source of wealth. Trade routes extended from the southern regions of the Indian Ocean zone southward to include the Xhosa-speakers of the eastern Cape, and westward across the high veld.[78] Since the Zambezi settlements of Sena, Tete and Zumbo had ready access to gold and other metals from both sides of the river, ivory was not the predominant commodity that it was elsewhere. It was, nevertheless, an important component of trade, and links were established at least as far west as the country of the Bisa.[79] By the 1780s, the trade routes had crossed Lake Malawi and subsequently fanned out to include many parts of north-eastern Zambia. The fact that such enormous distances were traversed in this single-minded pursuit attests to the perceived profitability of the endeavour.[80]

Commerce on the scale that had been achieved in the Indian Ocean zone by the eighteenth century demanded a fairly high degree of organisation. The superficial impressions that are obtained from records of earlier years suggest that trade in some regions was carried on in a fairly haphazard fashion and that merchandise often passed from 'one nation to another'.[81] Even when the producers attempted to take their goods to the coast, they often were obliged to pay tolls along the way, were denied passage or were subject to robbery. By the eighteenth century, many of these difficulties had been overcome. Some groups had begun to organise caravans that traversed specific routes and stopped at fixed destinations, carried larger quantities of ivory, travelled longer distances, and seemed to enjoy security either because their services had come to be valued or they had acquired the means to pay tolls. Yao traders, for example, emerged as specialists of the northern regions, in an orbit that encompassed the vast territories between the coastal sites of Mozambique Island and Kilwa and the lands to the west

77 During the middle of the eighteenth century, more than 230 000 pounds of ivory was being exported from the Zambezi; by the third quarter of the century, Inhambane exported 110 000 pounds and Lourenço Marques even more. Smith, 'The Struggle', pp. 192–6.

78 J. G. S. Bronkhorst, 'Bronkhorst se Verslaag van Potgieter se Reis Na die Noorde', in Louis Trichardt, *Dagboek van Louis Trichardt*, Capetown, 1938, p. 337; Louis Alberti, *Description Physique et Historique des Cafres sur la Côte Meridionale de l'Afrique*, Amsterdam, 1811, pp. 4–13.

79 Pedroso Gamitto, *King Kazembe and the Marave, Cheva, Bisa, Bemba, Lunda, and Other Peoples of Southern Africa*, Lisbon, 1960, vol. 1, pp. 203–4.

80 Isaacman, *Mozambique*, pp. 80–81.

81 Smith, 'The Struggle', p. 325.

of the Luangwa valley.[82] There they established intimate contacts with Bisa traders, who were recognised as specialists over a wide region of the middle of Central Africa.[83] In the south, groups of Tsonga professionals not only organised caravans but also began to establish trading communities in other regions and to direct hunting operations.[84] A mystique came to surround the trading communities: they were viewed as being shrewd, fair and the only ones from whom valuable trade goods could be obtained.[85]

International trade seems to have had an important impact on the economy of the Indian Ocean zone. Its significance has been obscured by the fact that imports were dominated by beads and cloth, commodities whose value is not readily apparent. These goods, however, served a variety of functions. Since the mode of production in many areas determined that much of the surplus gravitated towards a restricted class of persons, beads and other forms of adornments provided an ostentatious way of demonstrating social distinction. Imported goods also assumed the function of currency. Because they were relatively scarce and could not be duplicated, they were ascribed a high value within the regional economy. Beads and cloth, therefore, provided an additional source of storable wealth. Moreover, the price of exports continued to climb steeply, causing the surplus within the social formation also to grow. It would appear that contact with the wider world was an important stimulus for the growth of the material base of society in the Indian Ocean zone.[86]

As the volume of commerce grew during the eighteenth century, African merchants seized the opportunity to increase their profits by shifting their commerce from their traditional outlets to areas that promised better returns. Whereas Quelimane, the logical outlet for Zambezian produce, continued to be a major centre, other sites occupied by the Portuguese experienced mixed fortunes. By the middle of the eighteenth century, Inhambane had surpassed Sofala as an export emporium to become the major trading port of the southern zone. The change was primarily due to the efforts of Tsonga traders who operated in a radius that was described by contemporaries as 'vastíssimo'.[87] When English merchants from India, who paid better prices for their merchandise, began to frequent the harbour of Lourenço Marques, the Tsonga responded by diverting goods from Inhambane to the new outlet

82 Edward Alpers, *The East African Slave Trade*, Dar es Salaam, 1967, pp. 14–16.
83 Christopher St John, 'Kazembe and the Tanganyika–Nyasa Corridor, 1800–1890', in *Pre-Colonial African Trade*, Richard Gray and David Birmingham (eds), London, 1970, p. 212.
84 N. J. van Warmelo (ed.), *The Copper Miners of Musina*, Pretoria, 1940, p. 68.
85 Henry Fynn, *The Diary of Henry Francis Fynn*, Pietermaritzburg, 1950, p. 48.
86 Smith, 'The Struggle', pp. 332–45.
87 João Baptista de Montaury, 'Moçambique, Ilhas Querimbas . . .', in Andrade, *Relações*, p. 372.

in the south. By the last quarter of the eighteenth century, Lourenço Marques had replaced Inhambane as the leader in exports from the southern regions.[88]

The pattern of commerce in the northern zone was very similar. Traditionally the Yao marketed their ivory at Mozambique Island. Two important factors that developed in the mid-eighteenth century caused them to seek new avenues for their produce. One problem was that the Makua, whose territory they had to pass through in order to reach the coast, were beset by internal strife, making conditions unpredictable for travellers. The resurgence of Kilwa, after years of decay under Omani rule, proved to be an even greater factor in inducing the Yao to alter their patterns of commerce. Under Swahili leadership the trading port revived and offered better-quality merchandise and higher prices than those available at Mozambique Island. These conditions soon lured the Yao into trading most of their ivory at this non-Portuguese outlet.[89]

The alteration of trade routes to maximise returns reflected the successful way in which East-Central Africans coped with pressures introduced by Europeans. During the first centuries of contact with the wider world, trade had been used to broaden the material base of society. On the other hand, most attempts at encroachment had been successfully resisted. Even when apical conflict opened breaches that enabled Europeans to infiltrate and exploit a particular locality, the advantages they gained were usually ephemeral. As soon as a degree of unity was restored, Africans were able to re-establish their supremacy and to restrict the activities of the interlopers.

THE ERA OF NEGATIVE TRANSITION

The ability of Africans to act independently, especially in the commercial sphere, obliged Portugal to institute policies that were designed to limit freedom of choice. The proto-colonialism that ensued was one of a number of changes that adversely affected the Indian Ocean zone during the nineteenth century. Another was the growth of the slave-trade from its modest eighteenth-century beginnings to a phenomenon that profoundly disrupted social relations. The Indian Ocean zone was also subjected to devastating invasions from the south which resulted in the creation of a number of predatory states. In the midst of the general disarray, societies were confronted by a changing world economy that was able to apply more pervasive pressure to obtain various services and commodities.

Between the time of the Portuguese arrival in Indian Ocean waters and the middle of the eighteenth century, the fortunes of Portugal experienced a steady decline. This was partly because it was never able to make its

88 Alan K. Smith, 'Delagoa Bay and the trade of South-Eastern Africa', in Gray and Birmingham, *Pre-Colonial Trade*, pp. 283–4.
89 For a full discussion, see Alpers, *Ivory and Slaves*.

monopoly effective. It was not only in Central Africa that efforts to funnel commerce into the hands of its own nationals were unsuccessful, but also in the Red Sea and in the ocean to the east of Malacca, where it was obliged to trade on an equal footing with the indigenous merchants. As a result, by the later stages of the sixteenth century, as much pepper was reaching Europe by way of the old Red Sea route as was being carried in Portuguese vessels. The failure of Portugal to use the wealth obtained in Asian ventures to broaden its economic infrastructure was a far more significant factor. In fact, during the heyday of Portuguese expansion, the country ceased to be self-sufficient in commodities it had once exported and began to rely on imports from north-western Europe. In effect, the wealth that Portugal so painstakingly acquired helped to develop other European nations.[90]

Expansion actually drained Portugal of both financial and human resources. The peasantry, which was heavily taxed, deserted the land in large numbers, preferring the lure of riches in the far-off unknown to the drudgery of unremunerative tilling of the soil. Brazil, in particular, attracted numerous immigrants from the motherland. The drain on Portuguese resources was compounded by the necessity of fighting a global war against the Dutch. That the Portuguese should have been fighting the Dutch at all was one of the true ironies of modern history. Between 1580 and 1640 Portugal was incorporated into the Spanish kingdom because heirless King Dom Sebastião was killed in battle and, of the various pretenders, Philip II of Spain had the strongest army, if not the strongest claims to succeed. Thus, against their will the Portuguese were incorporated into Spain at the same time that the provinces of the Low Countries had revolted against the Habsburg monarch. Since the strength of the Netherlands was in maritime power, it directed its attacks on the Portuguese seaborne empire while virtually ignoring the land-based Spanish colonial empire. For nearly half a century the Portuguese in the Americas, Africa and Asia were forced to suffer the blows that nominally were directed at Spain. The impact proved extremely costly. Because of a lack of manpower and capital, colonisation schemes aimed at improving Portugal's position in East-Central Africa had to be abandoned while still in the blueprint stage.[91] The two Dutch India companies were the main agents in the dismembering of Portugal's territories. Although the Dutch West India Company was the less successful of the two, its attacks on Atlantic shipping and attempted conquests of Brazil and Angola severely taxed Portugal's resources. The East India Company, on the other hand,

90 For a discussion of the mechanics of the pepper trade, see Donald Lach, *Asia in the Making of Europe*, Chicago, 1965, vol. 1, pp. 92–149; an assessment of the impact of global commerce on Europe can be found in Eric Hobsbawm, 'The crisis in the seventeenth century', in *Crisis in Europe, 1560–1660*, Trevor Aston (ed.), London, 1965, pp. 5–59.
91 Teixeira Botelho, *História*, vol. 1, pp. 317–27, 339–53.

successfully ousted the Portuguese from virtually all of their bases in the eastern sphere of operation.[92]

The enervating effects of their struggles against the Dutch made the Portuguese increasingly vulnerable to the indigenous powers with whom they were in contact. In India much of their commercial activity fell victim to the rising power of the Marathas, and their sphere of operations was limited to the environs of Goa.[93] Similarly, Oman led a resurgence that severely restricted their activities in both the Persian Gulf and the Red Sea. Losses in East and Central Africa were no less significant. Towards the latter stages of the seventeenth century, armies of the Changamire moved northward and chased many of the *sertanejos* from the privileged positions they had acquired during the century.[94] With the fall of Fort Jesus to a combination of local and Omani forces in 1698 and the loss of control of the Swahili coast north of Cape Delgado, a catastrophic century came to an end. Their ability to hold out in Mozambique Island against a siege staged by the Dutch East India Company was one of the few successes in an otherwise dismal series of failures.[95]

By 1750, when the Marques de Pombal became the first minister of state in Portugal, the situation showed few signs of improvement. Although the discovery of gold and diamonds in Brazil provided some respite for the treasury, Pombal was concerned with the unequal relationship that had grown among Brazil, Portugal and Great Britain.[96] He was also concerned with the decadence that had overcome the official establishment in eastern Africa. A multitude of archaic and unworkable laws hampered progress. The civil service was corrupt, venal and self-serving, while military capacity existed only on paper and the religious orders were concerned more with self-aggrandisement than the propagation of the faith. With characteristic urgency Pombal instituted reforms that were designed to stop the decay.[97]

The principal aims of the first minister were to make Portuguese control more effective, to rationalise commerce so that it showed a profit for the state, to ease the burden that East and East-Central Africa placed on the government of India and to restrict the activities of foreigners in the Indian Ocean zone. Pombal was a pragmatist who was usually guided by the local situation rather than by a universal philosophy. With the notable exception of the expulsion of the Jesuits from the empire, policies designed for

92 Boxer, *The Portuguese Seaborne Empire*, pp. 106–28.

93 K. N. Panikkar, *Asia and Western Dominance*, London, 1959, pp. 58–9.

94 See below, chap. 7, p. 261.

95 Teixeira Botelho, *História*, vol. 1, pp. 261–72; Justus Strandes, *The Portuguese Period in East African History*, Nairobi, 1961, pp. 222–98.

96 Kenneth Maxwell, *Conflicts and Conspiracies: Brazil and Portugal, 1750–1808*, Cambridge, 1973, pp. 1–33.

97 Fritz Hoppe, *A África Oriental portuguesa no tempo do Marquês de Pombal*, Lisbon, 1970, pp. 63–155, 280–310.

particular locales were determined by local conditions. Thus, whereas Pombal could advocate intermarriage between Portuguese and indigenous peoples in parts of the empire where he thought this would strengthen Portuguese control, legislation was promulgated for the Zambezian *prazos* which specifically forbade such unions because of the fear that Portuguese control would otherwise be diluted.[98] Similarly, although commercial restrictions were imposed in Brazil, free trade was declared for all Portuguese nationals operating in eastern Africa. It was hoped that by opening trade to all, smuggling would decrease. In order to make the administration run more smoothly, the governments of East Africa and India were made separate concerns in 1752. To ensure that the reforms could be instituted properly, officials with administrative experience and reputations for honesty were appointed to oversee the new policies. Finally, to provide the officials with the means to enforce their will, 329 men were sent from Portugal to Mozambique in 1753. Although the number might not seem large, the effort involved many more Europeans than had previously manned the garrisons.[99]

The attempt to control a segment of the East African coast was not new. Pombal, however, was sufficiently pragmatic only to undertake ventures that could be afforded and accomplished. Planners who both preceded and succeeded him were unanimous in the opinion that other European nations must be prevented from securing a foothold along the coast. Portugal usually had little to fear, however, because eighteenth-century Europe showed scant interest in acquiring territory in the Indian Ocean zone. On the few occasions when other nations demonstrated a curiosity concerning Portugal's neglected sphere of interest, the Portuguese intervened in a defensive manner to preserve their monopoly. In 1721, for example, the Dutch East India Company established an outpost in the unoccupied harbour of Lourenço Marques. After several years of attempting unsuccessfully to make the settlement profitable, the Dutch began to look northwards along the coast for an alternative site.[100] Forewarned of Dutch intentions, the governor of Mozambique sent a small garrison to Inhambane in 1731 to establish effective control and to forestall a settlement by the East India Company.[101] The Dutch had already abandoned Lourenço Marques, and Portugal temporarily preserved the integrity of its sphere of influence.

Portugal again acted cautiously when its position was threatened in the latter half of the eighteenth century. In the 1760s English traders began to

98 Isaacman, *Mozambique*, p. 60.

99 Inácio Caetano Xavier, 'Notícias dos Dominios Portugueses', in Andrade, *Relações*, p. 152.

100 A full treatment of the Dutch period is given in Colin Coetzee, 'Die Kompanjie se Besetting op Delagoa-baai', in *Archives Yearbook for South African History*, part 2; Smith, 'The Struggle', pp. 47–111.

101 Smith, 'The Struggle', pp. 90–99.

pursue a vigorous trade in ivory at Lourenço Marques. The immediate effect was to divert commerce from the thriving port of Inhambane. The Portuguese, however, were reluctant to interfere with the English for fear of subsequent reprisals. In 1777, when sovereignty over the bay was claimed by an understaffed company that had been chartered in Austria, Portugal was able to take decisive action with few fears of retaliation. In 1781, the governor of Mozambique dispatched a force that with great bravado burned and pillaged the small station of the malaria-ridden and rapidly expiring company. Thus, with minimal expenditure and without a direct confrontation with a major power, Portugal laid claim to what subsequently would prove to be the very lucrative southern portion of Mozambique.[102]

Portuguese reforms instituted in the mid-eighteenth century had some impact, but not in the ways intended nor in crucial areas. For example, the free trade that Portuguese mercantile interests advocated actually benefited the Indian community, which, because of its close connections with India, was able to assume a dominant role in commerce. The inability of the Portuguese to establish a dominant military presence was, however, a much more important failure. After receiving reinforcements in 1753, the governor of Mozambique decided to settle a few old scores with Makua chiefs and to demonstrate the revitalised nature of the Portuguese establishment. The fact that he was obliged to retreat, leaving seventy of his men on the ground, demonstrated that Portugal lacked the resources to enforce its rule even in the area of its principal settlement at Mozambique Island. The Portuguese continued to remain an impotent force even after the admission of large numbers of Asians and Africans into the lower echelons of the army.[103]

As a result, Portugal resorted to the legal fiction of rule, a situation most interest groups were willing to tolerate. Only the Tonga around Inhambane submitted to a more effective Portuguese presence. Their cooperation was influenced by their need for the aid provided by the Portuguese commander and the mercantile community. On several occasions they joined forces to repel Tsonga attempts to take over the coast.[104] Elsewhere the pattern differed considerably. Lisbon's representatives resorted to such devices as conferring titles on rulers and perpetuating the notion that they were part of a wide administrative network. They also exploited local rivalries and made alliances with the strongest groups in a particular region. Although this approach achieved some successes, it often backfired and left the Portuguese alone, exposed and obliged to be submissive and apologetic. Their real problems, however, began when some officials mistook fiction for reality and

102 Alexandre Lobato, *História da fundação de Lourenço Marques*, Lisbon, 1948.
103 Xavier, 'Notícias', p. 152; Montaury, 'Moçambique', p. 339.
104 Smith, 'The Peoples', pp. 578–9.

attempted to impose their will. The result was everywhere the same. Whether it took the form of military defeat, elimination of over-zealous officialdom, or strategic evacuation by the local establishment, the Portuguese were soon reminded of their limitations.[105]

African toleration of the Portuguese paradoxically proved detrimental to the social formation. Allowing the Portuguese to remain dissuaded other traders from venturing into the coastal ports. The increasingly decadent Portuguese mercantile establishment could not, however, meet the demand of the Indian Ocean zone economy. The monopsony that they imposed occurred when there was a general contraction in the supply of principal exports. As intensive hunting depleted elephant herds and yields from old mines decreased, ivory and gold became more scarce. With the accumulation of a surplus no longer as easy, the fuelling of the regional economy became more difficult and the scale of transaction began to diminish. An anonymous African commentator of the 1830s captured the spirit when he mused of the 'old days' as a time when people were rich.[106]

The area of Natal, in the southern hinterland of Lourenço Marques, was one of the first regions to feel the impact of nineteenth-century contraction. Northern Nguni society had been greatly affected by international commerce. During the centuries of trade from Lourenço Marques, Natal had been both the most consistent and largest supplier of ivory.[107] Imports facilitated the manipulation of lineage domination so that there was a trend towards centralisation of power and consolidation of peoples and territories. Because ivory was a commodity of little internal value, social change had been effected at minimum cost. The conjuncture of Portuguese inability to supply necessary trade goods and declining sources of ivory, however, portended crisis. Reproduction of social relations depended upon the ability of rulers to maintain the flow of goods to their subordinates. With the decline in the ivory trade that was apparent by the beginning of the nineteenth century, it became necessary to substitute cattle for imported trade goods. Age-regiments which formerly had divided their time between fighting and hunting came to be employed increasingly in the seizure of cattle. Warfare on an unprecedented scale ensued, and the defeated and their herds were incorporated into ever-larger units. During the first twenty years of the nineteenth century, the Ndwandwe and the Mtetwa-Zulu emerged as the dominant contestants for power. When Shaka and his Zulu army inflicted a devastating defeat on the Ndwandwe

105 Nancy Hafkin, 'Trade, Society, and Politics in Northern Mozambique, *c.* 1753–1913', Ph.D. thesis, Boston University, 1973, pp. xii–xiii, 91–105; António Jóse Nobre, 'A Guerra dos Reis Vatuas Vizínhos do Presídio de Lourenço Marques em 1833', in *Documentação Avulsa Moçambicana do Arquivo Histórico Ultramarino*, Francisco Santana (ed.), Lisbon, 1964–6, vol. 1, pp. 219–23; Smith, 'The Struggle', pp. 271–4.

106 Andrew Smith, *The Diary of Andrew Smith, 1834–1836*, Capetown, 1939, vol. 2, p. 193.

107 Alan K. Smith, 'The Trade of Delagoa Bay as a Factor in Nguni Politics, 1750–1835', in *African Societies in South Africa*, Leonard Thompson (ed.), London, 1969, pp. 178–9.

and their Ncwangeni-Jere, Gaza and Msane allies, the way was opened not only for Zulu consolidation, but also for the explosive migration of peoples that was profoundly to affect the Indian Ocean zone.[108]

One section of the defeated Ndwandwe alliance that burst northward

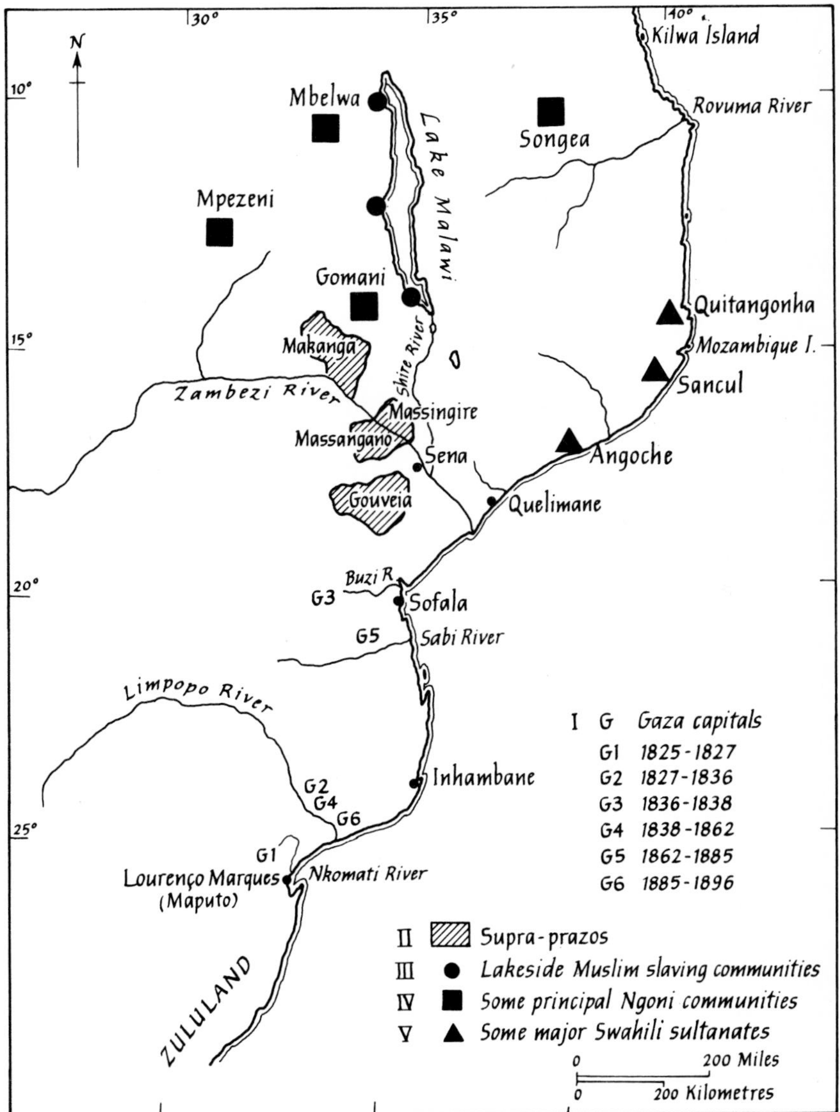

6:4 The Indian Ocean zone during the nineteenth century

108 Hedges, 'Trade and Politics' provides the best account of the impact of changes in the patterns of trade on the Nguni.

came to be known as the Ngoni. It consisted of several factions, some of which joined together at various times, fought with one another on occasion or moved on in different directions. Although small in numbers at the beginning, the Ngoni were able to wreak havoc partly by surprising their victims and also because the military training that had become a requisite of survival in Natal made them more effective fighters than their adversaries. The career of the branch led by Zwangendaba, which ultimately became the most numerous and important, is illustrative of the general pattern followed by the Ngoni. Between about 1821 and 1825, his band operated in southern Mozambique, where it maintained a loose alliance with the one led by Soshangane. When the two leaders quarrelled, Zwangendaba moved northward, where he defeated a related faction commanded by Ngwane Maseko. He was forced to flee again, however, when Ngwane Maseko was joined by Nxaba at the head of yet another Nguni-speaking faction. Zwangendaba then led his following westward along the banks of the Sabi river, whence, after several years of pillage, his following crossed the Zambezi.[109] Because of a succession dispute that accompanied his death, the section split into a faction headed by Mpezeni, which settled in Zambia, and another commanded by Mwambera, that remained in Malawi.[110] In addition to these two Ngoni states,[111] descendants of those who left Natal came to rest in Malawi and in the Songea region of western Tanzania.[112] More than fifty years elapsed after the flight from the south before permanent resting places were found.

Soshangane was the leader of a second group of the Ndwandwe alliance which moved northward to avoid Shaka's wrath. The main components of his initially small following were members of the Gaza, a name that continued to be employed in their new homeland. Whereas fragmentation and northward drift were continuing themes among the Ngoni, the movements of the Gaza were confined to the area south of the Zambezi river, and the body politic remained intact during the lifetime of Soshangane. By 1828 his following was strong enough to resist the war-weary and perhaps malaria-ridden army that Shaka sent to destroy him. Having parried what was to be the last Zulu challenge to their

109 William Rau, 'Mpezeni's Ngoni of Eastern Zambia, 1870–1920', Ph.D. thesis, University of California, Los Angeles, 1974, pp. 38–52.

110 J. A. Barnes, *Politics in a Changing Society*, London, 1954, pp. 17–23.

111 The languages of the South African coastland, including Zulu and Xhosa, are known as Nguni and are distinct from the highland languages west of the Drakensberg which are grouped as Sotho languages. When the *mfecane* war and the subsequent *difaqane* diaspora carried Nguni-speaking refugees northward, they influenced many peoples of Mozambique, Zimbabwe, Malawi and even Tanzania. The acculturated groups were called 'Ngoni' and spoke Ngoni languages, which bear similarity to the Nguni languages of South Africa.

112 Rau, 'Mpezeni's Ngoni', chap. 2, *passim*; E. A. Alpers, 'The nineteenth century: prelude to colonialism', in *Zamani*, B. A. Ogot and J. A. Kiernan (eds), pp. 242–3.

independence, the Gaza soon confirmed themselves as the strongest force in southern Mozambique. In 1834, the governor and *moradores* of Inhambane, during one of those periods when fiction was confused with reality, sent a force of 300 men to punish Soshangane for raiding peoples who had placed themselves under Portuguese protection. The rout of this 'colonial' army, and the subsequent successful demand for tribute from the inhabitants of Sena and Sofala, confirmed the pre-eminence of the Gaza over a wide expanse of territory. At various times, depending on the location of the capital, Tsonga-, Tshopi-, Tonga- and Shona-speaking peoples felt the wrath of the increasingly powerful Gaza state.[113]

Taken in conjunction with the similar set of circumstances that surrounded the career of the Ndebele, the impact of the Ngoni and the Gaza state of Soshangane represented a crucial transition in Central African history. The ability of these communities to survive and even to grow was a remarkable phenomenon. The different ways that each found for the incorporation of diverse peoples and for the regulation of their affairs demonstrated an eclectic and inventive approach to the resolution of the problem of survival. Nevertheless, the legacy for the social formation was negative in the extreme. Throughout the region there appeared groups in which exploitation was not limited to the lower ranks of society but was extended to all through regular raiding and expropriation. Under these circumstances, consumption by the non-productive sector of society attained a sufficiently large scale for successive regions to become depleted of resources, thus necessitating plunder in new areas. Many of the dispossessed joined war leaders because they preferred to eke out an existence in the lower echelons of society among the conquerors than to risk the vicissitudes of resistance against stronger foes. Others, however, adopted the techniques of the invaders, thus increasing the level of pillage.[114] Although the degree of impact of predatory states differed in both time and place, much of East-Central Africa was affected. In addition to the many who suffered directly from raiding and tribute collection, there were others who found no incentive to increase production because of the general instability.

The predatory states that depended on the expropriation of cattle and crops came into existence at the time when the slave-trade was growing in the Indian Ocean zone. Its beginnings in the second quarter of the eighteenth century were directly related to the needs of the world economy. The French governor of the islands of Mauritius and Réunion decided to convert the islands to plantations producing sugar and coffee.

113 Gerhard Liesegang, 'Aspects of Gaza Nguni History', *Rhodesian History*, vi, 1975, 1–14.
114 W. A. Elmslie, *Among the Wild Ngoni*, Glasgow, 1899, pp. 78–89; William Owen, *Narrative of Voyages to ... Africa, Arabia ...*, London, 1833, vol. 1, pp. 80, 123–4; 'Bronkhorst se Verslaag', p. 336; Alpers, 'The nineteenth century', pp. 242–3.

For this slaves were needed, and the Portuguese sphere of eastern Africa seemed the most likely source. With the connivance of the administrators of Mozambique, vessels from the islands began to undertake what officially was an illicit trade. Since the occasional governor of Mozambique actually lived up to the letter of the law by enforcing the mercantilistic proscriptions against French trading, the early years of the trade were marked by intermittent stoppages. By the 1770s, however, Lisbon had given official approval, and thereafter trade flourished openly.[115]

During the early stages, the Makua were both the principal agents of the slave-traders and the main victims. Stronger Makua chiefdoms made war on their weaker neighbours and sold their captives at Mozambique Island. The French had no qualms about providing fire-arms in return, even though they did not always have Portuguese approval. Guns, which helped the Makua to thwart Portuguese efforts to subdue them, also brought about their own destruction. Traders, whether French, Swahili or Indian, fomented trouble by providing rivals with weapons. It did not matter which side won, since the traders were supplied with captives in either case. Between the late eighteenth and early nineteenth centuries, most of the strong Makua chiefdoms were destroyed. Vast areas were depopulated, survivors congregated in larger settlements and servile forms of dependence entered the social relations of production.[116]

The Yao, who had pioneered the development of the ivory-trade, were quick to seize the opportunities presented by the slave-trade and soon became a principal supplier. While their ivory-trade was being diverted to Kilwa, they brought large numbers of captives to Mozambique. These they obtained from an equally vast area. Through Bisa intermediaries they acquired slaves from the Lunda kingdom of Kazembe. The slaving communities established in the environs of Lake Malawi by Yao and Swahili adventurers provided another important source. Moreover, like the Makua, the Yao were not loath to enslave their brethren; on the contrary, it appears that the majority of people whom they sold at the coast were fellow-Yao.[117]

A tremendous increase in demand during the nineteenth century led to the expansion of the slave-trade in the Indian Ocean zone. The French continued to exploit their Indian Ocean islands during much of the nineteenth century. Nevertheless, it was newcomers who accelerated the demand for labour. For the first time, Brazilian slavers found it worthwhile to undertake the long voyage around the Cape of Good Hope to acquire hands for their plantations. The development of plantation agriculture in the nearby islands of Zanzibar and Pemba was even more important. The

115 Alpers, *East African Slave Trade*, p. 7.
116 Hafkin, 'Trade, Society', pp. 26–8.
117 Alpers, *East African Slave Trade*, pp. 15–16, 23.

settling of the ruling dynasty of Oman on Zanzibar led to the cultivation of cloves and coconut palms on an extensive scale. As a result of the multiple demands on its human resources, eastern Africa exported an estimated 70 000 slaves annually in the 1860s.[118]

The increased demand for slaves resulted in a proliferation of the sites from which they were exported. For example, in the 1820s southern Mozambique, which had been virtually untouched by the slave-trade during the eighteenth century, was visited by French and Brazilian ships, and a brisk, if short-lived, commerce began. The wealth of the Swahili sultanates that dotted the coast north of Quelimane increased to the point where they no longer feared either the Makua or the Portuguese. Until prevailed upon by the British to declare the trade illegal, the Portuguese and Indians continued to export large numbers from Quelimane and Mozambique Island. Small, clandestine harbours all along the coast continued as points of embarkation even after abolition. Since slave-ships were difficult to monitor, their cargoes escaped the vigilance of the anti-slave-trade squadron. It was not until after 1873, when the British prevailed on Sultan Bargash to close the infamous slave-market on Zanzibar, that the trend was reversed.[119]

The ravages that resulted from the slave-trade were even worse than those caused by the Nguni successor states. Whereas the raiders often left enough people to allow farming to continue, slavers felt no such compunction. The reports of the various missionaries, explorers, traders and quasi-governmental officials who visited the area are vivid testimony to the often harrowing conditions. Descriptions abound of people forced to live in barricaded settlements in order to diminish the threat of surprise attacks.[120] Others were stunned to revisit places once described as idyllic and prosperous only to find that they had been ravaged and completely denuded of people, animals and crops.[121] Some of the most horrific conditions were seen in the fertile Malawi–Tanzania corridor. The frontier of slaving, however, did not end there. By the last quarter of the nineteenth century, it was being pushed hundreds of miles to the west.[122]

The emergence of the slave-trade and the arrival of predatory groups were important factors in transforming the nature of society in the Zambezi valley. The late eighteenth century witnessed a severe decline in the traditional exports of the Zambezi *prazeros*. Many responded by

118 *Ibid.*, p. 11.
119 Christopher Lloyd, *The Navy and the Slave Trade*, London, 1968, pp. 187–268.
120 Elton, *Travels*, pp. 345–7.
121 For vivid descriptions of slaving and its impact, see Elton, *Travels*; L. Monteith Fotheringham, *Adventures in Nyasaland*, London, 1891; E. C. Hore, *Tanganyika*, London, 1892; Frederick Moir, *After Livingstone*, London, 1923.
122 Andrew Roberts, 'Nyamwezi trade', in Gray and Birmingham, *Pre-Colonial Trade*, p. 68.

vacating their estates and emigrating to Brazil. Others sought salvation in the increasingly lucrative commerce in human beings. At first these *prazeros* functioned in much the same way as other traders. They acquired their cargo either by purchase from inland sources or by raiding weaker peoples north of the river. The significant profits proved too great a temptation, however, and many began to sell members of their own following. This breach in the contractual arrangement caused a wholesale flight from such estates to others where the traditional obligations of the *prazero* and rights of the *colono* were respected. In addition to the number of *prazos* that became vacant because the *prazero* overstepped his prerogatives, others were abandoned because of fear of the Gaza Nguni. Threats and demands for tribute by Soshangane created a climate of uncertainty that proved difficult to live with. Under these circumstances, a few skilled individuals who remained in the area were able to consolidate these holdings into *supra-prazos*.[123]

In some ways Portuguese policy with respect to these *supra-prazeros* continued along traditional lines. In others it reflected the changed material circumstances that became increasingly apparent towards the end of the century. By the mid-nineteenth century, the Zambezi valley had come to be dominated by the *supra-prazos* of Makanga, Massangano and Massingire and by the areas ruled over by Gouveia. The new *prazo* became less Portuguese in ethnic, cultural and political terms as generations passed, they were willing to accept the façade of a titular relationship as long as no obligations accompanied it. Agreements were ignored from the outset, unless it was in the interest of the particular *prazero* to honour them. As the century wore on, however, the Portuguese began to insist on compliance. In almost all instances hostilities followed. That the Portuguese could even contemplate confronting such powerful adversaries stemmed from the fact that they could often enlist the aid of the *prazeros* who were not being challenged. The new industrial technology to which Portugal was privy also made their fighting forces more effective than they had previously been. As a result, with the help of Gouveia, superior weaponry and the larger number of troops that became available, Massingire was defeated in 1882, Massangano in 1887 and Makanga in 1889.[124]

Supra-prazero penetration of the Shire valley brought chaos to a previously flourishing area. During the nineteenth century, Massingire, exhibiting all the characteristics of a *supra-prazo*, supplanted Portuguese interests that had infiltrated the lower river valley during the eighteenth century. At the same time the area immediately to the north came under the influence of Yao, and immigrant Muslim slave-traders who established themselves at various spots along the banks of the river and the shores of

123 Isaacman, *Mozambique*, pp. 124–54.
124 Newitt, *Portuguese Settlement*, pp. 234–341.

Lake Malawi. The influence of the slave-traders was compounded by the presence of several distinct groups of Ngoni who raided over an area that extended from the lower valley to the northern end of the lake. Thus, within a century, one of the most prosperous regions of the continent was transformed into one where there was security for neither life nor property.[125]

The ravages that beset the Shire highlands attracted a different type of outsider. These were Christian missionaries from Great Britain. In response to appeals contained in David Livingstone's journals and lectures, they sought to ameliorate the condition of the peoples by offering Christianity. In the 1860s, mission work was pioneered by the Universities' Mission to Central Africa, which was joined in the 1870s by the Church of Scotland and Free Church of Scotland missions. The missionaries soon learned that their belief in the regeneration of the area by exposure to the Bible had been naïve. They were unsuccessful either in protecting the lambs or in convincing the wolves to desist from their predation. They soon came to believe that the only solution was for Great Britain to assume control. During the 1880s, the church groups established an effective lobby in the press and Parliament which persuasively called for government intervention. Ultimately their appeals were answered.[126]

European encroachment was also becoming more pervasive in the south. The death of the Gaza ruler, Soshangane, in the late 1850s precipitated a succession dispute between his sons, Mawewe and Mzila. Although Mawewe was installed as heir and successfully concluded an alliance with his powerful Swazi neighbours, his attacks on ivory-traders and their associates convinced the Portuguese to side with Mzila. A combination of indigenous elephant-hunters, disaffected Tsonga chiefdoms and guns supplied from Lourenço Marques tipped the balance in Mzila's favour and enabled him to defeat Mawewe. In return for their help, Mzila signed one of those easily misunderstood documents that made him a 'vassal' of Portugal. A full-scale definition of what the treaties actually meant was delayed by subsequent Swazi intervention. Attacks that they launched against Mzila on the one hand and the Portuguese on the other convinced the new Gaza leader to return with his following to the north. As time passed, however, the vacuum left by Mzila's flight enabled the Portuguese to erect a few customs posts on the road to the Transvaal. Thus, when Ngungunyane, Mzila's successor, returned to the south during the 1880s,

125 Harry W. Langworthy, 'Central Malawi in the Nineteenth Century', in *From Nyasaland to Malawi*, Roderick Macdonald (ed.), Nairobi, 1975, pp. 12–33.

126 Alan K. Smith, 'The Anglo-Portuguese Conflict Over the Shire Highlands', *ibid.*, pp. 44–64; a detailed account of the career of the missionaries can be found in Michael Gelfand, *Lakeside Pioneers*, Oxford, 1964; the most interesting among the first-hand accounts provided by the missionaries themselves are William P. Johnson, *My African Reminiscences, 1875–1895*, London, 1924, and Robert Laws, *Reminiscences of Livingstonia*, London, 1934.

there was already a small Portuguese presence in the interior. Like his father, he signed a treaty that subsequently was to be the subject of very different interpretations by the signatories.[127]

In addition to the various documents that the Portuguese signed with successive Gaza rulers, they were able to produce other evidence to convince their European counterparts of their right to control southern Mozambique. In the 1820s, Captain William Owen of the British navy made an abortive attempt to annex the southern half of the harbour of Lourenço Marques. Since his actions were undertaken during an age when territorial expansion was anathema to the British government, it refused to sanction his activities. Fifty years later, however, the climate had changed. The introduction of sizeable amounts of capital into South Africa, and prospects for future development, increased the importance of surrounding areas. The port of Lourenço Marques was crucial because it was the proposed starting point of the Delagoa Bay–Transvaal railway. Under these circumstances, the British reasserted Owen's dormant claims to the bay.[128] When negotiations between Britain and Portugal reached an impasse, the matter was turned over to arbitration. The resulting McMahon award of 1875 dismissed British claims and ruled that Portugal was entitled to sole possession. The Portuguese had thus obtained a paper confirming their supremacy in southern Mozambique that not even the subsequent machinations of Cecil Rhodes could undermine.[129]

These diplomatic negotiations took place in an economic environment that was undergoing significant change. The increasing scarcity of ivory and the decline of cattle herds had an important impact on the social relations of production. The Gaza state had become very dependent on control of the remaining ivory-trade.[130] As the trade began to languish, lineage authority was undermined at its material base. At the same time, capital penetration in the form of intensive mining, commercialised agriculture, and railway development in South Africa, all reinforced the tendency towards social disintegration. Significant numbers of men began to engage in wage labour in the diamond and gold mines and on the farms and plantations of South Africa. The migrants included Tonga and Tshopi from the Inhambane region, who went not only to South Africa, but also contracted themselves as labourers on the French plantation islands. By

127 Philip Bonner, 'The Rise, Consolidation and Disintegration of Dlamini Power in Swaziland between 1820 and 1899', Ph.D. thesis, University of London, 1979, pp. 190–205; see below, chap. 7.

128 Documents aimed at substantiating Portugal's case can be found in *Memória Sobre Lourenço Marques*, Levi Maria Jordão Paiva Manso (ed.), Lisbon, 1870.

129 See Philip Warhurst, *Anglo-Portuguese Relations in South-Central Africa*, London, 1962, pp. 78–129, for an account of Rhodes's attempts to add the area to his empire.

130 Patrick Harries, 'Labour migration from the Delagoa Bay hinterland to South Africa: 1852–1895', University of London, Institute of Commonwealth Studies, *The Societies of Southern Africa in the Nineteenth and Twentieth Centuries*, London, 1977, p. 69.

1887 as many as one-half of the able-bodied male population of the Delagoa Bay region was working in South Africa.[131] Although at that stage most Mozambicans probably assumed that wage labour was a temporary expedient to solve specific and immediate problems, the truth is rather that the world economy was in the final stages of becoming synonymous with the economy of the world. A different set of variables would govern social relations in the future. As an agency of the world economy, colonialism served to maintain specific sets of articulation between various component parts.

The regions to the north of the Zambezi also entered a period of transition. With the decline of the coastal slave-trade, the population returned to the intensive cultivation of crops. The main source of demand for surplus agricultural produce had previously been the Portuguese, but by the late nineteenth century the more distant industrial world required these exports. The new interest was signalled by an increase in Asian and European shipping along the coast. People began to grow such cash crops as ground-nuts, sesame seeds, copra and rubber.[132] In areas where chiefs had monopolised the ivory- and slave-trades, production on small plots by family groups threatened to undermine their privileged positions. Some responded by establishing plantations that they cultivated with slave labour, whereas others simply attempted to increase the rate of taxation.[133] Although social relations varied from one area to another, the impact of the world economy introduced tensions everywhere. Before they had been resolved, colonialism was imposed.

CONCLUSION

The Indian Ocean zone passed through several stages during the five centuries before 1890. As its material base grew, the tendency everywhere was to move from egalitarian principles to various forms of social distinction. Although much of the change was associated with internal development, contact with the wider world was an important factor in stimulating economic diversification. The overseas connection, however, undermined the whole area. As in the case of the Zulu and the Gaza, failure to control the level of interaction led to extreme disorder. The world demand for primary commodities, best produced by non-free labour, was responsible for great depredations that destroyed once thriving mixed

131 *Ibid.*, pp. 61–6; David Webster, 'Migrant labour, social formations and the proletarianization of the Chopi of southern Mozambique', *African Perspectives*, 1978, 163–4; Liesegang, 'Aspects', 8.

132 Elton, *Travels*, p. 206; the board of trade of the Foreign Office produced annual reports which give estimates of exports; see, for example, 'Trade in the Province of Mozambique During the Year Ended 31 December 1889', C. 5895–15, 467–8.

133 Walters, 'Commodity Production', pp. 3–4.

economies. Elements within the social formation, however, must share part of the blame for the decay since there was no shortage of individuals and groups who were willing to mortgage the long-term interests of the Indian Ocean zone in exchange for personal gain. In so doing, East-Central Africans partly prepared the ground for their own downfall; they were ultimately deprived even of the benefits which that economic choice provided.

CHAPTER 7

The Zimbabwe plateau and its peoples

D. N. BEACH

The Zimbabwe plateau region of South-Central Africa is far smaller than the broad savanna belts of West-Central and North-Central Africa. It is also much more closely unified by culture, by language and by political experience. Its history is different from that of West-Central Africa: there were fewer markets, little slavery or slave-trading, no secret societies and no major American crop revolution until the nineteenth century. The towns of Zimbabwe were in sharp contrast to those elsewhere; although perhaps no larger than Kongo or Luba towns, the granite architecture of their central stone enclosures was dramatic and permanent. Migration, on a small scale and over medium distances, played a frequent role in the search for land, but did not create a permanent state of flux. Shona society organised many of its descent principles through men rather than through women. Its farming was mixed, and cattle-keeping was important, but there were no nomadic pastoralists. The most specialised sector of the economy was gold-mining, and at any one time as many as a thousand people could be involved in hacking the lode from deep pits and washing the crushed ore. The people who came to be known as Shona enjoyed reasonably stable political organisation, and even the disruptions of the nineteenth century were mild compared to the turmoil which engulfed Zaire and its neighbours in the decades before European partition.

The geographical compactness of the plateau, the relative uniformity of the Shona language, and the unity of the modern Zimbabwe republic are all historically important. It does not follow, however, that people in the past thought in such terms. Those of the west had strong links with neighbours beyond the middle Zambezi. Those of the south had links beyond the Limpopo with the Zoutpansberg and with Delagoa Bay. Those of the north and east had important interests in the lower Zambezi valley and beyond. The emergence of a common Shona language was probably a development of the later Iron Age; the Zimbabwe plateau had not always been predominantly Shona-speaking, and some non-Shona-speakers survived well into the modern period.

The fertility of the Zimbabwe plateau was very uneven. The red and black soils were richest for agriculture, and the sandy soils were the least fertile. In the south-west the plateau extends through wind-borne soils into the desert plain of the Kalahari. In the east rugged escarpments, cut by deep rivers, divide the high ground from the lower Zambezi valley and the dry, flat Mozambique coastlands. The granite country was the mining zone and the region of most extensive stone terracing. The old woodland cover was greatly thinned by Iron Age farming, leaving a broad grassland dotted with trees. Climate was dominated by a summer rain cycle, but every five years or so the rain was inadequate, or excessive or late. In the lowland good seasons were less common than bad ones. The Zambezi gradually became important along its two navigable stretches, but most of South-Central Africa had no fertile flood plains, no large lakes and no great swamps to attract fishermen. Some poor land had mineral resources such as salt to ease the poverty of those who lived there. Iron was found within reach of most communities. Thus the balanced and varied resources of the Zimbabwe plateau provided a wide range of environmental and economic factors to underpin the spectacular growth of Shona states.

The Indian Ocean played an important role in the economic development of the plateau. There is little evidence for regular commercial sailings to the far south of Zanzibar in the early centuries A.D. By the seventh century, however, the trade routes from Asia and the Mediterranean had begun to supply commercial beads to the Zimbabwe peoples. Beads were soon followed by Persian pottery, by Chinese porcelain and by Indian glassware. The sailing vessels ventured as far south as the Sabi river and beyond, but from there all goods had to be carried overland.[1] By the first part of the tenth century the Sofala coast was within easy range of traders from East Africa. Gold from Zimbabwe and ivory and iron from a wider area of South-Central Africa were exported. The first gold came from alluvial workings, but reef-mining began soon after, certainly by the thirteenth century. Trade was in the hands of Muslims, but Muslims never gained control of the gold-fields. The immigrant Muslim communities of Swahili-speakers at Sofala and on the lower Zambezi were supported by Shona-speakers and Sena-speakers who had adopted some of the cultural features of Islam and were known as Muslims. No Swahili settlements were established on the plateau. Along the Zambezi a few chiefs adopted Islam in the fifteenth century, but in general Muslims were more effective as middlemen than as rulers. They never gained a monopoly, however, and the plateau Shona continued to organise their own trading

1 Departmento de Arqueologia, Universidade Eduardo Mondlane, 'Arqueologia e conhecimento do passado', *Trabalhos de Arqueologia e Antropologia*, i, 1980, 4.

expeditions to the coast. By the fifteenth century the Zimbabwe plateau had become firmly tied to a long chain of coastal and river ports, Inhambane, Sofala, Sena and Angoche.

THE ORGANISATION OF SOCIETY

> He is weighed down by a great sorrow, for he already owns some twenty head of cattle, is already father of seven daughters and still has no son to whom he can leave his wealth as heritage.
>
> – K. Mauch, 1871, on a household dilemma

The basic social and economic unit of the south Zambezian plateau was the household. A small cluster of huts contained a man, his wife or wives, their children, and sometimes relatives, dependent clients and other allied or independent lineage-members. This basic unit of production and consumption sometimes cooperated with other units. Human and animal marauders usually prevented households from existing in isolation. A village of several such households was therefore the most viable unit of society. Several villages usually joined forces as a *nyika*, a territory under a hereditary ruler. Such rulers were often independent, but some became tributary to the six large Shona and Ngoni states that dominated the plateau. Territories were often subdivided into wards. Shona society was divided into lineages, and a male member belonged to his father's lineage; a married woman joined her husband's lineage. Each lineage was symbolised by an animal totem. Membership ensured that no-one might marry a close relative, and households, villages and territories had to collaborate to obtain marriage partners for their men. In a village usually only a third of the households belonged to the senior lineage. These dominant lineages naturally evolved their own traditions of legitimacy, which often represented both historical fact and kinship theory.[2]

The political economy was not based on an equal sharing of resources or wealth, in spite of a public ideology that often claimed equality. The fundamental political issue was land. Control of land use, of surface resources such as wild vegetables, of game and grazing grounds, of arable areas and of underground minerals, was the primary basis of relations between ruler and subject. Almost every tract of land was claimed by a ruler, though actual control was tenuous in the remote hunting or herding areas. Control of heavily populated areas, even those containing untouched woodland, was a feature of power politics. This control was theoretically vested in the leading living members of the senior lineage. The ideology of

2 R. M. G. Mtetwa, 'The "Political" and Economic History of the Duma People of South-western Rhodesia from the Early Eighteenth Century to 1945', D. Phil. thesis, University of Rhodesia, 1976, pp. 209–94; M. F. C. Bourdillon, *The Shona Peoples*, Gwelo, 1976, pp. 35–144.

the Shona symbolised this position. The ruler was given clods of earth at his installation, and hoes played an important part in ceremonies involving land grants or the right to work a gold-mine.[3] In theory the ruler had the right to withdraw land grants and reallocate them, even to claimants outside the group. In practice a 'house', or sub-group, could only be dispossessed by very strong pressures, and grants were virtually permanent. Usually the same fields were held by the same household, but the theoretical equality of land-holdings was altered by variations in land quality. In large territories which covered two or more environmental zones, highly prized, well-watered, well-wooded, fertile valleys on the edges of the plateau contrasted with the bleak, exposed high plateau and hot, dry lowland. Even in the micro-environment of the village, soil types, local rainfall, access to water, grazing or minerals and use of hunting grounds meant that land could not be shared equally because it was not equal in quality.

In the great political struggles between large territories the losers ended up holding the poorest land. Sometimes they were driven out altogether and migrated to new lands. Members of dominant lineages were not the exclusive holders of good land. Central lineages were often bitterly and bloodily divided, and each house sought useful marriage alliances with other lineages. A good marriage gained good land. New women, obtained with cattle bride-price, increased population, strengthened the military age group and increased the ruler's power.

Village ideology stressed communal activity in agriculture; the hardest annual work was done by working parties on each holding in succession. The working parties were rewarded with beer provided by the householder, and those who had more land, more family labour and more luck had more beer to offer. Success was reinforced by community effort, and the division between the wealthy and the poor persisted. A capricious climate, a shortage of hoes and axes, and a scarcity of labour to open a new landholding led to the persistence of a class of 'bondsmen'. Bondsmen attached themselves as servants to rich patrons in return for protection or for a wife. They were not slaves and could not be bought or sold, but formed the bottom level of Shona society.

Beyond the plateau, society probably functioned with some regional differences. In the Zambezi lowlands a husband usually attached himself to the household of his father-in-law and paid labour-service rather than bride-price. The matrilineal Tonga and Leya of the north-east were quite distinct. So too were the Tsonga-speakers of the south-east, who placed less emphasis than the Shona on agriculture. Over most of the area, however, there was a unity of social and economic purpose.

3 Arquivo Histórico Ultramarino, Moçambique, Maço 14, Luis Felix to Governor of Sofala, Zamve, 2 Oct. 1830.

THE LOCAL ECONOMY

> *Pagara murimi, pagara mupopoti.* Where there is a farmer there is a querulous man.
> *Hurudza inofa ichinzi inodya.* An expert farmer may starve while his neighbours believe he has plenty.
> *Gore harizi rakaze rimwe.* The same year can never come again.
>
> – Traditional source, on industry and fortune in the local economy

The plateau household was primarily an agricultural unit. Each household took part in hunting, vegetable-gathering, fruit-collecting, herding of cattle and small stock, and in mining, craftsmanship and industry. Agriculture was nevertheless the basic underlying activity. Even the Njanja, great makers and traders of hoes, put most effort into agriculture, and into herding the livestock they acquired through their trade in iron. The Shangwe had a reputation as tobacco traders, but they planted many

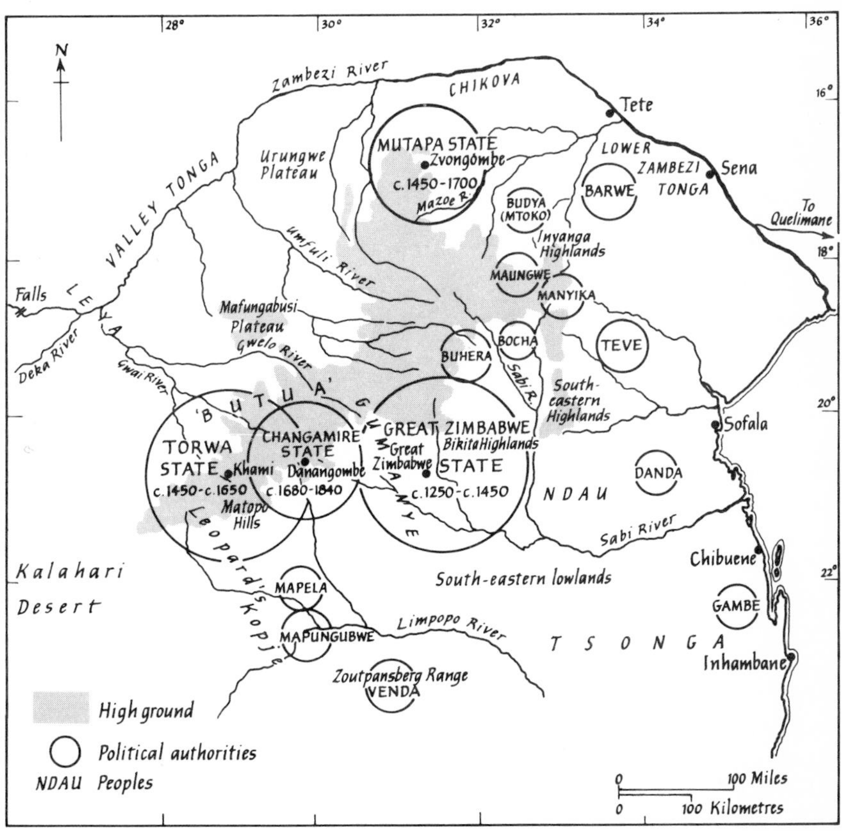

7:1 The Zimbabwe plateau before c. 1800

more fields of grain than of tobacco.[4] Even the Ndebele of the nineteenth century, once seen as primarily herdsmen, were basically agriculturalists.[5]

In the marginal lands, agriculture remained of vital importance. The Hlengwe of the south-eastern lowlands knew that only in one year out of three or four would they have sufficient rainfall for good crops. They therefore relied more heavily than plateau-dwellers on fishing, hunting and gathering. Yet they never abandoned agriculture, and continued to plant crops in the best-watered land available.[6] In the Inyanga highlands, poor soils, steep slopes and complex micro-climates made agriculture difficult,

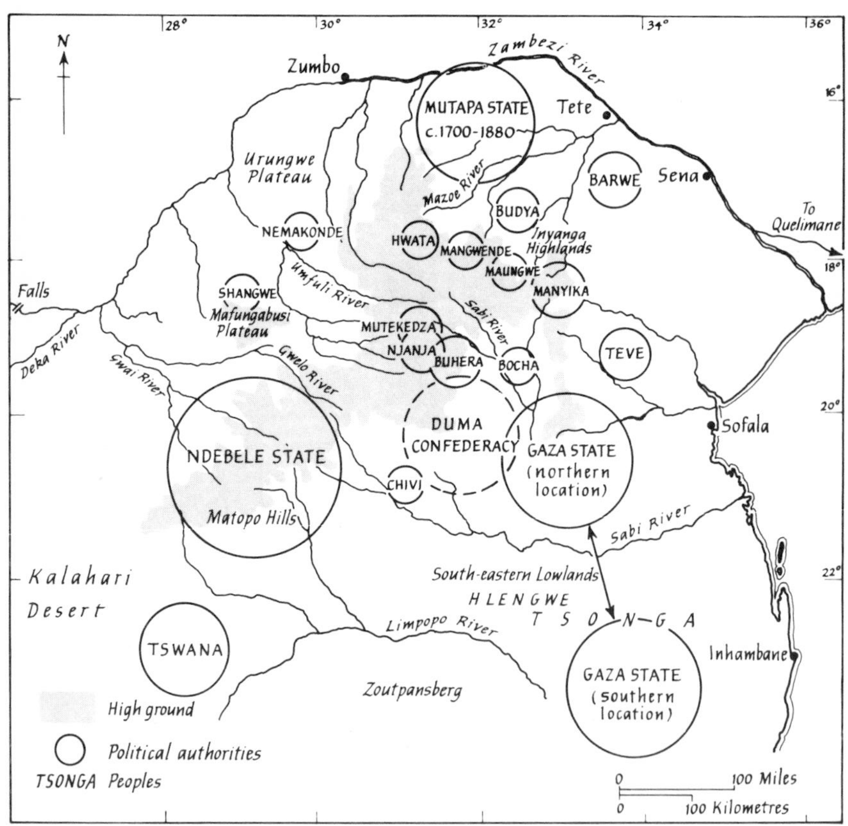

7:2 The Zimbabwe plateau in the nineteenth century

4 D. N. Beach, 'The Shona economy: branches of production' in *The Roots of Rural Poverty in Central and South Africa*, R.H. Palmer and Q. N. Parsons (eds), London, 1977, p. 51.
5 J. R. D. Cobbing, 'Ndebele under the Khumalos; 1820–1896', Ph.D. thesis, University of Lancaster, 1976, pp. 152–56.
6 Mtetwa, 'Duma', pp. 222, 263; J. H. Bannerman, 'Tsovani, Chisa and Mahenye', unpubl. paper. 1980, pp. 12–14.

yet the people put great energy into building miles of stone terracing and irrigation channels.[7]

Plateau agriculture had a mixed success in supplying people with their various needs. Despite constraints, most people got sufficient basic food from fields and vegetable gardens, but they needed wild vegetables and fruit, and hunted or herded animals to add vitamins and protein to the basic diet of millet-porridge. By careful choice of the right crop planted in the right soil, at the right time and according to the weather predictions of local experts, plateau people adapted to an unpredictable climate with much success. Storage techniques made it possible to keep grain for up to five years and so cushion the impact of famine. It is a tribute to the agricultural economy that most people managed to ride out the frequent famines on their own lands.[8]

Occasionally farmers faced a serious crisis. Neither selection of crops and soils nor expertise in predicting famine could ward off the worst disasters of climate, locust or blight. Nor could the granaries store sufficient grain to feed people through the really bad famines. There was no absolute security in agriculture by itself.[9] Although crops were carefully selected with a view to their suitability for the soils and expected weather, these were crops within a limited range. The original food crops of the Early Iron Age had been millets and sorghums and cowpeas, and they predominated for nearly two thousand years. New food crops were introduced, but they did not become staples until the twentieth century. Asian rice was grown extensively on the coast by the sixteenth century, but never became a plateau staple, being confined to small, marshy areas and to the gardens of women. Bananas, too, spread widely but never became a staple crop. Maize became available in the sixteenth century, but did not spread over most of the plateau until the 1890s, when it was generally eaten on the cob to supplement the basic millet-porridge.[10] It was to become a staple crop in the next century. Cassava remained practically unknown. Wheat was produced on the Jesuit estates in the Zambezi valley but never became common on the plateau.[11] The plateau people were quick to adopt a range of exotic vegetables and fruits, but the basic crops did not change until the last years of the nineteenth century. By then the demands of capitalism began to provoke a swift response. Similarly the agricultural techniques of

7 R. Summers, *Inyanga*, Cambridge, 1958.

8 Mtetwa, 'Duma', pp. 209–394; this is the optimistic view of the same basic data.

9 Beach, 'Shona economy', pp. 37–65; this is the pessimistic view.

10 The earliest reference to *milho zaburro* is in Andre Fernandes to the Society of Jesus in Portugal, Goa, 5 Dec. 1562; in *Records of South-East Africa*, G. M. Theal (ed.), Cape Town, 1898, Vol. 2, p. 129. Although it is assumed that this did mean maize as cited in M. P. Miracle, 'The introduction and spread of maize in Africa', *Journal of African History (JAH)*, vi, 1965, 39–40, 47–8, the traditions referred to in Beach, 'Shona economy', pp. 41–2, were adamant that maize was not a staple crop in pre-colonial times.

11 W. F. Rea, *The Economics of the Zambezi Missions, 1580–1759*, Rome, 1976, p. 103.

the Later Iron Age differed little from those of the Early Iron Age. Grain bins changed little in design, and hoes were made to a regular pattern, though iron hoes were not always available, and some people had to make do with wooden digging sticks.[12]

It was still possible for people to increase their production and trade their surplus where there was a market. Markets developed in the hinterland of Sofala, where there was a ready demand for crops at the port.[13] Markets also grew up around some of the inland fairs such as Manyika, where traders were accustomed to buying supplies.[14] In some areas, favoured by their climate and soils, it was possible to grow crops to trade with less fortunate zones. Thus, there existed an internal peasant economy unconnected with external trade. The best known of these areas was the Bikita section of the southern plateau, where the central 'houses' of the Duma people grew crops for sale to the lowlands. Another was in the middle Sabi valley, where the highland Ndau grew crops for sale to their relatives on the dry valley floor.[15] This was possible only where such favoured areas were close enough to unfavoured ones to make the transport of crops economic.

Stock-breeding offered a way out of the economic impasse of Iron Age agriculture. The advantages of keeping herds and flocks of cattle, sheep and goats were obvious. They could be bred and were a better long-term investment than perishable grain. Much of the ideology of the Shona and Ndebele was expressed in terms of cattle, exchanged between lineages as bridewealth. Even when cattle were not available to a household because of poverty or environment, they remained the ideal form of wealth. The large herds of Great Zimbabwe and of the Torwa state are well documented by archaeology. Both written documents and oral traditions stress the significance of cattle in the Torwa, Mutapa and Changamire states and in the north-eastern territories, but do not provide details of cattle management and distribution. The slaughter of young cattle, however, was always an unusual event, even when Great Zimbabwe was at its zenith.[16] The importance of cattle was noted at Khami from which the Torwa state exported cattle to the Zambezi valley in the sixteenth century.[17] The founder of the Changamire state started life as a herdsman in the transhumant grazing economy. Where cattle-rich and cattle-poor

12 Mtetwa, 'Duma', p. 226.

13 Beach, 'Shona economy', pp. 56–7.

14 H. H. K. Bhila, 'Trade and survival of an African polity: the external relations of Manyika from the sixteenth to the early nineteenth century', *Rhodesian History (RH)*, iii, 1972, 11.

15 Mtetwa, 'Duma', pp. 209–94; J. K. Rennie, 'Christianity, Colonialism and the Origins of Nationalism among the Ndau of Southern Rhodesia, 1890–1935', Ph.D. thesis, Northwestern University, 1973, p. 48.

16 C. Thorp, 'A Preliminary Report on Cattle Remains as Evidence for Social Differentiation in the Late Iron Age of Zimbabwe', paper in preparation.

17 D. N. Beach, *The Shona and Zimbabwe 900–1850*, Gwelo and London, 1980, pp. 99–100.

people existed side by side in the same community it was the custom to entrust cattle to clients or subjects.[18]

Cattle-herders were better protected than agriculturalists, but they too could succumb to severe adverse conditions. In time of famine, when cattle were exchanged for grain, herds could diminish rapidly. In 1895, for instance, the Shona of the Salisbury district had accumulated about two thousand head of cattle. By the end of that year of famine they had been forced to trade a thousand beasts and eat another five hundred.[19] Herds could be built up again by breeding and by a little judicious cattle-raiding, but stock-raising was nevertheless a precarious business, especially for the small stock-holder.

Industry and specialised agriculture were not adequate substitutes for wealth in crops and herds. Iron-working, iron-trading, the salt industry, cotton-growing, weaving, specialised pottery production and other industries were practised by groups excluded from the best agricultural and grazing lands. The salt-workers of the middle Sabi were economically important, and other groups also turned their skills to good advantage. There are few cases, however, where artisans became politically dominant. Two industries, none the less, became important: they were gold production and ivory-hunting.

The people of the Zimbabwe plateau turned to the difficult and dangerous production of gold and ivory because of the relative weaknesses of an economy based on agriculture and herding. However, gold and ivory trading were options available only to few people who lived in favoured regions. The gold-mining industry rose rapidly to a peak of prosperity based on the extremely efficient Shona mining of the upper reefs. As the mines were exhausted, however, the industry dwindled and was not a constant economic resource. Elephant-hunting provided wealth over a longer time span. It was only in the last decades of the nineteenth century that guns led to the widespread extinction of elephants. Before then, ivory-hunting was a specialised activity with about four hundred hunters operating at any one time.[20] Thus, although the limitations of agriculture and herding forced people into local industries and intercontinental trade, the agrarian economy remained the cornerstone of society. This basic situation changed only after 1860. More plentiful guns, trade with the south and opportunities for labour migration were introduced. After 1890 the change became more pervasive as local markets for peasant produce developed.

The development of agriculture was, in the end, the most significant feature in plateau history before 1900, more indeed than that of its intercontinental trade. Its evolution was more important than that of the

18 S. I. G. Mudenge, 'Role of trade in the Rozvi empire: a re-appraisal', *JAH*, xv, 1974, 389.
19 Beach, 'Shona economy', p. 44.
20 *Ibid.*, p. 54.

magnificent, but ephemeral, urban communities around the stone-built *zimbabwe* sites. Extensive rather than intensive agriculture involved a constant struggle to control uncleared land. There was little natural grassland on the plateau, and cleared or semi-cleared land represented the cumulative victory of Iron Age people over the bush. The growing population of man and beast tamed the environment, and by 1900 there were about 700 000 people and 500 000 head of cattle on the plateau. This steady growth did not occur with uniformity. A particularly rapid increase in both human and cattle populations occurred at Great Zimbabwe before about 1400. This build-up was followed by outward emigration. Gradually, from about 1450 to 1750, the old Zimbabwe heartland was depopulated. During this same period, population appears to have increased in the north and the east. Later, a return movement resettled the central plateau between 1700 and 1800, and the southern plateau between 1750 and 1850. The wars with the Portuguese played some part in these later trends, but agricultural demography was a more important factor.[21]

THE EARLY SHONA STATES BEFORE 1700

Ushe idova: hunoparara. Authority is dew, it evaporates.
Chikuriri chine chimwe chikuriri chacho. Every power is subject to another power.

– Proverbs on power

The word 'state', in Zimbabwe plateau history, is most appropriately applied to six political units. They were governed on similar lines to the 'territories', but on a larger scale. Each state exacted tribute from several territories, in a wide area, over a long time period. Some states also built prestige stone buildings and enclosures. The Great Zimbabwe state that flourished in the thirteenth to fifteenth centuries was based on the southern edge of the plateau. The Torwa state dominated the south-west from the fifteenth to seventeenth centuries. It was superseded by the Changamire state from the seventeenth to the nineteenth centuries. Meanwhile, the north was dominated by the long-lived Mutapa state, from the fifteenth to the nineteenth centuries. Much later, in the nineteenth century, two Nguni-speaking states[22] ruled by the Ndebele and by the Gaza came to prominence. Each of these states achieved military success and economic wealth at the expense of neighbouring or preceding political units. The great 'conquest' states of the Changamire and Ndebele were founded by immigrants who took over states that had existed before and incorporated many of the administrative personnel. Two earlier states, Torwa and Mutapa, started as outgrowths of the Great Zimbabwe state. This great

21 Beach, *Shona and Zimbabwe, passim.*
22 See above Chapter 6, p. 236, fn. 111.

polity, known in detail from its archaeological record, was the earliest large polity of the plateau and lay at the origin of Zimbabwean state formation.

The two main factors underlying the rise of Great Zimbabwe were intercontinental trade[23] and the control of cattle.[24] In addition, a religious factor played its role in state growth.[25] Gold production was almost certainly linked to the rise of the state. Several centuries later it was the decline of gold-mining which led to the decline of the whole Zimbabwe–Khami building culture. Despite the importance of mining and trade, however, it should nevertheless be borne in mind that the mundane branches of production were also important at Great Zimbabwe; it represented a flourishing, integrated, economic whole.

The roots of Great Zimbabwe go back to the tenth and eleventh centuries. At this time, increased cattle-herding and gold-mining created new wealth among the Shona-speaking Leopard's Kopje people of the south-west. They imported more beads, they produced refined pottery for their rulers, they used some gold for ornaments and they began building upper-class huts on hillside terraces. The best and earliest expressions of this new culture were at Mapungubwe and Mapela in the Limpopo basin. These first stirrings of state formation in the south-west were soon challenged by new initiatives in the south-east.[26] The new site which became so important was Zimbabwe hill, overlooking a valley in the long southern edge of the plateau. There was no obvious reason why this spot should have become important, for it was not environmentally better favoured than the rest of the plateau edge, nor did it command any particularly advantageous route to the Indian Ocean. It is likely that the local, Shona-speaking, Gumanye community began to turn the valley into a state by using their cattle to acquire wives and so increase the population. Their success led them to create a military force with which they dominated a part of the trade-route system to the seashore. Traders from the Leopard's Kopje mining areas could be compelled to pay a transit tax. The success of the new-born state was such that it rivalled, and finally choked off, the Mapungubwe competition.

Great Zimbabwe became a state probably about 1250. The 'city' at the core of the state flourished a little later.[27] The great mass of packed huts that

23 T. N. Huffman, 'The rise and fall of Zimbabwe', *JAH*, xiii, 1973, 361–5.

24 P. S. Garlake, 'Pastoralism and *zimbabwe*', *JAH*, xiv, 1978, 479–93.

25 D. N. Beach, 'Great Zimbabwe as a Mwari-cult centre', *Rhodesian Prehistory*, xi, 1973, 11–12, shows the thinness of the traditional evidence on religion at Great Zimbabwe. Mtetwa, 'Duma', pp. 90–107, goes even further.

26 M. Hall and J. C. Vogel, 'Some recent radiocarbon dates from southern Africa', *JAH*, xxi, 1980, 450–51, confirm the suspicion in Beach, *Shona and Zimbabwe*, pp. 38–41, that the rise of Great Zimbabwe was at the expense of Mapungubwe and Mapela.

27 Only Pta 1984 a.d. 1130 ± 40 has a corrected calendar date that is clearly in the twelfth century. Pta 1985 a.d. 1280 ± 45 comes out at A.D. 1260–1290 on the Ralph scale and A.D. 1335 on the Clark scale, while even M–915 a.d. 1440 ± 150 and Pta 2429 a.d. 1410 ± 40 come

(continued on next page)

spread across the valley, between the marshes and up the hillside terraces, was constructed in the fourteenth century. The huts of the rulers, hidden behind their great stone walls, were also built after 1300. By the last phase of the city, in the early fifteenth century, the social distinction between rulers and subjects was most marked. There were contrasts in housing, in living space, in diet and in imported goods. The urban area of Great Zimbabwe was about 7 kilometres in circumference. This was too large for the environment to bear permanently. After more than a hundred years of spectacular achievement, environmental stress eroded the settlement, and in the fifteenth century it collapsed. The ecological damage was such that certain trees will still not grow in the area today.[28]

The ruling dynasty at Great Zimbabwe can no longer be identified from traditions. Its influence, however, had spread far. Off-shoot 'houses' left the valley seeking better grazing, better agriculture, better ivory-hunting, more gold-mines and shorter trade routes; perhaps they even sought political independence. Some of these 'houses' found suitable stone with which to build miniature copies of the granite walls of Great Zimbabwe. Others settled in sites without walling. In the north and east the migrant houses can be linked to later dynasties described in traditions and documents. The Mutapa dynasty, which emerged in the north in the fifteenth century, came to rule the best-known, although not the most important, of the states that succeeded Great Zimbabwe.

The true immediate successor of Great Zimbabwe was the Torwa state, known to the Portuguese as 'Butua'. Its first great capital buildings were at Khami, which was founded soon after the middle of the fifteenth century, and lasted nearly two hundred years until destroyed by fire in the first half of the seventeenth century.[29] A second capital was built at Danangombe in the later seventeenth century. The second phase was troubled, and eventually Torwa fell to the incoming Changamire, who took over the stone buildings.[30] The culture of the Torwa state was a progressive development from Great Zimbabwe, with similar architecture, pottery, urban lay-out and economy. In terms of scale, however, Torwa was much

(27 *continued*)

out at A.D. 1390 and A.D. 1380 on the Ralph scale. The statistical error must be applied to corrected dates as well. Beach, *Shona and Zimbabwe*, pp. 321–24; Hall and Vogel 'Some radiocarbon dates', 452.

28 J. H. Bannerman, 'Trees at Great Zimbabwe', unpubl. paper, 1979.

29 Khami was built after SR 94 a.d. 1455 ± 95 (corrected to A.D. 1410 or A.D. 1420 plus statistical error) but probably not long after, since two heartwood posts (Pta 744 and 748) have corrected dates of A.D. 1360 or A.D. 1390 and A.D. 1430 or A.D. 1445 plus statistical error, while the outer ring of a post Pts 1978 is dated at a.d. 1445 ± 40 or A.D. 1400–1420 plus statistical error. The thatch burnt in the final occupation of Khami, formerly thought to be linked to the much-maligned Nguni, is Pta 2430, a.d. 1710 ± 40 corrected to A.D. 1630 plus statistical error. (Personal communication from T. N. Huffman.)

30 Danangombe has upper occupation posts (not heartwood) dated Pta 1914, a.d. 1770 ± 40 or A.D. 1650 plus statistical error, and Pta 1915, a.d. 1840 ± 35 or A.D. 1670–1710 plus statistical error.

less grand. Khami was smaller than Great Zimbabwe had been, and Danangombe was smaller still. The prestige buildings were less magnificent, the urban area was less sprawling, and provincial centres were less numerous.[31] The finest buildings in Torwa were constructed in the early phase, and no fresh construction took place under the Changamire dynasty after the conquest of 1685 to 1696. The tradition of building even more elaborate enclosures of stone seems to have come to a halt in the south-west by 1700,[32] and thereafter only defensive walls were built. Since cattle remained abundant, the decline in stone masonry cannot be associated with a decline in herding. It was more likely linked to a parallel fall in gold exports. Such a change was associated with a general decline in the strength of plateau state-building, although political tradition continued, particularly in the north.

The fall of Great Zimbabwe, in the fifteenth century, brought the rising northern state of Mutapa into prominence as the second most powerful Shona state after Torwa. By 1500 the Mutapa dynasty had gained control of a large wedge of gold-rich plateau country, a viable agricultural base, and a section of the Zambezi valley which commanded the trade routes. At first the Mutapa rulers attempted to extend their control to the sea, at the Zambezi mouth and at Sofala. These attempts failed, either because the local people resisted, or because 'houses' sent to control the lowland trade routes rebelled and became independent.

The Mutapa state started as a branch of the Great Zimbabwe culture. Several *zimbabwe* buildings within the state, particularly the Zvongombe complex, were probably early Mutapa capitals. Stone-building was still practised as late as 1512, but by the middle of the sixteenth century it seems to have stopped except on defensive sites. From then on, capital sites consisted of large stockades. One measuring 11 kilometres in circumference was bigger than Great Zimbabwe. It may, however, have had a smaller population since huts were more widely spread out.

Territories run on much the same lines as the Mutapa state occupied some of the land between the capital and the sea. Barwe, Manyika, Teve, Gambe and Danda were all established by the sixteenth century and possibly Maungwe, Bocha and Buhera as well. Some territories near the coast were extended by the Shona into non-Shona areas, carrying Shona as the dominant language. In other areas non-Shona-speakers assimilated immigrant Shona rulers. Between the sixteenth and eighteenth centuries, a colonising process also drew Shona dynasties into the west and south-west to push the Shona language frontier across the Urungwe and Mafungabusi plateaux.

31 P. S. Garlake, *Great Zimbabwe*, London, 1973, 162–6.

32 Beach, *Shona and Zimbabwe*, pp. 188–203, 325. The 1630 terminal date for Khami shows how unreliable traditions linking it to the Changamire Rozvi can be.

The early states operated on much the same lines as the basic territories. They were governed by a central lineage which dominated land resources through the armed men at its command. Mutapa, and other powerful territorial rulers, could command a bodyguard of several hundred, whose function was to strengthen levies of ordinary people in time of war, and to ensure internal security in time of peace. A wise ruler offset his dependence upon his own central lineage by forming alliances with houses who had previously ruled the land. The captain-general or *mukomohasha* of both the Mutapa and the Barwe states was usually chosen from the subject 'tonga' people. Although ideology and ritual stressed the supreme power of a ruler, he had to defend his position in every way possible and was constantly prey to rival houses waiting to stage a *coup d'état*.

The court, the capital and the army were supported by a small tax on trade ranging from 5 to 15 per cent. A larger tax of 50 per cent was levied on the gold and ivory of the miners and hunters. Those living near the capital paid a tribute in agricultural labour or regional produce. Legal court fees were also charged. By the 1640s the legal system had become in effect a branch of the economy; the prosecution of wealthy defendants brought riches to claimants and to the men who ran the courts. When intercontinental trade declined, traders became particularly tempting targets of litigation.[33]

Religion played an important role throughout the community. The high god of the Zimbabwe plateau was the remote Mulungu. At an everyday level, *mudzimu* spirits and their mediums cared for the well-being of society. The widespread belief in *uroyi*, or witchcraft, required the intervention of numerous *nganga*, or diviners. At a later date the high-god cult of Mwari spread among the Shona. New super-spirits such as Chaminuka and Nehanda were introduced. Some local territorial cults derived from the pre-Mutapa era, but others such as the *shave* spirits may have been a later addition, since they were not recorded until after 1700.

INTERCONTINENTAL TRADE AND THE PORTUGUESE

> These kings are already accustomed to cloth. ... It will be hard to go backwards. Having gold extracted as he orders, he will know: he will need someone to buy it.
>
> – Anonymous, 1683, on the basis of intercontinental trade

The important developments in the history of the Zimbabwe plateau before 1900 lay in agriculture, yet gold-mining attracted most international attention. Gold brought Muslims and Portuguese to the Sofala coast, and gold was the force behind two Portuguese attempts to seize control of the plateau. In the 1570s the Barreto–Homem expedition

33 Bhila, 'Trade and survival', 23–4.

set out to conquer not only Mutapa but also Manyika and Torwa. Its European- and Asian-trained commanders failed to adapt to African conditions of warfare, and were defeated. Furthermore, the mines of Manyika were not suited to European, American or Asian mining methods. Later, in the 1620s and 1630s a much larger invasion was mounted. This assault did succeed in conquering Mutapa and Manyika, and the better-prepared Portuguese leaders recruited African mercenaries. By the 1670s and 1680s, however, the long-term Portuguese economic strategy failed when they were unable to sustain, let along increase, gold production. Brutal methods of labour coercion which initially induced a slight rise in gold production rapidly became counter-productive; local agricultural peoples who were expected to work in the mines fled in a large-scale abandonment of their land. In the 1690s the rise of Changamire definitively drove the Portuguese off the plateau and confirmed their failure.

The Portuguese failed because they could not increase gold production without destroying the agricultural base of the economy. Their efforts were in any case misdirected. The more perceptive Portuguese realised that the expense and effort involved in controlling production were unnecessary. Conditions in the economy naturally encouraged people to mine gold and hunt for ivory. Once the commodities were produced they had no choice but to trade them with the contemporary controllers of the coast. For gold and ivory, there was only a limited local market. The natural trade routes all led to the sea and to Asia. Nearly all trade, whether through Inhambane, or the Sabi river, or Sofala or the navigable lower reaches of the Zambezi, reached the north Mozambique coast. Thus whoever controlled the coast north of the Zambezi controlled the terms of trade. For most of the intercontinental trading era a single power, Mogadishu or Kilwa Island or Mombasa or the Portuguese island of Mozambique, monopolised coastal navigation to the north. Shona producers therefore had little choice of trading partner and had to accept the prices offered. In theory, a Shona ruler could stop trade with a boycott or hold-up, could declare a *mupeto* and insist on forced payment or could seize the goods of a trader on his land. In practice, the demand for imported cloth and beads to supplement the locally produced varieties was so great that plateau peoples never held out for long and eventually resumed trade. After the seventeenth century foreign traders therefore no longer aspired to conquer the interior.

When the Portuguese took Sofala from the Muslims in 1506 it was intended that a royal monopoly should be imposed upon the trade. This proved unworkable, and instead an unofficial private trade developed, which was then taxed by the royal captains at Mozambique Island. To avoid this taxation an illegal private trade grew up which was difficult to detect. Individual Portuguese entrepreneurs moved out from Sofala, Sena and Quelimane to set themselves up as businessmen under the Shona rulers of the interior. By 1541 traders were already living in the Mutapa state, and a 'Captain of the Gates' was appointed as the leader of their community. The split was thus recognised between 'royal' Portuguese, subject to the government of Mozambique Island, and 'free' Portuguese, subject to the Mutapa. The backwoodsmen came to be known as the *sertanejos*.

In spite of initial hostility, some Muslim traders coexisted reasonably well with the Portuguese, and 'trusty' Muslims became Portuguese agents. Many of the Muslim community, however, were gradually squeezed out of their *comprador* role by Portuguese traders. By 1700 the Muslim hold had been lost not only in the Portuguese sphere but also in the independent Shona territories and in the Torwa state. Islamic culture was also eroded, and by the eighteenth century the remnants of Muslim society had become absorbed into Shona and Venda craft communities known as 'Lemba'.[34]

The transformations in plateau society under alien influence began in the interior in the early sixteenth century. The Portuguese who settled in the Shona territories concentrated on trade, took little part in the actual production of gold,[35] coexisted with Muslims, and lived under the authority of recognised African rulers. The arrival of the Barreto–Homem expedition on the Zambezi in 1571 threatened to upset their system. This expedition used the death of a missionary in Mutapa in 1561 as an excuse to conquer the plateau and crush the Muslims. The optimistic venture failed to get beyond the lower Zambezi drylands and returned to Sena. It was weakened by disease, by drought and hunger, and by the resistance of the Tonga. A second attack from Sofala through Teve was more successful, but was still inadequately equipped to take the Manyika mines. A third attempt to reach the Mutapa mines at Chikova was also crushed by local resistance. The old system of trade triumphed for at least another quarter-century.

In the early 1600s the Mutapa state grew weaker. The *sertanejos* began recruiting African slave armies along the Zambezi valley in a bid for power. The opportunity came when Mutapa was simultaneously threatened by Marave invaders from the north and by internal rebels in the south. The Mutapa sought *sertanejo* support, and in 1607 a treaty conceding the mines was wrung from him. A twenty-year period of 'cold war' and trading conflict ensued. In 1628–33 the Portuguese finally manipulated Shona dynastic divisions so effectively as to gain control not only of the Mutapa state but of Manyika as well. Within the new sphere of influence, however, it was not the Portuguese royal government but the free backwoodsmen who held sway. These powerful free agents raised African

34 G. J. Liesegang, 'New light on Venda traditions', *History in Africa*, iv, 1977, 171; D. C. Chigiga, 'A preliminary study of the Lemba of Rhodesia', unpubl. paper, Central African Historical Association Conference, 1972.

35 Beach, *Shona and Zimbabwe*, p. 109.

armies, flouted Shona authority, recruited allies among Mutapa dissidents and coerced gold producers. The disintegration of plateau society was so severe that in 1644 a Portuguese expedition briefly succeeded in reaching the Torwa state in the south. By 1663 the chaos reached such a peak that the Mutapa himself was killed.

After 1663 the tide began to turn in the Afro-European confrontation. A measure of African control over the Portuguese backwoodsmen was achieved by the astute Mutapa Mukombwe, who reigned from 1663 to the 1680s. He also fomented anti-Portuguese risings among the Tonga of the lower Zambezi, and sought an alliance with Manyika. A more effective challenge to the Portuguese than organised political resistance was the response of the ordinary people. They left the gold-producing areas and migrated to places in the hills where neither the Portuguese nor the Mutapa state could reach them. This loss of labour was worsened by an epidemic of disease. The Portuguese were forced by circumstance to retreat to the Zambezi ports in the mid-1680s. This retreat, though few realised it at the time, marked the end of any Portuguese hope of mining their own gold on the plateau.

The 1690s saw the African recovery of the great African markets on the plateau. The meteoric rise to power of the Changamire dynasty challenged not only Mutapa and Torwa, the great successor states of old Zimbabwe, but also the traders. A temporary alliance between the Changamire and the Mutapa drove the Portuguese out in 1693. Soon the Portuguese were removed from Manyika as well. Some Portuguese vowed vengeance and reconquest, but others admitted the extent to which their policies had provoked retribution. In the end no Portuguese attempt to reconquer the plateau was launched until the late nineteenth century, two hundred years later. Instead the Portuguese remained in the Zambezi valley and on the coast; they opened a new *feira* at Zumbo on the middle river. Eventually the Manyika *feira* was reopened in cooperation with the local rulers. Afro-Portuguese trading relations after 1700 were similar to those before 1600. The men of the coast could not conquer the interior, and rulers of the interior could not find independent outlets on the coast. The Shona reverted to trading through agents of the Portuguese, but this time the agents were Zambezian Africans rather than immigrant Muslims. In the new situation it was ironic, but not entirely surprising, to find the Portuguese looking on the Changamire who had driven them out as a protector who could impose order on the trade routes and settle disputes with minor rulers.[36] The Changamire powerfully controlled the last phase of the international gold trade. During the eighteenth and nineteenth centuries, however, the gold production of Zimbabwe diminished. By the time the first 'Rhodesian' settlers arrived in the country in 1890, all the

36 Mudenge, 'Role of trade', 386–7; Bhila, 'Trade and survival', 19–28.

upper-level gold had long been removed. Only some alluvial working continued.[37]

Intercontinental trade was not exclusively tied to gold production, and ivory remained a major export during the entire pre-conquest period. Elephants were more widely distributed than gold, so offering more people a chance to take part in the export trade. Elephant-hunting, moreover, may have been less subject to control by rulers than gold-mining, especially when the kill took place in a remote area. The scale of elephant-hunting may have been smaller before guns became available, but the hunting territories were more remote once the elephants had been pushed back into marginal land.[38]

It is surprising, in view of the impact of the slave-trade in other areas of Central Africa, that the Zimbabwe plateau was remarkably little affected by slaving. This was partly because the East Coast was not connected to large-scale slave markets until the eighteenth century. When the labour demand from the Mascarene Islands and the Brazilian market developed in the nineteenth century, most slaves were taken from Inhambane, from the lower Zambezi and from the north. The Shona-speaking areas on the plateau behind Sofala and Sena supplied only a small number of slaves, probably not more than 8 per cent of total exports.[39] The reluctance of the Shona to trade in slaves is interesting. The institution of slavery was known in Shona society,[40] as it was in the Zambezi lowlands.[41] However, whereas Portuguese slave-buying provoked an indirect expansion of slavery and of slave-exporting in the lowlands, it did not much affect the plateau. On the contrary, the plateau itself was a net importer of purchased slaves who came from the lowlands and from beyond the Zambezi.[42] These slaves particularly included women, and were bought with grain from famine-struck lowlanders. After 1840 both young men and young women were bought by the Ndebele.[43] This internal use of labour ran against the trend elsewhere in Central Africa of succumbing to the foreign pressures to export slaves. Plateau agriculture constantly needed more hands.[44]

37 I. R. Phimister, 'Precolonial goldmining in southern Zambezia: a re-assessment', *African Social Research*, xvii, 1976, 16–17; W. G. L. Randles, *L'Empire du Monomotapa du xve au xixe siècle*, Paris, 1975, pp. 113–14.

38 Beach, *Shona and Zimbabwe*, p. 289; D. N. Beach, 'Second thoughts on the Shona economy', *RH*, iv, 1978, 411. The traditions do not all stress elephant-hunting, but Rimuka certainly hunted and south-east Buhera probably contained elephants; southern Bocha had elephants in recent times.

39 E. A. Alpers, *Ivory and Slaves in East Central Africa*, London, 1975, p. 152; A. F. Isaacman, 'The origin, formation and early history of the Chikunda of Central Africa', *JAH*, xiii, 1972, 449.

40 C. S. Lancaster, 'The Zambezi Goba ancestral cult', *Africa*, xlvii, 1977, 229–41.

41 This includes slaves acquired by raiding or trade as well as voluntary 'service' husbands; slaves in Teve are often referred to in the documents of the 1830s; Beach, 'Shona economy', p. 56.

42 A. F. Isaacman, *The Tradition of Resistance in Mozambique*, London, 1976, p. 48.

43 Beach, *Shona and Zimbabwe*, *passim*.

44 Beach, 'Shona economy', p. 56.

Portuguese overseas trade proved to be surprisingly resilient in South-Central Africa. It survived the *mfecane* of the 1830s with less damage than might have been anticipated. The decline of the Changamire led to the occasional closing of the Zumbo *feira*, but it was reopened in 1861 and Portuguese traders pushed up-stream to the 'Victoria' falls.[45] Manyika fair was formally closed between 1835 and 1854, following Ngoni attacks, but some trade continued conducted by African agents.[46] In 1857 Sena continued to be a centre of trade linked to the remaining gold-workings on the plateau.[47] In the 1850s the Portuguese traded regularly with the new Ndebele state in the south.[48] Even in this reputedly turbulent period, old trade links continued to be maintained.

Between 1860 and 1890, a new breed of *prazo*-holders living on the great Zambezi estates enhanced the plateau trade. The *prazo*-holders of Zumbo had close ties with the Urungwe district on the north-western plateau, and until 1890 Vicente José Ribeiro continued to maintain a trading-post on the upper Mazoe.[49] In the 1870s and 1880s Manuel António de Sousa established extensive trading links with the central and eastern plateau; his nickname, 'Kuvheya', became the African term for all 'Portuguese' traders.[50] These two *prazo*-holders in particular supplied much of the military force behind a Portuguese attempt to seize control of the plateau in 1889.

An important question concerns the extent to which international trade affected the life of the plateau peoples. The trade was popularly associated with cloth, with beads and with wars. Imports also included a variety of prestige goods for the rulers: *ndoro* shells, cowries, fashionable clothing, a few guns, the occasional small cannon, distilled drinks, Chinese celadon and Persian porcelain.[51] In terms of sheer bulk, cloth and beads predominated. Cloth formed a kind of currency, a measure of value and means of exchange, before ultimately ending up in daily use. Imported textiles were in competition with excellent but expensive local cotton cloth, which was laboriously woven on small looms. It had great advantages over cured skins, and became more than a luxury requirement in a climate that saw frost in winter. Beads also played an important role in

45 S. I. G. Mudenge, 'The Dominicans at Zumbo', *Mohlomi*, i, 1976, 52–5; D. N. Beach, 'Ndebele raiders and Shona power', *JAH*, xv, 1974, 640; Cobbing, 'Ndebele under the Khumalos', pp. 191–2.

46 H. H. K. Bhila, 'Manyika's relationship with the Portuguese and the Gaza Nguni', *RH*, vii, 1976, 31–4.

47 Izidoro Correia Pereira, 'Mappa das minas conhecidas no Districto de Senna', *Annaes do Conselho Ultramarino, Parte Não Official*, Série II, Lisbon, 1867, 186–7.

48 Cobbing, 'Ndeble under the Khumalos', p. 189.

49 National Archives, Zimbabwe, CT 1/1/6, Valligy Mussagy to F. C. Selous, Nyota, 23 Nov. 1890.

50 University of Zimbabwe History Department Texts, 31–108.

51 Mudenge, 'Role of trade', 387–8.

the agricultural economy and facilitated exchange relations in household production.[52]

The exports which paid for these exotic goods were intrinsically valuable: both gold and ivory had to be won with a high expenditure in labour hours. Gold-washing was merely tedious, but gold-mining was dangerous as well: pit collapses frequently claimed lives. Elephant-hunting could also be dangerous. Local economic forces nevertheless drove people to sink deep reef mines down to the water-table and to tackle angry elephants with nothing more than an axe. These entrepreneurs were so successful that they financed the Shona states which claimed half of their gold and ivory winnings.

THE NEW STATES, THE WARRIORS AND THE MIGRATIONS

> The men and the women are of a disproportionate size, very swift in running, strong and brave and extremely resolute in their undertakings, so arrogant in speech that they click their tongues with each word with such strength that they seem to pull the voice violently from their inside . . .; the said Borozes, although they are coarse unruly and ignorant obey their superiors in a way that seems equal to that of the European troops.
>
> – Anonymous account of the Rozvi, about 1794

Between about 1650 and 1750, new types of state emerged on and around the plateau. Both the Torwa and the Mutapa states were on the verge of extinction by 1650, ravaged by civil war and by the Portuguese. The Mutapa state survived in a modified form until the mid-nineteenth century. The Torwa state fell to the Changamire Rozvi, who came from the north-east to erect a new state on old foundations. In each case aspects of the old system survived, but new elements became prominent.

The efforts of Mutapa Mukombwe and his immediate successors did not restore the state to its pre-1629 frontiers. Much of the plateau was reallocated by Mukombwe to new, outside immigrant groups. Prominent among these were Budya migrants from Barwe on the lower Zambezi. They set up a complex of new dynasties by about 1650.[53] Some migrants reached Urungwe in the north-east, but most settled in the heartlands of the old Mutapa state at the invitation of the ruler. By 1720 the Mutapa held little of the plateau, as it drifted out of his control; the heart of the state was concentrated in the Zambezi lowlands between Zumbo and Tete.

A change occurred in the eighteenth-century military and social structure of the Mutapa state. The state had traditionally had no regular

52 Beach, *Shona and Zimbabwe*, pp. 30–31.

53 Beach, *Shona and Zimbabwe*, pp. 164–5, wrongly locates the Budya homeland of Mungari as being near Tete. It should have been clear from Isaacman, *Tradition of Resistance*, p. xvii, that Mungari was the Barwe centre 120 kilometres to the south. (Personal communication from J. H. Bannerman.)

military force apart from the Mutapa's bodyguard. Young men exchanged cattle bride-price to obtain wives and settled in their fathers' communities. About 1695, however, a new warrior class called *nyai* became prominent.[54] These young men lacked cattle to obtain wives, and so became the military clients of influential heads of 'houses'. In return for military and other service, they were given wives by their patrons. Each patron was a regular contender for the Mutapa royal title, and each maintained his own army to further his claim. These armies were sometimes used in direct conflict over the succession to royal office. They could also be turned against foreigners, and were a sufficient military force to keep Portuguese *prazo*-holders out of Mutapa until the second half of the nineteenth century.

The most successful military group to emerge from the new political situation were the Rozvi. The origin of the Rozvi was connected to groups who coalesced around the great Changamire leader of the late seventeenth century. He was probably descended from unsuccessful rebels who resisted the rule of Mutapa between 1490 and 1547. This ancestral Changamire rose to power in the war-torn north-east. He was first a cattle-keeping client of the Mutapa, and then a rebel against him. His 'Rozvi' soldiers or destroyers soon became powerful enough to eject the Portuguese from nearby Manyika and then to make two major raids into Mutapa itself. The Changamire became a dynasty, captured the Torwa state in the south-west, and with some of their Rozvi followers, settled around the Torwa capital at Danangombe.[55] The new Changamire state had a strong military element. Armies of 2 000 and even 4 000 men could be sent as far away as Zumbo and Manyika. The Rozvi soldiers lived in a cattle-rich part of the plateau, and probably did military service in exchange for cattle and for wives. They probably herded the ruler's cattle, as did the Ndebele *amabutho* in the next century.

Local heads of 'houses' had the difficult task of controlling armies of adolescents in both the Changamire and the Mutapa states. Mutapa soldiers successfully fought off the Portuguese, but they also waylaid travellers between Zumbo and Tete in their own interest rather than that of the state. At least one Rozvi army rebelled and had to be defeated by more disciplined troops. In the 1760s the Hiya, a group of emigrants from the Sabi valley, set off on an astonishing career of raiding from the Mazoe valley to the Gwelo river system. They were not crushed by the Rozvi until the 1790s, and their thirty years of raiding gave the central plateau a fore-taste of the *mfecane* raids of the next century. Migrants seeking agricultural

54 Beach, *Shona and Zimbabwe*, pp. 150–1. There is one reference to a Mutapa centre 'Camanhaya', which might relate to *nyai* in 1512; see Gaspar Veloso, 'Notes', in *Documents on the Portuguese in Moçambique and Central Africa, 1498–1840*, A. da Silva Rego and T. W. Baxter (eds), Lisbon, 1964, vol. 3, p. 182.

55 'Danangombe', as originally spelt in the 1900s, could mean 'cattle enclosure' (*danga*) or *dana*, a bare hill. Both would fit the site aptly.

and grazing land were never averse to raiding herds and villages, and raiding easily became a career. Between 1820 and 1840 the passage of the Ngoni led two groups of young Shona to adopt the Ngoni raiding and fighting methods. One group was defeated by the Duma,[56] but the other had a flourishing career on the southern plateau before being absorbed into the rising Ndebele economic system.[57] The speed with which many young Shona adopted a raiding way of life and later new Ndebele and Gaza identities suggests an ardent dissatisfaction with the old social system. It was old age, marriage and increased responsibility which mellowed each generation of raiders.

The migrations on the plateau during the eighteenth and early nineteenth centuries had more significant facets than raiding alone. They represented a new stage both in the battle to control the environment and in the search for a new social structure among Shona. The change moved people geographically and ideologically away from the old states and territories of the north and east. A factor behind the original move of the Changamire and his Rozvi followers from the north-east may have been population pressure. Some Rozvi settled on the central plateau, but many more undertook a major migration to the south-west to compete for land with earlier migrants from Great Zimbabwe. Other Rozvi moved into lowland Teve and took over the state from the old dynasty, driving the 'Tonga' people into the hills.[58]

The Rozvi movements were only the beginning of widespread resettlement in the eighteenth and nineteenth centuries. When the Changamire moved to the south-west, other peoples from the north, the east and even the south came to fill the relative vacuum that had been left. Most of the modern dynasties of the central plateau date from the first half of the eighteenth century. What their traditions represent in historical terms is difficult to tell, since the explanatory role of the migrant tends to be exaggerated in oral history. By the end of the eighteenth century, however,

56 Mtetwa, 'Duma', p. 149. Beach, *Shona and Zimbabwe*, p. 320, incorrectly implies that they preceded the *mfecane*.

57 J. D. White, 'Esitshebeni', unpubl. book, Shabani, 1974, National Archives, Zimbabwe, pp. 252–358.

58 J. L. Ferreira, to Secretário Geral, Moribane, 20 Oct. 1916, Resposta E/20, SGL, Nos. 1, ; Beach, *Shona and Zimbabwe*, chap. 5, incorrectly assumes a continuum in dynastic control of Teve from the sixteenth century onwards. Ferreira's account refers to a group who by 1916 were known in traditions as people from Urozvi or Mbire, who came into the land of the Teve, tried to build a tower to reach the moon (a common Rozvi tradition), failed and returned to their land, coming back later to make a final settlement. This sounds very much like the Changamire campaigns of the 1690s preceding an immigration like that in the Ndau country. This would account for the short reign-list recorded by Silva in the 1830s and 1840s and the connection between the later Teve dynasty and the Changamire noted by him and by Ferrão. On the other hand, if Mtetwa is right in dating the original Duma departure from Teve to the mid-seventeenth century, then the early Teve dynasty must have been *moyo* (the heart clan) as well as the latter. As stressed in *Shona and Zimbabwe*, this is quite likely.

the movement had led the south to become the most heavily populated section of the plateau.

In the resettlement areas new dynasties moved away from the old structure used in Mutapa. No new state was founded, and even the Changamire Rozvi gradually lost their wide-ranging control. The typical new political unit was a small territory that rarely reached 70 kilometres across. Few of the social institutions of the north and east survived in the centre and south. The granting of political office to the wives and sisters of rulers, common in the Mutapa state, in Manyika and in Teve, was discontinued in the centre and never used in the south. Special grain tribute to rulers became rare. Rulers received only token tribute except where elephants could be caught. Little gold was available to finance a regular military force or to build a state capital, though some quite large *zimbabwe* stone structures continued to be used in the north-east. Even the title of *mambo* was dropped by local rulers. These moves away from the early ideal state structure became more striking over time. The earlier migrants maintained the old institutions, and the Rozvi in the Deka–Gwaai and the Zoutpansberg initially built capitals. Continuity of institutions was also maintained among migrants into Teve and into the south-eastern highlands. However, the migrations into the central and southern plateau carried less complex political notions. The new units were in the tradition of small coexisting territories and may have resembled old Shona settlements, or the political formations of an earlier phase of the Iron Age.

In the north and east the religious system had been based on ancestor spirit cults, especially those relating to the ruling lineage. By the late eighteenth century diverse and specialised religious entities were emerging. Spirit cults such as Chaminuka, Nehanda and Kaguvi became prominent, though they bore no relationship to local lineages. The Rozvi high god Mwari, a combination of sky-god and ancestor spirit,[59] became important in the north-east, where the Rozvi originated, and in the Changamire state. Rozvi migrants to Venda country took Mwari with them, and there the cult was syncretised with an older Venda cave-cult. A modified version of this Rozvi–Venda Mwari cult, by now based on mediums operating from caves, was re-exported to the Matopo hills of south Zimbabwe in the early nineteenth century. This revitalised cult appealed to people who had had no connection with the Rozvi, and it spread rapidly. Alternative cults based on rain charms flourished alongside the ancestor cults of the new settlers.

59 Beach, *Shona and Zimbabwe*, 247–53, attempts to combine the compatible elements in the various theories on the origin of Mwari, but is difficult to follow because the matter is treated historiographically, working backwards from the more recent evidence. The argument that the Mwari cult in its earliest form started in the north-east in association with the Rozvi and *moyo* dynasties, already implicit in G. Fortune, 'Who was Mwari?', *RH*, iv, 1973, 13, where Mwari is seen as a Rozvi ancestral spirit, is reinforced by early reference to prayers to Mwari in the old *moyo* nuclear area before the arrival of the Mwari cave-cult; see J. T. Bent, *The Ruined Cities of Mashonaland*, London, 1892, pp. 310–41.

The 'new frontier' involved a great land rush and clearly required religious intervention of every kind.

THE MFECANE STATES

> They have completely taken over the language, costume and customs of the Ndebele and do not want to know that they are descendants of the Karanga – although they keep visiting their Karanga relatives.
>
> – Rev. Knothe, 1888, on Shona members of the Ndebele state

In the 1830s the history of the plateau was fundamentally altered when permanent settlements of Nguni-speakers appeared. It was from this time that the term 'Shona' came into use, initially as an Ndebele word to describe the Rozvi. Gradually, after 1890, Shona-speakers adopted the name for themselves in preference to regional names like 'Karanga', 'Kalanga' and 'Zezuru'. The *mfecane* of Ngoni migrants brought widespread raiding to Zimbabwe. It is common, however, to exaggerate the cataclysmic suddenness of the disruption. It was not, for example, the Ngoni who ended the construction of prestige stone buildings; that had already tapered off by 1700 even at the Changamire capital of Danangombe.

The first *mfecane* bands appeared on the plateau in 1826, but most communities did not see invaders until after 1831. The Ngoni migrant groups ranged fast over the plateau, fighting each other until the last of them had left in 1838. The unlucky Rozvi had to contend with many groups in succession, but other Shona probably did not suffer so severely. The establishment of the Ndebele was quite a different matter. They settled permanently in the south-west about 1840. The Gaza did the same in the south-east. They extended their raiding only slowly, and many areas saw no marauders until the 1860s. Some Shona and Tsonga actually lived happily under Ndebele rule, and others managed successfully to resist their encroachments.

The first Ngoni migrants kept on the move and eventually crossed the Zambezi, travelling north. They failed to set up their own states on the Zimbabwe plateau. Nxaba's group spent a decade after 1827 in the eastern highlands. It restocked its human and cattle population by raiding Manyika, the Teve and even Sofala. Its development as a major state was thwarted in 1836 by Soshangane of Gaza, who drove the Nxaba north of the Zambezi. After his victory Soshangane stayed in the north for two years and then went south again. On the opposite, south-western side of the plateau the Changamire state, already hard-pressed by an advancing Tswana frontier, was overrun by several Ngoni and Sotho bands from 1831. The Changamire was killed, and the battered Rozvi were no longer capable of resisting the Ndebele. On the central plateau Zwangendaba attempted to found a state on the middle Mazoe, but was driven off by

Ngoni rivals. By 1836, however, all of the contenders for the middle plateau had crossed the Zambezi. The five-year struggle along the Ngoni migration routes was disruptive but brief. For many central Shona, raiding became a severe problem only in the 1860s.[60]

Once the migrants had left, the only Nguni-speakers remaining on the plateau were the Ndebele and the Gaza. Despite their similarity, due to a common origin in Natal in the 1820s, there were significant differences between these two Ngoni-inspired states. The Ndebele arrived in the Changamire state in about 1840 and took it over, complete with most of its population. They remained there until conquered by the Rhodesians in the 1890s. They exacted regular tribute from a small, tightly controlled area. In this closely governed area the Ndebele, unlike the Gaza, retained their linguistic and cultural identity. They also converted many of their Shona subjects, so that by 1893 about 60 per cent of the Ndebele were of Shona origin.

The Gaza experience was rather different. They influenced a much larger area and shifted the centre of their state frequently. Soshangane based his empire on the lower Limpopo valley. After a short stay in the eastern highlands he returned to the Limpopo in 1838–1839, and the area remained the centre of the Gaza state for a full generation. In 1862 Mzila, son of Soshangane, moved the Gaza court north once more, to the upper Buzi river in the south-eastern highlands of Zimbabwe. A generation later, in 1889, Mzila's son Ngungunyane returned once more to the Limpopo. It was there that the Gaza court was conquered by the Portuguese in 1895. The mobility of the Gaza political centre considerably affected the structure of the state. The area within which the Gaza exacted regular tribute was very great. They maintained frontier relations with Delagoa Bay in the south; in the north they imposed tribute on the Zambezi people near Sena between 1844 and the 1880s; their eastern border almost reached the sea at Inhambane, and their western border ran from Manyika to the Limpopo. This huge area was controlled by a core of Nguni-speakers which was smaller than the ruling core of the Ndebele state. It is therefore not surprising that Gaza control of its tributary area was looser than that of the Ndebele. The smallness of the Nguni nucleus, and the frequent shifting across the Shona–Tsonga ethnic frontier, caused the Gaza to be largely absorbed into the culture of their subject peoples. Even the court was too small to retain the Nguni language. The contrast with the Ndebele was very marked.[61]

The Ndebele state both resembled and differed from the Changamire

60 G. J. Liesegang, 'Nguni migrations between Delagoa Bay and the Zambezi, 1821–1839', *African Historical Studies*, iii, 1970, 317–37; Beach, *Shona and Zimbabwe*, chaps 4, 5, 7 and 8, neglects to mention the Nguni conflicts in the central plateau area, although covering their activities in the north, south-west and east.

61 G. J. Liesegang, 'Aspects of Gaza Nguni history 1821–1897', *RH*, vi, 1975, 1–14.

state whose old area it occupied. In the Ndebele state, as in Shona ones, the hierarchy of society was based on households, villages and territories. Over the fifty years of Ndebele rule, whole Rozvi or Kalanga villages became culturally absorbed. The economy was basically agricultural, with a strong herding component, some hunting and gathering, and craft and trading sectors. The position of the king was not very different from that of a Shona state ruler. The same theoretical supremacy was supported by ritual, and the same practical politics necessitated a constant guard against an attempted *coup*. The great Ndebele rulers Mzilikazi and Lobengula survived all internal opposition during their reigns, but not without anxiety. The political trials and executions of potential Ndebele rivals to the king were sometimes accompanied by the killing of whole lineages and villages. Such violent measures forestalled rebellion and kept the king in power.[62]

The main difference between the Ndebele and the Shona states lay in the *amabutho* regiments. They were composed of young men called by the king to live together in separate residential units when the state was threatened by external or internal enemies. The ideology of the *amabutho* was that of defensive and offensive military units; in practice they spent the majority of their labour-hours herding the cattle of the state. There was a military parallel with the Mutapa *nyai*, but the latter did not herd cattle. The Ndebele soldiers, unlike their contemporaries in the tightly regimented Zulu state, did not remain unmarried until they were stood down from their regular units. Gradually they married and formed villages and territories like those from which they had been called. Not all young men joined the *amabutho*, and the regimental villages evolved in parallel with ordinary villages.[63]

In the Gaza state, more than in the Ndebele state, the basic units of Shona and Tsonga society retained their identity, remained in their own territory and practised their own local economic activity. Some Shona leaders fled from the south-east and took refuge west of the Sabi during the period 1862–1889.[64] Large numbers of Shona recruits were compelled to join in the Gaza march to the Limpopo in 1889, but adjacent highland communities survived unscathed.[65] Gradually the small, scattered Gaza communities

62 Cobbing, 'Ndebele under the Khumalos', chaps 2, 7.

63 Cobbing, 'Ndebele under the Khumalos', chap. 3; J. R. D. Cobbing, 'The evolution of Ndebele amabutho', *JAH*, xv, 1974.

64 G. J. Liesegang, 'Beitrage zur Geschichte des Reiches der Gaza Nguni im südlichen Moçambique 1820–1895', D.Phil. thesis, Köln, 1968, is the fullest account, but is known to be undergoing revision; Rennie, 'Ndau', deals only with the 1836–38 and 1862–89 periods of 'purely' Gaza history in details; Rita-Ferreira, 'Etno-história e cultura tradicional do grupo Angune (Nguni)', *Memórias do Instituto de Investigações cientificas de Moçambique*, xi, série c, 1974, is the most recent general coverage in print.

65 Rennie, 'Ndau', chap. 3.

from Manyika to the Limpopo were transformed.[66] Gaza kingship had much in common with Ndebele kingship, though the war of 1859–1862 between Mawewe and Mzila was a far more serious civil war than that of 1870–1872 between Lobengula and his opponents.[67] The *amabutho* of the Gaza were not like the *amabutho* of the Ndebele and did not create separate territorial and dynastic units. Instead, they retained links with their home areas and maintained their fighting force by the occasional recruitment of young members. They were not full-time soldiers but took part in herding the king's cattle and working his fields. The Ndebele *amabutho* declined over the decades, but Gaza actually increased recruitment during the reign of Mzila.[68]

Both Ndebele and Gaza had a remarkable appeal for young Shona and Tsonga recruits. Already in the eighteenth century Shona bands of raiders presented young men with an opportunity to escape the shackles of a society largely controlled by its elders. The young men who joined the *amabutho* of the Gaza and of the Ndebele were also escaping, and enthusiastically assumed a Nguni identity. Men of Shona origin readily adopted the Ndebele language, though women continued to speak Shona into the twentieth century.[69] Although the Nguni language did not survive among the Gaza, many Nguni words were adopted, and people changed their clan names to Nguni ones. Gaza military fashion was widely affected, and Shona warriors adopted Gaza dress and weapons.[70] The name 'Shangana', borrowed from Soshangane's name, became a prized title among south-eastern Shona- and Tsonga-speakers, and 'Shangaans' later received higher pay in the South African mines.

The impact of the Ndebele and Gaza raiding on the older societies surrounding them has sometimes been exaggerated. It used to be thought that raiding had caused a wide, depopulated, scorched-earth zone around the Ndebele state. This was not so. Many southern Shona actually moved towards the Ndebele state in their resettlement migrations. Few areas were completely abandoned as a result of raiding, and those were mostly in the thinly peopled west and north-west.[71] The majority of the plateau inhabitants remained on their land, and in the north and east nearly all the old communities remained intact. The Gaza wars were more disruptive, but even they did not force whole peoples off their lands. The main Gaza raiding areas in Manyika and Maungwe remained heavily populated.

The Ndebele had a blunt policy towards their Shona neighbours. Those

66 Bhila, 'Manyika, Portuguese and the Gaza Nguni', 35–6; Bannerman, 'Tsovani, Chisa and Mahenye', pp. 6–7.
67 Liesegang, 'Aspects of Gaza', 4–9; Cobbing, 'Ndebele under the Khumalos', chap. 7.
68 Rita-Ferreira, 'Etno-história', 201–3.
69 National Archives, Zimbabwe, Hist. Mss. BU 1/1/1, C. Bullock to C. Doke, Fort Victoria, 17 Sept. 1929.
70 Rennie, 'Ndau', p. 146.
71 Cobbing, 'Ndebele under the Khumalos', chap. 4.

who submitted and paid a small tribute were exempt from raiding, and attacks concentrated on those who resisted or, worse still, who invited retaliation by themselves raiding the Ndebele. Raids could occasionally be forestalled by payment. Tributary peoples were rarely attacked and often identified themselves closely with the new state. Ndebele raids often hit the neighbours of a target group as the small bands swept forward over a wide front up to 70 kilometres across.[72] Some independent Shona states, such as Chivi, though geographically quite close to the Ndebele, survived and resisted incorporation throughout the nineteenth century. The more distant tributary states in Mutekedza, Hwata, Nemakonde and Shangwe were cut off from the court by independent territories.[73]

The distinction between tributary territory and independent territory was less clear in Gaza than in Ndebele. The distance between territory and capital could vary by 400 kilometres with the movement of the court. This naturally limited the effectiveness of government over the wide area between Zambezi and Limpopo. Outside the two main centres of the state, territories fluctuated between paying tribute and resisting. In Manyika, where a unitary system of Shona territorial government was maintained, relations with Gaza fluctuated in this manner.[74] The loose confederal system of the Duma broke up because each section of Duma society organised its own defence against the Gaza return. By 1889 the Duma territories had the same autonomy as other southern Shona.[75]

Throughout the later nineteenth century a large segment of the Zimbabwe plateau effectively lay beyond the range of either the Gaza or the Ndebele; some territories were raided once or twice, but others escaped entirely. The failure of either state to expand northward was partly due to the survival of the Mutapa state. The strong north-eastern territories of the Budya and the well-armed *prazo*-holders on the Zambezi also kept potential invaders out. Many central and northern Shona therefore enjoyed relative peace in the nineteenth century, though raids against one another mobilised a few soldiers and did occasional damage.[76]

THE ADVANCE OF CAPITALISM

> I go to the Madzwiti [Ndebele], but I shall not return: but mark you, some eight years hence, behold the stranger will enter, and he will build himself white houses.
>
> – F. W. T. Posselt, 1926, quoting the Chaminuka medium on the changes to come after his death in 1883

72 Beach, 'Ndebele raiders', 633–51.
73 N. M. B. Bhebe, 'Some aspects of Ndebele relations with the Shona', *RH*, iv, 1973, 31–8; Beach, 'Ndebele raiders', 633–51; Cobbing, 'Ndebele under the Khumalos', chap. 4.
74 Bhila, 'Manyika, the Portuguese and the Gaza Nguni', 31–7.
75 Mtetwa, 'Duma', pp. 147–206.
76 M. D. D. Newitt, *Portuguese Settlement on the Zambesi*, London, 1973, pp. 251–340.

The *mfecane* did not destroy the economy or society of most plateau peoples. The fields were tilled and planted, the cattle herds continued to be grazed where the Ndebele and Gaza had failed to appropriate them, the Shangwe and Njanja continued to sell tobacco and hoes, a few traditional gold-washers and elephant-hunters still operated. The steady build-up of population on the southern plateau presented problems of unequal access to land, and the growing differentials between householder and bondsman meant that life was not Utopian. Over the past thousand years there had been few permanent changes. The 'gold boom' had come and gone; the stone buildings were in ruins. In the *mfecane* period there was rather more raiding than in the fairly violent times that preceded it. Compared with the Atlantic zone of Central Africa, however, change on the Zimbabwe plateau had been on a muted scale.

All this was to change quickly. Within a generation the countryside was dotted with towns, crossed by roads and railways, and pierced by deep mines. The land had begun to be divided into 'commercial' farms and 'traditional' reserves. Yet all the sudden changes of the 1890s did not come out of a clear sky. In the 1880s a perceptive observer on the plateau would have noticed the distant rumble of economic thunder from the south. The growth of the capitalist economy of southern Africa had been having an effect on the plateau well before 1890. The first sign was the new availability of guns in the nineteenth century and an upsurge in the demand for ivory. The Ndebele gun- and ivory-trade with the Portuguese from the Zambezi was overtaken by traders based on the South African ports. As early as 1851 a large consignment of guns arrived from the south for sale to Mzilikazi; after that time the trade was unchecked. Ndebele ivory-hunting boomed, and from the 1860s licensed hunting by whites became common. By the 1880s most of the easily accessible elephants had been killed.[77] The central part of the plateau may have been the last area to gain fire-arms in quantity, but by 1890 it had caught up. A gun, originally bought with a tusk, became a profitable investment in later elephant hunts, as well as supplying meat and providing security.

By the mid-1860s the Ndebele began to trade cattle with the south. The rise of the Kimberley mines in the late 1860s, of the Transvaal mines in the 1880s and of the Mashonaland mines from 1890 made the cattle business a profitable one. Both cattle- and ivory-traders were partially, but by no means fully, controlled by the Ndebele monarchy. Independent southern Shona communities also began to export their animals. The new wealth led to greater social mobility, but it tied the Ndebele to an external supply of consumer goods from the south. Not only guns, but imported blankets and manufactured clothing became common.[78] In the Gaza state, by contrast,

77 Cobbing, 'Ndebele under the Khumalos', pp. 193–203.
78 *Ibid.*, pp. 207–13.

the maintenance of the royal herds led to an over-all shortage of cattle among commoners, and there is little evidence of cattle exports to South Africa.[79]

The migration of labour soon became a more significant response to the developments in the south than the sale of cattle. Migrant labourers brought back goods and an increased knowledge of southern African affairs. The Kimberley mines began large-scale working in 1869–1870, and already by 1873 the first southern Shona and Ndebele labourers were returning to Zimbabwe.[80] The southward stream grew steadily, but never to the same proportions as the migrations by Gaza workers who had already begun to seek southern employment on Natal sugar plantations in the 1860s. Soon afterwards the 'Shangaans' of Gaza were to become one of the most important elements in the Kimberley labour force, and in the 1880s they began to work on the Rand gold-mines as well.[81]

The reason for these great southward migrations was a drive for economic opportunity. The long walk to the mines might be dangerous, the working conditions unpleasant and unhealthy, and the wages relatively low, yet many people north of the Limpopo were so poor that they could better their condition by going to South Africa. Among the Ndebele it tended to be people of Shona origin who migrated. Among the independent Shona communities it was people from the poorest territories and households who went. In the Gaza state drought, famine and royal levies had so impoverished people that a broad cross-section of society went south. Elsewhere in South-Central Africa labour migrants remained a small minority of the population until the pressures of twentieth-century capitalism became overwhelming. The rapid initial response to the opportunities for migrant labour were an indication of the economic pressures felt at the lower level of some societies. The rewards were significant; a gun bought with mine wages could kill an elephant and so recover its investment value overnight. One elephant tusk could pay the bride-price for a wife, and so enable a returned migrant to establish a household. Thus a single journey might enable a man to claw his way to success in the local economy. In the meantime, however, an unprecedented agricultural burden was placed on women in the absence of men.[82]

In the 1880s a perceptive plateau-dweller might have concluded that the growth of capitalism in the south offered significant benefits. There had,

79 Mtetwa, 'Duma', p. 274.

80 J. Ford, *The Role of Trypanosomiases in African Ecology*, Oxford, 1971, pp. 311–12, 333–53; S. Young, 'Fertility and famine: women's agricultural history in southern Mozambique', in *Roots of Rural Poverty*, Palmer and Parsons (eds), p. 72; Rita-Ferreira, 'Etnó-historia', 189.

81 Beach, 'Shona economy', p. 57; Cobbing, 'Ndebele under the Khumalos', p. 215.

82 Young, 'Fertility and famine', pp. 73–5.

however, already been signs of the dangers and drawbacks. In the 1860s the rediscovery of gold on the Zimbabwe plateau by prospectors from the south led white miners to seek mineral rights from Lobengula, the Ndebele ruler. They ominously demanded that exclusive mining rights be granted to commercial companies whose shares could be bought and sold on the stock market. Luckily for Lobengula there was insufficient capital in the south for the early concessions which he granted, in the 1870s, to be pursued actively. In the meantime the Ndebele became aware that concessions brought with them a potential danger of conquest.[83]

During the 1870s both governments and companies in the south began to take interest in the Zimbabwe region. Shepstone intervened in the Ndebele succession crisis of 1870–1877 to further Natal's interest in the north.[84] Erskine led missions to the Gaza state in 1871–1872, and Beningfield was interested in Gaza and Manyika in the 1880s.[85] Meanwhile, the long-standing Portuguese interest in the Zimbabwe plateau began to shift its stance from mercantilism to capitalism. Portuguese claims to the plateau, dating from the seventeenth century, became more significant as a struggling succession of companies began to exploit the plateau's resources in the late 1870s. The Mozambique Company, incongruously allied to semi-feudal *prazo*-holders such as Sousa and Ribeiro, started to extract Manyika gold in 1890. It was a step ahead of its British–South African rival.

The African rulers of South-Central Africa were perfectly aware of the problems they faced and took steps, albeit unsuccessful ones, to solve them. Mzila of Gaza attempted to sign a treaty with Natal in 1870, and, although nothing concrete came of this initiative, the Gaza continued to seek an accommodation with the British that would keep the Portuguese at bay.[86] They failed to do so, and the Portuguese continued to control the Gaza trade routes until in 1891 Britain and Portugal partitioned the whole region between themselves. Meanwhile in the west a treaty of 1885 gave Kgama's Tswana a British police force to back up his internal authority and protect him from the Ndebele. In 1887 Lobengula protected Ndebele interests by making a similar deal with the Afrikaners of the Transvaal. In return for minimal concessions he gained an alliance with a strong military power in southern Africa. His diplomatic *coup* was short-lived, however, and Afrikaners proved to be more interested in an eastern route to the sea than

83 *Ibid.*
84 Cobbing, 'Ndebele under the Khumalos', pp. 203–5.
85 *Ibid.*, chap. 7; N. A. Etherington, 'Labour supply and the genesis of South African confederation in the 1870s', *JAH*, xx, 1979, 235–54.
86 E. Axelson, *Portugal and the Scramble for Africa 1875–1891*, Johannesburg, 1967, pp. 10, 135; H. H. K. Bhila, 'The 1896–97 Southern Rhodesian war reconsidered', *Pula*, i, 1980, 139–62.

in expansion to the north. The Ndebele were soon abandoned to the mercy of the British.

The Shona also took an active part in diplomacy. They were more worried by Ndebele than by the European powers. Southern Shona rulers tried to hire Afrikaner mercenaries in the 1880s, but few Afrikaners seriously contemplated moving north.[87] The big chance for the central Shona came in 1889 when the Mozambique Company tried to gain their allegiance and thus forestall Cecil Rhodes and the British South Africa Company. Two expeditions reached Nemakonde and Mangwende laden with guns and ammunition. In return for flying the Portuguese flag, and for resisting Ndebele and British encroachment, the Shona received a supply of fire-arms. They responded eagerly, and larger political gatherings were seen on the plateau than at any time since the 1680s.[88] When the conquering enemy did appear, however, it was not the Ndebele but the heavily armed British column of 1890. The Shona guns were quietly hidden away. They came out again only in the great uprising of 1896.

After 1890, the immediate future of Zimbabweans was no longer in doubt. The Ndebele and the Gaza were diplomatically isolated and surrounded by unsympathetic powers; their subjection by the Rhodesians and Portuguese was only a matter of time, though each maintained its political unity until conquered in 1893 and 1895. Once these military giants had been defeated, many of their subject peoples rapidly switched their allegiance to the new imperial powers.[89] Among the Shona, numerous individual factions made their own response to the initial Rhodesian occupation. Rivalries between territories and within dynasties caused many groups to see the 'Rhodesians' as potential allies in local conflict. Manyika and Teve played off Rhodesians against Portuguese in 1890–1891. Improbable alliances led to several notorious incidents in 1892 as Shona politics followed a pragmatic patchwork pattern. Only when they were subjected to the first hut taxation in 1894 were the Shona spurred to opposition and more effective efforts at resistance. Even in 1895 a single ruler might resist Company hut tax by force while at the same time trading peacefully with a European storekeeper.[90] This fluid pattern of alliances and responses changed only with the great revolts of 1896.

The great *chimurenga* of 1896–1897 involved many separate uprisings. The Ndebele and Gaza rose in anti-colonial rebellion in 1896 and 1897 after they had been defeated in war. The Ndebele fought to restore their state under a new king. The Gaza fought to get Ngungunyane back from

87 Axelson, *Portugal and the Scramble for Africa*, pp. 9–11, 117–281.
88 D. N. Beach, 'The Adendorff trek in Shona history', *South African History Journal*, iii, 1971, 30–48.
89 Beach, 'Ndebele raiders', 648–9.
90 Cobbing, 'Ndebele under the Khumalos', pp. 389–90; Liesegang, 'Aspects of Gaza', 13.

exile.[91] The central Shona, on the other hand, had not been defeated in battle. They had watched the gradual infiltration of Rhodesian miners, traders, farmers and tax-collectors, but still thought of themselves as independent. When the news of the successful Ndebele rising spread in June 1896, most central Shona territories decided that the elimination of foreigners would preserve their independence. The southern Shona, on the other hand, came to different conclusions since they still saw the Ndebele as a greater threat than the British.[92] All the various political and military responses proved to be in vain, however, and the peoples of the Zimbabwe plateau vanished from view beneath the colonial steam-roller to re-emerge only eighty years later.[93]

91 D. N. Beach, 'Chimurenga: the Shona rising of 1896–97', *JAH*, 1979, xx, 403–4; Beach, 'Ndebele raiders', 649–50.
92 J. R. D. Cobbing, 'The absent priesthood: another look at the Rhodesian risings of 1896–7', *JAH*, xviii, 1977, 61–84; Liesegang, 'Aspects of Gaza', 13.
93 Beach, 'Chimurenga', 395–420.

Sources and Further Reading

SOCIETY AND ECONOMY BEFORE A.D. 1400

Two pioneering surveys of Central African history were prepared in the 1960s and made possible the growth of new interest, new teaching and new research at a time when African scholarship was striding forward in the ten universities of the region. They were Jan Vansina, *Kingdoms of the Savanna*, Madison, 1966, and Terence Ranger (ed.), *Aspects of Central African History*, London, 1968. A slightly later survey, prepared originally as separate chapters for the *Cambridge History of Africa*, is David Birmingham, *Central Africa to 1870: Zambezia, Zaire and the South Atlantic*, Cambridge, 1981. A number of good country histories have been published for the nations of Central Africa as cited in other bibliographical essays below, but their emphasis has naturally been on recent history. Three with early history sections are Englebert Mveng, *Histoire du Cameroun*, Paris, 1963, A. D. Roberts, *A History of Zambia*, London, 1976, and Bridglal Pachai (ed.), *The Early History of Malawi*, London, 1972.

Central Africa has been fortunate in the number of scholars who have been interested in its prehistory through archaeological and related studies. J. Desmond Clark began his researches in the 1950s in Zambia, and his continental survey, *The Prehistory of Africa*, London, 1970, remains a valuable and readable guide to the development of early man and his society. The highly important history of crops in North-Central Africa has been much advanced by the work of many scholars brought together in Jack R. Harlan, Jan M. J. de Wet and Ann B. L. Stemler (eds), *Origins of African Plant Domestication*, The Hague, 1976, and cited in the footnotes. The classification of Central Africa's many languages into the four great language families of Africa was established in broad outline by Joseph H. Greenberg, *Languages of Africa*, The Hague, 1963. Greenberg's approach is more valuable in seeking an historical overview than the detailed work of David Dalby, *The Language Map of Africa*, which emphasises the 'fragmentation' of language groups in North-Central Africa resulting from their stability and antiquity. The material cultures of Central Africa's peoples were put into pan-African perspective by George P. Murdock, *Africa: Its Peoples and Their Culture History*, New York, 1959. The later prehistory of East-Central and South-Central Africa is surveyed in great detail in D. W. Phillipson, *The Later Prehistory of Eastern and Southern Africa*, London, 1977. A set of essays on the western area has been prepared by F. van Noten (ed.), *The Archaeology of West-Central Africa*, Graz, forthcoming. Nicholas David, 'History of crops and peoples in North Cameroon to A.D. 1900' in J. R. Harlan *et al., Origins*, is a valuable contribution to the prehistory of North-Central Africa which will be elaborated by the author's forthcoming works. Further new work on Central Africa will also be found in the *UNESCO History of Africa*, in progress.

Regional studies concerning history before A.D. 1400 in Central Africa are not numerous, but a few are exceptionally valuable. Peter S. Garlake, *Great Zimbabwe*, London, 1973, has strongly historical conclusions based on archaeological evidence. When published, the doctoral thesis of Pierre de Maret, 'Chronologie de l'Age du Fer dans la Dépression de l'Upemba' will provide material for historians as well as very detailed site reports for archaeologists. The work of Brian M. Fagan, *The Iron Age Cultures in Zambia*, two volumes, London, 1967–9, was of pioneering importance for the methodology as well as the substance of Central African prehistory.

The most important historical debate to occur in Central Africa during the 1960s concerned the 'origin' of the Bantu-speaking peoples. Many articles were published, notably four, by a linguist, an historian, a statistician and an anthropologist, which stand out for their lasting influence: Malcolm Guthrie, 'Some developments in the prehistory of the Bantu languages', *Journal of African History*, iii, 1962; Roland Oliver, 'The problem of the Bantu expansion', *Journal of African History*, vii, 1966; Alec Henrici, 'Numerical classification of Bantu languages', *African Language Studies*, xiv, 1973; J. Hiernaux, 'Bantu expansion: the evidence from physical anthropology', *Journal of African History*, ix, 1968. For a major recent synthesis see Roland Oliver and Brian M. Fagan, 'The emergence of Bantu Africa' in J. D. Fage (ed.), *The Cambridge History of Africa*, Cambridge, 1978, volume 2, chapter 6.

The use of oral tradition has been of fundamental importance to Africa's historians since long before its value was discovered in Europe. The pioneer was Jan Vansina, and his latest work, *The Children of Woot: a History of the Kuba People*, Madison, 1978, is an exemplary study of a people at the very heart of Central Africa. But oral tradition rarely reaches back to 1400, let alone earlier. One important innovative study which re-explores its uses at the limits of the time frontier is Joseph C. Miller, *Kings and Kinsmen: Early Mbundu States in Angola*, Oxford, 1976. This work is made doubly valuable by the fact that Angola is a region still little known to archaeologists.

In Central Africa it is particularly hard to penetrate beyond the memory of tradition because very few literate travellers of the Muslim Middle Ages reached even the Saharan and Indian Ocean frontiers of Central Africa. Historical reconstruction must draw a picture of each society by making imaginative use of later information, much of it extensively compiled by Portuguese sailors, missionaries and soldiers. The documents have been collected and published in such sources as Louis Jadin's seven contributions to the *Bulletin de l'Institut Historique Belge de Rome*, 1961–70; G. M. Theal, *Records of South-Eastern Africa*, nine volumes , reprint, Cape Town, 1964; and António Brásio, *Monumenta Missionária Africana*, eleven volumes, Lisbon, 1952–71. Recent use of such material includes W. G. L. Randles, *L'Empire du Monomotapa du XVe au XIXe siècle*, Paris, 1975, and Anne Hilton, *The Kongo Kingdom to the Seventeenth Century*, Oxford, forthcoming.

THE SAVANNA BELT OF NORTH-CENTRAL AFRICA

Just as North-Central Africa was the last area conquered by Europeans, so it has been the last to be 'subjected' to scholarly scrutiny. It remains a '*tâche blanche*', or blank spot, on the historical map of the continent. In part, this is the result of a paucity of source materials. Virtually no written documents record the early history of the area. Its southern reaches had neither a Pigafetta nor a Dapper, and in the north early Muslim travellers and writers focused their attention primarily on states of the Sahel such as Kanem-Borno and the more obscure Gaoga. Other types of sources, used with encouraging and impressive results elsewhere, do not exist for North-Central Africa. In the heart of the savanna no well-established states existed with institutions designed to preserve a formalised oral history; throughout the region, archaeological research has been scattered and uneven.

For the Muslim fringe zones and Cameroun, research has inched ahead in recent years, although very slowly in comparison with work in West, East or southern Africa. But the situation remains dire in the central and southern parts of North-Central Africa. A unified and in-depth historical perspective demands a much better understanding of the evolution of areas adjacent to the major rivers which linked the savanna with the forest and coast. Studies are needed in all fields to carry out the type of interdisciplinary enquiries that have contributed much to knowledge about the past in other parts of the continent.

Abubakar, Sa'ad. *The Lamibe of Fombina: a political history of Adamawa, 1809–1901*, London and Zaria, 1977. Although focusing on Yola, this study considers Adamawa as a whole.

Azevedo, Mario Joaquim. 'Sara Demographic Instability as a Consequence of French Colonial Policy in Chad, 1890–1940', Ph.D. dissertation, Duke University, Durham, N.C., 1976. The early chapters include information on pre-colonial history.

Barth, Heinrich. *Travels and Discoveries in North and Central Africa*, London, 1965, 3 volumes. The second volume treats North-Central Africa.

Bayle des Hermens, Roger de. *Recherches préhistoriques en République centrafricaine*, Paris, 1975. Part of the series *Recherches oubanguiennes*, published by the Laboratoire d'ethnologie et de sociologie comparative at the Université de Paris X (Nanterre).

Bjorkelo, Anders J. 'State and Society in Three Central Sudanic Kingdoms: Kanem-Bornu, Bagirmi, and Wadai', Ph.D. dissertation, Universitet i Bergen, 1976.

Bruel, Georges. *Bibliographie de l'Afrique équatoriale française*, Paris, 1914. The best bibliography yet available for the pre-colonial period.

Burnham, Philip. *Opportunity and Constraint in a Savanna Society: the Gbaya of Meiganga, Cameroon*, New York and London, 1980. An excellent study of Gbaya history, social organisation and environment, and of Fulani–Gbaya relations.

_______. 'Permissive ecology and structural conservatism in Gbaya society', in *Social and Ecological Systems*, Philip Burnham and Roy F. Ellen (eds), New York and London, 1979, pp. 185–202. A basic essay outlining Burnham's concept of a 'permissive ecology', a central theme in savanna history.

_______. 'Raiders and traders in Adamawa', in *Asian and African Systems of Slavery*, J. Watson (ed.), Berkeley and Los Angeles, 1980, pp. 43–72. A study of the Muslim (Fulani, Hausa, Borno) penetration in the nineteenth century.

Chevalier, Auguste. *Mission Chari–Lac Tchad, 1902–1904: l'Afrique centrale française, récit du voyage de la mission*, Paris, 1907. An essential survey of the ethnography, geography and history of the northern CAR and southern Chad on the eve of colonial conquest.

Collins, Robert O. *King Leopold, England, and the Upper Nile, 1899–1909*, New Haven, Connecticut, 1968.

_______. *Land beyond the Rivers: the Southern Sudan, 1898–1918*, New Haven, Connecticut, 1971.

_______. *The Southern Sudan, 1883–1898: a Struggle for Control*, New Haven, Connecticut, 1962.

_______. 'Sudanese factors in the history of the Congo and Central West Africa in the nineteenth century', in *Sudan in Africa*, Yusuf Fadl Hasan (ed.), Khartoum, 1971, 156–67. These items form one exhaustive study of the southern Sudan and its impact on neighbouring regions in the late nineteenth century.

Cordell, Dennis D. 'Blood partnership in theory and practice: the expansion of Muslim power in Dar al-Kuti', *Journal of African History*, xx, 3, 1979, 379–94. Illustrates how the growing Muslim community used a non-Muslim institution to consolidate its position.

_______. 'Dar al-Kuti: a History of the Slave Trade and State Formation on the Islamic Frontier in Northern Equatorial Africa (Central African Republic and Chad)', Ph.D. dissertation, University of Wisconsin, Madison, 1977. A study of a Muslim state placed in the larger context of the expanding Muslim economy in the eastern part of North-Central Africa.

Dampierre, Eric de. *Un Ancien Royaume bandia du Haut-Oubangui*, Paris, 1967. The major study of the Nzakara, their history, social organisation, internal politics and relations with neighbouring societies.

Ehret, Christopher, *et al.* 'Some thoughts on the early history of the Nile–Congo watershed', *Ufahamu*, v, 2, 1974, 85–112. An important article which uses the techniques of historical linguistics to reconstruct early history.

Evans-Pritchard, E. E., *The Azande: History and Political Institutions*, London, 1971. The major work on the Azande, including case studies of important individual leaders.

Gaud, F. *Les Mandja (Congo-Français)*, Brussels, 1911. A detailed ethnographic survey undertaken before the end of European conquest.

Kalck, Pierre. *Histoire de la République centrafricaine des origines préhistoriques à nos jours*, Paris, 1974. A broad survey based on the author's *doctorat d'état*.

———. *Historical Dictionary of the Central African Republic*, trans. Thomas O'Toole, Metuchen, N.J., and London, 1980. Short but useful.

Mohammadou, Eldridge. *Fulbe Hooseere: les royaumes Foulbe du plateau de l'Adamaoua au XIXe siècle*, Institute for the Study of Languages and Cultures of Asia and Africa, Tokyo, 1978. The latest volume in Mohammadou's collections of Fulani oral traditions. He proposes a periodisation, attempts a synthesis and presents oral testimonies.

Nachtigal, Gustav. *Sahara and Sudan II: Kawar, Bornu, Kanem, Borku, Ennedi; Sahara and Sudan III; Sahara and Sudan IV: Wadai and Darfur*, ed. and trans. Allan G. B. and Humphrey J. Fisher, London, respectively 1980, forthcoming and 1971.

———. *Sahara und Sudan: Ergebnisse Sechsjähriger Reisen in Afrika*, Graz, 1967. This reprint of Nachtigal's travel account, and the masterful translations by the Fishers which include useful notes, constitute an invaluable overview of the Muslim zone on the desert edge.

Njeuma, M. Z. *Fulani Hegemony in Yola (Old Adamawa), 1809–1902*, Centre for Teaching and Research (CEPER), Yaoundé, 1978. This study concentrates on Yola, the *jihad*, efforts to consolidate the conquest, and ends with European intervention.

Renouf-Stefanik, Suzanne. *Animisme et Islam chez les Manza (Centrafrique): influence de la religion musulmane sur les coutumes traditionnelles manza*, Société d'Etudes Linguistiques et Anthropologiques de France (SELAF), Paris, 1978.

Santandrea, Stefano. *A Tribal History of the Western Bahr al-Ghazal*,

Bologna, 1964. A compendium of data on the south-western Sudan including oral traditions, information taken from missionary journals in restricted circulation and tax records.

Saxon, Douglas Esche. 'The History of the Shari River Basin, ca. 500 B.C. – 1 000 A.D.', Ph.D. thesis, University of California at Los Angeles, 1980. A reconstruction of early history from linguistic sources.

Schweinfurth, Georg. *The Heart of Africa*, trans. Ellen Frewer, New York, 1874. An invaluable survey of the south-western Sudan and north-eastern Zaire during the Khartoumer era.

Tardits, Claude. *Contribution de la recherche ethnologique à l'histoire du Cameroun*, CNRS (Centre National de la Recherche Scientifique), Paris, in press. Unfortunately in press for a long time, the essays in this collection should promote a synthesis of research on the Cameroun past.

al-Tunisi, Muhammad b. Umar (Mohammad Ibn-Omar el-Tounsy). *Voyage au Darfour*, trans. S. Perron, Paris, 1845.

———. *Voyages au Ouaday*, trans. S. Perron, Paris, 1851. These two accounts offer the best Muslim view of the Sahelian states; they also indicate the state of knowledge about regions further south.

Vergiat, A. M. *Moeurs et coutumes des Manjas*, Paris, 1937. An ethnographic survey.

Vidal, Pierre. *La Civilisation mégalithique de Bouar: prospections et fouilles, 1962–1966*, Paris, 1969. Also a part of the series *Recherches oubanguiennes.*

———. *Garçons et filles: le passage à l'âge d'homme chez les Gbaya Kara*, Paris, 1976. Another volume in the series *Recherches oubanguiennes*, this book analyses the place of initiation in Gbaya society.

El-Zubeir Pasha. *Black Ivory, or the Story of El-Zubeir Pasha, Slaver and Sultan, as Told by Himself*, ed. and trans. H. C. Jackson, New York, 1970. The personal account of one of the most famous (infamous) of the Khartoumers.

THE PEOPLES OF THE FOREST

General research in the forest area has lagged behind that conducted elsewhere in Africa. Truly rich background data exist only for lower Zaire and the Loango coast, for the Gabon estuary and northern Gabon, for Douala and central Cameroun and for portions of Zaire's Equateur province. Good general information is also available for the southern fringe of the forest between the upper Zaire and Lake Mayi Ndombe. Other research exists for southern Maniema, for the 'People of the water' between Malebo Pool and the Mongala river, and for the northern fringe of the Uele river. In general the areas with the lowest population densities are the least known. The available bibliography is dispersed in languages ranging from Hungarian to Japanese with French, German and Dutch being more prominent than English.

Historical research lags even further behind than general research but exhibits similar characteristics. French and English are the dominant languages of recent scholarship. Historiography has been slow to develop when compared to West Africa, but the situation is rapidly changing. Several works, including doctoral dissertations, are ready to go to press. Research output has greatly accelerated under the influence of the Central African universities. Many master's theses have been written, though most are, unfortunately, not accessible. So far, only a tiny fraction of the historical output deals with pre-colonial history. The northern savanna and forest areas of Central Africa remain the least studied parts of the continent.

Ambouroue-Avaro, J. *Un Peuple gabonais à l'aube de la colonisation: le Bas-Ogooué au XIXe siècle*, Paris, 1981.

Ardener, E. 'Documentary and Linguistic Evidence for the Rise of the Trading Polities between Rio del Rey and Cameroons, 1500–1650', in *History and Social Anthropology*, I. M. Lewis (ed.), London, 1968, pp. 81–126. Historical geography of the coast. Complements Bouchaud.

Austen, R. 'Slavery among Coastal Middlemen: the Duala of Cameroon', in S. Miers and L. Kopytoff, *Slavery in Africa: Historical and Anthropological Perspectives*, Madison, Wisconsin, 1977, pp. 305–34. Formation of social strata.

Austen, R., and Jacob, K. 'Dutch Trading Voyages to Cameroun, 1721–1759: European Documents and African History', *Annales de la Faculté des Lettres*, University of Yaoundé, 1974, xi, vol. 6, 1–27. The slave-trade.

Bouchaud, J. *La Côte du Cameroun dans l'histoire et la cartographie*, Paris, 1952 (Mémoires IRCAM). Still basic on written sources.

Brunschwig, H. *Brazza Explorateur: l'Ogooué 1875–1879*, Paris, 1966.

———. *Brazza Explorateur: les traités Makoko: 1880–1882*, Paris, 1972. These two volumes are collections of texts and commentary. Like other works in this series (Coquery-Vidrovitch, Mazenot) they contain much data about societies on the eve of the colonial conquest.

Bucher, H. 'Mpongwe origins: historiographical perspectives', *History in Africa*, ii, 1975, 59–89. Sources and problems of early history. Bucher's doctoral dissertation deals with the Mpongwe to 1860.

Chamberlin, C. 'The migration of the Fang into Central Gabon during the nineteenth century: a new interpretation', *International Journal of African Historical Studies*, xi, 1978, 429–56. Part of a doctoral dissertation about bulk trade in central Gabon. Reviews the question of 'Fang migrations'.

Coquery-Vidrovitch, C. *Brazza et la prise de possession du Congo: 1883–1885*, Paris, 1969. Collection of texts and commentary.

De Calonne Beaufaict, A. *Les Ababua*, Brussels, 1909. Should be a classic. The earliest sociological work on Central Africa.

Dupré, G. 'Le Commerce entre sociétés lignagères: les Nzabi dans la traite à la fin du XIXe siècle (Gabon-Congo)', *Cahiers d'etudes africaines*, 12, xlviii, 1972, 616–58. Trade, social stratification and expansion.

Harms, Robert W. *River of Wealth, River of Sorrow: the Central Zaire Basin in the Era of the Slave and Ivory Trade, 1500–1891*, New Haven and London, 1981. The great Congo trade.

Hulstaert, G. 'Anciennes Relations commerciales de l'Equateur', *Enquêtes et documents d'histoire africaine*, ii, 1977, 31–50. Nineteenth-century trade history.

______. 'La Société politique Nkundo', *Etudes Zairoises*, ii, 1974, 85–107. Precolonial situation. This prolific author, a linguist with over fifty years of experience in the area, wrote much of historical importance.

Janzen, J. *Lemba, 1650–1930: the Regional History of an African Drum of Affliction*, forthcoming, 1983. The only social history of its kind.

Jewsiewicki, B., (ed.) 'Contributions to a history of agriculture and fishing in Central Africa', *African Economic History*, vii, 1979. Strong emphasis on environment. For the forest, see especially the contributions by Harms, Van Leynseele and Mumbanza.

Laburthe-Tolra, P. *Minlaaba*, Lille, 1977, 3 vols. Exhaustive treatment of pre-colonial history for Bane country, south of Yaoundé.

Martin, P. M. *The External Trade of the Loango Coast 1576–1870*, Oxford, 1972. The standard reference on the topic.

Mazenot, G. *La Likouala-Mossaka: histoire de la pénétration du Haut Congo, 1878–1920*, Paris, 1970. Collection of texts and commentary.

Mbokolo, E. 'Le Gabon précolonial: étude sociale et économique', *Cahiers d'études africaines*, xvii, nos. 66/67, Paris, 1977, 331–44. To be contrasted with Bucher for interpretation of eighteenth-century Gabon society.

Metegue N'Na, Nicolas. *Economies et sociétés au Gabon dans la première moitié du XIXe siècle*, Paris, 1979.

Mumbanza mwa Bamwele. 'Fondements économiques de l'évolution des systèmes de filiation dans les sociétés de la Haute-Ngiri et de la Moeko, du XIXe siècle à nos jours', *Enquêtes et Documents d'histoire africaine*, ii 1977, 1–30.

Patterson, K. D. *The Northern Gabon Coast to 1875*, Oxford, 1975. Especially valuable for the Ogowe delta.

Rey, P. P. *Colonialisme, néocolonialisme et transition au capitalisme: l'exemple de la Comilog*, Paris, 1971. The major marxist interpretation. Includes much on pre-colonial times.

______. 'L'Esclavage lignager chez les Tsangui, les Punu et les Kuni du Congo Brazzaville. Sa place dans le système d'ensemble des rapports de production', in *L'Esclavage en Afrique précoloniale*, C. Meillassoux (ed.), Paris, 1975, pp. 509–28. Slavery and relations of production.

Sautter, G. *De l'Atlantique au fleuve Congo*, Paris, 1966, 2 volumes. The classic human geography.

Vansina, J. *The Tio Kingdom of the Middle Congo 1880–1892*, London, 1973.

A society in the nineteenth century.
———. *The Children of Woot: a History of the Kuba Peoples*, Madison, Wisconsin, 1978. The making of a society and its culture.
Walker, R. *Notes d'histoire du Gabon*, Brazzaville, 1960 (Mémoires de l'institut d'études centrafricaines, 9). Still very useful despite later work along the coast by Bucher, Mbokolo, Patterson and Chamberlin. Walker was Gabon's foremost scholar in the pre-university age.
Wirz, A. 'La "rivière du Cameroun": commerce pré-colonial et controle du pouvoir en société lignagère', *Revue française d'histoire d'outre-mer*, lx, no. 219, 1973, 172–95. Part of the author's study in German: *Vom Sklavenhandel zum Kolonialen Handel: Wirtschaftsräume und Wirtschaftsformen in Kamerun vor 1914*, Zurich, 1972.
Yogolelo Tambwe Ya Kasimbwa. *Introduction à l'histoire des Lega: Problèmes et mèthode*, Brussels, 1975 (Cahiers du CEDAF no. 5). The only historical study for the eastern half of the area. Good exposé of problems involved.

THE PARADOXES OF IMPOVERISHMENT IN THE ATLANTIC ZONE

My inferences from monographic studies cited in the footnotes may not always conform to the emphases of authors from whose works I draw. I intend not to contradict directly what their careful research has revealed but rather to use the perspective of the 'Atlantic zone' to enrich the significance of their conclusions. Footnotes thus guide the reader to the accessible authorities on the various topics raised more than they document specific conclusions.

Historical writing on the region termed here the 'Atlantic zone' of West-Central Africa grew out of a pre-1965 concern with the Portuguese 'civilising mission' in Angola, passed through a 1965–78 phase of Afro-centric interest, and has moved recently toward a balanced synthesis of African with world historical themes. The present outline strives to integrate the Afro-centric studies of the 1965–78 period, mostly conceived on a local scale, with the newest, large-scale work on European and world economic history.

The older studies emphasised the missionary, military and administrative histories of the Portuguese conquest, with secondary concern given to the maritime slave-trade. Historians in the period focused narrowly on the best-documented Kongo and Luanda regions. In Portuguese, Ralph Delgado, *História de Angola*, four volumes, Benguela and Lobito, 1948–55, revised edition 1961, exemplifies these tendencies in the scholarship of Salazar's Portugal. In English, David Birmingham, *Trade and Conflict in Angola*, Oxford, 1966, adds significant emphasis to the African side and broadens the geographical range, while retaining the sixteenth- and seventeenth-century focus of the historical writing of that era. The main ethnographic literature is in Portuguese, French, German and other languages. The bibliography is readily accessible in Phyllis Martin, *Historical Dictionary of Angola*, Metuchen, N. J., 1980.

Jan Vansina, *Kingdoms of the Savanna*, Madison, Wisconsin, 1966, marked the turn toward an Afro-centric history of West-Central Africa, still with emphasis on political and cultural history. The major landmarks of the ensuing period focused on ethnically-defined regions. The historical section of Gladwyn Childs, *Umbundu Kinship and Character*, London, 1949, reprinted as *Kinship and Character of the Ovimbundu*, London, 1969, anticipated the Afro-centric trend for the Ovimbundu and remains the only work to date on the important central highlands. Joseph C. Miller, *Kings and Kinsmen: Early Mbundu States in Angola*, Oxford, 1976, and Beatrix Heintze's several essays (footnotes 10, 30, 42, 52) carry forward the historical study of the Mbundu in the sixteenth and seventeenth centuries. Recent Ph.D. dissertations by Anne Wilson, 'The Kongo Kingdom to the Mid-seventeenth Century', University of London, 1977, and John K, Thornton, 'The Kingdom of Kongo in the Era of the Civil Wars, 1641–1718', University of California at Los Angeles, 1979, both soon to be published, supersede a substantial volume of earlier work on Kongo. Phyllis M. Martin, *The External Trade of the Loango Coast 1576–1870*, Oxford, 1972, remains basic for the northern coast. Two bibliographical essays by Joseph C. Miller, 'Angola before 1900: a review of recent research', *African Studies Review*, xx, 1, 1977, 103–16, and 'Angola before 1840: a progress report', forthcoming in the proceedings of the 1980 Bad Homburg Colloquium on Portuguese-Speaking Africa, give details on recent work on other regions.

The forthcoming collection of essays edited by Franz-Wilhelm Heimer, *The Formation of Angolan Society* or *A formação da sociedade angolana* in Portuguese, will incorporate the new emphases on economic history, political economy, demography and history of climate that link earlier work to larger world historical patterns. For the moment, one may consult preliminary studies by Thornton (footnote 74), Dias (footnote 3), Vellut (footnotes 2, 80), Clarence-Smith (footnotes 3, 5, 12, 78), and Miller (footnote 1).

The eighteenth century remains generally neglected by historians, but Joseph C. Miller, *Way of Death: the Angolan Slave Trade, 1730–1830* (in preparation) is intended to fill a gap. The nineteenth century, a period also long left without adequate attention, is emerging clearly from the studies of Jill Dias (footnotes 76, 78) and W. G. Clarence-Smith, *Slaves, Peasants, and Capitalists in Southern Angola*, Cambridge, 1979.

Most known documents for the sixteenth century and many of those for the first half of the seventeenth century have been published. The largest collection is António Brásio (ed.), *Monumenta missionária africana – Africa occidental (Série I)*, eleven volumes, Lisbon, 1952–71. One may also consult

Arquivos de Angola, Luanda, série I (1933–9) and série II (1943–). Virtually complete references to published documents may be compiled from the bibliographies in Anne Wilson, 'Kongo Kingdom', John Thornton, 'Kingdom of Kongo', and Joseph Miller, *Kings and Kinsmen*. The two vital seventeenth-century sources are João António Cavazzi de Montecuccolo, *Descrição histórica dos três reinos do Congo, Matamba, e Angola*, Graciano Maria de Leguzzano (trans. and ed.), two volumes, Lisbon, 1965, and António de Oliveira de Cadornega, *História geral das guerras angolanas, 1680*, José Matias Delgado and M. Alves da Cunha (eds), three volumes, Lisbon, 1940–42, reprinted 1972.

The less plentiful eighteenth-century published sources are the 'Catálogo dos governadores do Reino de Angola', published in several versions, including in Elias Alexandre da Silva Corrêa, *História de Angola*, two volumes, Lisbon, 1937. See the critique in François Bontinck, 'Bréves remarques relatives au "Catálogo dos Governadores do Reino de Angola"', *Studia*, xxxix, 1974, 69–78. One may also consult Ralph Delgado, *Ao Sul do Cuanza (Ocupação e aproveitamento do antigo reino de Benguela)*, two volumes, Lisbon, 1944, and *O reino de Benguela (do descobrimento à criação do governo subalterno)*, Lisbon, 1945, and Alfredo de Albuquerque Felner, *Angola: Apontamentos sôbre a colonização dos planaltos e litoral do sul de Angola*, three volumes, Lisbon, 1940. Two nineteenth-century bulletins, the *Annaes do Conselho Ultramarino* (*parte não official*) and the *Annaes marítimos e coloniaes*, also include documents from this period.

Beyond documents published in the collections indicated above, sources for the nineteenth century include a number of travel memoirs. Among the principal ones: Raimundo José da Cunha Mattos, *Compêndio histórico das possessões de Portugal na Africa*, Rio de Janeiro, 1963; Jean Baptiste Douville, *Voyage au Congo et dans l'intérieur de l'Afrique équinoxiale*, two volumes, Paris, 1832, but see Joseph C. Miller, 'A note on Jean-Baptiste Douville', *Cahiers d'études africaines*, xiii, 1, no. 49, 1973, 149–53, and Pierre Verger, 'Jean Baptiste Douville, naturaliste calomnié ou imposteur démasqué?' *Afro-Asia*, xii, 1975, 91–108; José Joaquim Lopes de Lima, *Ensaios sôbre a statistica das possessões portugueses na Africa Occidental e Oriental: Vol. III, Angola e Benguela*, Lisbon, 1846; David Livingstone, *Missionary Travels and Researches in South Africa*, London, 1857; Joaquim Rodrigues Graça, 'Viagem feita de Loanda ...', *Annaes do Conselho Ultramarino* (*parte não official*), 1, 1854–8, 104–14, 117–29, 133–46, republished in *Boletim da Sociedade de Geographia de Lisboa*, ix, 8–9, 1890, 365–468; Ladislau Magyar, *Reisen in Süd-Afrika in den Jahren 1849 bis 1857*, Pest und Leipzig, 1859, but compare Judith Listowel, *The Other Livingstone*, Lewes, 1974, pp. 75–145; Verney Lovett Cameron, *Across Africa*, two volumes, London, 1877; Paul Pogge, *Im Reich des Muata Yamvo*, Berlin, 1880; A. A. da Serpa Pinto, *Como eu atravessei a Africa*, two volumes, Lisbon, 1881; A. F. da Silva Porto, *Viagens e apontamentos de um portuense em Africa*, J. Miranda and A.

Brochado (eds.), Lisbon, 1942; Henrique Augusto Dias de Carvalho, *Expedição portugueza ao Muatiânvua*, eight volumes, Lisbon, 1890.

Basic works on the slave-trade begin with Philip D. Curtin, *The Atlantic Slave Trade: a Census*, Madison, Wisconsin, 1969. With particular reference to the Angolan trade (in addition to those mentioned in footnote 64): E. Correia Lopes, *A escravatura: subsídios para a sua história*, Lisbon, 1944; Maurício Goulart, *Escravidão africana no Brasil (das origens à extinção do tráfico)*, São Paulo, 1949; Affonso de Escragnolle Taunay, 'Subsídios para a história do tráfico africano no Brasil colonial', *Anais do Museu Paulista*, x, 2, 1941, 5–311; Herbert S. Klein, *The Middle Passage*, Princeton, 1978.

The principal archives housing documents bearing on the history of West-Central Africa are in Lisbon (Arquivo Histórico Ultramarino and others), Rome (Vatican), The Netherlands (Algemeen Rijksarchief, The Hague) and Luanda (Arquivo Nacional de Angola). Oral sources are described most fully in Joseph Miller, *Kings and Kinsmen*, but have not generally been exploited for much of the region.

Previous general surveys include Jan Vansina, *Kingdoms of the Savanna*; Douglas Wheeler and René Pélissier, *Angola*, London, 1970; and David Birmingham, *Central Africa to 1870: Zambezia, Zaire, and the South Atlantic*, Cambridge, 1981, reprinted from the *Cambridge History of Africa*, Cambridge, 1975–7; Lawrence W. Henderson, *Angola: Five Centuries of Conflict*, Ithaca, 1979. Martin's *Historical Dictionary of Angola* will guide readers efficiently toward nearly all topics.

THE SOCIETIES OF THE EASTERN SAVANNA

There are several surveys and anthologies of pre-colonial savanna history whose texts and bibliographies are worth consulting. The best work is Andrew D. Roberts, *A History of Zambia*, London, 1976. Others include Richard Gray and David Birmingham (eds), *Pre-Colonial African Trade: Essays on Trade in Central and Eastern Africa before 1900*, London, 1970; B(ridglal) Pachai (ed.), *The Early History of Malawi*, Evanston, Illinois, 1972; and Jan Vansina, *Kingdoms of the Savanna*, Madison, Wisconsin, 1966.

Europeans, Afro-Europeans and Afro-Arabs crossed the region in the nineteenth century and left published accounts of their journeys. The earliest substantial body of published material was generated by Portuguese and Luso-African attempts to establish trade relations with Kazembe from the 1790s to 1832. The name of David Livingstone stands out among mid-nineteenth century travellers. His *Missionary Travels and Researches in South Africa*, London, 1857, and *The Last Journals of David Livingstone in Central Africa*, two volumes, London, 1874, should be consulted along with the many other works by and about him. The books of a host of Livingstone's peripatetic contemporaries are fundamental sources: Frederick S. Arnot, *Garenganze, or Seven Years' Pioneer Mission Work in Central Africa*, 1889;

reprint, London, 1969; Verney L. Cameron, *Across Africa*, two volumes, 1877; reprint, New York, 1969; H. Capello and R. Ivens, *De Angola á contracosta*, two volumes, Lisbon, 1886; Henrique A. Dias de Carvalho, *Ethnographia e história tradicional dos povos da Lunda*, Lisbon, 1890; Alexandre Delcommune, *Vingt Années de vie africaine: récits de voyages, d'aventures et d'exploration au Congo Belge 1874–1893*, two volumes, Brussels, 1922; Victor Giraud, *Les Lacs de l'Afrique equatoriale*, Paris, 1890; Christa Johns (translator), *Emil Holub's Travels North of the Zambezi 1885–6*, Manchester, 1975; Paul Pogge, *Im Reich des Muata Jamvo*, Berlin, 1880; A. A. de Serpa Pinto, *How I Crossed Central Africa*, translated by Alfred Elwes, two volumes, London, 1881; Hermann von Wissmann, *My Second Journey through Equatorial Africa from the Congo to the Zambezi in the Years 1886 and 1887*, translated by Minna J. Bergmann, London, 1891. Tippu Tip's informative Swahili-language autobiography has been translated twice in recent times. The better version is the fully annotated French translation by François Bontinck entitled *L'Autobiographie de Hamed ben Mohammed el-Murjebi Tippo Tip (ca. 1840–1905)*, Brussels, 1974, but see also the English translation by W. H. Whiteley, *Maisha ya Hamed bin Muhammed el Murjebi yaani Tippu Tip* (supplement to the *East African Swahili Commitee Journals*, no. 28/2, 1958, and no. 29/1, 1959.

Africans have made significant contributions to the historiography of their respective cultures. There are three lengthy presentations of oral traditions from Zambia: Simon J. Chibanza, 'Kaonde History' in *Central Bantu Historical Texts I*, Rhodes-Livingstone Communication no. 22, Lusaka, 1961, pp. 41–144; Jacques C. Chiwale, translator and annotator, *Central Bantu Historical Texts, III. Royal Praises and Praise Names of the Lunda Kazembe of Northern Rhodesia: their Meaning and Historical Background*, Rhodes-Livingstone Communication no. 25, Lusaka, 1952; and Mwata Kazembe XIV, *Central Bantu Historical Texts, II. Historical Traditions of the Eastern Lunda*, translated by Ian Cunnison, Rhodes-Livingstone Communication no. 23, Lusaka, 1961. Antoine Mwenda Munongo has written articles about Msiri's régime which are anthologised as 'Pages d'Histoire Yeke', in Collection de Mémoires, vol. 25, Lubumbashi, Centre d'Etudes des Problèmes Sociaux Indigènes, 1967, pp. 1–243.

Anthropologists have often done the important spade work for the historian. There is the anthology edited by Elizabeth Colson and Max Gluckman, *Seven Tribes of British Central Africa*, Manchester, 1951. Ian Cunnison, *The Luapula Peoples of Northern Rhodesia, Custom and History in Tribal Politics*, 1958; reprint, Manchester, 1967, is important, as are his articles and translation work cited in the footnotes. Luc de Heusch has presented a provocative analysis of savanna intellectual history in *Le Roi ivre, ou l'origine de l'état*, Paris, 1972.

The history of the eastern savanna is more understandable today than it was fifteen years ago, because so many of the individual pieces of the mosaic have been researched by doctoral candidates. The list of monographs and dissertations is impressive: Michael S. Bisson, 'The Prehistoric Coppermines of Zambia', Ph.D. dissertation, University of California at Santa Barbara, 1976; Pierre de Maret, 'Chronologie de l'Age du Fer dans la Dépression de l'Upemba en République du Zaïre', Ph.D. thesis, Free University of Brussels, 1977–8, 3 vols.; Nancy J. Fairley, 'Mianda ya Ben'Ekie: a History of the Ben'Ekie', Ph.D. thesis, State University of New York at Stony Brook, 1978; Eugene L. Hermitte, 'An Economic History of Barotseland, 1800–1940', Ph.D. thesis, Northwestern University, 1974; J. Jeffrey Hoover, 'The Seduction of Ruwej: Reconstructing Ruund History (The Nuclear Lunda; Zaire, Angola, Zambia)', Ph. D. thesis, two vols., Yale University, 1978; Harry W. Langworthy, 'A History of Undi's Kingdom to 1890: Aspects of Chewa History in East Central Africa', Ph.D. thesis, Boston University, 1969; Stephen A. Lucas, 'Baluba et Aruund; Etude comparative des structures socio-politiques', Ph.D. thesis, two vols., Ecole Pratique des Hautes Etudes, Paris, 1968; Mutumba Mainga, *Bulozi under the Luyana Kings, Political Evolution and State Formation in Pre-colonial Zambia*, London, 1973; Timothy I. Matthews, 'The Historical Tradition of the Peoples of the Gwembe Valley, Middle Zambezi', Ph.D. thesis, University of London, 1976; Robert J. Papstein, 'The Upper Zambezi: a History of the Luvale People, 1000–1900', Ph.D. thesis, University of California at Los Angeles, 1978; Kings M. Phiri, 'Chewa History in Central Malawi and the Use of Oral Traditions, 1600–1920', Ph.D. thesis, University of Wisconsin at Madison, 1975; Gwyn Prins, *The Hidden Hippopotamus, Reappraisal in African History: the Early Colonial Experience in Western Zambia*, Cambridge, 1980; William F. Pruitt, Jr., 'An Independent People: the Salampasu of Luisa Territory', Ph.D. thesis, Northwestern University, 1974; Thomas Q. Reefe, *The Rainbow and the Kings, a History of the Luba Empire to 1891*, Berkeley and Los Angeles, 1981; Allen F. Roberts, 'Heroic Beasts, Beastly Heroes: Principles of Cosmology and Chiefship among the Lakeside BaTabwa of Zaire', Ph.D. thesis, University of Chicago, 1980; Andrew D. Roberts, *A History of the Bemba: Political Growth and Change in North-Eastern Zambia before 1900*, London, 1973; Robert E. Schechter, 'History and Historiography on a Frontier of Lunda Expansion: the Origins and Development of the Kanongesha', Ph.D. thesis, University of Wisconsin at Madison, 1976; N'Dua Solol Kanampumb, 'Histoire ancienne des populations Luba et Lunda du Plateau du Haut-Lubilash, des origines au début du XXe siécle (Bena Nsamba, Inimpimin et Tuwudi)', Ph.D. thesis, two vols., National University of Zaire at Lubumbashi, 1978; Albert J. Williams-Myers, 'The Nsenga of Central Africa: Political and Economic Aspects of Clan History, 1700 to the Late Nineteenth Century', Ph.D. thesis, University of California at Los Angeles, 1978; John C. Yoder,

'A People on the Edge of Empires: a History of the Kanyok of Central Zaire', Ph.D. thesis, Northwestern University, 1977. Some dissertations have to be consulted at the author's degree-granting institution, but most are available on microfilm or in bound photocopy form.

THE INDIAN OCEAN ZONE

Source material for the Indian Ocean zone varies considerably both with respect to time and place. Although the consistent presence of the Portuguese on the coast dates from the sixteenth century, the legacy in terms of documentation is disappointing. Records of the Zambezi valley and its southern hinterland are rewarding in terms of their quality and consistency over time. Elsewhere, however, the information they provide is more sporadic and less accurate. The inconsistency with which records were kept and deposited in archives determined that there are long intervals when there is virtually no information about even those coastal areas that the Portuguese claimed to have occupied. Moreover, because of the increased administrative vigilance that attended the separation of Mozambique from the Estado da India in 1752, documentation for the eighteenth century is often better than for the periods that either preceded or followed.

Published documentation reflects the general archival pattern. The most important collection is contained in G. M. Theal's nine-volume *Records of South-Eastern Africa*, which reproduces many Portuguese documents in translation, as well as many Dutch and English reports in the original. *Documents on the Portuguese in Mozambique and Central Africa* is an ambitious project which, when completed, will probably supplant the Theal volumes in importance. Francisco Santana's *Documentação Avulsa Moçambicana do Arquivo Histórico Ultramarino* contains accurate summaries of the nineteenth-century records contained in the collection known as the *maços*. Several important eighteenth-century manuscripts are reprinted in António de Andrade's *Relações de Moçambique Setecentista*. One may also consult the extracts known as 'Inventário do Fundo do Século Dezoito', which began appearing in *Moçambique*, number 72. Finally the *Arquivo das Colonias* reprinted many otherwise unobtainable documents.

The absence of first-hand travellers' accounts is a serious drawback. With the exception of the diaries kept by the survivors of sixteenth- and seventeenth-century shipwrecks, they are virtually non-existent until the nineteenth century. Even the nineteenth century, however, is exceedingly sparse when compared with West Africa or even the South African high veld. The only significant exception was provided by the British missionaries and their associates who infiltrated the Lake Malawi region in the second half of the nineteenth century. Elsewhere, in terms of the information provided by missionaries and explorers, the Indian Ocean zone remained one of the least studied areas of Africa.

The scholarship on much of the Indian Ocean zone is equally disappointing. Serious academic work during the colonial era was limited almost exclusively to those peripheral regions that came under British rule. The nature of Portuguese rule not only prevented research, but also precluded free access by travellers. Nevertheless, there was no shortage of amateurs who delved into a wide variety of investigations. Although much is useless, one occasionally encounters material that is extremely helpful. The best guide to this not inconsiderable body of literature is the *Bibliografia do Ultramar Português Existente na Sociedade de Geografia de Lisboa, Fascículo V, Moçambique*.

Ethnography was the favourite subject of investigation during the colonial era. There are a variety of capable works for the English-speaking territories, ranging from monographs such as J. Clyde Mitchell's *The Yao Village* and J. A. Barnes's *Politics in a Changing Society* to edited collections like Elizabeth Colson and Max Gluckman's *Seven Tribes of British Central Africa*. Moreover, Tanzania, Malawi, Eastern Zambia and Zimbabwe are covered by a number of volumes in the Ethnographic Survey of Africa series. Mozambique, unfortunately, has not been nearly so well served. Henri A. Junod's *The Life of a South African Tribe*, E. Dora Earthy's *Valenge Women*, and Jorge Dias's five-volume *Os Macondes de Moçambique* are the major studies. Otherwise one must depend on numerous articles of varying quality. The *Bibliografia Etnológica de Moçambique* by António Rita-Ferreira is a useful starting point.

During most of the colonial era, history in Mozambique was synonymous with studies of the Portuguese. The only notable works in English were Eric Axelson's *South-East Africa, 1498–1530* and *The Portuguese in South-East Africa, 1600–1700*, Mabel Jackson Haight's *European Powers in South-Eastern Africa* and, for the later period, Philip Warhurst's *Anglo-Portuguese Relations in South-Central Africa* and Richard Hammond's *Portugal and Africa*. There are a number of studies in Portuguese that are worth consulting. Among the works of the prolific historian Alexandre Lobato, *A Evolução Administrativa de Moçambique* and *A História do Presídio de Lourenço Marques* should be noted. The two-volume *História Política e Militar dos Portugueses em Moçambique* by José Teixeira Botelho is useful and provides information not found elsewhere. The more recent *Africa Oriental Portuguesa no Tempo do Marquês de Pombal* by Fritz Hoppe is an important addition to the literature.

More recent scholarship in English has begun to establish a more balanced historiography. For the northern regions there is Edward A. Alpers' pioneering *Ivory and Slaves* and Nancy Hafkin's Ph.D. thesis, 'Trade, Society, and Politics in Northern Mozambique, c. 1753–1913'. The central zone is more than adequately served by Allen Isaacman's

Mozambique: the Africanization of a European Institution and M. D. D. Newitt's *Portuguese Settlement on the Zambesi*. For the south there is Alan K. Smith's 'The Struggle for Control of Southern Mozambique, 1720–1835' Ph.D. thesis, University of California at Los Angeles, 1970 and David Hedges' 'Trade and Politics in Southern Mozambique and Zululand in the Eighteenth and Early Nineteenth Centuries'. In addition, recent dissertations by Philip Bonner, H. H. K. Bhila. S. Mudenge, Albert Williams-Myers, William Rau, Kings Phiri, and Cyril Hromnik touch, in varying degrees, on aspects of the history of the Indian Ocean zone. Fuller citations are given in the footnotes to Chapter 6.

THE ZIMBABWE PLATEAU AND ITS PEOPLES

Archaeological work, which is the basis of knowledge in the pre-1400 period, is rather thin for the centuries covered by this chapter. The exciting new developments cover the last centuries of the stone-building culture in the Torwa state and in the Inyanga highlands, but practically nothing is known from archaeology about the ordinary people of the plateau or about the capital sites of the north and the east. Documents and traditions have greatly expanded our knowledge of the area in the last ten years, though considerable gaps remain. Documents are good on the lower Zambezi valley, on the Mutapa state and on the *feiras* of Zumbo and Manyika. The wealth of traditional material is concerned mainly with political succession and with land rights. The traditions are particularly thin in the west.

Much of the research on the north-eastern borders of the plateau has been published. Books and articles are available on the *prazos* of the lower Zambezi and of Manyika. For the plateau as a whole, before 1850, a general survey has been published, as well as a study of the religious aspects of Ndebele history. Much good work remains in the form of unpublished theses, for instance, studies of the Gaza, the trade system of the bay of Maputo, the south-eastern Ndau-speakers, the Duma confederacy, the Teve territory, the *feira* of Zumbo, the Changamire state, Shona communications and a general history of the Ndebele state. Although there is currently a slight gap in the flow of fresh publications on pre-1900 history, the progress in the 1970s was remarkable, and the pre-colonial history of the whole zone is on a far sounder footing as a result.

Beach, D. N. 'Ndebele raiders and Shona power', *Journal of African History*, xv, 1974, 633–51.

———. 'The Mutapa dynasty: a comparison of documentary and traditional evidence', *History in Africa*, iii, 1976, 1–17.

———. 'The Shona economy: branches of production', in *The Roots of Rural Poverty in Central and South Africa*, R. H. Palmer and Q. N. Parsons (eds), London, 1977, pp. 37–65.

———. 'Chimurenga: the Shona rising of 1896–97', *Journal of African History*, xx, 1979, 395–420.
———. *The Shona and Zimbabwe 900–1850*, Gwelo and London, 1980.
Bhebe, N. M. B. 'Some aspects of Ndebele relations with the Shona', *Rhodesian History*, iv, 1973, 31–8.
———. 'The Ndebele and Mwari before 1893: a religious conquest of the conquerors by the vanquished', in *Guardians of the Land*, J. M. Schoffeleers (ed.), Gwelo, 1978, pp. 287–95.
———. 'Ndebele politics during the scramble', *Mohlomi*, ii, 1977, 28—37.
———. *Christianity and Traditional Religion in Western Zimbabwe 1859–1923*, London, 1979.
Bhila, H. H. K. 'Trade and the survival of an African polity: the external relations of Manyika from the sixteenth to the early nineteenth century', *Rhodesian History*, iii, 1973, 11–28.
———. 'Manyika's relationship with the Portuguese and the Gaza Nguni', *Rhodesian History*, vii, 1976, 31–7.
———. 'The 1896–97 Southern Rhodesian war reconsidered', *Pula*, i, 1980, 139–62.
———. *Trade and Politics in a Shona Kingdom*, London, 1982.
Cobbing, J. R. D. 'The evolution of Ndebele *amabutho*', *Journal of African History*, xv, 1974, 607–31.
———. 'The absent priesthood: another look at the Rhodesian risings of 1896–7', *Journal of African History*, xviii, 1977, 61–84.
———. 'The Ndebele under the Khumalos, 1820–1896', Ph.D. thesis, University of Lancaster, 1976.
Costa, A. Nogueira da, 'Penetração e impacto do capital mercantil Português em Moçambique nos séculos XVI e XVII: o caso do Muenemutapa', roneo, Universidade Eduardo Mondlane, 1977.
Garlake, P. S. *Great Zimbabwe*, London, 1973.
———. 'Pastoralism and *zimbabwe*', *Journal of African History*, xix, 1978, 479–93.
Huffman, T. N. 'The rise and fall of Zimbabwe', *Journal of African History*, xiii, 1973, 353–66.
———. 'Ancient mining and Zimbabwe', *Journal of the South African Institute of Mining and Metallurgy*, lxxiv, 1974, 328–42.
———. 'Zimbabwe: southern Africa's first town', *Rhodesian Prehistory*, vii, 1977, 9–14.
Isaacman, A. F. *Mozambique: the Africanization of a European Institution: the Zambezi Prazos, 1750–1902*, Madison, Wisconsin, 1972.
———. 'The origin, formation and early history of the Chikunda of Central Africa', *Journal of African History*, xiii, 1972, 443–61.
———. 'Madzi-manga, *mhondoro* and the use of oral tradition – a chapter in Barwe religious and political history', *Journal of African History*, xiv, 1973, 395–409.

———. *The Tradition of Resistance in Mozambique*, London, 1976.

Liesegang, G. J. 'Beitrage zur Geschichte des Reiches der Gaza Nguni im südlichen Moçambique 1820–1895', D.Phil. thesis, Köln, 1968.

———. 'Nguni migrations between Delagoa Bay and the Zambezi, 1821–1839', *African Historical Studies*, iii, 1970, 317–37.

———. 'Aspects of Gaza Nguni history 1821–1897', *Rhodesian History*, vi, 1975, 1–14.

Mtetwa, R. M. G. 'The "Political" and Economic History of the Duma People of South-western Rhodesia from the Early Eighteenth Century to 1945', D. Phil. thesis, University of Rhodesia, 1976.

———. 'Labour supplies for the construction of the *zimbabwe* and their implications', *Rhodesian Prehistory*, xvii, 1979, 8–10.

Mudenge, S. I. G. 'The Rozvi Empire and the *feira* of Zumbo', Ph.D. thesis, University of London, 1972.

———. 'An identification of the Rozvi and its implications for the history of the Karanga', *Rhodesian History*, v, 1974, 19–31.

———. 'The role of trade in the Rozvi empire: a re-appraisal', *Journal of African History*, xv, 1974, 373–91.

Newitt, M. D. D. *Portuguese Settlement on the Zambesi*, London, 1973.

Phimister, I. R. 'Alluvial gold mining and trade in nineteenth-century South-Central Africa', *Journal of African History*, xv, 1974, 445–56.

———. 'Precolonial goldmining in southern Zambezia: a re-assessment', *African Social Research*, xvii, 1976, 1–30.

Randles, W. G. L. *L'Empire du Monomotapa du XVe au XIXe siècle*, Paris, 1975.

Ranger, T. O. 'The meaning of Mwari', *Rhodesian History*, v, 1974, 5–17.

Rea, W. F. *The Economics of the Zambezi Missions 1580–1759*, Rome, 1976.

Rennie, J. K. 'Christianity, Colonialism and the Origins of Nationalism among the Ndau of Southern Rhodesia, 1890–1935', Ph.D. thesis, Northwestern University, 1973.

———. 'From Zimbabwe to a colonial chieftaincy: four transformations of the Musikavanhu territorial cult in Rhodesia', in *Guardians of the Land*, J. M. Schoffeleers (ed.), Gwelo, 1981, 257–85.

Rita-Ferreira, A. 'Etno-história e cultura tradicional do grupo Angune (Nguni)', *Memórias do Instituto dos Investigações cientificas de Moçambique*, 11, Série C, 1974.

Zachrisson, P. *An African Area in Change: Belingwe 1894–1946*, Gothenburg, 1978.

Acknowledgements

The editors wish to thank the British Social Science Research Council for a grant to enable the authors to discuss their work at a conference in Canterbury in July 1980. They also wish to thank all those from Central African universities and elsewhere who attended the conference or sent advice. Eliot College in the University of Kent at Canterbury, the African Studies Program and History Department of Indiana University and the publisher all contributed generously to the administrative work of preparing and distributing the typescripts of successive drafts. Several Indiana graduate students helped translate the contributions submitted in French. The editors also wish to thank Bettina Wilkes for her careful copy-editing, N. S. Hyslop for his skilled rendering of the numerous maps, and Roger G. Thomas for his meticulous page-proof corrections.

David Birmingham would like to thank David Phillipson, Nicholas David, Pierre de Maret and A. P. Smyth for their advice on archaeology and prehistory.

Dennis Cordell expresses particular gratitude to Joel W. Gregory, Philip Burnham, Christopher Ehret, William J. Samarin and K. David Patterson as well as to the American Philosophical Society and the American Council of Learned Societies.

Jan Vansina received financial support from the William F. Vilas Estate and from the Guggenheim Foundation. He also thanks C. V. for map work, R. Harms, J. Ewald, M. Dawson and G. Noeske who assisted with bibliographical research, and the many scholars who read previous drafts of the chapter.

Joseph Miller's chapter represents a preliminary result of thinking and research conducted since 1977 under the financial sponsorship of the Joint Committee on Africa of the American Council of Learned Societies and the Social Sciences Research Council, the Sesquicentennial Associateship program of the University of Virginia Center for Advanced Studies, and the National Endowment for the Humanities. The American Council of Learned Societies and the University of Virginia provided travel grants. He is grateful to them all.

Thomas Reefe received a travel grant from the American Council of Learned Societies.

Index

abortion, 109, 115
Acheulian hand-axe, 4
Adamawa plateau, 13, 30, 32, 34, 38, 52, 61, 67, 68
Adamawa-Ubangian languages, 13, 38, 42
Afonso I, king of Kongo, 136–7, 138
Africans in the Portuguese army, 233, 259
Africanus, Lao *see* Leo Africanus
Afrikaners, 275–6
age grades, 85, 95, 125, 215, 216, 234
agoardente, 133, 147, 153, 158–9
agriculture:
  extensive, 210–11, 281, 254
  intensive, 210, 211, 213, 218, 243
  productivity, 55, 87, 97, 108, 119–22, 161
  and ritual, 12, 169, 213
  storage, 251, 252, 254
  surpluses, 56, 69, 97, 107, 109, 209, 210, 214, 228, 234, 243, 252
  women and, 107, 108, 109, 125, 211–12, 213, 251, 274
  see also animal husbandry; crops *and* plantations
al-Sanusi *see* Muhammad al-Sanusi
al-Zubayr Pasha, 64, 65
Albert, Lake, 82
Alima river, 98, 106, 109
Alvaro I, king of Kongo, 137
Alvaro II, king of Kongo, 137
amabutho regiments, 265, 270, 271
Ambaca, 134
'Ambakistas', 134
Ambriz, 103
Americans in Zaire, xii
Americas:
  food crops from the, 49, 51, 54–5, 70, 97, 98, 107–8, 109, 161, 190, 211, 245
  plantations, 51, 118, 131
  slave trade, x, 51, 118, 133, 134–5, 147–8, 150, 151, 152, 153, 155, 238, 262
  trade, 130, 153, 232
ancestors, x, 20, 26, 27, 57–8, 86, 91, 93, 96, 125, 135, 168, 169–70, 171, 173, 176, 177, 188, 203, 268
Angoche, 247
Angola, x, xi, 3, 5–6, 15, 22, 27, 97, 118–59, 173, 188, 189, 193, 197, 201, 202, 230
animal husbandry, 4, 11, 12, 16, 17, 40, 58, 212, 239, 248, 252
  European animals, 109, 111
  see also specific animals and cattle
animals:
  sacred, 166, 178
  totems, 247
  in the Upemba depression, 163
Annobon, 102
Antonio I, king of Kongo, 144
anvils, 185
Arabic:
  charms, 50
  language, 60
  literacy in, 50
Arabs, x, 45, 52, 197
Aruwimi river, 91, 105, 106, 108
Asia, trade with, 243, 246, 259
Asians in the Portuguese army, 233, 259
associations, 85, 94–6, 98, 216
  bambudye, 186–7, 188
  bwami, 95–6
  epanga, 114
  healing, 91, 94

hunting, 212, 216, 219
jengu, 114
lemba, 112, 113
luhuna, 95–6
men's, 45, 94–5
ritual, 86, 91
secret, 44, 186–7, 188, 212, 216, 245
and status, 95, 186, 216
and talent, 216
trading, 216, 219
and wealth, 95, 216
women's, 44
Atlantic trade, 26, 29, 32, 45, 49, 50–1, 54, 70, 72, 73, 77, 80, 98, 100–7, 111–17, 118–21, 123, 129–59, 166, 188, 189, 190, 197
Avongara states, 53–7
axes as insignia, 20, 165
Azande states, people and language, 13, 30, 37, 52, 53–60, 65, 67, 70, 73, 92, 96, 97, 106

Baboua, 67
Bafut, 45
Bagirmi language (Barma), 37
Bagirmi state and people, 35, 39, 47–9, 52, 59, 60, 66–7, 68, 72, 73
Bahr al-Ghazal, 70
Bali, 45
balungu (Msiri's overseas), 199
bambudye secret society, 186–7, 188
Bamenda hills, 45, 52
Bamileke chiefdoms, 52
Bamum, 45
Banana, 103
bananas, 16, 28, 107, 109, 251
Banda people and language, 13, 30, 34, 35, 38, 39, 42, 44, 49–50, 58, 60, 65, 66, 68, 69, 217
Bandia state and people, 52, 53, 57–8, 59
Bangssou, 58, 70
Bangui, 51, 70
Bangweulu, Lake, 161, 169, 186
Bantu languages and Bantu-speakers, ix, 1, 14, 15–19, 20, 59, 92, 123, 169, 179, 196, 202, 205–6
Banziri people, 51
Bargash, Sultan of Zanzibar, 239
barley, 9
Barma language *see* Bagirmi language
Barotse *see* Lozi kingdom
Barreto–Homem expedition (1571), 222–3, 258–9, 260
barter, 161, 172, 173, 180, 186
Barth, Heinrich, x
Barwe state, 257, 258, 264
Basoko, 115
Batanga, 105
Baya people, 13
Beach, D. N. 245–77
beads:
glass, 21, 22, 24, 188
gold, 24
ornamental, 6, 21
porcelain, 188
shell, 188, 199
stone, 188
trade, 22, 24, 63, 68, 97, 132, 174, 177, 188, 228, 246, 255, 259, 263–4
beans, 19, 23, 107, 108–9
beer-brewing, 12, 16, 201, 248
beeswax *see* wax
belaka, 52, 53
Belgian colonialism, xi, 70, 72, 202, 204
Belgian Congo *see* Zaire
bellows, iron-smelting, 15
bells, 20, 82, 165, 183
Bemba people and languages, 17, 177, 192, 194, 199, 204
Benghazi, 48
Bengo river, 133, 147
Benguela, 121, 123, 128, 134, 135, 143, 145, 146, 147, 149, 150, 152, 153, 155
Benin, 131, 220
Beningfield, 275
Benue river, 13, 53
Berbers, 45
Beti people, 82
Biafra, Bight of, xi, 51
Bihe kingdom, 149
Bikita, 252
bilabi (*bilaba*) (gift-giving), 87–8
Binga people, 58
Bioko (Fernando Po), 14, 94, 100, 107
Birmingham, David, 1–29
Bisa people, 193–4, 227, 228, 238
Biti people, 92
blacksmiths, 15, 19, 27, 41, 42, 127, 173, 185, 190, 201, 213, 214
blankets, 273
blight, 251
blood brotherhood and partnership, 43–4, 55, 84, 88
Bobangi traders, 32
Bocha, 257
body decoration, 6, 38

Bolobo, 115
Boma kingdom, 94, 99, 100
Bomokandi, 79
bondsmen, 248, 273
bone:
  jewellery, 20
  tools, 7, 8, 14
Bonga, 115
Bongo massif, 34
Borno, 39, 45, 47, 52, 60, 66–7, 74
  see also Kanem-Borno empire
Botswana, cattle, 22
Bouar megaliths, 34, 36
Bozoum, 34
Brazil, x, 133, 134–5, 147–8, 152, 153, 155, 230, 231, 232, 238, 240, 262
Brazza, Pierre Savorgnan de, 105
bride-price (*lobola*), 35, 68, 88, 89, 151, 175, 213, 216, 248, 252, 255, 265, 274
British:
  colonialism, xi, xii, 54, 70, 72, 105, 118, 204, 241, 242, 275–6, 277
  and the slave trade, 64, 118, 146, 152, 239, 241
  trade, 102, 118, 135, 147, 148, 149, 152, 153, 222, 232–3
British South Africa Company, 275, 276
Budya people, 264, 272
Buhera, 257
buildings, 11, 17, 59
  daga laterite, 24
  pole and *daga*, 19
  stone, 23, 24–5, 26, 245, 254, 256, 257
Bulawayo, cattle, 22
'bulls', 167, 169
Bulu people, 82
Bum, 45
Bumwele clan, 113
Bungu principality, 98
Bunkeya, 200–1, 202
bureaucracy, Lozi empire, 184, 185
Bushi, 95
Butua *see* Torwa state
Buunzi, 98, 99, 112
Buvanji dynasty, 98
Buzi river, 269
bwami associations, 95–6

cabbages, 107
Cabinda, 102
Caconda, 134, 143, 149
Calabar, trade, 102
Cameroun, xi, 3, 13–14, 30, 38, 45, 67, 70, 72–3, 79–82, 102, 103, 105, 114
Cameroun, Mount, 106, 114
Canbembe (a blacksmith), 173–4
cannibals, 137, 139–40
canoes, 7, 19, 83, 87, 160, 161, 163, 172, 184, 196, 202
  trade, 106, 172
Cão, Diogo, 129
'Captain of the Gates', 260
Caribbean, x, 107
cassava (manioc), 51, 69–70, 107, 108, 109, 161, 185, 190, 194, 201, 211, 251
  trade, 108, 109
'Cassava People', 190
'catchers', 190
cats, 109
cattle, 1, 3, 4, 11, 17–19, 22, 24–7, 37–8, 123, 124, 163–4, 167, 202, 211–13, 216–17, 234, 242, 245, 247, 249–57, 265, 268, 270, 271, 273–4
  diseases, 4, 11, 19, 25, 26, 59, 163, 212
  figurines, 22, 24
  raiding, 126, 157, 158, 185, 196, 197, 234, 237, 253, 266
  social and ritual role, 22, 24, 213
  trade, 131, 132, 133, 214, 234, 252, 253, 273–4
cave-cults, 170, 267
celadon ware, 24, 26, 263
Central Africa, area defined, ix
Central African Republic (CAR), 7–8, 30, 32, 34, 35, 37, 42, 43, 65, 69
Central Sudanic peoples and languages, 37–8, 42, 58–9
  see also specific tribes
cereals, ix, 9–11, 12, 13, 14, 16, 28, 58, 59, 64, 161, 183, 250, 252, 253, 262, 267
  see also specific cereals
Chad, 7–8, 32, 37, 38–9, 42, 72–3
Chad, Lake, 3, 8, 32, 34, 37, 38, 44, 45, 47, 59, 65
Chambeshi river, 192, 194
Chaminuka (a spirit), 258, 267, 272
Changamire state, dynasty and people, 231, 252, 254, 256, 257, 259, 261, 263–70
charms, 50, 86, 115, 192
Chedzurgwe copper mines, 22
Chewa languages and Chewa-speakers, 21, 206–7, 209, 211, 213, 215, 216, 217, 219
chickens, 11, 19, 214
chiefdoms, 55, 91, 92, 94, 95, 97, 165, 167, 169–71, 187, 190–1, 215, 219, 238, 241
Chikangombe (Malawi snake-god), 20

Chikova, 260
Chikunda traders, 197, 204
chimurenga (1896–7), 276
Chinese porcelain, 24, 26, 246, 263
Chinko river, 53
Chivi people, 272
Chokwe people, 155–6, 158, 197, 199, 200, 204
Christianity, x, xi–xii, 119, 131, 135, 136–7, 149
  as a cult, 143, 144, 157
  missionaries, 105, 118, 131, 141, 165, 220, 222, 231, 239, 241, 260
  see also Jesuits
Church of Scotland Mission, 241
circumcision, 38, 56, 173
city-states, 44, 177, 186, 199–200
  see also Great Zimbabwe
clans, 40–3, 54, 55, 57, 67, 89, 98, 111–14, 124, 165, 166, 190–1, 194, 203, 215, 271
  see also specific clans
Clarence, 105
clay:
  cattle figurines, 22, 24
  weights, 26
  see also pottery
clients *see* patrons and clients
climate, ix, 3, 4, 5, 6, 10, 37, 38, 44, 108, 135, 158, 246, 248, 251, 252, 263
  see also rainfall
cloth *see* textiles
clothes, 263, 273
  military, 271
  Muslim, 60
  skin, 6, 26, 263
  textile, 26, 60
coconuts, 239, 243
cocoyam (*macabo*), 107
coffee plantations, xi, 158–9, 237–8
colonialism, x–xii, 84, 89, 107, 108, 205, 243
  see also specific colonial powers
colours, symbolism of, 179
commerce *see* trade
Congo State, 27, 54, 72, 92, 97, 116, 118
cooking, 5, 6, 8, 12, 13, 19, 108
copper, 180, 203
  currency, 21, 127, 172
  ingots, 21, 22, 172, 173, 174, 175
  jewellery, 1, 19, 20, 22, 35, 68, 173, 191
  mining, ix, xi, 1, 4, 21, 22, 24, 27, 28–9, 98, 127, 128, 192
  nails, 20
  ornaments, 1, 21, 127, 173, 175, 198, 214
  and status, 22, 173
  trade, x, 1, 20–2, 24, 26, 28–9, 60, 68, 97, 127, 128, 131, 133, 172–5, 177, 178, 180, 193, 214, 222
  wire, 22, 173
  working, 14, 128, 201
Copperbelt, 4, 21, 22, 160, 172, 173, 174, 186, 191, 192, 193, 197, 201
Cordell, Dennis D., 30–74
cosmetics, ochre, 6
cotton:
  growing, 253
  plantations, 158–9
  trade, xi, 158, 214
  weaving, 26, 213, 214, 253
cowpeas, 251
cowrie shells, 19, 21, 25, 263
Coya (a king), 127
craftsmen and craftsmanship, 19, 20, 22, 29, 41, 60, 212, 213, 214, 217, 249, 260, 270
  see also specific crafts
creoles *see* Euro-Africans
crops, xi, 3, 4, 9–14, 29, 56, 69–70, 87, 119, 122, 123, 161, 177, 209–12, 237, 239, 243, 250–2, 271, 273
  from the Americas, 49, 51, 54–5, 70, 97, 98, 107–8, 109, 161, 190, 211, 245
  bush fallow cultivation, 210–11
  diseases, 251
  fertilisation, 210, 213
  irrigation and drainage, 208, 210, 211, 251
  ridging, 210
  rotation, 107, 108
  terracing, 23–4, 25, 246, 251
  see also cereals; fruit crops; tree crops *and* vegetable crops
Cross river, 105
'Crushing of Peoples', 196–7
cults, 95, 169–72, 174
  of afflictions, 91, 94, 170
  cave, 170, 267
  Christian, 143, 144, 157
  of High Gods, 169–70, 171–2, 258
  Mwari, 258, 267
  rain, 3, 27, 170–1, 267
  of sacred kings, 93, 94
  spirit, 86, 93, 98, 115, 258, 267, 272
  territorial, 170, 258
  see also ancestors

currency:
  copper, 21, 127, 172
  cowries, 21
  gold, 26
  imported goods, 228
  metal, 87, 89
  nzimbu shells, 27, 128, 132
  salt, 147, 148, 172
  textiles, 26, 27–8, 87, 146–7, 148, 263
'Cutter of Ears', 182

dambos, 161
Dambwa villages, 19
Danangombe, 256, 257, 265, 268
Danda, 257
Dande river, 141
Dar al-Kuti, 63, 66, 67–8, 69, 73, 74
Dar Fur, 8, 35, 39, 48, 49, 60, 63, 64, 72
  see also Fur state
Dar Runga, 66, 67
  see also Runga people
defence:
  and political organisation, 49, 111, 194
  and settlement, 44–5, 68, 69, 123, 126–7, 181–2, 196, 201, 202, 239
Deka-Gwaai, 267
Delagoa Bay, 242, 243, 245, 269
Delgado, Cape, 231
demography *see* population
depopulation, 49, 66, 70, 145, 150–1, 196, 201, 238, 254
Dia principality, 99
'Diana's Vow', 6
Dibamba river, 114
diseases, xi, 29, 208, 209
  cattle, 4, 11, 19, 25, 59, 163, 165–6, 212
  crop, 251
  human, 11, 19, 47, 49–50, 53, 69, 70, 109, 122, 158, 163, 233, 236, 260, 261
diviners and divination (*nganga*), 56, 170, 258
  Muslim, 50, 60
Diwan, 50
dogs, 11
dos Santos, Joãos, x
Douala and the Duala people and language, 1, 82, 102, 103, 105, 111, 114, 116
'down-river people', 190–1
dress *see* clothes
drinks, alcoholic, 12, 16, 133, 147, 153, 158–9, 201, 248, 263
drought, 9, 10, 11, 13, 47, 53, 119, 121–2, 125, 126, 135, 139, 140, 143, 145, 146, 147, 150–1, 155, 158, 159, 160–1, 168, 171, 203, 260, 274
Duala *see* Douala
ducks, 109
Dugumbi, Mwene, 116
Duma people, 252, 266, 272
Dutch:
  colonialism, 134
  and the Portuguese, 230–1, 232
  traders, 102, 113–14, 118, 132, 143, 144, 222, 230–1, 232
Dutch East India Company, 230–1, 232
Dutch West India Company, 230
dye-stuffs trade, 152

earth priests, 41, 45, 168–9, 170, 173, 203
ecological factors, ix, 3, 27, 32, 34–6, 39–40, 44–5, 56, 58–9, 77, 79, 121–3, 126–7, 150–2, 158, 160–4, 167, 190, 208, 254, 256
  see also climate *and* natural resources
economic organisation, xii, 1, 37, 40, 61, 106, 249–54
  see also trade
education:
  colonial, xii
  Muslim, 67
Egypt, 54, 60, 63–5, 97
elephant hunting, 1, 22, 155–8, 197, 199, 212, 219, 226–7, 234, 253, 256, 258, 259, 262, 264, 267, 273
  see also ivory
eleusine, 201
élites, xii, 45, 47, 55, 56, 58, 143, 174–5, 192, 203
emblems *see* insignia and regalia
enclosures:
  Muslim, 60
  stone, 23, 24–5, 26, 245, 254, 256, 257
  wooden, 181–2
environment *see* ecological factors *and* geographical factors
epanga association, 114
epidemics, xi, 49, 53, 69, 158, 261
Erskine, Townsend, 275
ethnic groups, 30, 32, 34, 50, 81, 89, 92, 93, 96, 122, 123, 164, 195, 207, 210
Euro-Africans, 132–5, 137, 140, 143, 145, 146–8, 149, 151, 152–3, 155, 157, 158–9, 193, 223
European:
  animals, 109, 111
  conquest and colonialism, 52, 54, 70–4,

92, 111, 114, 116, 119, 120, 131, 151–2, 158, 164–5, 197, 202, 203, 220–2, 229, 242, 276
missionaries, 105, 118, 131, 141, 165, 220, 222, 231, 239, 241, 260
trade, 49, 50–1, 70, 72–4, 100, 105, 113, 118, 133, 135, 151, 165, 221–2, 230, 239, 243, 276
travellers, x, 29, 42, 57, 71, 118, 165, 208–9, 210, 239
see also specific European countries
executioners, 182

family and kinship, x, 20, 21, 40, 43–4, 60, 84–9, 91, 92, 93, 96, 122, 123, 124, 128, 143, 151, 166, 167, 173, 175, 201, 215, 223, 247
perpetual kinship, 189–90, 191, 192
see also lineage *and* marriage
famine, 43, 53, 81, 108, 122, 145, 146, 150–1, 158, 159, 161, 166–7, 190, 194, 203, 253, 262, 274
Fang migrations, 82, 105–6
farming *see* agriculture
Fashoda, 72, 73
feathers, 128
trade, 152
feiras, 222, 261, 263
Fernan Vaz, 113
Fernando Po *see* Bioko
ferrymen, 160
fertility rites, 21, 168
Feti (a king), 127
Fezzan, 45, 47
figurines:
cattle, 22, 24
clay, 22, 24
wooden, 27
fire rituals, 21
firearms, 5, 65, 68, 105, 119, 195, 196, 198, 219, 253, 262, 263, 276
trade, 63, 66, 68, 102–3, 143, 148–9, 152, 155, 156, 157, 198–9, 200, 201, 223, 238, 241, 273, 274
fish-drying, 1, 19–20, 121, 172, 214
fish-smoking, 212
fishing and fishermen, ix, x, 3, 4, 6–8, 9, 11, 17, 19, 54, 59, 79, 80, 81, 168–9, 183, 187, 212, 250
trade, 20, 98, 121, 128, 161, 165, 172, 212, 214
food:
gatherers, 4, 5, 8–10, 14, 16, 54, 109, 167, 247, 249, 250, 251, 270
preparation *see* cooking
supply *see* agriculture *and* famine
trade, 106
Fort-Crampel, 74
Fort Jesus, 231
forts, Portuguese, 221
'Forty-Day Road', 48
Free Church of Scotland Mission, 241
French:
colonialism, xi, xii, 54, 69, 70, 72, 73, 74, 105, 114
language, 147
plantations, 237–8, 242
and the slave trade, 146, 147, 149–50, 237–9
trade, 102, 118, 135, 147, 148, 149
fruit:
crops, 16, 26, 168, 210, 214, 251
wild, 249, 251
see also specific fruits
Fulani people, 52, 63, 66–7, 68, 73
funerary objects, 17, 19, 20
see also royal graves
Fur state, 48, 49, 52
see also Dar Fur

Gabon and Gabon river, 14, 75, 81, 82, 86, 95, 102, 103, 105, 111, 113–14
Gama, Vasco da *see* Vasco da Gama
Gambe, 257
game *see* hunting and hunters
Gaoga kingdom, 39
Garcia II, king of Kongo, 144
Gaza state and people, 67, 235, 236–7, 240–3, 254, 266, 268–77
Gbaya people and language, 34, 39–42, 58, 63, 67, 68
genealogies *see* lineages
genesis myths, 39, 75, 165, 178–80, 185, 186, 196, 203, 207
Gentil, Emile, 73
geographical factors, ix, 3, 27, 58, 77–9, 160–4, 205, 206, 208, 245–6
see also eccological factors
German colonialism, xi, 72–3, 118
gift-giving, 87–8, 96, 99, 192, 224
glass, 246
beads, 21, 22, 24, 188
goats, 11, 17, 26, 37, 87, 192, 252
trade, 106, 214
gold:
beads, 24

gold (continued)
currency, 26
jewellery, 1
mining, xi, 4, 25, 28–9, 225, 231, 234, 242, 245, 247, 253, 255, 256, 258–64, 267, 273, 274, 275
ornaments, 1, 255
trade, x, 4, 22, 24, 25–9, 129, 132, 214, 217, 221–2, 225, 227, 234, 246, 253, 257, 258, 260, 261, 264, 267
Gold Coast, 129, 131
Gouveia, 240
grains *see* cereals
Great Britain *see* British
Great Zimbabwe, 19, 22, 24–7, 252, 254–7, 261, 266
grindstones, 11, 17
groundnuts, 106, 107, 108, 109, 161, 201, 243
groves, sacred, 170
guardian spirits, 115
guests, 125–6
Guinea, Gulf of, 131, 132
Gula people, 58
Gumaye, 255
guns *see* firearms
Gwelo river, 265
Gwembe valley, 170–1, 174, 197

Hamed bin Muhammed el-Murjebi *see* Tippu Tip
harpoons, 7, 8
Hausa-Fulani states, 66–7
Hausa people, 52, 61, 67, 74, 82
Hausa-Tuaregs, 74
healing associations, 91, 94, 170
health care, xi, 21
Muslim, 50
hides *see* leather
hierarchy *see* social stratification *and* élites
Hindu traders *see* Indian traders
hippopotamus, 183
Hiya people, 265
Hlengwe people, 250
'Holding Up the Sun' ceremony, 173
Homo sapiens sapiens, 5
horses and horsemen, 11, 82
hostages, 199, 200, 201
house-firms, 114–15
household possessions, 11, 40
households, Zimbabwe, 247, 248, 249, 270, 273, 274
'houses' (sub-groups), 84–90, 91, 92, 93–4, 95, 100, 111, 113–14, 115, 116, 248, 252, 256, 257, 265
Hufrat al-Nuhas, 35, 60, 68
Huila kingdom, 126, 149–50
human sacrifice, 20, 181
Humbe, 149
Humpata, 126, 149–50, 159
'Hunters', 201
hunting and hunters, ix, 1, 3, 4, 5–6, 8, 11, 13, 16, 19, 21, 26, 54, 79, 80, 83, 84, 87, 93, 105, 109, 161, 163, 167, 168, 178, 180, 202, 212, 219, 228, 241, 247–51, 270
associations, 212, 216, 219
of elephants, 1, 22, 155–8, 197, 199, 212, 219, 226–7, 234, 253, 256, 258, 259, 262, 264, 267, 273
hut taxation, 276
Hwata, 272
Hyläa, 75

Ikelemba river, 109
Ikongo, 81
Ilonga, 81
Ilunga Sungu, king of the Luba empire, 187, 188
Imbangala (Jagas), 137, 139–40, 141, 149, 156
implements *see* tools
independence, xii
India, trade with, 226–7, 228, 231, 233, 246
Indian Ocean trade, x, 4, 20, 25, 29, 77, 188, 197, 212, 214, 216–23, 225–44, 246, 255, 259
Indian traders, x, 25, 217–18, 223, 233, 238, 239
Indonesian seafarers, 16, 25
infanticide, royal, 186
Ingombe Ilede, trade, 22, 174
Inhambane, 27, 212, 215, 228–9, 232, 233, 237, 242, 247, 259, 262, 269
initiation ceremonies, 38, 44, 60, 82, 91, 94, 95, 178
insignia and regalia, 93, 127, 169, 173, 188, 190, 191, 199
axes, 20, 165
bells, 20, 165, 183
chairs, 96
firearms, 198
Inyanga highlands, 250–1
Irebu, 115
iron:
bells, 20, 82, 183
implements, 1, 14, 15, 17, 127, 172, 173, 186, 190, 214, 249, 252, 273

jewellery, 15, 19
mining and working, 14–15, 16, 28–9, 41, 98, 127–8, 138, 173, 180, 185, 188, 203, 213–14, 246, 253
ritual, 15
trade, x, 20, 26, 28–9, 87, 106, 138, 172, 173, 177–8, 180, 183, 186, 194, 246, 249, 253
as wealth, 27
Iron Age, 1, 4, 6, 14, 15–16, 17, 18, 19, 20, 21, 22, 23, 25, 27, 127, 161, 172, 206, 208, 209–20, 245, 246, 251–2, 254, 267
iron-masters, status, 15, 213–14
irrigation and drainage, 208, 210, 211, 251
Islam, 45, 47–8, 50, 52, 70, 246, 260
Isma'il Fasha, Khedive of Egypt, 64
Itimbiri river, 93
Ituri, 80, 82
Ivindo river, 80
ivory:
jewellery, 20
trade, x, xi, 22, 24–6, 60, 61, 63–5, 97, 102, 103, 116, 118, 152, 153, 155–6, 188, 197, 199, 204, 212, 217, 219, 222, 225–7, 229, 233, 234, 238, 241–3, 246, 253, 256, 258, 259, 262, 264, 267, 273, 274

Jagas *see* Imbangala
jallaba (pedlars), 60, 61, 63, 64, 67
João III, king of Portugal, 132
jemba witchcraft, 82
jengu association, 114
Jesuits, 132–3, 148, 231, 251
jewellery:
bone, 20
copper, 1, 19, 20, 22, 35, 68, 173, 191
gold, 1
iron, 15, 19
ivory, 20
jihads, 67
Jos plateau, iron smelting, 15
Jukun confederation, 53
justice:
centralised system, 93, 100, 114, 258
court fees, 258
dispute settlement, 41, 42

Kafue river, 162, 164, 166, 167, 168, 197
Kaguvi (a spirit), 267
Kakongo principality, 98
Kalahari desert, 122, 123, 155, 246
Kalala Ilunga (a warrior), 180
Kalambo Falls, 5
Kalanga people, 268, 270
Kalemba, 6
Kalonga kingdom, 233–4, 225
Kamerun, 72
Kanem-Borno empire, 35, 39, 47, 48, 49, 50, 60, 72
Kanem state, 37, 45, 47, 50
Kanongesha polity, 176, 191
Kanuri, people and language, 8, 37, 44
Kanyembo I, Mukulweji chief, 192
Kanyok kingdom, 176, 181–2, 187, 199
kaolin ointment, 94
Kaporolo river, 124
Kapwirimbwe, salt manufacturing, 17
Kara people, 58
Karanga people, 268
Kasai chiefdoms, 94
Kasai river, 99, 122, 124, 155, 160
Kasanje kingdom, 141, 149, 156, 157, 189
Kasongo, 115, 199
Kasongo Kinyama (an adventurer), 198–9
Katanga, stone tools, 16
Katende, 187
Kazamba, 69
Kazembe kingdom, 177, 178, 181, 182, 192–3, 194, 200, 238
Kazembe title, 191, 201
Kenga people, 34–5, 60
Kenya pottery, 18
Kere-speakers, 81
Kgama, 275
Khami, 252, 255, 256, 257
Khartoum, x, 60, 63, 97
Khartoumers, 63–5, 67, 68
Khoisan-speakers, 16
Kikoto kya Kaumba, 187
Kilwa, 25, 26, 227, 229, 238, 259
Kimbangu, Simon, xii
Kimberley mines, 273, 274
kingship and kingdoms, x, 20, 25, 44, 45, 47, 48, 95–100, 111–13, 117, 128, 135, 136, 143, 157, 160, 163, 166, 175–95, 203, 236, 258, 270–1
cult of the sacred kings, 93, 94
lineages, 216–17, 218, 224–5
succession disputes, 167, 180, 186, 188, 194, 200, 203, 218–20, 223–5, 229, 265, 270, 275
see also specific kings and kingdoms
Kingsley, Mary, 75
Kinguri title, 139
Kinkondja kingdom, 187
Kinshasa, neolithic culture, 14

Kisale, Lake, 19–20
Kisama mines, 128, 138
kitome lords of Kongo, 127
Kololo people, 196, 198, 200, 204,
Kom, 45
Kona confederation, 53
Kongo kingdom and region, x, 1, 15, 17, 22, 27–8, 98, 102, 103, 111, 112, 113, 123–4, 127–8, 129–59, 220
Korarafa empire, 52–3
Kordofan, 60
Kotoko people, 38–9, 44–5, 47
Kotto river, 51
Kounde, 67
Kresh people, 44, 49–50, 58, 60, 63, 65
Kuba kingdom and people, 97–8, 109
Kubango river, 122, 156
Kukuya plateau, 79
Kulembe, lords of, 126
Kunene river, 122, 123, 124, 125, 143, 146, 147, 148, 149, 156, 157
Kusseri, battle of (1900), 73
Kutomboka dance, 178
Kuvelai river, 124
Kuvo river, 147, 149
Kwa river, 99, 157
Kwakwa river, 114
Kwale pottery, 18
Kwange (cassava bread), 108
Kwango river, 122, 124, 127, 139, 140, 141, 142–3, 144, 145, 146, 149, 150, 153, 154, 156, 189
'Kwanyama' people, 124
Kwanza river, 123–4, 125, 126, 132, 133, 139, 141, 148, 149, 150, 154, 155, 156
Kwilu, 79
Kwilu-Nyari river, 111

labour:
- coercion, 259
- corvée, 56–7, 69, 93, 184, 248, 258
- division of, 40, 56–7, 83–4, 85, 87, 97, 107, 109, 125, 166, 211–12, 213, 248
- exploitation, xi, 55, 132, 153
- labour-intensive production, 218
- migration, 253, 274
- slave, 67, 69, 109, 131, 133, 146, 151, 159, 197, 243
- specialisation, 97
- supply, 163, 188, 197, 248, 261
- trade, 131
- wages, 242–3, 274

land:
- arable, 39, 247
- availability, 10, 11, 13, 40, 44, 55, 57, 119, 151, 163, 167–8, 209, 218–19, 245, 266, 273
- clearance, 36, 39, 83, 109, 211, 254
- grants, 133
- tenure, 100, 107, 125–6, 166, 215, 216, 247–8, 258, 271, 273
- terracing, 23–4, 25, 246, 251, 255, 256
- use, 3, 11, 20, 40–1, 84, 85, 167–8
- wealth in, 83
- *see also* soils

languages, 1, 5, 7, 8, 13, 17, 30, 33, 34, 36–9, 54, 58, 96, 123, 124, 195, 206–8, 277
- *see also specific languages*

leather:
- bellows, 15
- trade, 155, 157

lemba association, 112, 113
'Lemba' craft communities, 260
Leo Africanus, x
leopards, 26, 91, 94
Leopard's Kopje, 22–3, 24, 255
Leopold II, king of the Belgians, 72, 202
Lewanika, king of the Lozi kingdom, 197
Leya people, 248
Leza *see* Nzambi
Libreville, 105
likundu (evil spirits), 56
Limpopo river, 22, 23, 24, 208, 219, 245, 255, 269, 270, 272, 274
lineages:
- dual descent, 85, 93, 189
- matrilineal, 84–5, 89, 94, 99, 115, 166–7, 191, 192, 214–16, 219, 248
- multiple collateral, 224–5
- patrilineal, 43, 84, 85, 89, 115, 167, 169, 186, 214–16, 245, 247
- royal, 216–17, 218, 224–5
- segmentary, 75, 77, 85–6, 125, 127–8, 131, 135, 136, 140, 141, 145, 150, 159, 167, 175, 187, 218, 219
- and status, 93, 94, 125–6, 127
- unilateral, 189

Lingala trade language, 53
lions, 82
Lisala, 92
literacy in Arabic, 50
livestock *see* animal husbandry
Livingstone, David, 196, 241
Loango kingdom, 98, 99, 100, 102, 103, 107, 108, 111–13, 121, 133, 144, 145, 146,

147, 149, 152, 157
Lobengula, Ndebele ruler, 270, 271, 275–6
lobola see bride-price
locusts, 11, 251
Logone river, 34, 36, 38, 42, 44, 45, 47, 68
Lokenye river, 94, 97
Lomami river, 82, 88, 93, 116, 173, 179–89, 185, 186
Lomela river, 94
Lopez, Cape, 102, 113, 114
lord of the earth *see* earth priests
'lord of the people', 169, 170
'Lord of the Viper', 182
'lord of the weir', 169
Lourenço Marques, 228–9, 232, 233, 234, 241, 242
Lozi kingdom, 176, 177–8, 181, 183–5, 197, 200, 204
Lualaba river, 82
Luanda, 121, 128, 131, 132, 133, 134, 135, 138, 140, 141, 142, 143, 144, 146, 147, 148, 149, 152
Luangwa river, 201–2, 228
Luapula river, 162, 166, 192, 193, 194
Luba empire, 21, 22, 176, 177, 178, 179–80, 181, 182, 185–8, 197, 198, 199, 200, 217
Luba language, 17, 191, 192
luhuna associations, 95–6
Lujenda river, 219
Lukala river, 123–4, 138
Lukwesa I, *Kazembe*, 192–3
Lulonga river, 109
Lunda empire, 1, 139, 141, 144, 155, 156, 176, 177, 178, 181, 182, 189–92, 193, 197, 200, 201, 238
Lundu (a warlord), 171
Lundu kingdom, 223–4
Lupemban tools, 5
Lurio river, 208
Luvua river, 171, 173
luxury goods *see* prestige goods

Maba people, 52
Mabiti political order, 96
macabo (cocoyam), 107
machira cloth, 26
McMahon award (1875), 242
Madi people, 8, 56
Mafungabusi plateau, 257
Mahdi and the Mahdists, 65, 70
maize, 51, 107, 108, 161, 201, 211, 251
Majingay people, 43
see also Sara Majingay language
Makandza, 115
Makanga, 240
Makoko treaty, 105
Makonde people, 205–6, 210, 212, 215
Makua language and Makua-speakers, 206–7, 210, 212, 215, 216, 224, 229, 233, 238, 239
malachite, 21, 173, 191
malaria, 19, 109, 233, 236
Malawi, 4, 18, 20–1, 27, 167, 186, 189, 197, 202, 236, 239
Malawi, Lake, 3, 160, 166, 193, 194, 202, 206, 210, 213, 227, 238, 241
Malebo Pool, 87, 98, 102, 103, 105, 108, 109, 112, 136, 157
malunga (wooden figurines), 27
malunga chiefs of the Kwango, 127
mambo title, 267
Mamvu-Lese people, 59
Mandara mountains, 32
Mando warriors, 92
Manekweni, 26–7, 213
Mangbele conglomerate, 92, 96
Mangbetu kingdom and people, 8, 56, 59, 81, 92, 96–7, 100, 109
Mangwende, 276
mani lords of Kongo, 128, 135, 137, 144, 157
Maniema, 80, 82, 95, 116
manioc *see* cassava
manufacturing *see* craftsmen and craftsmanship
Manyika, 22, 252, 257, 259, 260, 261, 263, 265, 267, 268, 269, 270, 271, 272, 275, 276
Manza people, 39, 42, 43–4, 69
Manziga, king of the Mangbetu, 96
Mapaha house, 92
Mapela, 23, 24, 255
Mapungubwe, 24, 255
Maputo river, 208
Marave states, 217, 219, 223–4, 225, 260
Marchand expedition, 72
markets, 1, 20, 21, 87, 103, 112, 128, 132, 245, 252, 253, 261
maroons, 102
marriage, 80, 88–9, 91, 100, 114, 115, 123, 125, 131, 134, 156, 189, 247, 270
alliances through, 43–4, 55, 57, 86–9, 96, 127, 128, 131, 140, 143, 149, 201, 248
bride-price (*lobola*), 35, 68, 88, 89, 151, 175, 213, 216, 248, 252, 255, 265, 274
dowries, 21

marriage (continued)
exogamous, 39, 41, 44, 86, 166, 203, 215, 216
intermarriage, 232
polygynous, 215, 218
sacrificial wives, 20
Marshaga polity, 97
Mascarene Islands *see* Mauritius and Réunion
Mashonaland, 273
Massa people, 38–9, 45
Massangano, 240
Massingire, 240
'Masters of the Land', 98
Matamba, 141–2
Matopo hills, 267
Maungwe, 257, 271
Mauritius plantations, 237–8, 242, 262
Mawewe, son of Soshangane, 241, 271
Mayi Ndombe, Lake, 93–4, 96, 97–8, 100
Mayumba, 103, 112
Mazoe river, 263, 265, 268
Mbailundu kingdom, 143, 149
Mbali, 58
Mbamba, 137, 143
mbang (political and religious leader), 60
mbanza Kongo, 137, 138, 143
Mbata people, 144
see also Zombo people
Mbemba Nzinga *see* Afonso I, king of Kongo
Mbere people, 52
Mbidi Kiluwe (a hunter), 180
Mbomu river, 30, 34, 36, 38, 51, 52, 53, 57, 58–9, 73, 92
M'Bona *see* Nzambi
Mbondo, 139
Mbres, 66
Mbuji Mayi river, 189, 190–1
Mbum states and people, 52–3, 67, 68
Mbundu region and people, 124, 127, 128, 132, 135, 138–9, 143, 156
Mbunza, king of the Mangbetu, 97
Mbwela, 144–5
Mbwila, 144–5
measles, 49
medicine, Muslim, 50
Mediterranean trade, 77, 106, 129, 246
mediums, 170, 258, 267
megaliths, 34, 36
men's associations, 45, 94–5
mercenaries, 131, 140, 156, 191, 200, 223, 259, 276
Meroe, iron smelting, 15
metalwares trade, 132, 133
metal-working, x, 4, 14, 20
metals, 132, 214, 225, 227
mfecane, 263, 265, 268–72, 273
microlithic tools, 5
Middle Passage, 148
middlemen, 103, 147–8, 189, 246
migration, 13–19, 34–9, 47, 52, 55, 57, 61, 63, 66, 67, 75, 80–3, 88, 97, 104–6, 115, 117, 124–6, 134, 155–6, 158, 165, 167–9, 180–1, 183, 185, 192, 196, 202, 203, 217–19, 235–6, 245, 248, 254, 256, 259, 261–2, 264–9, 271
and disease, 49
forced, xi, 99, 161
labour, 253, 274
Miller, Joseph C., 118–59
millet, 9, 10, 12, 13, 23, 27, 36, 37, 38, 51, 69, 107, 108, 121, 124, 190, 211, 251
Mina, gold dust, 132
Mindouli, 98, 112
minerals and mining, xi, xii, 4, 19, 35, 112, 209, 213, 217, 242, 246, 248, 249, 271, 273, 274
trade, 98, 118, 136–7, 222
see also specific minerals
miners, training of, xi
missionaries *see* Christianity
Moçâmedes bay, 149, 159
Mogadishu, 259
mokota (headmen), 116
Mombasa, 259
Mondunga-speakers, 92
money *see* currency
Mongo, 34–5
moradores (townsmen), 224–5, 237
mounds in the Lozi kingdom, 183, 184
Mozambique, xi, 4, 16, 21, 25, 26, 169, 197, 204–44, 246, 259
Mozambique Company, 275, 276
Mozambique Island, 221, 224, 227, 229, 231, 233, 238, 239, 259, 260
Mpezeni, Ngoni leader, 236
Mpongwe, 114
Msane people, 235
Msiri, Nyamwezi conqueror, 197, 198–9, 200–1, 202
Mtetwa–Zulu people, 234
mudzimu spirits, 258
Muhammad al-Sanusi, 63, 69, 73, 74
Muhammad 'Ali, 63
Muiro (a blacksmith), 173–4

mukomohasha (captain-general), 258
Mukulweji river, 191–2
mulattos *see* Euro-Africans
Mulungu (high god), 258
Mungo river, 105, 114
mupetos, 259
Musgu people, 38–9
Mushie, 115
Muslims, x, 26, 27, 29, 30, 32, 35, 45, 49, 57–72, 218, 222, 240–1, 246, 258, 260, 261
and European colonists, 72–4, 221, 223, 259
slave raids, 39, 42, 45–8, 52, 57, 59–70, 73
see also Islam
Musumba (war camp), 178
Mutapa state, people and ruler, 22, 27, 132, 252, 254, 256, 257, 258, 259, 260–1, 264–5, 267, 270, 272
Mutapa Mukombwe, 261, 264
Mutekedza, 272
Mutombo Mukulu kingdom, 176, 190
Mutumba mountains, 173
Mwambera, Ngoni leader, 236
mwami kingship, 95, 96
Mwanza, 168
Mwari cult, 258, 267
Mwe Pwati, 112
Mwene Dugumbi, 116
Mwene Mutapa, 222, 225
Mweru, Lake, 162, 172
mwiri cult, 86
Mzila, Gaza ruler, 241, 269, 271, 275
Mzilikazi, Ndebele ruler, 270, 273

Nabiembali, king of the Mangbetu, 96–7
Nachikufan hunters, 6
Nachtigal, Gustav, 72
Nama people, 157
Natal, 234, 236, 269, 274, 275
natural resources, 35, 162, 167, 168, 172, 185–6, 188, 189, 202–3, 247
depletion of, x, 151, 155, 157, 158, 197, 201, 227, 234, 237, 239, 242, 253, 256, 273
scarcity of, 161, 168, 175, 180–1, 184, 194, 214
nature spirits, 86, 93, 98
Naweej I, Lunda conqueror, 190–1
Ncwangeni-Jere people, 235
Ndala Kisua, 139
Ndau people, 252
Ndebele state and people, 237, 250, 252, 254, 262, 263, 265, 266, 268–77
Ndele, 66, 69
ndembu chiefs, 126, 139, 141, 142, 144
Ndogo people, 38
'Ndombe' people, 124
ndoro shells, 263
Ndwandwe people, 234–6
Nehanda (a spirit), 258, 268
Nemakonde, 272, 276
Netherlands *see* Dutch
New World *see* Americas
Ngalama, king of the Lozi empire, 184
nganga see diviners and divination
Ngangela people, 124, 125, 139, 146, 148
Ngaoundéré, 52, 67
Ngbandi people, 57
Ngbetu (Mangbetu ancestor), 96
ngola (iron regalia), 127, 138
Ngola a Kiluanje ('conquering Ngola'), 133, 138–9, 140, 141
Ngola state, 133, 138–9, 140
Ngombala, king of the Lozi empire, 184
Ngombela, 87
Ngonde people, 213
Ngoni people, 196, 198, 199, 210–2, 204, 236–7, 241, 247, 263, 266, 268–9
Ngoyo principality, 98, 102, 112–13, 145
Ngungunyane, ruler of the Gaza, 241–2, 269, 276–7
Nguni language and Nguni-speakers, 209, 213, 234, 236, 239, 240, 254, 268, 269, 271
Ngura, Azande ruler, 53
Ngwane Maseko, Nguni-speakers' leader, 236
Niger, 74
Niger-Congo languages, 13, 14
Niger river, 72, 131
Nigeria, 12, 15
Nile river, x, 3, 7, 13, 15, 30, 32, 45, 48, 52, 58, 59, 60, 61, 63, 64, 65, 70, 72
Nilo-Saharan people and languages, 7, 8, 9, 13
Nilotic peoples, 8
Njanja people, 249, 273
Njau, lords of, 150
Nkambo Kayembe (spirit of the salt industry), 173
Nkhumbi people, 124, 157, 159
Nkisi river, 27, 122, 123, 144
nkobi (portable shrines), 113
Nkomati river, 208
Nkomi kingdom, 103, 113
Nkongola (mythical chief), 179–80

Nkope style pottery, 18
Nkulu (refugees), 168
nkum (princes), 93–4, 97, 99
Novaes, Paulo Dias de, 132–3, 138, 139
Nsenga language, 202
Nsundi, 112
Nunu principality, 99
Nupe kingdom, 53
Nxaba, Nguni-speakers' leader, 236, 268
nyai (warriors), 265, 270
Nyakusa people, 213
Nyambe *see* Nzambi
Nyamwezi people, x, 197, 198, 199, 201, 204
Nyangwe, 115, 116, 196, 199
nyika see territories
Nzabi people, 107, 109
Nzakara people and language, 57–8, 65, 67, 69, 70, 73
Nzambi (Leza, M'Bona, Nyambe), a god, 169, 171
nzimbu shells, 27, 128, 132
Nzinga, woman-ruler of Matamba, 140–2
Nzinga a Nkuwu, king of Kongo, 135

ochre cosmetics, 6
Ogowe river, 80, 82, 85, 87, 102, 103, 105, 113
oil palms *see* palm and palm-products
Omani rulers, 229, 231, 239
ondro (evil spirits), 56
oracle, Mangbetu poison, 56
oral traditions, 3, 39, 54, 63, 75, 81–2, 160, 165, 168, 171, 178–80, 181, 182, 185–7, 188, 196, 203, 206, 207, 219, 252, 256, 266
ordeals, poison, 56
ornaments, 228
  bead, 6, 21
  copper, 1, 21, 127, 173, 175, 198, 214
  gold, 1, 255
  shell, 21, 188, 199
  see also jewellery
Orungu kingdom, 103, 113
Ouaka river, 51
Ovambo people, 124, 146, 157, 158
'Ovimbali', 134
Ovimbundu people, x, 124, 155, 197, 198, 199, 200, 201, 204
Owen, Captain William, 242

paddlers *see* canoes
painting:
  body, 6
  rock, 6
palm and palm-products, 1, 12–13, 17
  cloth, 27–8, 87, 102, 106, 133, 140, 143, 147, 174, 190
  coconuts, 239, 243
  trade, 1, 27–8, 87, 98, 102, 106, 133, 140, 143, 147, 174, 190
pastoralists *see* animal husbandry
patrons and clients, 43–4, 47, 72, 84–6, 106, 111, 114–16, 126, 128, 140, 151, 153, 183, 187, 188, 190, 191, 193, 200, 203, 247, 248, 253, 265
pawns, 84, 85, 89, 166, 175
peas, 23, 251
pedlars, 60, 61, 63, 64, 67
Pemba, plantations, 238–9
Pende people, 124, 141
'People of the Eyes' and 'People of the Tail', 178
peppers, 107
perfumes trade, 25
Persian porcelain, 263
Philip II, king of Spain, 230
Phiri clan, 21, 217
pigs, 109
pirates, 106
plantations, x, 51, 69, 177, 188, 242, 243
  cassava, 109, 190
  cloves, 239
  coconut, 239
  coffee, xi, 158–9, 237–8
  cotton, 158–9
  sugar, xi, 102, 131, 133, 139, 158, 237–8, 274
political organisation *see* state formation
Pombal, Marques de, 231–2
pools, sacred, 170, 171
population, ix
  distribution, 32, 34, 39, 40, 45, 49, 52, 55, 69, 70, 79–83, 98, 109, 110, 115, 119, 121–6, 161, 163, 165, 180–1, 189, 192, 194, 199, 203, 208–9, 271
  growth, 3–4, 11, 12, 14, 15–16, 17, 54, 80, 119, 151, 158, 159, 218–19, 248, 254, 255, 273
  see also depopulation *and* migration
porcelain *see* pottery, porcelain
Portuguese:
  administration, 231–2
  colonisation, x, xi, xii, 102, 118–20, 130–59, 189, 193, 211, 220–43, 254,

258–65, 269, 275, 276
and the Dutch, 230–1, 232
explorers, 129, 193, 220
forts, 221
intermarriage, 232
introduction of pigs, 109
mariners, 21
missionaries, 118, 220
slave trade, 238, 262
trade, 51, 100, 102–3, 118, 127, 131–59, 188, 193, 220–3, 225–9, 234, 237–44, 258–63, 273, 275
Portuguese Order of Christ, 157
'potlatch', 88
pottery, x, 8, 11, 14, 16, 17, 27, 253, 256
beads, 188
bellows, 15
Chinese porcelain, 24, 26, 246, 263
Kisale, 19
Kwale, 18
Nkope style, 18
Persian porcelain, 246
trade, 24, 26, 106, 188, 246, 263
wavy-line decoration, 8
prazos (estates) and *prazeros*, 224–5, 239–40, 263, 265, 272, 275
prestige goods, 20, 21, 22, 24, 29, 41, 48, 68, 69, 135, 145, 146, 172, 173, 174, 175, 177, 178, 185, 188–9, 190, 193, 203, 228, 263
prices, 228, 229, 259
of slaves, 102, 197, 240
Príncipe, 131
prisoners, 185, 188, 201
as slaves, 181
proverbs, 165, 183
Pungo Andongo, 126–7, 134
pygmies, 13, 79, 80, 83, 84, 109

Quelimane, 228, 239, 260

Rabih Fadlallah, 65–8, 69, 73
Rafai, 70, 73
raffia cloth:
as currency, 27–8, 87
trade, 27–8, 102, 106, 140, 174, 190
railways, xi, 242, 273
rain-forest *see* forests and forest-dwellers
rain-makers, 19, 21, 127, 168, 170–1, 177, 203, 267
rain-shrines, 3, 27, 170
rainbows, 179, 180
rainfall, ix, 3, 6, 42, 119, 121–2, 139, 146, 150, 160–1, 168, 170–1, 180, 183, 203, 208, 246, 248, 250
see also drought
Rand gold-mines, 274
Ranger, Terence, xii
Reefe, Thomas Q., 160–204
regalia *see* insignia and regalia
religion:
traditional, 3, 20–1, 26, 27, 41, 42, 43, 44, 48, 50, 52–3, 56, 58, 59, 86, 93, 99, 135, 136, 168, 169–72, 173, 177, 179–80, 182, 185, 188, 201, 203, 255, 258, 267–8
see also Christianity; cults *and* Islam
Réunion plantations, 237–8, 242, 262
Rhodes, Cecil, 242, 276
Rhodesians, 261, 269, 276, 277
Ribeiro, Vicente José, 263, 275
rice, 9, 201, 214, 251
Rio del Rey, 102, 103, 114
Rio Muni, 79
ritual, 48, 60, 61, 91, 99, 173, 177, 178, 188, 247
agricultural, 12, 169, 213
associations, 86, 91
authority and, 44, 45
blood partnership, 43–4, 55
circumcision, 173
court, 180, 184, 185, 187, 258, 270
fertility, 21, 41, 180
fire, 21
genesis, 179
of healing, 91, 94, 170
initiation, 38, 44, 60, 82, 91, 94, 95, 178
in iron smelting, 15
rain-making, 171
see also cults
roads, xi, 273
rock art, 6, 11
rock shelters and fastnesses, 5, 11, 34, 69, 123, 126–7, 128, 139
Rovuma river, 205, 206, 208, 218, 219
royal barge, Lozi, 184
royal courts, 177–8, 184, 185, 187, 192, 258
royal graves, 177, 181
royal lineages, 216–17, 218, 224–5
Rozvi dynasty, 225, 264, 265–7, 268, 270
rubber, 243
trade, x, xi, 118, 153, 155, 156, 158
Ruki, 80
Runga people, 66
Ruund cultural tradition, 189, 190, 191
see also Lunda empire
Ruzizi river, 95

Sabanga people, 30
Sabi river, 208, 236, 246, 252, 253, 259, 265, 270
Sahara, 11, 26, 29, 32, 35, 45–50, 64, 65, 66, 73, 129
Sahel, 30, 32, 35, 50, 59, 66, 72
Sa'id Baldas, chief of the Kresh, 65
Salamat river, 32
Salisbury, 253
salt, 1, 17, 27, 35, 99, 121, 127, 173, 180, 185, 188, 192, 194, 203, 213, 246, 253
  as currency, 147, 148, 172
  trade, 17, 20, 35, 87, 97, 98, 106, 121, 126–7, 128, 131, 132, 133, 138, 147, 172, 177, 178, 180, 186, 191, 193, 194
Sanaga river, 82
Sangha river, 53
Sango people and language, 51, 53, 56
Sankuru river, 85, 88, 97, 105, 106
Sanusiyya brotherhood, 73
Sao civilisation, 36, 44, 47
São Salvador, 143, 157
São Tomé, 100, 102, 131–2, 133, 134, 137–9, 140, 143
Sara Majingay people and language, 37, 60
Sara people 8, 39, 42–3, 48, 49, 58, 60, 65, 68
Schweinfurth, Georg, x
Sebastião, king of Portugal, 132, 222, 230
Sebitwane, leader of the Kololo, 200
secret societies *see* associations
Selenge, 81
Sena, 27, 222, 223, 224, 227, 237, 246, 247, 259, 260, 262, 263, 269
'Senzalas', 173
sertanejos (backwoodsmen), 224, 231, 260–1
sesame seeds, 201, 243
Sewisha, Lozi chief, 185
sex and associations, 44, 45, 94–5
Shaba, trade, 97
Shaka, Zulu leader, 197, 198, 234–6
'Shangaans', 271, 274
Shangana title, 271
Shangwe state and people, 249–50, 272, 273
Shari river, 8, 32, 34, 35, 36, 38, 43, 44, 47, 48, 59–60
sheep, 11, 16, 37, 109, 192, 214, 252
shells, 1, 19, 21, 27
  currency, 21, 27
  ornaments, 21, 188, 199
  trade, 1, 25, 121, 128, 132, 133, 188, 263
Shepstone, Sir Theophilus, 275
Shire river, 171, 209, 210, 214, 240–1
Shona language and Shona-speakers, 1, 22, 25, 26, 208, 209, 210, 213, 219, 224–5, 237, 245–77
shrines, x, 3, 21, 24, 27, 56, 91, 98, 99, 113
Shuwa Arabs, 52
silver, 132, 139, 221
slave armies, 224, 260
slave raids, 39, 42, 45–50, 52, 57, 59, 61–70, 73, 82, 106, 143, 189, 197, 238–41
slave trade, x, 30, 35, 45, 47, 49–51, 54, 57, 60–8, 75, 102, 103, 106, 107, 108, 111, 113–14, 116, 118–19, 131–57, 166, 188–9, 197, 198, 204, 219, 229, 237–41, 243, 245, 262
sleeping sickness, xi, 163
smallpox, 49, 69
Smith, Alan K., 205–44
smuggling, 135, 147, 148, 232
'Snake-Destroyers', 179
'Snake-Rainbow', 180
snakes, 179, 182
social stratification, 24, 52, 55–7, 69, 73–4, 91, 93, 97, 99, 100, 111, 114, 116–17, 124–5, 166, 174–5, 185, 209, 215–20, 228, 237, 238, 248, 256, 273
  see also élites *and* status
societies *see* associations
Sofala, 22, 26, 221, 228, 237, 246, 247, 252, 257, 258, 259, 260, 262, 268
soils, 3, 4, 23, 79, 80, 108, 158, 161–3, 183, 208, 209, 210, 218, 246, 248, 250, 251, 252
Sokoto Caliphate, 66–7
Songea region, 236
Songhai people, 8
Songye town-states, 177, 186, 199–200
Sonyo, 137, 143–5
sorcerers *see* witchcraft
sorghum, 9–10, 13, 23, 36, 37, 38, 51, 69, 107, 108, 121, 124, 126, 201, 251
Soshangane, Gaza leader, 236–7, 240, 241–2, 268, 269, 271
Sotho people, 268
Sousa, Fernão de, 140
Sousa, Manuel António de ('Kuvheya'), 263, 275
Sousa Coutinho, Francisco Innocencio de, 148
South Africa, xi, xii, 196–7, 227, 234–5, 241, 242–3, 245, 271, 273–6
Spanish colonialism, xi, 133
spice trade, 25
spirit cults, 86, 93, 98, 115, 258, 267, 272

see also ancestors
squashes, 19
state formation:
decentralised states, 148–9, 153, 190–1, 194, 204
segmentary states, 127–8, 131, 135, 136, 140, 141, 145, 150, 159, 175, 187, 199, 218, 219
see also city-states
status, 11, 15, 19, 21, 22, 25, 26, 27, 52, 60, 77, 85, 111, 114, 116–17, 125, 173, 176, 181, 203, 213–17
hereditary, 93, 94, 125–6, 127
and wealth, 93, 95, 97, 125, 217
see also élites; prestige goods *and* titleholding
stone:
beads, 188
buildings, 24, 26, 254–7, 267, 268, 273
enclosures, 23–6, 245, 254, 256, 257
megaliths, 34, 36
terracing, 246, 251, 255, 256
tools, 5–6, 8, 11, 12, 13, 14, 16, 36
Stone Age, 4–6, 14, 16, 17
'Striking the Anvil' ceremony, 185
Sudan, ix, 32, 34, 35, 37, 44, 54, 63–5, 70, 73, 161
sugar:
plantations, xi, 102, 131, 133, 139, 158, 237–8, 274
trade, 106, 131–2
Sulayman (son of al-Zubayr), 64, 65
sultani, 116
supra-prazos, 240
Swahili:
language, 195
sultanates, 239
traders, x, 25–6, 115, 197, 198, 199, 204, 218, 229, 238, 246
Swazi people, 241
syphilis, 49

Tanganyika, Lake, 3, 5, 160, 213
Tanganyika, lineages, 167
Tanzania, 16, 18, 167, 194, 197, 201, 206, 236, 239
taxation, 60, 132–4, 146, 148, 216, 217, 224, 243, 255, 258, 259, 274, 276, 277
technological development, 1, 3, 4, 5–6, 8, 11, 12, 13, 14–16, 17, 128, 184, 221, 240
terracing, 23–4, 25, 246, 251, 255, 256
territories (*nyika*), Zimbabwe, 247, 254, 257, 258, 267, 270, 272, 276
Tete, 27, 222, 224, 227, 264, 265
Teve, 257, 260, 266, 267, 268, 276
textiles:
cotton, xi, 26, 158–9, 213, 214, 253
as currency, 26–8, 87, 146–8, 263
imported, 133, 146–7, 152
machira, 26
palm cloth, 1, 27–8, 87, 102, 106, 133, 140, 143, 147, 174, 190
trade, 1, 22, 24, 26, 27–8, 60, 63, 68, 87, 97, 102, 106, 131–4, 140, 143, 146–7, 152, 158, 174, 188, 190, 214, 228, 259, 263, 273
weaving, 26, 27, 213, 214, 253, 263
Tikar kingdoms, 45, 52
timber, xi
trade, 102, 152
Tio kingdom, 94, 98, 99, 105, 112, 113, 136, 144
Tippu Tip, 115, 116, 197, 199–200
titleholding, 93–4, 95–6, 97, 99, 100, 115, 141, 182, 184, 189–90, 191, 192, 201, 203, 233, 267, 271
tobacco, 107, 108, 249–50
trade, 106, 108, 109, 249, 273
Tonga language and Tonga-speakers, 208, 212, 215–16, 219, 233, 237, 242, 248, 258, 260, 261, 266
tools, 4–6, 20, 247
bone, 7, 8, 14
iron, 1, 14, 15, 17, 127, 172, 173, 186, 190, 214, 249, 252, 273
microlithic, 5
ownership, 40
stone, 5–6, 8, 11, 12, 13, 14, 16, 36
wooden, 5, 8, 11, 14, 252
tooth extraction, 38, 164
tortoises, 178
tortoiseshell trade, 25
Torwa state (Butua), 252, 254, 256–7, 259, 260, 261, 264, 265
totems, animal, 247
Toupouri, Lake, 45
trade, 1, 35, 52, 56, 109, 126, 255, 258–64
associations, 216, 219
Atlantic, 26, 29, 32, 45, 49, 50–1, 54, 70, 72, 73, 77, 80, 98, 100–7, 111–17, 118–21, 123, 129–59, 166, 188, 189, 190, 197
boycotts, 259
caravans, 3, 66, 106, 109, 111, 112, 115–16, 153, 155, 156, 190, 198, 199, 227–8

trade (continued)
carriers, 106
competition, 106, 114, 115, 203, 219
credit, 146, 148, 150–1, 153
free, 232, 233
Indian Ocean, x, 4, 20, 25, 29, 77, 188, 197, 212, 214, 216–23, 225–44, 246, 255, 259
inter-village, 87, 91, 95, 172
languages, 54
Mediterranean, 77, 106, 129, 246
monopolies, 73, 102, 131, 147, 217, 221, 222, 230, 232, 246, 259
monopsony, 234
pedlars, 60, 61, 63, 64, 67
prerogatives, 224
specialisations, 106, 109
taxes and tolls, 153, 157, 227, 241, 255, 258, 259
trans-Saharan, 26, 29, 45–50, 64, 65, 66, 73, 129
treaties, 105, 193, 241, 242, 260, 275
see also markets *and specific trade commodities*
trade routes:
power centres on, 189, 200
protection of, 20, 112, 227
transhumance, 25, 123, 124, 162, 184, 252
Transvaal, 241, 242, 273
trapping and trappers, 79, 83, 93
tree crops, 13, 107
see also palm and palm-products
tribute, 21, 27, 55, 56–7, 69, 91–2, 93, 96 99, 100, 137, 145, 150, 169, 177, 178, 185–93, 224, 237, 240, 247, 254, 258, 267, 269, 272
trypanosomiasis, 11, 163
Tshitolian stone-knappers, 5–6
Tshopi people, 210, 219, 237, 242
Tsonga language and Tsonga-speakers, 208, 209, 210–11, 213, 215, 216, 217, 219, 228–9, 233, 237, 241, 248, 268, 269, 270, 271
Tswana, 268, 275
Tumba, Lake, 94
Tumbuka people, 20
Twin Rivers rock shelter, 5

Ubangi river, 8, 13, 32, 34, 38, 43, 51, 52, 53, 56, 57, 58, 72, 73, 77, 81, 82, 91, 95, 105, 106, 108
Ubangi-Shari, 74
Ubangian peoples and languages, 13, 38, 42, 58–9
Uele river, 38, 51, 52, 58, 70, 79, 91, 92, 106
Universities' Mission to Central Africa, 241
Upemba depression, 17, 19–20, 162–3, 168, 171, 172, 174, 181, 186, 187, 198
Upoto, 115
uroyi see witchcraft
Urungwe, 257, 263, 264
Usuman dan Fodio, 67

Vansina, Jan, xii, 75–117
Vasco da Gama, 130, 220, 221
vegetable crops, 12–13, 16, 58, 59, 69, 210, 251
see also specific vegetables
vegetable oils, 152
vegetables, wild, 12, 247, 249, 251
Venda people, 260, 267
Victoria Falls, 263
'vidye', 170
Vili people, 15, 144, 149, 157
villages, 1, 11, 19, 23, 59, 68–9, 80, 81, 83–96, 100, 116, 124, 163, 165–75, 177, 181, 183, 186, 193, 195–6, 200, 201, 203, 204, 211, 214–16, 247–8, 270
clusters, 91, 92–3, 100, 165, 169, 171, 189, 197, 209
conglomerates, 92–3, 96, 97, 100
dynastic, 93
headmen, 84, 85, 92, 93, 116
principalities, 92–100, 112
trade between, 87, 91, 95, 172
warfare, 88–9, 92, 160
Vunda plain, 128

Wadai, 8, 34, 39, 48, 49–50, 60, 65, 66, 67, 68, 72, 73
Wambu kingdom, 143, 149
warlords and war leaders, 41–3, 45, 88, 126–8, 141, 143, 145, 146, 149, 160, 171–2, 191, 195, 199, 200, 202, 237
warriors in genesis myths, 178, 180
warthogs, 109
water:
for cooking, 12
pots, 12
supply, 12, 24, 99, 122, 160, 162, 170, 208, 209, 248, 250
see also drought; irrigation and drainage *and* rainfall
wax trade, x, 118, 152, 153, 155, 156, 157, 197
wealth, 52, 55–7, 69, 73–4, 127, 166

and associations, 95, 216
from cattle, 11, 22, 25, 167, 181, 213, 216–17, 248, 252, 255, 265
from fish, 20, 212
inherited, 20
iron as, 27
from ivory, 227
from land, 83
slaves as, 151, 181
and status, 93, 95, 97, 125, 217
storable, 209, 212, 216, 217, 228
from textiles, 26
from trade, 128, 129, 146–7, 153, 175, 228
weapons, 29, 92, 119, 127, 135, 160, 173, 190, 195, 214, 240, 264, 271
see also firearms
weaving, 26, 27, 213, 214, 253, 263
West Indies *see* Caribbean
wheat, 9, 251
wine trade, 106, 132, 133, 134, 153, 159
witchcraft (*uroyi*), 56, 82, 86, 115, 182, 258
Wolarbe clan, 67
women:
and agriculture, 107–9, 125, 211–12, 213, 251, 274
and iron smelting ritual, 15
kidnapping of, 88, 89
pawns, 166
road gangs, xi
sacrificial wives, 20
slaves, 66, 145, 155–6, 197, 262
societies of, 44
status of, 85, 124–5, 267
see also marriage
wood-carving, x
wooden tools, 5, 8, 11, 14, 252
Wuri river, 105, 111, 114

Xhosa-speaking people, 227

Yaka, 144
Yakoma people, 51, 92
yams, 10, 12–13, 108, 201
Yao people, 205–6, 210, 212, 215, 216, 219, 227–8, 229, 238, 240–1
Yaoundé, 82
Yav a Nawej, king of the Lunda empire, 191
yellow fever, 109
Yeta I, king of the Lozi empire, 184
Yola, 67
Yoruba kingdoms, 53
Yusuf, sultan of Wadai, 66

Zaire, xii, 14, 15, 17, 19–20, 21, 35, 37, 56, 63, 79, 96, 202, 245
Zaire river, ix, 5, 13, 17, 32, 51, 58–9, 72, 77, 79, 81, 87, 91, 100, 102, 103, 105–6, 108, 111, 114–15, 117, 123, 129, 136, 143, 144, 152, 161, 167, 168, 191
Zambezi river, ix, 5, 27, 122, 160, 161, 162, 164, 183, 188, 191, 197, 222, 223–5, 227, 228, 239–40, 245, 246, 257, 259, 260
Zambia, xi, 4, 5, 6, 16, 17, 19, 21–2, 174, 202, 227, 236
Zande expansion, 104
Zanzibar, x, 54, 93, 97, 106, 111, 115–16, 238–9, 246
zaribas (trading settlements), 63–5, 67
Zemio (Azande state), 70, 73
Zemio, Azande sultan, 65
Zezuru people, 268
Zimbabwe, xi, xii, 1, 6, 8, 16, 19, 22–7, 170, 174, 245–77
Zimbabwe hill *see* Great Zimbabwe
Zombo (Mbata) people, 144, 157
Zoutpansberg, 245, 267
Zulus and Zululand, 196–7, 211, 234–7, 243, 270
Zumbo, 227, 261, 264, 265
Zvongombe, 257
Zwangendaba, Ngoni leader, 201, 202, 236, 268–9